ENOCH POWELL AND THE POWELLITES

Enoch Powell
and the Powellites

DOUGLAS E. SCHOEN

ST. MARTIN'S PRESS NEW YORK

To my parents

Contents

List of Tables

List of Figures

Preface

It is important for me to state at the outset what the nature of my contact with Enoch Powell has been. I approached Mr Powell in October 1975 with a request to interview him for this study. Mr Powell replied that he could not grant me an interview as this would imply collaboration between the two of us. Nevertheless he agreed to provide (and subsequently did provide) copies of speeches he had delivered in Ulster since 1973 plus additional requested materials. Unfortunately Mr Powell took exception to my interviewing other M.P.s about him and made his feelings known to my supervisor. Both my supervisor (R. W. Johnson of Magdalen College) and I indicated to Mr Powell that I was doing serious academic research and was not, as he maintained, engaging in 'political gossip'. Mr Powell did not respond to either Mr Johnson's or my letter except by directing his secretary to send me a bill for £1 for duplicating the speeches he had earlier provided. I did get a chance to question Mr Powell about his views on devolution at a Nuffield College seminar in January 1976, but have not otherwise seen or spoken to him.

Acknowledgements

A great many people have contributed substantial amounts of time and effort to this work and in so doing have made it an infinitely better product. I must start by thanking E. J. Dionne who initially suggested the idea and offered numerous helpful suggestions through the period while the book was being written; also A. H. Brown of St Antony's College, who gave me my preliminary training in British politics and was a source of advice throughout the early months of my research.

I have received help from people on two continents in guiding me in the use of the computer. Richard Lyon, Don Ferree and Murray Dalziel of Harvard University, Professor Herbert Klein of Columbia University, as well as Clive Payne of Nuffield College, Oxford, all went out of their way to assist me. A wide number of people have either provided data from their files or done computer analysis for me. The staff of the Roper Center at Williams College, Williamstown, Massachusetts, kindly provided tables from old Gallup surveys, as did Robert Wybrow of Gallup Poll Ltd, London. Nick Spencer of the Opinion Research Centre provided materials from his organisation's files and was very prompt in meeting my requests for additional information. John O'Brien and John Barter of National Opinion Polls also provided much material from their files. Additional N.O.P. data were provided by the Social Science Research Council (S.S.R.C.) Survey Archives at the University of Essex. Ivor Crewe and Tony Fox of the British Election Study at Essex University were especially helpful in running tables for me from the 1974 wave of the Butler-Stokes Panel Study.

Robert Worcester of Market & Opinion Research International (M.O.R.I.) also gave me access to many data and was a source of stimulation throughout. I have learned a great deal about the workings of British politics from him and am deeply grateful for his wise counsel.

I, of course, would like to thank people who consented to be interviewed for this project. I have tried to protect the confidentiality of informants whenever it was requested. In the course of interviewing, I had occasion to impose upon many people. In London, Player and Bobby Crosby, David and Deena Roskies, David Caploe, Diana and Anthony Fawcett and Peter Hutton were particularly hospitable. In Belfast Frank Wright provided friendly lodging for a very scared New Yorker.

Professors William Schneider and Samuel Beer of Harvard University,

Philip Williams of Oxford University, and William Craig, M.P., all read the manuscript and offered much useful criticism. Professor Schneider has also taught me much of the methodology embodied herein and offered a number of important suggestions which have been incorporated into the book. I have benefited too from discussions with Daniel P. Moynihan, David Butler, Garry Orren, Martin Kilson and Kenneth Kirkwood.

My deepest debt, though, is to R. W. Johnson, who supervised the research. He helped focus my research initially and read the work twice with extraordinary care. His influence will be found on virtually every page of the book and it is not an overstatement to say that his assistance was essential to the completion of the work. On a personal level, he, Anne, Rebecca and Dicken Johnson all treated me like a member of their family even when my work was disrupting their own lives.

Bibi Rehana Khan typed successive drafts of the manuscript with care and diligence and Robert Holland and Eric Breindel proof-read it meticulously. The Warden and Fellows of St Antony's College made my stay in Oxford enjoyable and profitable. Finally, John Winckler at Macmillan made a number of useful suggestions and was a source of encouragement throughout the process. But despite all the assistance I have received, it remains to be said that any errors of fact or judgement must lie with me.

DOUGLAS SCHOEN

May 1976

Introduction

Interviews with residents of Ealing and Southfields (London) who told Market & Opinion Research International in 1973 and 1974 that Enoch Powell best represented their views were conducted by the author and E. J. Dionne in March 1975. Names of respondents have been changed.

Winifred Winston lives in Ealing, where she has resided since she was three years old. She says that Ealing used to be a good neighbourhood to live in, but now she has her doubts. Her block of well-preserved terrace houses is now inhabited by a number of West Indians and Asian families whom she does not understand and fears:

> The foreigners have interfered with our lives. They have loud parties and have children out in the streets until all hours of the night. These people claim they have passports. So what, anyone can have a British passport. We wouldn't be treated as well if we went to a foreign country.

Mrs Winston gave up hope a long time ago that either the Conservative or the Labour parties would do anything about the immigration problem. In her opinion 'the problem is that all the parties want the immigrants in. There's no real difference between them.' She was so upset by the economic crisis and immigration that she did not vote in the October 1974 general election.

There was one man Mrs Winston believed could do something to help Britain: Enoch Powell. 'Enoch Powell is the man. He's seen it all. He's got it at his finger tips. He knows what we go through. . . . If Enoch were prime minister we'd be at the top of the tree.'

George Jefferson and his wife Joan live in a very different London neighbourhood – Southfields, an area relatively free of coloured immigrants. But they share Mrs Winston's concern over the immigration problem and have much the same response. As Mrs Jefferson puts it: 'Enoch Powell is the man. The fact is that if he promises to do something, he stands by it. He's the only man who really stands by it. He's powerful.'

Mary Whyle, a neighbour of Mrs Winston, moved to Ealing nine years ago from Kensington. Her street is quiet, though children – mostly non-white – can be seen playing in their gardens and on the pavements.

She says that she used not to have anything against the coloured population, but her views have changed over the past few years:

> This was a nice neighbourhood when I moved here. Now it's full of blacks. I never had a colour prejudice before, but I do now. It was a nice road when I moved in here. Now it's coloured. Now I'm not against the coloured, but we're getting a rough lot. I was waiting in a bus queue with a group of people, and a whole lot of them cut in front of us. And if you say anything, they haul you before the Race Relations Board.

Like Mrs Winston, Mrs Whyle is not satisfied with the way any of the major parties are handling the country's problems, and hasn't voted for a long time. But there is one man who could conceivably have induced her to vote in February and October 1974:

> I *would* have voted if Enoch Powell had been head of the Tories. Because Powell's not afraid of what he thinks, and doesn't give a damn about the other people. I was canvassed by this lady from the Tories here, and I told her I wasn't voting, but that I would if Powell was the Tory leader. She said, 'But he's much too controversial.' I replied: 'You silly thing. That's just what we need. He's one of the few truly honest men.'

Mrs Winston, Mrs Whyle and the Jeffersons are not the only people upon whom Enoch Powell made a tremendous impact during the late 1960s and early 1970s. After his April 1968 speech on immigration at Birmingham, dockers and meat porters marched to Westminster to support his position and protest against his dismissal from the Shadow Cabinet by Edward Heath, the Tory leader. He is probably also the only British politician ever to be the subject of a fictional account of his own assassination, in this case provocatively entitled *Who Killed Enoch Powell?*[1] His immigration speeches aroused such intense passions that gangs of London 'skinheads' in the late 1960s reportedly chanted 'Enoch, Enoch' while attacking Pakistanis.

It would be a mistake to conclude that Powell simply created a great stir, making no lasting impact. After the 1968 Birmingham speech, over two-thirds of the public told the opinion pollsters they agreed with what he said and overnight he became the leading candidate to succeed Heath as the Conservative party's leader. Nor was his massive following a nine-day wonder. Market & Opinion Research International (hereafter referred to as M.O.R.I.) found a full one-quarter of their respondents in February 1973 – five years later – saying that Powell was the M.P. who best represented their views and a fifth said he was their choice to be prime minister for the next five years. Moreover Powell played a decisive role in both the 1970 and February 1974 general elections. The purpose of this book, then, is to discuss how he built up that measure of support and to explain the reasons why such a large portion of the electorate came to identify with him.

This commentary is necessarily incomplete – Powell is still very much an active politician with a still considerable following. A definitive biography (or autobiography) may have to wait many years. Nonetheless, whatever course future events may take, it is surely already the case that Powell's career and popularity have had a sufficiently great effect on British politics to warrant our unapologetic attention.

The book is divided into two main parts. The first part follows Powell's career in British politics from 1950 when he entered the House of Commons. Particular attention has been given to the period since July 1962 when he first attained Cabinet rank and a correspondingly larger measure of public prominence. The first chapter deals with Powell's early years in the House and his efforts to win support for *laissez-faire* capitalism within the Conservative party. The next chapter seeks to explain the reasons behind Powell's decision to take up the immigration issue and to document the amount of mass support he won through his appeals. The third continues the discussion of Powell's anti-immigration efforts and discusses in some detail his role in the 1970 election. Chapter 4 is devoted to one of the most damaging defeats in Powell's career – his failure to keep Britain out of the E.E.C. It also touches on Powell's criticisms of the Heath Government's U-turn on economic issues evident by 1972. The fifth chapter deals exclusively with Powell's speeches on Northern Ireland between 1968 and 1973 and seeks to explain the essence of his Unionist commitment. Chapter 6 concentrates on Powell's increasing alienation from the Conservative party over the E.E.C. and economic policy, and explains the reasons behind his February 1974 endorsement of Labour as well as assessing his electoral impact. Chapter 7 explains how Powell came to get a constituency in Northern Ireland and discusses the problems he has faced as the only Englishman in the Ulster Unionist parliamentary delegation.

The second part deals with the mass support Powell won nationally between 1968–75. Chapter 8 tries to provide a clear picture of how Powell's national support changed during this period. In addition to showing the peaks and troughs in his national support, the chapter shows how his following changed by party, class, age, region and sex. The next three chapters seek to explain *why* he won the support he did. Chapters 9 and 10 test the applicability of two epiphenomenal explanations – mass society and status theories. Chapter 11 seeks to provide an alternative explanation of his rise and is supplemented by interviews with Powellites in the London area. The conclusion attempts to assess Powell's impact on British politics during the 1960s and 1970s and the broader significance of his rise to the working of the British political system.

PART I

PART

1 Campaigning as a Free Marketeer

From the age of three, Enoch Powell was referred to as 'the professor' around his family's household on the outskirts of Birmingham.[1] And for the first twenty-five years of his life Powell sought to earn that title. As a young boy he proved to be an outstanding student – so outstanding that he was to win scholarships to the leading grammar school in Birmingham and subsequently to Cambridge.

He was born in June 1912 to lower middle class parents in Stechford, outside Birmingham. Although both his parents were school teachers, his mother proved to be the decisive force in his early educational development. Before Powell began school she taught him the alphabet and imbued him with the determination and dedication which, as even his bitterest critics would concede, have been characteristic of the man in all his later life. Powell became one of four boys to win a scholarship to King Edward VI grammar school, where he found himself a contemporary of Dennis Hills (the writer who the President of Uganda, Idi Amin, threatened to execute) and Alan Nunn May (who was later convicted of spying on the British Government).

At King Edward's Powell discovered his initial interest in the classics and learned Greek with the assistance of his mother. His progress was so rapid that he began a translation of Herodotus while still a schoolboy. In his last two years at King Edward's he also became tremendously excited by German culture and language. He was later to be influenced profoundly by the German philosopher Nietzsche.

Powell's academic success won him a classics scholarship to Trinity College, Cambridge, where if anything his life became even more ascetic that it had been at school. He did not mix socially with his fellow undergraduates or with the dons. His life was devoted totally to scholarship, so much so that virtually none of his contemporaries knew him. His dedication and ability won him virtually every classics prize Cambridge offered. Resolutely 'unclubable' as he may have been, his brillance was not in doubt. He was elected a Fellow of Trinity after his graduation in 1933, whereupon he began work on his major academic text, *A Lexicon to Herodotus*, a work he brought to fruition and published with the Cambridge University Press.

Powell felt stultified at Cambridge and sought to broaden his horizons. He spent much time on the Continent doing academic research during

3

the mid-1930s and finally took up the chair in Greek at Sydney University, becoming the youngest professor in the Commonwealth at 25. Barely a year after taking the post, however, he left Australia to join the British Army. Entering the Army in 1939 as a private, he emerged six and a half years later as a brigadier, after service in North Africa, the Middle East and India. Having won high honours in academic and military spheres, he now chose to enter politics. He got a job at the Conservative Research Department in 1947, where he joined another young army officer, Iain Macleod, on the staff. Eager to enter Parliament, Powell fought a hopeless by-election in a mining constituency in 1947 before being adopted a year later as the Conservative candidate in marginal Wolverhampton South West. The Tories lost the 1950 election, but Powell managed to capture the constituency by 691 votes. He thus became part of the celebrated parliamentary crop of 1950–51 which was to dominate Conservative politics for the next two decades. His narrow victory in 1950 seemed to destine him for a rather precarious career in a highly marginal constituency. But through assiduous nursing of his constituency, aggressive campaigning, as well as some good fortune, his majority grew through the 1950s. In 1951 he held the seat with a 3196 vote majority, an increase due in part to the absence of a Liberal opponent. Four years later a redistribution before the poll added about 2000 more Tory voters to the constituency, helping Powell increase his majority to 8420. In the 1959 election his margin increased to 11,164 so that his seat was no longer a marginal. He had established himself in Wolverhampton so well that the national swing back to Labour in the 1964 and 1966 elections did not jeopardise his seat. In fact he actually slightly increased his majority between 1959 and 1964.

THE EARLY YEARS IN THE HOUSE OF COMMONS

Powell entered the House as an ardent imperialist and became a low-profile member of the Tories' Suez group (which opposed British troop withdrawals from the Canal area). Once troops were pulled out of the Canal zone in 1954, however, he began to question his commitment to the Empire. His questions were voiced openly in a lecture he delivered to a Conservative summer school in 1954. He concluded that the British Empire had dissolved and would not be reconstructed. He noted that 'the inherent instability of the (imperial) connection was for a long time veiled by the circumstances of the time – by the overwhelming preponderance of British power'.[2] What was surprising to Powell was that it took such a long time for the Empire to be dissolved. When the final crisis developed at Suez in 1956, he was unconcerned about the need for a strong show of force. After Britain had pulled its troops out of the Canal in 1954, it was foolish to try to exert military influence. During the whole Suez crisis, he was more concerned with performing adequately in his job as Parliamentary Secretary for Housing and Local Goverment, a position Sir Anthony Eden had appointed him to in 1955. So surprising was his public silence that there was even some speculation that he might withdraw from the Suez group so as not to offend the party leadership.

Advancement did not come as quickly for Powell as it did for his former colleague at the Conservative Research Department, Iain Macleod. But in January 1957 the Prime Minister, Harold Macmillan, made Powell Financial Secretary to the Treasury under Peter Thorneycroft, the Chancellor. However, Powell, Thorneycroft and another colleague, Nigel Birch, felt compelled to resign in early 1958 when Macmillan failed to agree to his ministers' budgetary estimates for the year. Their resignation was prompted by the disclosure that the Prime Minister's estimates for the next year provided for a £50 million increase in expenditure, while the Government was publicly committed to keeping expenditures at the present level. To maintain solvency, there would have had to have been massive cuts in the social services, something Macmillan was not prepared to accept. Upon resigning, neither Powell nor Thorneycroft sought to use the issue to build a faction on the Tory back-benches. Nor did Powell join Sir Cyril Osborne's anti-immigration group in the late 1950s and early 1960s, despite some personal sympathy with Sir Cyril's position. As Andrew Roth has noted: 'There were plenty of targets about for a man of his intelligence and very strong views; but he kept his mouth shut.'[3] Instead Powell temporarily faded into the background, while making clear he was still loyal to Macmillan.

His adoption of a low profile did not mean that he had abandoned his principles. After the 1959 election, Macmillan offered him the post of Parliamentary Secretary of Education. He refused on the grounds that he could not rejoin the Government unless his former colleagues at the Treasury also returned. Another of his conditions for return was that the principles of restricted expenditure should be accepted by the Government. Despite this show of independence Powell was careful not to offend the leadership during debate over the 1960 Budget. Expenditure was still too high in his judgement, but he did not damage his own position by speaking out too strongly. His loyalty was rewarded in July 1960 when he returned to the Government as Minister of Health, along with Thorneycroft who became Minister of Aviation. His first major crisis in that post came in early 1962 during Selwyn Lloyd's pay pause. Wage increases were to be limited to 2·5% and National Health Service nurses were pressing for increases of up to 25%. Since Powell was a devoted foe of government control of wages and prices, there was some initial doubt whether he would enforce the Chancellor's limits. But Powell refused to ask for an exception to be made for nurses and vigilantly enforced them. Although his stand against the nurses drew some criticism in the press, his loyalty was again rewarded. In July 1962 Macmillan elevated him to Cabinet status. Yet this elevation brought little reaction from the press. Most of the attention centred on Macmillan's other sackings and appointments. In all, Macmillan sacked seven of his twenty-one Cabinet ministers.[4]

During his first year in the Cabinet Powell remained inconspicuous. Virtually all his speeches in Parliament and to public audiences were on issues relating to his job as Minister of Health.[5] Because he had been closely associated with R. A. Butler while at Smith Square and had been a member of the One Nation Group, he had as yet no press reputation as a spokesman for the Tory Right. Rather the 1962 Cabinet reshuffle (which saw Selwyn Lloyd depart) had been perceived as victory for the modernising wing of the party.[6]

Powell's stock within the party gradually rose. After a Cabinet meeting at Chequers in April 1963, James Margach wrote in the *Sunday Times* that 'Mr Enoch Powell proved to be the "Man of Chequers". His vision of the type of society which will emerge over the next ten years and more, and how Government policies and social services can be developed was compelling.'[7] Nonetheless he was still getting little public attention. The only other time he got any mention on an extra-health matter in the first half of 1963 was in June during the Profumo scandal. Reports – most probably planted by anti-Macmillan backbenchers – began appearing in a number of newspapers that Powell was considering resigning. The press went to Powell's houses in London and Wolverhampton looking for comment, but he withheld judgement until 16 June. Then in two speeches, one at Narborough and another on behalf of a by-election candidate, he backed the Prime Minister and defended his integrity.[8] Macmillan was no doubt relieved by the action, for Powell now enjoyed a substantial reputation within the parliamentary party as an austerely upright guardian of the party's principles. In a negative way he thus enjoyed considerable influence at this point.

Nonetheless poll data collected during the Profumo controversy showed that Powell had only minimal support in the electorate and among M.P.s as a potential successor to Macmillan. Both the *Daily Express* and *Daily Telegraph* sponsored surveys of the electorate and M.P.s during June and July. The polls in the *Express* and *Telegraph* showed that Powell had the support of 5% and 6% of Conservative M.P.s respectively should Macmillan resign. In analysing these surveys Roth concluded that 'while Powell was not in the first rank with Maudling, Butler and Hailsham, he was in the second rank with Edward Heath and far ahead of the Earl of Home.'[9] Powell's support in the mass electorate at this time was even lower than his standing in the party. A *Daily Express* poll in June showed that he was in fifth place with 3% of the electorate in the choice of a replacement for Macmillan.[10]

Powell played a central role in the behind-the-scenes manoeuvring around the selection of a successor for Macmillan, who resigned in October 1963. Despite their ideological difference, Powell felt a strong sense of loyalty to R. A. Butler, his political patron, as did Iain Macleod.[11] Macmillan on the other hand felt nothing but antipathy for Butler and did everything he could to block his succession by initially supporting Lord Hailsham. It became apparent however that Hailsham could not get the necessary support among party leaders and Macmillan turned to Sir Alec Douglas-Home. When word leaked out that Home was about to be asked to form a government, Powell and Macleod made a last-ditch attempt to block him. They organised a late-night caucus of Conservative M.P.s at Powell's house which was attended by the party's Chief Whip. At the meeting they expressed their displeasure about the impending appointment and hoped the Chief Whip would convey their dissatisfaction to Macmillan. This effort failed and Home was called to the Palace. The contest was not over, as Home acknowledged by not actually kissing hands with the Queen on receiving her commission. He was not sure he would be able to recruit a Cabinet to serve with him.

Powell and Macleod both announced they would not serve in a Home Cabinet and urged Butler and Sir Edward Boyle to hold out also. However both Butler and Boyle agreed to serve, leaving Powell and Macleod as the only members of the Macmillan Cabinet not to accept Sir Alec's invitation. There seems to be little doubt that Home would have failed to form a government had Butler accepted the bold course proposed by Powell – a fact which later led Powell to criticise Butler for his lack of political nerve.

Powell's refusal was apparently motivated by personal loyalty to Butler rather than by any ideological objection to Home, to whom he promised to be as loyal out of the Cabinet as he would have been were he in the Government.[12] Nonetheless, given that Butler himself had joined the Home Government, this attitude appeared at best quixotic and was more generally interpreted as a continuing attempt to threaten the Home experiment. Commentators widely saw the refusal as having an added sociological significance. Macmillan's effort to subvert the normal party machinery, according to *The Times*, marked an effort by the traditional party élites to block the growing influence of grammar-school educated Tories like Powell. In the aftermath of the contest *The Times* noted that Powell and Macleod knew 'as most observers know, that the Conservative Gentlemen had taken on the Conservative Players and had won hands down in a day when everybody thought the Conservative Gentlemen had given up'.[13]

Powell himself was not popularly seen as a contender. A National Opinion Polls (N.O.P.) survey conducted in July did record minimal (3%) backing for him. But Butler was and remained the clear popular favourite – a follow-up N.O.P. in October showed 64% preferring him as prime minister. Powell received no mention in this poll. The only favourable mention Powell got came after his decision not to serve in

Sir Alec's Cabinet. By a 38–25% plurality a Gallup sample agreed with this decision.[14]

The Home victory was initially regarded as a triumph for the Tory Right. A member of the One Nation Group, Powell's failure to serve was taken as confirmation of this view.[15]

Such an interpretation was misleading in regard to both men, as T. E. Utley noted in 1968:[16]

> It is true that Home was generally classified as a man of the right, an epithet which is now beginning to be applied to Powell. It was nevertheless a totally different kind of right from that which Powell represented. Home's thinking on the Commonwealth and foreign policy was still cast in the old-fashioned liberal imperialist mould from which Powell had escaped. Home had few views on domestic policy but he might be suspected of inclining toward a tradition of Tory paternalism which Powell now strongly rejected.

NEW FREEDOM FOR POWELL

By retreating to the back-benches Powell obtained a new freedom to speak out on issues which he felt to be important, launching wholesale attacks on state economic planning, state intervention in the economy, and a prices and incomes policy. He was immediately elected chairman of the Conservative back-benchers' Education Committee, and if anything his coverage in the press got better.[17] Early in 1964 he made a number of major statements on the country's economic situation which resembled quite closely those he had delivered the summer before, but this time he received much wider coverage. He argued that it was impossible to hold down prices with a National Economic Development Council and an incomes policy. Market forces, he suggested, were the only way the economy should be regulated. He also derided the Confederation of British Industry's attempt to hold down prices, saying that their only job was to maximise profits. Powell's skill in presenting his opposition to a prices and incomes policy received editorial commendation from *The Times*, but also brought him criticism not only from Harold Wilson but also from a rather wounded C.B.I.[18] Following his attack on their policy of voluntary price restraint, the C.B.I. responded by saying that Britain did not then have a free economy and that market forces were not always the only determinant of price policies.[19] Powell also came under attack after the publication of three anonymous articles in *The Times*, generally attributed to his authorship.[20] In the articles, the author reviewed the development of post-war Conservative policy and criticised the party for accepting a mixed economy. He also reiterated his call for market forces to be allowed to operate in the economic realm, while non-economic criteria should be applied only in health care, education and defence. The articles were immediately seized upon by Harold Wilson, the new Labour leader, to suggest that they demonstrated the degree of internal strife existing within the Tory party. Powell was now seen by Wilson as 'the arch-priest of high Toryism',[21] and his views were so abrasively *laissez-faire* that they did not go uncriticised in his own party.[22]

Quite undeterred, Powell continued to give speeches in praise of the free market and free enterprise.[23] In spring 1964 he delivered a most provocative speech in Glasgow.[24] While noting that unemployment was invariably higher in Scotland than in England, he nonetheless suggested that industry should locate itself in the areas it found to be most profitable. As for the Scots, it was their job to move to more prosperous regions if they could not find suitable employment in Glasgow.

Powell also broadened his economic critique to consider the role of trade unions.[25] While he was as ready as any Conservative to condemn trade union 'coercion' he maintained that unions do not have any important effect in holding wages down below what they might be if there were no price fixing in the labour market.[26] He was quite ready to accept that this meant that no blame for inflation could be levelled at the unions. Inflation was caused by increased government expenditure, not by rising pay packages won by militant trade unionists.

Throughout 1964 the Conservative party girded itself for the coming election. As it turned out, Sir Alec waited until October to call for a national poll. Because he was out of the party leadership, Powell played a relatively minor role in the national campaign. He deliberately avoided mentioning the immigration issue during his own campaign for re-election in Wolverhampton. By this time immigration had become a particularly intense issue in the West Midlands, and a number of Tory candidates (most notably Peter Griffiths in Smethwick) gained wide-spread publicity for their anti-immigration stance. Powell's election address contained only a brief reference to the subject. He supported controls on immigration but fought the election as an integrationist, arguing that immigrants already in the country were entitled to the same treatment as the native population.

THE 1964 DEFEAT: VICTORY FOR POWELL?

The Conservatives' defeat in the 1964 election produced a new and by no means disadvantageous situation for Powell. He was both freer than before to express his opinions and more likely to have them taken seriously. Many Conservatives – including many of the younger M.P.s – reacted predictably, in the wake of the 1964 defeat, against the Butskel-lite consensus of the 1951–64 period. After the 1945 defeat, in an altogether less friendly climate, Rab Butler had led a fundamental reconstruction of Conservative thinking to produce that consensus; it now seemed not impossible that Powell, irrevocably one of Butler's protégés, might lead an analogous though ideologically contrary movement of reconstruction. On a more personal level Powell felt the election defeat freed him to join Sir Alec Douglas-Home's Shadow Cabinet as spokesman on Transport.[27] He had maintained that out of loyalty to Rab Butler he could not accept Home's offer in 1963, but following the election defeat he felt no more constraint.[28]

Despite Powell's new Transport portfolio, most of his public pronouncements were still on economics. Transport policy seems to have been the subject of only one of his major public addresses during 1965. During November and December 1964 Powell intensified his campaign against a statutory prices and incomes policy. He told the Birmingham Young Conservatives that an incomes policy was 'foolish nonsense' and that market forces should be allowed to reign.[29] The only way a prices and incomes policy could be successful was through 'universal detailed control' similar to that found in fascist states.

By the end of 1964 he was beginning to establish himself as one of the foremost spokesmen against consensus politics in Britain. His targets, it was clear, were not only Labour proponents of an incomes policy but also their Tory counterparts such as Selwyn Lloyd and Reginald Maudling. Powell's objective, it seemed, was to wrest the initiative from such figures and change the face of the Conservative party. As Andrew Roth has noted:[30]

> In this new-style Conservative party, businessmen, shopkeepers and skilled workers would be led by radical right wing intellectuals. Therefore he continued with his attacks on the ideas and structure of the Establishment, hoping that by doing so he could eventually bring about a political realignment. This explains why he used every occurrence, every major Labour speech, as a lever to shake increasing numbers of Conservatives free from consensus politics.

With less public attention, but no less significantly, Powell also set out his own conception of English nationalism during 1964. These speeches – one delivered in April to the Royal Society of St George and the other in November at Trinity College, Dublin – provided the logical (as well as emotional) underpinning for his subsequent pronouncements on immigration, defence, the E.E.C. and Ulster, and as such deserve special attention.[31]

In seeking to forge a new national identity for Britain, he argued that people could no longer take pride in the Empire and should now hold in high regard that which is distinctively British. It was important for Britain not to overestimate her role in the world. To do so would in the long run contribute to the mood of demoralised self-consciousness which had developed in response to the belief that Britain had declined from her former imperial position. In fact Powell maintained in his Trinity College speech, Britain had never really reached the heights others had given her credit for. The Empire had largely been a myth, something Conservative politicians like Joseph Chamberlain convinced the electorate existed so that their party would have a cause around which they could unite the nation. A consideration of British history in the 1880s and 1890s revealed to Powell that Britain's connection with her overseas dependencies was anything but imperial. Because for fifty years British schoolchildren had been taught there was once an Empire, the populace now believed their country's position had declined. They were also taught that their country had once been the workshop of the world and had slowly seen its economic and industrial position eroded. Yet Britain's position was bound to decline simply because she started producing before other nations. There was a natural conservatism about any nation which was ahead of others, while competing nations were bound to be innovative in order to catch up. This was perfectly natural and no cause for despair. The end of Empire found Britain a richer and more productive nation than ever before; the national feeling of malaise was hardly warranted.

This malaise of political and cultural insecurity rested squarely on a misconception of the past, on entirely mythical beliefs about the British Empire and England's role as workshop of the world. For the British people to be truly happy, they needed, said Powell, a realistic sense of their past and their evolution into the present. Happiness could only come to people who appreciated their particular strengths and values:[32]

> True success and happiness are not to be had by a nation so long as it views its life and the life of the world around it through the refracting, distorting medium of false beliefs about its own past and about the way the past has grown into the present. To be happy it is not necessary to beat the statistical record of all comers. Happiness and success are likeliest to come to the nations which knows themselves as they really are, without delusions of height or depth.

For Britain to know itself as it really is, he felt the nation had to be proud of the country's institutional and cultural heritage. The England he looked to in his speech to the Royal Society of St George was one which existed before the nation's expansion. The British people in 1964 could reassert their national and cultural identity by recognising that they were 'once more akin with the old English' of the days before Elizabeth I and the Tudors.[33] If one could go back to those times and ask what it was that bound the British people together, the answer would provide a clue to what form English nationalism should take today.

Powell did try to answer as the old English would have done. His answer was extraordinarily romantic and sentimental for a politician who earned his reputation for being a coldly logical thinker. Despite his logician's mind, he has always maintained that instinct and sentiment are on 'the highest plane in political and national life'.[34] Thus his response, which stressed the beauties of pastoral England, should not be considered surprising:[35]

> What would they say? They would speak to us in our own English tongue, the tongue made for telling truth in, turned already to songs that haunt the hearer like the sadness of spring. They would tell us of that marvellous land, so sweetly mixed of opposites in climate that all the seasons of the year appear there in their greatest perfection; of the fields amid which they built their halls, their cottages, their churches, and where the same blackthorn showered its petals upon them as upon us; they would tell us, surely, of the rivers, the hills and of the island coasts of England.

The other major element which bound the English people together through the ages was its governing institutions. Powell said the old English would speak in reverential tones about Parliament and the monarchy:[36]

> They would tell us too of a place near the great city which the Romans built at a ford of the River Thames, a place with many chambers and one lofty hall, with angel faces carved on the hammer-beams, to which men resorted out of all England to speak on behalf of their fellows, a thing called 'parliament'; and from that hall went out men with fur-trimmed gowns and strange caps on their heads, to judge the same judgements and dispense the same justice to all the people of England.

> One thing above all they assuredly would not forget, Lancastrian or Yorkist, squire or lord, priest or layman; they would point to the kingship of England, and its emblems everywhere visible. Symbol yet source of power; person of flesh and blood, yet incarnation of an idea; the kingship would have seemed to them, as it seems to us, to embrace and express the qualities that are peculiarly England's.

The previous two passages have been quoted at great length because of the language Powell used. It is not difficult to get a sense of the deep emotional commitment he had to English institutions. Anthony Sampson's comment that Powell 'resorts to a semi-mystical view of Parliament as the embodiment of the nation's soul', neatly summarises his attitude towards it.[37]

He was also particularly proud that Parliament had remained unaltered for centuries. In other nations government institutions are often 'recent or artificial creations' while in England they are 'as works of nature, spontaneous and unquestioned'.[38]

He stressed particular values which were distinctive in Britain: unity, continuity and homogeneity. Again his rhetoric reveals the deep passion he has for this idyllic concept of pre-Tudor England:[39]

The unity of England, effortless and unconstrained, which accepts the unlimited supremacy of Crown in Parliament, so naturally as not to be aware of it; the homogeneity of England, so profound and embracing that the counties and regions make it a hobby to discover their differences and assert their peculiarities; the continuity of England, which has brought their unity and this homogeneity about by the slow alchemy of centuries. . . .

The deepest instinct of the Englishman – how the word 'instinct' keeps forcing itself in again and again – is for continuity; he never acts more freely nor innovates more boldly than when he most is conscious of conserving or reacting.

Nonetheless, despite his speeches on economics and nationalism, it is clear that the electorate was taking no notice of Powell. An N.O.P. survey[40] in June 1964 (before the election) and a Gallup Poll in December 1964 (after the election) alike recorded no support for him as a candidate for the top two or three positions in the Tory party.[41]

At the élite level – among Tory M.P.s – he made a considerable impact but won no personal following. 'Observer' in the *Financial Times* noted 'in one or two crises he had been discussed as a possible party leader. His intelligence is enormous and he has been a good departmental minister. The real Right has no leader, and on paper he is the ideal man; yet he seems to have no steady support except from his old companion in the wilderness, Mr Nigel Birch.'[42]

While Powell was eager to build a following he was not willing to make any concessions to even the most sacredly bipartisan objectives of national policy.

M.P.s and the public have heard an unbroken line of Tory, Whig, Liberal, Conservative and Labour Chancellors stress the need for export promotion. On this subject, indeed, the consensus is older than party itself. Nonetheless Powell did not hesitate to attack the Government's encouragement of exports and discouragement of imports as mistaken interference with the operation of the market. He was clearly encouraging his listeners to ignore the incessant government appeals to the 'Dunkirk spirit' to protect the value of sterling by a greater export effort.[43] He could go no further without incurring the charge of preaching devaluation. To go even this far caused grave discomfort to his more conventionally minded colleagues and potential supporters. Meanwhile, his attention began to turn to the perhaps even thornier issue of immigration.

He played a behind-the-scenes role in developing Sir Alec Douglas-Home's repatriation plan in early 1965, but personally was not a vocal advocate of tighter restrictions.[44] He did move away from support for the unrestricted right of dependants to enter, after getting intense pressure from local constituents about the problem in Wolverhampton.

His public justification for supporting tighter controls was cast largely in economic terms. The country's liberal immigration policy restricted productivity, because the presence of a large unskilled work-force retarded mechanisation and reorganisation.[45]

THE 1965 LEADERSHIP CONTEST

It was at this juncture that Sir Alec Douglas-Home resigned as Tory leader, giving way under the pressure of precisely the younger, more business-minded Conservative M.P.s among whom Powell's most likely supporters were to be found. Nonetheless it was clear that the ensuing leadership contest had come far too soon for Powell to have had a realistic chance against either of the main contenders, Reginald Maudling or Edward Heath. He entered the ring nevertheless, wishing to test the impact he had made in the evident hope that if he received a sizeable vote on the first ballot his importance in the party would be bolstered. He felt moreover that it was important for Conservative M.P.s to have the chance to express support for the sort of alternatives he offered. The advance indications were that he would not get much support. A *Sunday Times* poll of M.P.s conducted early in 1965 showed that Powell was unlikely to get more than twenty votes.[46] The data from public polls on his standing in the electorate were hardly more encouraging. An N.O.P. poll in February had shown that Maudling (34%), Heath (15%) and Macleod (9%) were the candidates with significant popular support in the event of a Home resignation. The effect of the resignation itself was to solidify support for Maudling (44%) and Heath (28%);[47] true, Powell rose slightly in the polls – from 1% to 3% – but this merely restored him to his June 1963 rating, and still left him with only half the level of support enjoyed by a non-leadership candidate, Macleod.

In the event Powell received only 15 votes (5% of Tory M.P.s), Heath led on the first ballot with 150 votes and became Leader when Powell and Maudling withdrew before the second ballot. The fact that Maudling and Heath were relatively closely matched may possibly have hurt Powell – those Tory M.P.s determined on a more abrasive style of leadership had evidently decided that Heath was their man. Given that Maudling was the popular front-runner it had been clear to such M.P.s that they could not afford to 'waste' a vote on Powell who, ironically, might have done better in a larger field of candidates – the type of contest which developed a decade later after Heath had, in turn, resigned.

Who were the potential or actual supporters? Andrew Roth concludes that his support at the élite level came from two sources – young Tory intellectuals like Nicholas Ridley and John Biffen, and advocates of tighter immigration control such as Sir Cyril Osborne, Harold Gurden and Peter Griffiths.[48] *The Times* political correspondent predicted before the vote that whatever support Powell would get would come from young free-marketeers elected in 1964.[49] Ten years after the contest John Biffen recalled nine of the fifteen members who supported Powell. According to Biffen, John Hay nominated Powell and Biffen seconded him. Other supporters of Powell were Bernard Braine, Tom Galbraith, Ridley, Edith Pitt, Michael Allison, Sir John Vaughan-Morgan, and Sir Harry d'Avigdor Goldsmid. It seems clear the party Establishment really did not take his candidacy seriously. One senior back-bencher dismissed Powell as the 'British Goldwater' while another said his standing represented 'an act of mischief'.[50] Ten years after the event a Tory M.P. who was involved in the selection process commented, 'Powell entered the race to make himself known. He didn't have a chance to win and by standing he got his name in the papers for a week.'

Thus we have seen that Powell at this time (1965) had failed to generate support at either the mass or élite level. He had also failed to win much general approval from the electorate. In a special N.O.P. survey on the electorate's attitudes towards leading Conservatives, respondents were asked which of six leaders (Maudling, Heath, Macleod, Lloyd, Soames and Powell) they would give the highest rating on a set of personal criteria, thus providing a chance for electors to express approval for Powell short of support for him as leader. They did not take the opportunity. On all eleven criteria offered, Maudling and Heath were placed above all the others by wide margins. Despite his leadership candidature Powell was given only one third-place rating over Macleod (for being 'more in touch with ordinary people'). Otherwise he was given his best approval ratings for ability to handle trade unions (11%), toughness (10%) and being straightforward and plain-speaking (10%). Asked to rate the six in order as 'most pleasant person', voters placed Powell joint last with Selwyn Lloyd, at that point possibly the least popular major figure in British politics.[51]

Despite Powell's quite striking failure to win any significant level of personal support, virtually all journalistic analyses of his influence written during the spring and summer of 1965 stressed the impact his thought had made on the development of Conservative policy. Conservatives near the heart of the party, at least implicitly considering Powell's deficiencies as a potential leader or popular spokesman, emphasised that his intellectual influence could hardly be exaggerated. Reviewing *A Nation Not Afraid* (a collection of Powell's speeches published in July), Iain Macleod wrote that 'Powellism is gaining converts every day. Much of our programme when the general election comes will be based on ideas in this book.'[52] Similarly the *Sunday Times* commented that Powell 'has driven the true concept of the market forces back into Tory thinking and it is not necessary to travel every yard of the road with him to acknowledge his contribution.'[53] David Wood, *The Times* political correspondent, noted that 'the lesson according to St Enoch has been read eloquently inside [Mr Heath's] policy study groups.'[54] Powellism, Wood noted, 'has made converts among young Tories who want to break out from the semi-socialist web woven by expediency in three Tory administrations, and has revived hope among older Tories – a hope that Conservatism can again be what they always thought it was.'[55] While, in the aftermath of the Tory leadership contest, Alan Watkins of the *Spectator* suggested that Powell's intellectual influence within the party had been destroyed by his poor showing, he amended that judgement two months later. After Powell's appearance at the Conservative party conference in October, Watkins recognised he had been too quick to dismiss him. He wrote that 'Powell is no more than a stimulating theorist. But the reception he evoked at the Tory conference will not have escaped Mr Heath. He remains a potential threat to Conservative party unity.'[56]

Specifically, Powell's views had clearly been influential in four fields. His call for a change from universal social services to selective benefits available only to those in need was now accepted by virtually all Tories; on the question of the trade unions he had had 'a considerable impact in making the party less tolerant of private coercion'.[57] He had moved the Tories away from their strong commitment in the 1964 campaign to a prices and incomes policy. Finally, his campaign against central state economic planning had succeeded in deleting the stress on planning from the prominent position it had occupied in the Tories' 1964 election manifesto. There was no doubt that he had achieved a status which would have made his dropping from the Shadow Cabinet hard to envisage, politically awkward as his presence might be at times for his colleagues.

A PROMOTION UNDER HEATH

Shortly after Heath was elected Leader, he appointed his former challenger Shadow Secretary of Defence, a clear promotion from his Transport brief under Home. For Powell the appointment meant 'a return from the wilderness', according to the *Sunday Telegraph*.[58] It also meant an opportunity for him to expand upon his controversial views on Britain's place in the world – an opportunity he took at the Conservative party conference in October 1965. Powell implicitly questioned Britain's East of Suez commitment, arguing that Britain was primarily a European power which could do little to halt communist advance in either Africa or Asia. In fact he suggested that in the absence of Western powers a natural balance would come into play in developing areas threatened by communism. Western powers, he suggested, might delay rather than hasten the arrival of a balance of influence in such areas.[59] While the speech had been read in advance and apparently approved by Sir Alec Douglas-Home, now Shadow Foreign Secretary, it created a furore within the party, where it was interpreted to be a questioning of Britain's commitments abroad. One Conservative M.P. demanded that Powell resign from the Shadow Cabinet, and other Tory M.P.s organised a private party meeting a few weeks later to offer Powell a sharp rebuke.[60] Sir Alec meanwhile tried to 'clarify' Powell's remarks. Britain, Sir Alec insisted, would not abandon its obligations and leave a vacuum. In many cases, indeed, Britain had treaty commitments to fulfil which she could not avoid even if she wanted to.[61]

Again Powell received very extensive press coverage for his provocative speech but won little extra popular support. In mid-October N.O.P. asked a sample of the electorate to name the most outstanding figures in the Conservative party. Heath, the new Leader, now moved ahead of Maudling, but Powell's position remained relatively unchanged from the summer. He was the fifth leading Conservative with 7%, trailing substantially behind Heath (50%), Maudling (36%), Home (16%) and Macleod (14%).[62] After the Tory conference, Gallup again asked its respondents who should be the first three men in a Conservative government. Six per cent named Powell, putting him sixth in preference.[63] While there was some indication that Powell had provoked a considerable response from Tory party workers with his conference speech, there was no indication that he made any impact on the electorate.[64] Despite the furore, he gave no indication of wishing to modify his position before the storm or of wishing to abandon his *enfant terrible* role, and in the months that followed he displayed a continuing tendency to speak on issues quite unrelated to his Defence brief.

Early in January 1966 he clashed almost openly with Reginald Maudling, the Shadow Chancellor, over the value of a prices and incomes policy.[65] Powell argued that Britain could control its rate of inflation and improve its internal monetary stability without any wage and price controls. Trade unions played no role in increasing the rate of inflation; it was only government expenditure which raised the cost of living. Prior to Powell's speech, Maudling had argued for a prices and incomes policy, suggesting that trade unions' influence over wage settlements was proof that the liberal economists' free market was not fully operative in Britain. Powell was not the only monetarist in the Tory party. Others followed his lead and attacked the leadership for accepting a prices and incomes policy. *The Times* political correspondent noted 'there are enough Powellites in the party to make the point that if the Opposition's business is to attack the Government then the Government must be attacked for their mistakes and failures – that is, among other things, a prices and incomes policy. In short, some Conservatives argue that Mr Powell could put the Opposition into a strong position' if he were to be unleashed to attack Mr Wilson and Mr Brown.[66] Powell himself covered this point in part by stressing the need for a constantly attacking Opposition (in an article in the *Swinton Journal*).[67]

One supporter of Powell's, Angus Maude, also attacked the Heath leadership during January 1966 in two articles he wrote for the *Spectator* and *Encounter*, calling the Opposition a 'meaningless irrelevance' and criticising it for failing to take a strong enough line against trade union power and a prices and incomes policy.[68] Heath, clearly furious, asked Maude to resign from the Tory front bench. The point was lost on nobody that this was a very clear shot across Powell's bow, for Maude had done little more than echo Powell.[69]

But Powell did not take the hint. He followed up his attack on Maudling with a speech which questioned 'the myth of the Commonwealth'.[70] Starting from the premise that the British people did not perceive themselves as belonging to such a body, he went on to launch implicit broadsides against official Tory policy on Rhodesia, foreign aid and immigration. Because the Government mistakenly still believed it had some influence over lands that were under dominion or protection of the crown at the time of the outbreak of World War II, it had fallen into the trap of acting as if it had some official influence over internal Rhodesian politics. The same mistaken paternalism led both to extremely questionable programmes of foreign aid to some countries and to the adoption of foolishly open immigration policies. Britain had reached the point, he said, of seeing its European neighbours as aliens and the inhabitants of Asia and Africa as British.

When Powell criticised the Defence Secretary, Mr Healey, for reneging on Britain's commitment in Aden, Healey tartly inquired how Powell could criticise a withdrawal from Aden when he himself had questioned British commitments in the Far East.[71] Powell's response was almost provocatively lacking in conviction: he merely stated that he was echoing party policy. He seemed happier when, more controversially (for a Tory), he criticised Healey for Britain's alleged over-dependence on America.[72]

The Conservatives lived almost daily in expectation of a general election. Heath, a new and untried Leader, could hardly have risked disunity by disciplining Powell had he wanted to. Therefore he went out of his way to mute any potential cleavages between himself and Powell. In early March Heath, perhaps making virtue out of necessity, suggested Powell had 'done considerable good for the Tories by the provocative attitude he has taken in Opposition on a number of subjects'.[73] Nonetheless he can hardly have thanked Powell for the major piece of provocation he did offer when the election was duly called in March 1966. Powell dramatically alleged that Britain had a contingency plan to send troops to Vietnam to help the Americans – a charge vociferously denied by Mr Healey. Heath was forced to concede not only that he had no information to support Powell's allegation, but also that Powell was speaking his own mind; Conservative party policy towards America had not changed.[74]

Powell took an extremely active role in the national campaign, delivering as many as eight speeches daily, mainly on economic issues, stressing that the major issue of the election campaign was the value of sterling.[75] He did not generally attract much press attention except for one screaming headline in the *Daily Sketch* following an isolated immigration speech. After the campaign Alan Watkins wrote in the *Spectator* that 'the principal point to take account of is that, Vietnam apart, Mr Powell made no particular impression on the campaign'.[76]

Heath's position was initially no stronger after Labour's overwhelming win and Powell quickly asserted his right to determine the expected reshaping of Tory policy. While the party leader had declared that the Tories needed to articulate a clearly formulated set of policies, Powell demurred, indicating that the Tories needed to be more philosophical. Where the Tory election manifesto suggested 'action and not words', Powell now advocated 'words and not action'. Then with Heath out of the country, Powell unilaterally issued a statement opposing the Government's blockade of Rhodesia. Before issuing the statement Powell failed to consult Reginald Maudling, the acting party leader in Heath's absence.[77]

A TEMPORARY RETREAT

As a result of Powell's actions both in the campaign and after it, Heath called him to his Albany flat to see if the two could reach some accord as to how much leeway Powell was to have in developing his own interpretations of party policy. The two men apparently reached an agreement and Powell stayed on the front bench. Initial reports in the *Sunday Times* indicated that Powell had agreed not to speak outside his area of responsibility and agreed to consult his colleagues if he chose to venture away from Defence.[78]

During the spring of 1966 Powell stuck to his Defence job, making only one speech criticising Government intervention in the economy.[79] There was no indication that he had changed his views but he kept his part of the bargain struck at Albany, even though it meant adopting a low profile. It was Heath who, unwisely, broke the spirit of the Albany compact in a rare unguarded moment before the party conference saying (in answer to a question) that 'Powell is under wraps'. Heath joked that Powell now restricted himself to speaking about milk prices and co-ops.[80] The comment infuriated Powell and the Albany bargain was dead. He returned to economics in the autumn, making eight major speeches attacking national economic planning, the coercive power of trade unions, and the prices and incomes policy.[81] While Heath was urging voluntary wage restraints, Powell ridiculed the whole concept and suggested that shopkeepers should defy the price freeze.[82] His Defence speeches both in Parliament and to the party conference all stressed his belief in Britain's need to restrict her concerns to the defence of the British Isles and Western Europe.[83] He also reiterated his calls for

Britain not to interfere with Rhodesia's internal affairs.[84] These speeches did get him some press attention, but still did not bring him any popular following. While the *Spectator* could write during his clash with Maudling that Powell was the 'leading radical force in British politics' and thus 'a man to be cherished', the electorate did not hold a similar opinion.[85] An N.O.P. survey showed that of the 30% that wanted Heath replaced only 2% mentioned Powell as a possible successor.[86] When Gallup repeated in August the question it had asked in November 1965 about which three Conservatives the electorate would put in for prime minister and the other top jobs, Powell's showing improved only slightly. Table 1.1 sets out the comparative standing of Heath, Maudling, Macleod, Home, Hogg and Powell from 1964 to 1966. Powell's showing had improved steadily but he was still not in the top rank of Tory leaders.

TABLE 1.1   First three men for Conservative government, 1964–66*

	December 1964 %	November 1965 %	August 1966 %
Heath	14	52	52
Maudling	35	25	32
Macleod	7	11	18
Home	41	18	15
Hogg	10	4	15
Powell	0	6	8

* Percentages add up to more than 100% because of multiple responses.

Source: Gallup Political Index (Dec 1965) 177; and (Sep 1966) 117.

The August 1966 Gallup Poll also provided a means of determining whether support for Powell was at all related to his position on the prices and incomes policy.[87] More generally, examination of these data gives some indication how much impact Powell had made at the mass level. Despite the clarity – even starkness – of Powell's distinctive policy alternatives his supporters were less likely than anyone else's to have a clear opinion about incomes policy. Among supporters of the leading six Tory politicians, Powell's supporters were the *least likely* to oppose an incomes policy and gave it only slightly less support than the whole sample. The Maudling-Powell clash over incomes policy had clearly eluded their respective supporters, who gave about equal amounts of support to the policy.

True, the poll was taken after a period of Powell's enforced silence on economic issues but it seemed clear, at the least, that he had not made and probably could not make any large or lasting popular impact with this talk. He persevered however and, after Heath's Washington comment, returned to developing his economic critique in earnest. Between August 1966 and January 1967 (when the next Gallup Poll on support for party leaders was conducted), he made ten speeches on economics, at least seven of which dealt entirely or at least in part with

TABLE 1.2 Support for prices and incomes policy by support for leading Conservative politicians, Aug 1966

	All %	Heath %	Maudling %	Macleod %	Home %	Hogg %	Powell %
Prices and incomes policy a good thing	47	44	46	57	43	45	44
Prices and incomes policy a bad thing	25	27	24	28	31	31	20
Qualified answer/ don't know	28	29	30	15	26	24	36
	100	100	100	100	100	100	100
	(2132)	(549)	(331)	(178)	(162)	(152)	(79)

Source: Roper Center, Williams College.

the prices and incomes policy and state intervention. Thus the January 1967 Gallup poll perhaps is a better test of whether support for Powell in his pre-immigration period was related to any of his positions on economic issues. Once again the answer was negative. The 1967 sample was asked whether the Government should lay down strict directives for employers and employees to follow or whether they should be left to settle their own disputes. Powell had of course long been an outspoken advocate of the second alternative. As Table 1.3 shows, his message had not been received.

TABLE 1.3 Government policy on intervention in wage disputes by support for Conservative leaders, Jan 1967

	All %	Maudling %	Powell %
Government should lay down firm directives	39	41	40
Government should leave it to unions and employers to settle disputes	45	49	49
Don't know	16	10	11
	100	100	100
	(2347)	(419)	(152)

Source: Roper Center, Williams College.

The same sample was asked whether economic restrictions should be lifted or continued. Again the picture was a contrary one.

TABLE 1.4   Support for economic restrictions by support for Conservative leaders, Jan 1967

	All %	Powell supporters %	Maudling supporters %
Government should ease restrictions	41	43	46
Government should continue restrictions	36	39	38
Don't know	23	18	16
	100	100	100
	(2344)	(152)	(418)

Source: Roper Center, Williams College.

While the January 1967 Gallup poll showed no relationship between support for Powell and opposition to an incomes policy, it did reveal that his personal following had increased. Fig. 1.1 provides a picture of the support each of the leading Conservatives received between 1964 and 1967. By early 1967, then, Powell had made sufficient impact with his speeches to be visible and acquire a certain measure of support. He had not however mobilised a distinctive, issue-oriented constituency. Most likely his support can be explained largely as a result of general awareness of his name.

During 1967 Powell continued his implicit criticisms of official Tory policy and the party leader. In January for example he attacked Government efforts to increase exports, knowing full well that Heath was a founding member of the National Export Council.[88] In direct opposition to Tory policy, he called for a floating exchange rate for sterling and attacked political interference in the housing market. He also differed publicly again with Maudling over the prices and incomes policy.[89]

But Heath took no action against Powell and indirectly praised him at a Young Conservative convention in Brighton. When asked whether Powell was proving to be an embarrassment, the Conservative leader said: 'He has to some people a provocative way of putting things which greatly stimulates them and he is therefore an asset to the party'.[90] Powell also continued to oppose a British presence East of Suez and called for a concentration of efforts in Western Europe. In other respects, of course, Defence was an 'easy' brief – Powell could sternly warn

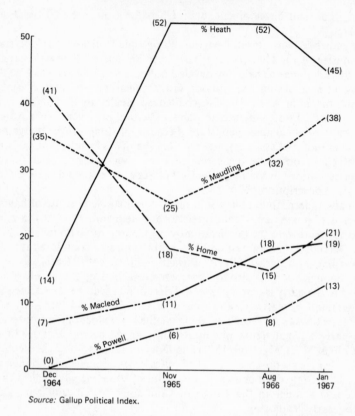

Source: Gallup Political Index.

Fig. 1.1   First three men for Conservative government 1964–67

against over-dependence on nuclear weapons, for example, without ruffling Conservative opinion.[91]

Meanwhile some of Powell's chickens had, gratifyingly, come home to roost on George Brown and Harold Wilson with the collapse of the Government's prices and incomes policy in late 1966. Press commentators were not slow to give credit where it was due. Alan Watkins wrote in the *Spectator* that Powell was laying the basis for a new theoretical Toryism.[92] David Wood in *The Times* credited him with spearheading the anti-planning reaction in the Conservative party which came in the wake of the failure of the Labour economic plan.[93] A year later, just before his Birmingham speech, Auberon Waugh gave Powell even more credit for developing Conservative economic policy. He wrote that the main body of the Conservative party has 'now broadly accepted Mr Powell's diagnosis of incomes policy, and this is surely the most important development in British politics since the Clause Four debate'.[94]

Meanwhile with typical vigour Powell had turned the Defence committee of the Conservative party into an active body with weekly meetings designed to help him develop policy. As in 1966, he stuck to the party line in urging the Labour Government not to renege on its commitments in Aden. He also challenged Healey in Parliament over Labour's tactic of announcing dates of withdrawal years in advance of the troops' actual departure because of long-range budgetary considerations. Less comfortably for the Tory leadership, Powell remained in obstinate disagreement over issues such as aid to the American troops in Vietnam, the East of Suez presence and the need for military conscription.[95]

Heath, indeed, found himself in the uncomfortable position of having a Defence spokesman of model energy and dedication and at the same time having to veto the publication by the Conservative Political Centre of a Defence pamphlet written by Powell because he considered it to be out of line with party policy.[96] Powell's conflict with Heath was now clear enough for pollsters to start perceiving him as a possible alternative to the party leader. A *Sunday Times* poll in October conducted by the Opinion Research Centre (hereafter O.R.C.) found that only 6% of the electorate said Powell would make the best leader of the Conservative party.[97] That figure put him in fifth place behind Heath (38%) Maudling (27%), Macleod (15%) and Duncan Sandys (10%). Moreover, while there was no shortage of tributes to his intellectual influence, Tory M.P.s remained generally distrustful of someone who was such a maverick, a loner in the House of Commons, and a constant critic of the party leadership.

The vetoing of Powell's Defence pamphlet may have been the last straw. He had agreed to keep to his own brief and then had been refused publication of his views even so. He was now completely hemmed in. He was still making little – and possibly diminishing – public impact. At this point he began to turn to the great sleeping issue of the day – coloured immigration. Since 1964 he had been articulating an increasingly hard line against Commonwealth immigration, and the intensity of people's emotions on the issue had clearly made an impact on him. During late 1967 a controversy developed over the right of Kenyan Asians to enter Britain freely. Passions were again aroused and neither party seemed to be taking a strong stance against allowing more immigrants to enter. Public feeling undeniably ran strong; it was largely unrepresented on the front benches. Powell, having strained the tolerance of the Conservative hierarchy to breaking point, had paid a high price and achieved a very limited success. Hemmed in and frustrated, he realised he had to change tactics. In the boldest thrust of his career, he decided to attack the bipartisan consensus at its weakest point.

2 The Turn to Immigration

Enoch Powell's immigration speeches from 1968 on are noteworthy because of his effort to go beyond statistics and personalise the concern he felt about the problem. The former classics don was trying – and he is still the only front-ranking politician to have done so – to narrow the gap between élite and mass attitudes on this particularly emotive issue by showing that he saw the problem in the same way as the man in the street. The positions he advocated in 1968 were neither very novel nor very different from official party policy. It was the way he expressed himself that created all the furore. During the 1960s he became steadily more convinced that tighter controls had to be employed on coloured immigration – as early as 1965 he had publicly supported voluntary repatriation. But what made the 1968 speeches so important was that they revealed a 'new' Enoch Powell, willing to risk not merely the disagreement but the utter wrath of the reigning (vaguely liberal) bipartisan consensus. This he did by moving away from discussions of issues which created little popular interest, and instead sought to win the popular following that had so far eluded him by evoking and echoing mass fears.

During the late 1950s and early 1960s Powell resisted any temptation to speak out publicly for tighter immigration control. Sir Cyril Osborne was the leading Tory back-bench advocate of control but he got no public support from Powell.[1] There is some indication that he supported tighter controls inside party conferences, but he did not begin to speak out publicly on the subject until 1964. From that point on Powell became more and more resolute in his desire to curb Commonwealth immigration.

SET LIKE FLINT AGAINST RACIAL DISCRIMINATION

The 1964 general election campaign presented Powell with an opportunity to confront the immigration issue directly. However he avoided mentioning it during his own campaign for re-election in Wolverhampton. Immigration had become an issue particularly in the West Midlands, most notably in the Birmingham constituency, Smethwick.[2] There is some question what Powell's attitude was towards the Smethwick Conservative candidate, Peter Griffiths, who took a very strong position against coloured immigration. An appearance Powell was to have made on behalf of Griffiths was cancelled at the last minute, leading the Labour candidate Patrick Gordon Walker to announce, 'Enoch Powell is known for his forthright view against introducing racialism into politics'.[3] Despite one published report that Powell had personally cancelled the engagement, it is unclear what the exact circumstances were.[4] Powell himself claimed that the Conservatives in Smethwick had made a mistake and double-booked speakers, hence necessitating the cancellation. Powell also showed no hesitation in speaking for another anti-immigration Tory, John Oxford, who stood in Bilston. Oxford, Foot reports, delivered a speech 'of which Peter Griffiths would have been proud'.[5]

Powell's major comments on immigration during the 1964 campaign came in newspaper articles, not campaign speeches. He reviewed a book on apartheid in South Africa for the *Sunday Times* which concluded with a distillation of his own views on the subject.[6] He argued that the case for immigration control was based on the view that the United Kingdom and the Commonwealth were not part of the same community. He did believe in the free movement of labour within communities, but the Commonwealth and the U.K. were separate entities. His own evolving concept of British nationalism led him to see the U.K. as being culturally and politically distinct from its former dependencies. The particular brand of British nationalism he advocated at Trinity College, Dublin, was reinforced by cultural and social homogeneity. Immigrants destroyed that homogeneity and made the forging of a positive and patriotic British nationalism more difficult.[7]

But Powell in 1964 was willing to accept that immigrants already in Britain had to be integrated into the populace as well as possible. Economic forces were to be the main vehicle for pushing social integration. He accepted the existence of a multi-racial society and advocated tighter controls in restrained and intellectual terms. Thus, during the summer preceding the election, he resisted inducements from other Conservative M.P.s to take the lead in criticising the Government's immigration policies. His election address played down the issue, and contained only a small reference to the question. *The Times* reported in a brief article that Powell supported controls so that 'Britain might avoid the colour question.'[8] There was no hint that he supported tighter controls than those the Tories were pledged to impose.

His other major mention of immigration came in a newspaper article written for the *Wolverhampton Express and Star*. While conceding that the issue had become one of the most important problems in his constituency, he set himself firmly against racial discrimination.[9]

I have and always will set my face like flint against making any difference between one citizen of this country and another on grounds of his origin.

I am certain that not only the Conservative party but the overwhelming majority of people in this country are of the same mind and wish – that is what it amounts to – to see the coloured immigrants no less integrated into the life and society of what is now their homeland than any other group, such as the Jewish community or the thousands of Poles living in Britain. No other prospect is tolerable.

He also indicated his support 'as an inescapable obligation of humanity' to allow the wives and children of immigrants to join their husbands and fathers in Britain.[10] Neither of his Labour and Liberal opponents indicated subsequently that Powell had made unfair use of racial issues in the campaign and the Institute of Race Relations newsletter praised him for his moderate views on the immigration issue.

If he believed – as many did – that the racial issue could be disposed of by taking a staunchly principled stand for integration, then he too must have been shaken by the clear electoral potency of the issue in the eventual results. While the country as a whole swung by 3.2% to Labour, an almost unparallelled contrary swing to the Conservatives of 0·6% occurred in the Black Country, where the immigration issue had been most intensely felt. Overall, three of the five Tory gains in 1964 can probably be attributed to racial backlash.[11] The Smethwick result was particularly striking – Gordon Walker, the Shadow Foreign Secretary no less, was trounced by the hitherto obscure Griffiths, whose unbridled banging of the racial drum achieved a Conservative swing of 7·5%. Griffiths and Smethwick understandably became the focus of enormous media attention.

It was not merely that the Black Country had contributed to reducing the Labour majority to an insecure four seats and had produced precisely the situation Harold Wilson had always declared he dreaded most. Perhaps more importantly still, the election brought the race and immigration issue to the very centre of British politics. While all three major parties had been united behind a liberal, integrationist stance, the election demonstrated the depth and intensity of popular feelings. The potency of the issue was dramatically clear; it was certain that Griffiths had merely scratched the surface. Nor was its potency merely regional, as the even more dramatic second defeat of Gordon Walker at the Leyton by-election quickly proved.

Powell's seat lay in the heart of the Black Country and he too won in 1964 with a slightly increased majority, possibly attributable to anti-immigration feelings. Whether he liked it or not he was clearly sitting on a store of electoral dynamite. Wilson might attack Griffiths as a 'parliamentary leper' and term his election a 'disgrace', but there was no gainsaying the fact that Griffiths was clearly in some senses a tribune of the people. His public utterances might help drive him out of politics (he disappeared, quietly, in the 1966 Labour landslide) but it could not put the issues he had raised back into the Pandora's box he had helped to open.

After the election results had been counted and fully analysed, Powell did gradually modify his posture. He said he did not consider Griffiths's Smethwick victory a disgrace, and defended the use of immigration in the campaign as a partisan issue. Still, he kept his distance from Griffiths. A report in the *Wolverhampton Express and Star* indicated he was not supporting or defending Alderman Griffiths's views but was defending his own line.[12] Such tactical moves apart, the Smethwick result and the ensuing furore must have given Powell, the most cerebral of politicians, cause for deep thought. It is worth noting that it was immediately after the 1964 election that he delivered his major speech on the meaning of British nationhood at Trinity College, Dublin. As with his earlier St George's Day speech of that year, it was plain that his stress on the importance of the British homogeneity of tradition and culture had clear though still unworked-through implications for immigration policy.

ADVOCATING A MORE RESTRICTIONIST LINE

Powell did not return to immigration again until early 1965. During the early part of the year he aligned with the restrictionists inside the Shadow Cabinet and played a role in developing Sir Alec Douglas-Home's repatriation plan, which was first presented at Hampstead in early February 1965.

At that point however the leading supporter of tighter immigration restrictions was not Powell but Peter Thorneycroft, the newly appointed spokesman on Home Affairs. Powell refused to speak in the Commons on the issue, but did support a resolution of Sir Cyril Osborne's calling for a ban on all immigration except for people whose parents or grand-parents had been born in England. Still, Foot attributes Powell's movement towards a stricter immigration policy in the spring of 1965 to events in the West Midlands. Two health reports, one issued in late 1964 the other in early 1965, aroused fears about the indigeneous immigrant population. The reports cited immigrant families' high birth-rate and the relatively large percentage of hospital confinements which immi-grants accounted for. When immigration again became a national issue in early 1965, local Conservatives in Wolverhampton seized on the statistics in these reports to demand tighter controls from their M.P., Enoch Powell. Peter Farmer, the chairman of the Wolverhampton South West Conservative constituency association, came away from a meeting with Powell during this period convinced his M.P. would support tighter controls.[13]

After the meeting with Farmer, Powell addressed the Wolverhampton Conservative women on the subject of immigration, and backed away from the position he had taken in October 1964 when he had endorsed the unrestricted right of entry for the dependants of immigrants. Now he suggested that all Commonwealth immigrants be treated in the same way as aliens.[14] It is important to note that he explained much of his opposition to unrestricted immigration in terms of its effect on the free market. Immigration, he said, was not increasing productivity. Rather:[15]

> It is a mistake to think that because immigrants were willing to be hewers of wood and drawers of water they are increasing productivity by releasing indigeneous workers for more productive tasks. The actual effect is probably that some mechanisation, reorganisation and capital investment which would otherwise take place does not happen and consequently our productivity all around is lower than it would have been.

Powell did not return to immigration until autumn 1965, after his failure in the Conservative leadership election. While he had created, as we have seen, a considerable stir at the party conference by his questioning of Britain's East of Suez commitment, this had been quite overshadowed by the debate on immigration. The weakest of thirty-one resolutions was selected for debate at the conference, with no reference being made to further controls. The Conservative leadership, it was clear, was determined for reasons of both principle and tactics to hold a very firm line against any danger of being engulfed by a tide of disreputable and populist racial feelings from within its own ranks. It was clear in any case that the Wilson Government, despite its execration of Griffiths, had been panicked towards making concessions to the anti-immigrant lobby. After the Tory conference, the *Sun* noted that 'the taint of Smethwick and colour prejudice was effectively and officially rubbed out of the party record during a debate on immigration'.[16]

Powell was one of the first to break the delicate consensus which had been forged on immigration. He made another call for tighter immigration standards at Birmingham during late November.[17] Even with the controls already in effect because of the Labour Government's White Paper, over 10,000 people from the West Indies and India had entered Britain in August and September. For the first time Powell advocated support for a policy of voluntary repatriation for those 'elements which are proving unsuccessful or unassimilable'.[18]

He did not speak again on immigration until the March 1966 general election campaign. In general race was not as important nationally as it had been in 1964 though the issue was far from dead – indeed in Wolverhampton it had gained even greater prominence when, two weeks before the national poll, anti-immigration candidates had done surprisingly well in local borough elections. Powell's election address contained a brief reference to his support for tighter immigration controls, and he made a speech on the topic in the closing days of the campaign. But again his message was the same; he emphasised the need for integration and his opposition to racial discrimination. However, he also renewed his call for the voluntary repatriation of the 'small minority' who were not successful in Britain.[19]

On this latter point he was careful: 'Of course I stress the word voluntarily – except for deportation after a criminal offence, there can be no question of any kind of duress.'[20] There was no hint of his later appeals for 'massive, albeit voluntary' repatriation of up to half the immigration population. To be sure, he spoke in favour of drastic reductions in the entry of immigrants and his hope of balancing the outflow against the inflow. But he carefully eschewed the emotive rhetoric which already marked the speeches of some local politicians and which was to be the hall-mark of his own later statements. After the election the Institute of Race Relations newsletter acknowledged that Powell had not tried to win popular support by appealing to anti-immigration sentiment.[21]

Thereafter he neglected the immigration issue until the summer of 1967 when he wrote an article for the *Sunday Express*.[22] For the first time he now opposed letting dependants of Commonwealth immigrants enter the country. For families to be reunited, he suggested that immigrants in Britain rejoin their kin in their native lands. But according to Paul Foot he did not join the escalating anti-immigration campaign during the summer and early autumn of 1967. Moreover, his opinions were expressed in newpaper articles – he made no speeches on the subject.

THE KENYAN ASIANS

The immigration issue was re-heated by the controversy over the status of Kenyan Asians which developed in late 1967. In the 1963 Act granting Kenya independence the British Government gave Kenyan residents a two-year period in which to choose British and Kenyan citizenship, with the chance to retain their British passports in the interim. The plan was designed to give British whites the right to return, but it left the Kenyans of Asian descent in an ambiguous position. It was not clear for example whether the Kenyans would continue to hold U.K. citizenship after the two year grace period – thus exempting them from the 1962 Commonwealth immigration control legislation. The question became of central importance between 1964 and 1967 as the Kenyan government made it clear that the Asians were no longer welcome in the country. As a result, part of the 100,000 who had retained their British passports elected to enter the U.K., thus provoking sharp dispute as to whether they had the unrestricted right to do so.

Iain Macleod had been one of the architects of the Kenyan independence agreement in 1962, which now proved to be so controversial as to damage his position inside the Tory party. He countered with a determined defence of the 1962 free entry clauses: his actions in 1962 had earned him a liberal reputation and he was in no position to back down in 1967. Thus in a February 1968 *Spectator* article, Macleod wrote that the Conservatives meant to exclude the Kenyan Asians from the 1962 Immigration Act and so had an obligation to let them enter the country freely.[23]

Initially the Conservatives sought to avoid public debate over the issue of the Kenyan Asians and the question was not selected for discussion at the party conference in Scarborough. During the conference Powell became the first politician to raise the issue of controlling the number of Kenyans allowed into Britain. He issued his call for controls at a meeting held in Deal, where he argued that when the Kenyan government decided the Asians were not citizens, they had unexpectedly become eligible to hold British passports, a situation never anticipated by the framers of the Kenyan Independence Act. Thus no implicit or explicit promise had ever been given to the Kenyan Asians about their right to enter Britain. As for the 'loophole' in the 1962 Commonwealth Immigrants Act, he suggested that an amendment to that legislation should be passed limiting the entry right of Kenyan Asians. He also suggested that the High Commission be instructed to issue British passports only in exceptional circumstances. He continued to call for tighter immigration controls at meetings in Bournemouth and Wolverhampton in December, on each occasion suggesting that the number of immigrants allowed in was too high and reiterating his call for voluntary repatriation.[24] He returned to the theme at a Conservative dinner in Walsall at the beginning of February 1968. The Walsall speech, though less publicised than his dramatic speech in Birmingham later in April, clearly foreshadowed it. For the first time Powell attempted to identify with his constituents' fears. Rather than speak as an M.P. who was in some way above the mass electorate, he chose to speak as a man experiencing the same problems as his constituents.[25] He told of 'the sense of hopelessness and helplessness' felt by 'those of us living in the Midlands'· or 'we in Wolverhampton'. He called present British immigration policy 'crazy' and spoke graphically of schools having only one white student in a class. The whole tenor of the speech was such as to portray the outside world as being hostile and insensitive to the particular problems Midlanders like himself and his constituents were experiencing.

The Walsall speech marked a clear change in his approach to the immigration problem and won him editorial praise from the *Sunday Express* and the *Daily Sketch* and condemnation from the *Sunday Times*.[26] He also drew criticism from his colleagues in the Shadow Cabinet, most notably Quintin Hogg and Iain Macleod.[27] Nonetheless the speech may have had an impact on Government policy, for only five days later the Labour Government conceded that it was prepared to introduce controls to limit the entrance of Kenyan Asians.[28] Mr Callaghan, the Home Secretary, presenting statistics to show that the number of African immigrants had doubled since 1965,[29] pushed a Bill incorporating such controls through the Commons in three days and Powell, inevitably, took most of the credit and blame for having panicked the Government into a change of mind.[30] While fifteen Tory liberals had opposed the Bill, there was a clear change of emphasis in the Conservative party too, where attitudes hardened against the Race Relations Bill which would come before the House in April. It was clear indeed that Powell had helped split the Conservative party to the grave embarrassment of Heath. The party's tough opposition to the free entry of Kenyan Asians had alienated some left-wing Tories, including Humphry Berkeley, who resigned from the party because of its immigration policies. This liberal minority was determined to restore the balance by supporting the Government's anti-discrimination legislation. The Tory right, led by Powell and Duncan Sandys, opposed the legislation and demanded that the party take a firm stand against the Bill. To avoid a public worsening of those divisions Heath and his allies inside the Shadow Cabinet decided to draft a reasoned amendment criticising the method, rather than the actual intentions, of the legislation. By such a tactic Heath hoped to placate the Tory left by not directly opposing the Government's Bill and to appease the right by the inclusion in the reasoned amendment of the suggestion that further immigration should by drastically cut.[31] Powell served on the sub-committee which drafted the reasoned amendment and supplied some of the language which was incorporated.[32] In addition, a Tory M.P. remembered that Powell had agreed to support Quintin Hogg's approach to the measure in the parliamentary debate.[33]

It was against this background that Powell delivered his April 20 speech at Birmingham, timing it to achieve maximum attention with the Race Relations Bill due for a second reading the next Tuesday in Parliament.

'LIKE THE ROMAN'
Despite his Walsall speech, Powell must have surely realised as he rose to speak in Birmingham that the address in his hands was bound to have a sensational impact on his listeners, the Tory party, the electorate at large and his own career.[34] While he was careful to preface his remarks by saying he advocated nothing beyond official party policy, he acknowledged that people would criticise him for the remarks he was about to make; but, he said, he felt an obligation to make them anyway. The speech was a strange mixture of populist assertion and ancedote, statistics and classical allusion. Powell spoke as a tribune with sacred duty to voice the discontent and despair brought to him by his constituents, to repeat their stories of harassment and unhappiness, as ancient natives of the land now displaced by an engulfing alien tide. The emotive incident best recalled by the public later was of the (anonymous)

old lady who had complained to Powell of how immigrants had pushed excrement through her letter box. Having stated the problem in these terms, Powell turned his passionate attack to both the Race Relations Bill and the continuing inflow of immigrants. The Bill would add insult to injury by elevating immigrants into a privileged class; its passage, he warned, would be 'throwing a match into gunpowder'. The situation was already critical and yet, against all reason, the influx was allowed to continue. A country and its rulers who tolerated this 'must be mad, literally mad. It is like watching a nation busily engaged in heaping up its own funeral pyre.' As he looked ahead he was filled with foreboding; 'Like the Roman, I seem to see "the River Tiber foaming with much blood".' He concluded that the 'tragic and intractable phenomenon which we watch with horror on the other side of the Atlantic' might yet come to Britain unless drastic action was taken.

The speech was a major incident in its own right. It was true enough that Powell's policy recommendations were in advance of the official Tory line only as regards the technical (if highly material) question of the status of dependants of immigrants already in Britain, and in his flat opposition to the Race Relations Bill, although this hardly distinguished him from a very considerable body of Conservative opinion both at Westminster and in the country. Shortly after the speech, indeed, Conservative Central Office issued a statement acknowledging that the speech was not out of line with official policy.[35] Heath himself issued a call for voluntary repatriation and a drastic cut in the number of immigrants allowed into the country in a *News of the World* article which appeared the day after the Birmingham speech.

Such considerations were doubtless important to Powell himself; to the media and the party leadership they were quite beside the point. The headlines next day in the mass circulation *Sun*[36] ('Immigration: the Powell Explosion') and the *London Evening Standard*[37] ('Race: Powell's Bombshell') expressed accurately enough the real excitement and fury generated by the speech. The press was in little doubt as to the extraordinary spectacle it had just witnessed. One of the country's leading political figures, a man of Cabinet rank and experience with a powerful aura of cerebral severity, had made all his own the cause of the pubs and clubs, the bingo-halls and the football terraces. The bitter anecdotes of a thousand Coronation Streets had poured forth from an apparent stalwart of the Establishment and were set amidst the classical allusions so long the hall-mark of the authoritative in British political rhetoric. Powell had moreover trodden an ambiguous line in his talk of the holocaust to come. While he had averred merely that racial conflict of some kind was sadly predictable, given the strength of native English resentment against the incoming immigrants, he had voiced the resentments sympathetically and had not condemned them. The implication was strong to both his supporters and opponents that he was siding with a righteous assertion of yeoman English wrath against the threatening alien tide.

Heath took firm and immediate action, telephoning Powell to tell him he was being sacked from the Shadow Cabinet for making a speech the Leader considered 'to be racialist in content and liable to exacerbate racial tension'.[38] The Conservative party opposed racialism and discrimination, Heath said, and Powell's speech could lead possibly even to civil strife. Powell responded to Heath with a letter which got headlines across the country.

Powell conceded, somewhat patronisingly, that Heath might one day be a good, or even great, prime minister, but implicitly criticised his Leader for lacking courage. He spoke of his anxiety at 'the impression you often give of playing down and even unsaying policies and views which you hold and believe to be right for fear of clamour from some sections of the press or public'.[39]

There was naturally much speculation about why he delivered the speech in the first place. He stuck to the simple position that he felt an obligation to speak out. The last sentence of the Birmingham speech read: 'All I know is that to see, and not to speak, would be the great betrayal'.[40] There was however much speculation both inside the Shadow Cabinet and in the press as to whether Powell was using the speech as a means of challenging the Heath leadership.[41]

Certainly there was general consensus inside the Conservative party that Heath had to take a strong line against Powell to maintain any hope of emerging as a strong leader.[42] Thus Heath's immediate sacking of Powell was seen as strengthening his position as Leader, temporarily at least. A potentially heated debate in the Commons over the Race Relations Bill was averted and the split in the party over immigration was muted for a short period.

THE SPEECH'S IMPACT

The impact of the Birmingham speech continued to reverberate however, with some commentators asking whether Powell had not inflicted real damage on the post-war political consensus. Others focused on the scale of his popular support, attributing it to the fact that the electorate had finally alighted upon someone who bridged the gap between élite and mass opinion. (This interpretation will be dealt with at some length in Part II.) Questions were also raised as to the impact of the speech (and the response to it) in different strata of British society. Needless to say it produced widely varying responses within the Conservative party, in the electorate and from the press.

Determining the extent of support for Powell inside the Conservative party is difficult. It does seem clear, however, that the most antagonistic reaction to the speech came from those at the highest levels of the party while the most favourable response came from the bottom of the party hierarchy. In the Shadow Cabinet itself he had absolutely no support. Every member supported Heath's decision to sack him and considered the speech to be detrimental to the development of party policy on immigration.[43] Inside the Parliamentary party it is doubtful whether he had as many as forty-five supporters. A *Daily Mail* poll of M.P.s just before the second reading of the Race Relations Bill showed that twenty of twenty-one Conservative Members surveyed felt the speech had been destructive and that Heath had taken the proper action.[44] This survey probably underestimates Powell's support in the party. There were three wings of the party on race relations at this time, Powell being part of the extreme right-wing faction which opposed the Race Relations Bill and favoured an almost total ban on coloured immigration. The largest possible membership figure one could give to this grouping would be forty-five – the number of Tory rebels who opposed the third reading of the Race Relations Bill. However, David Wood in *The Times* analysed the political outlooks of the forty-five M.P.s and concluded that hard-core right-wing opponents of the legislation numbered only about seventeen. The bulk of Tory M.P.s were in the middle on race relations and supported the Heath policies. There were also about twenty-four left-wing Conservatives (including a Shadow Cabinet member, Sir Edward Boyle) who did not support the Government's reasoned amendment.[45] To be sure, a number of Powell's supporters were highly vocal (such as Sir Gerald Nabarro) or prolific journalistically (such as Angus Maude), but they had little influence within the Shadow Cabinet or the 1922 Committee. Hard-core support for Powell probably did not extend beyond ten or fifteen men – including (besides Nabarro and Maude) John Biffen, Ronald Bell, Harold Gurden and John Jennings. The weakness of Powell's parliamentary supporters was clearly seen in two events the week following his Birmingham speech. First no effort was made by the Tory right to oppose the second reading of the Race Relations Bill. True, Powell had played a role in framing the reasoned amendment. But the clear implication of his Birmingham speech was that this was a wholly inadequate gesture. Powell's position would certainly have been bolstered by a large right-wing rebellion against both the Government's Bill and the Tories' amendment. In the event – and perhaps because of the furore over Powell's speech – the right assented to supporting the reasoned amendment while the left wing opposed it. Secondly, when Sir Edward Boyle abstained on the reasoned amendment, Nabarro made an effort to have the 1922 Commitee recommend that he too be sacked from the Shadow Cabinet. Nabarro was very poorly received and his suggestion evoked very little response.[46] Journalistic commentary strongly emphasised Powell's relative isolation. Peter Jenkins of the *Guardian* called him more of a 'symbol' than a leader.[47] James Margach in the *Sunday Times* stated flatly that Powell 'has no power base at Westminster'.[48] At best, Margach suggested, he could get between forty and fifty votes against Heath in a straight leadership contest. Even this may have been unduly optimistic, for Powell had actually alienated some of his free-market supporters by his views on immigration. As David Wood noted in *The Times*:[49]

> It is true that Mr Powell, an unmistakably ambitious man, is now on the back-benches as a potential leader of the freelancing right, but he has a long way to go before he looks like a convincing leader. Mr Powell has been winning followers lately among youngish M.P.s who are in love with his economic message, but some of these happen to be far removed from his position on race matters.
>
> The Powellite group, in so far as it identifiably exists, is not yet a tightly knit force or arrangement of political subjects and to that extent Mr Heath has no need for the present worry about his right flank.

However, down in the party the response was more favourable, but there was no orchestrated criticism of Heath's action. A number of constituency associations in the Midlands, including Sir Gerald Nabarro's in South Worcestershire, did pass resolutions condemning Heath's action,[50] and some moderate M.P.s also drew criticism from their local associations for not coming to Powell's defence.[51] But there was no organised outpouring of support. Moreover the speculation that the solid front against Powell might crumble, once the shock had passed away, proved erroneous.[52] There was no challenge to the Heath leadership at the 1968 party conference and, though Powell's speech there for tighter immigration restrictions received a standing ovation, so too did Quintin Hogg's defence of the Shadow Cabinet's position. The immigration resolution debated was relatively non-controversial and easily passed.[53]

There were scattered traces of support for Powell in the borough council elections held in May. In Southall, Orpington and Lambeth, Tory candidates put out literature saying 'We back Powell, don't you?' It was only too clear to most Conservatives however that such divisions would be exploited by Labour, for Robert Mellish (the Labour M.P.) immediately sought to embarrass Heath by challenging him to repudiate these local candidates.[54] There may have been more support for Powell within Tory local ranks than was visible on the surface,[55] but if so the main point was clearly that it was submerged under the greater principle of party unity behind the leadership.

Press response was heavily negative. Of forty-five local and national newspapers examined, twenty-eight were unfavourable, ten had mixed reactions and only seven were favourable.[56] It is worth noting, however, that the combined circulation of the only two nationals favourable to Powell (the *Daily Express* and the *News of the World*) at 10 million nearly matched the total circulations (11.3 million) of the seven that were unfavourable. Moreover, although Powell's own local paper (the *Wolverhampton Express and Star*) was unfavourable, a number of important local papers (including the *Glasgow Herald*, *Birmingham Evening Mail* and *Liverpool Daily Post*) displayed the same mixed editorial reactions as did the *Daily Telegraph* and *Daily Sketch*.

The press in fact was caught between an almost uniformly anti-Powell establishment and a mass public whose reactions were starkly different. As Table 2.1 shows, polls completed after his speech showed that between 60 % and 75 % of the electorate were in sympathy with him and disapproved of Heath's sacking of him from the Shadow Cabinet. Feeling ran deep as well as wide: London dockers and meat porters, traditionally strong Labour supporters, actually marched to Westminster to demonstrate support for Powell – an event which made almost as great an impact as the Birmingham speech itself.[57] But it was not just the working class that supported him: all sections of the electorate gave him high levels of support. Whether analysed by class, party, age or region, all groups in the electorate were heavily pro-Powell after the speech.[58]

TABLE 2.1 Attitudes to Powell's speech and sacking, Apr 1968

	Gallup %	O.R.C. %	N.O.P. %	Daily Express %
Agree or disagree with what Powell said about immigrants				
Agree	74	82	67	79
Disagree	15	12	19	17
Don't know	11	6	14	4
	100	100	100	100
	(928)			
Heath right or wrong to sack Powell				
Right	20	18	25	—
Wrong	69	73	61	—
Don't know	11	9	14	—
	100	100	100	
	(928)			

Source: Gallup Poll CQ 576, provided Gallup Polls Ltd; *NOP Political Bulletin*, May 1968, 9; *South Wales Echo*, 25 Apr 1968 for O.R.C. data; and Jack Field, 'Race Relations and the Polls', *Race Today* 1, June 1969, 37 for the *Daily Express* data.

If Powell's intent in making his Birmingham speech had been to increase his popular following, he had certainly succeeded. Gallup recorded a 23 % rise in the percentage of respondents favouring him as a successor to Heath. N.O.P. recorded a similar – though much less pronounced – finding. Three months after the speech, Gallup found that his support fell to the levels recorded in the April N.O.P. poll.

TABLE 2.2   Choice for Tory leadership should Heath resign, Apr–July 1968

	Gallup* *March* %	*Gallup* *April* %	*N.O.P.* *April* %	*Gallup* *July* %
Powell	1	24	13	13
Maudling	20	18	11	14
Douglas-Home	10	8	9	7
Macleod	6	7	7	9
Hogg	6	5	5	6
Lloyd	5	1	—	2
Other	6	3	3	2
Don't know	46	34	52	47
	100	100	100	100

* The fieldwork for the two Gallup polls was done within two weeks of one another in April, before and after the Birmingham speech.

The considerable disparity between N.O.P. and Gallup initial findings is perhaps explicable by the fact that Gallup prefaced its questions on the party leadership by two questions about the Birmingham speech, both of which drew largely positive responses and provided a probably biased context for the question about a sucessor to Heath; the net effect of this bias seems to have been to move 'don't knows' from the March survey into the Powell camp. If figures are computed on the basis of only those with definite opinions, the disparity narrows, as Powell receives 36% (Gallup) and 27% (N.O.P.).

Source: *Gallup Political Index*, May 1968, 47 and July 1968, 86; and *N.O.P. Political Bulletin*, May 1968, 6.

Powell's huge popularity appears to have been single-issue based. A July 1968 Gallup poll asking respondents whether they favoured more or less economic planning found that 36% of Powell supporters, but only 32% of the whole sample, favoured state intervention. There did appear to have been some relationship between being on the right of the Tory party and supporting Powell. Of those people saying they would be more inclined to support Heath if he 'shifted his policy to the right – became more strongly Tory', 47% said they would be more inclined to support the Tories if Powell were the leader, and only 28% said they would be less inclined. Of those people saying they would be less inclined to support Heath if he moved right, only 25% said they would be more inclined to vote Conservative with Powell as leader and 52% said they would be less inclined.[59] The Birmingham speech thus gave the electorate a general sense that Powell was on the right of the party, but it apparently did little to win support for his economic views. It seems possible indeed that many of his supporters did not know of his views on issues besides immigration.

In the wake of the Birmingham speech the chief charge levelled against Powell was that he had worsened race relations both by hardening racial attitudes and by lending a new veneer of respectability to racialist feeling, encouraging those who were anti-immigrant to be more confident and assertive in their demeanour. On the first point the evidence gathered by Studlar suggests that his speech produced an increase in anti-immigrant feeling which was both very slight and merely temporary.[60] There is no clear evidence one way or another to support or disprove the second charge. All that one may say is that, thus far at least, his more dire predictions ('the Tiber foaming with blood') have not been fulfilled, let alone self-fulfilling.

What does seem possible is that he may have had some effect, temporarily at least, in slowing the progress of public opinion towards more liberal positions on race. The speech (as Table 2.3 shows) apparently reversed public attitudes towards the Race Relations Bill then before Parliament.

TABLE 2.3 Attitudes toward Race Relations Bill during April 1968 (Birmingham speech, 20 April)

	Gallup Mid-Apr %	O.R.C. Apr 18–21 %	Gallup Apr 26–29 %
Approve	42	53	30
Disapprove	29	36	46
Don't know	29	11	24
	100	100	100

Source: For the O.R.C. data, *Evening Standard*, 25 Apr; for the Gallup data, *Daily Telegraph*, 25 Apr, *Gallup Opinion Index*, May 1968 2.

Powell was relatively silent during the summer of 1968, making no contribution to the debate on the third reading of the Race Relations Bill in July.[61] During September most of his speeches were devoted to defence policy and to denationalisation of industry,[62] where his views went far beyond the official Conservative party study then about to be published. He called for widespread denationalisation of even the most unprofitable concerns, while official policy emphasised merely the need to halt any extension of denationalisation.[63] He also made the first speech on Scottish and Welsh nationalism during autumn 1968. While both the Government and the Conservatives had moved towards the idea of limited devolution of power to the regions, Powell suggested that Wales and Scotland should either be totally independent from the U.K. or should remain members on the same terms as other regions.[64] Both parties had to face the fact that he had enormous popular support, with his contrary views now spanning prices and incomes policy, defence, nationalisation, the allocation of social services race and devolution – he was almost offering a complete alternative programme. At the October 1968 Labour party conference Harold Wilson spoke about Powell as if he and not Heath were the leader of the Conservative party. Wilson compared Powellism to a virus and said it had infected the Conservative party at every level of the organisation.[65] On the Conservative side none other than Iain Macleod, formerly one of Powell's closest friends, became the first front-bench spokesman since April 1968 to attack him directly on anything beside his racial views.[66] Macleod said that the market had not operated in the way Powell suggested it did since the Middle Ages. While he did concede that his defence views were worth debating, he said that Powell 'from his ivory tower' dreamt of a society where the biggest employer, customer and consumer refrained from regulating currency rates and avoided taking a role in labour-management disputes. Without state intervention, Macleod suggested, much of the country would work for low wages. Without strong unions people would be forced to take whatever they were offered. On immigration Macleod simply labelled Powell 'a demogogue'. At the Tory conference Macleod repeated his jibes at Powell and said 'this is the year of the hotheads and the demogogues and the pedlars of panaceas'.[67] Powell and Quintin Hogg did clash at the conference over immigration as has been noted, but neither on that issue nor on the broader front did Powell show any sign of wishing to take up a personal trial of strength with the party leadership. On the contrary his speech was surprisingly moderate. He clearly wished to establish that he could, while maintaining the views he held, remain within the Conservative mainstream.[68] Benefiting from Powell's tactical discretion, Heath emerged from the conference in a much stronger position than many had anticipated. In contrast, Powell's mass support showed signs of erosion during the conference, as Table 2.4 shows. Moreover after the conference O.R.C. reported that, while in October they had found a 73–18% majority disapproving of Heath's action in sacking Powell, in November this majority had declined to a 53–32% split.[69]

A pre-conference N.O.P. poll had also confirmed Gallup's earlier findings in that there was still no relationship between support for Powell and support for the issues he advocated other than immigration. In the aftermath of his speech on denationalisation, N.O.P. found that equal proportions of all respondents and Powell supporters (53%) favoured keeping gas a nationalised industry. Similarly, almost equal

TABLE 2.4   Heath or Powell choice for prime minister, Sep–Oct 1968

	N.O.P. (*pre-conference*) %	O.R.C. (*pre-conference*) %	O.R.C. (*post-conference*) %
Heath	41	48	49
Powell	37	41	30
Don't know	22	11	21
	100	100	100

Source: *N.O.P. Political Bulletin*, Sep 1968; *Sunday Times*, 17 Nov 1968 for a report of the O.R.C. data.

percentages of the electorate (56%) and Powell supporters (55%) felt that a prices and incomes policy was still necessary. But N.O.P. did find a clear relationship between dissatisfaction with Heath's leadership and support for Powell. Fifty-seven per cent of Tories who were dissatisfied with Heath supported Powell for the Conservative leadership, while a similar proportion of those who were satisfied with Heath's performance favoured him to maintain his position.[70]

Powell's response to this situation was to make another address on immigration, this time at Eastbourne before the Greater London Rotarians.[71] Despite his discreet demeanour at the party conference he was, he made it clear, entirely unrepentant. He had not, he said, violated party policy by his Birmingham speech and had been unjustly sacked from the Shadow Cabinet. A dangerous gap had developed in Britain between 'the overwhelming majority of the people throughout the country on one side and, on the other side, a tiny majority with almost a monopoly hold upon the channels of communication, who seem determined not to know the facts and not to face the realities, who will resort to any device or extremity to blind both themselves and others'.[72] He predicted that with a minimum immigrant population of 4·5 million by the year 2000, a number of little Washington D.C.s would develop in Britain. To alleviate the problem he again advocated refusal of entry to immigrants' dependants and 'large-scale voluntary, but organised, financed and subsidised repatriation'. He envisaged such a programme being supervised by a Ministry of Repatriation, which he offered to head.[73]

Both these proposals ran counter to official Conservative policy: the precarious harmony achieved at the party conference lay in ruins. Heath, to whom the challenge was provocatively clear, responded furiously, charging Powell with 'racial character assassination' and adding that 'the party would never accept a total ban on coloured immigration'.[74] There was also some talk of prosecuting him for a violation of the Race Relations Act, but the Attorney General decided against bringing any action.[75]

Press opinion hardened against Powell. Of thirty-four post-Eastbourne newspaper editorials studied, only 9% were favourable to him, down from 16% in April. Hostile editorials increased from 62% to 89%. Every major national newspaper, with the exception of the *News of the World*, condemned him. Even formerly favourable papers such as the *Telegraph*, and the *Express* came out against him.[76]

There had also been a clear drop in public support, as Table 2.5 shows.

TABLE 2.5 Attitudes towards Powell's immigration views, Apr–Dec 1968

	Apr 1968 %	Dec 1968 %
Agree	74	58
Disagree	15	26
Don't know	11	16
	100	100

Source: *Gallup Political Index*, May 1968 and Dec 1968.

Powell's position with the public remained strong nonetheless — O.R.C. found 74% of their sample in agreement with his repatriation plan while only 19% disagreed.[77] This despite the fact that 55% said he made race relations in Britain more difficult and only 11% said he had made things better. In another O.R.C. survey, 38% of coloured immigrants drawn from a sample of questionable validity said they wanted to be repatriated if the Government would provide financial assistance.[78] Almost half the immigrants surveyed (47%) also said they favoured further controls on the number of immigrants let into the country. While immigrants were hardly supporters of Powell, with only 3% saying he had made their lives better and 27% saying he had made their lives more difficult, 70% said he had made no difference or were not able to offer an opinion.

Having now made it clear that he was fully maintaining his views on immigration to the plain contempt both of his own party leadership and the entire liberal establishment, Powell went no further. Nor did he need to. His every appearance was news, particularly since he chose to speak before a number of university audiences despite (or because of?) the large hostile demonstrations which invariably marked such occasions.[79] Powell also engaged in a highly charged debate with David Frost on television in January, generating intense audience reactions.[80] While he did concede in one speech that one could not lay down strict numerical quotas for entering immigrants,[81] he joined twenty-three other Conservatives in voting against the second reading of a Bill setting up an appeals mechanism for immigrants denied admission into the country.[82]

Meanwhile Heath, having shown he was capable of a firm stand against Powell's initial challenge, now began to edge towards his former colleague's position. Consciously or not choosing to speak before the same audience which had heard Powell's first major immigration speech, Heath addressed the Walsall Conservatives in tones not dissimilar to those used by Powell almost a year before. Getting down to 'brass tacks' – as he put it – Heath urged that only the closest relatives of immigrants should be let into the country. Entry for all other immigrants should be strictly limited with the Government reserving the right to remove people after a yearly review, permanent residence being granted only after passage through four consecutive reviews. In addition, the entry of any immigrant should be made conditional on Home Office investigation into whether both 'room' and jobs were available for him in the area he wished to go to.[83]

With Heath apparently suggesting that each individual immigrant should have to pass through the eye of a needle in order to enter Britain, the Tory leader's popularity *vis-à-vis* Powell picked up smartly, as Table 2.6 shows.

TABLE 2.6   Heath or Powell for leader of the opposition and prime minister, 1968–69

| | Sep 1968 | | Jan 1969 | |
	For Tory leader %	For PM %	For Tory leader %	For PM %
Heath	40	41	47	49
Powell	37	37	36	34
Don't know	23	22	17	17
	100	100	100	100

Source: *N.O.P. Political Bulletin*, Sep 1968 and Jan 1969.

While the data did reveal a slippage in Powell's support since April 1968, there was no sign at all of his support slipping back to the level of his 'pre-immigration' days. While in December 1967 only 13% of Gallup's respondents had named Powell as one of their first three men for a Conservative government, 33% mentioned him in January 1969.[84] This left him an easy second to Heath, his popular standing now on an entirely new plateau. Heath had narrowly contained the challenge, first by standing firm and then by stealing some of his antagonist's clothes. Powell, though he was to return to immigration from time to time, now began to turn to other issues.

3 Powell and the 1970 Tory Election Victory

By 1969 the Labour Government was in deep trouble. After the 1967 devaluation its credit was now unlikely to recover; its incomes and industrial relations policies were running into deep and increasing trade union resistance. Unemployment mounted. The Left was utterly disenchanted by Government support for the U.S. in Vietnam. Despite the failure of the public to take Heath entirely to its heart, the Conservatives led the opinion polls by record margins, and by-elections told the same story. Wilson, jettisoning his former opposition to the E.E.C., sought a way out in a renewed application for British membership.

The Conservative party generally and its Leader particularly were supporters of such a move. But Powell's position was less clear. Conservative anti-Marketeers had approached him immediately after he was dropped from the Shadow Cabinet, urging him to speak against E.E.C. membership.[1] Although he rejected these approaches, his attitudes to the E.E.C. had indeed moved away from his 1967 support for British entry. Even then he had been fearful that the U.K.'s identity would be submerged if it joined with other European nations.[2] Now he moved to a position of outright opposition to E.E.C. membership, thus again aligning himself against all three major party leaderships. Prudently, however, he did not at first seek to emphasise his differences with his party's leadership over Europe. Immigration had made him an outcast. The anti-Market cause had a vast potential following, including many Conservatives as well as the Labour left. This new constituency required gentle cultivation. For Powell the Market issue was primarily one of parliamentary sovereignty. In his initial anti-Market speech he spoke of the humiliation and degradation Britain had faced with the loss of Empire, the revelations of its weak position East of Suez, and its declining trade. Britain needed a new self-image which could best be created outside the Community.[3]

No sooner had the Labour left found themselves with this uncomfortable new bedfellow on the E.E.C. issue than they also found themselves in an embarrassing collaboration with him in defeating their leaders' bipartisan consensus on House of Lords reform in April 1969. Powell opposed the reform largely because it would involve large-scale

tampering with an institution which was acceptable because it had
functioned effectively for so long. The left disliked the huge extension
of prime-ministerial patronage involved in the measure and were, in
many cases, abolitionists anyway. The 'unholy alliance' – as Iain
Macleod bitterly called it – of Powell and the Labour left helped upset
the Bill by the most consummate exploitation of parliamentary procedure, finally forcing the Government to abandon it with its legislative
schedule in complete disarray. Some Labour opponents of reform such
as William Hamilton and Andrew Faulds (Griffiths's successor as M.P.
for Smethwick) confessed themselves 'ashamed' of Powell's support.
Many were more struck however by the sheer brilliance of the victory
won by the collaboration of Michael Foot and Enoch Powell, undeniably
the two most distinguished parliamentarians in the House.[4]

Powell returned to immigration in a speech given in June 1969.[5] He
accused Heath of failing to grasp the magnitude of the problem and
suggested that Britain now faced a threat from within to its nationhood.
The only solution was repatriation. For the cost of eighteen months of
aid to underdeveloped countries, Britain's entire immigrant population
could be repatriated. On the basis of the O.R.C. poll of immigrants,[6]
he predicted that half would want to return to their native lands. On the
other hand he also sought to minimise his specific policy differences with
Heath after the latter's Walsall speech: the only question they disagreed
about, according to Powell, was the right of dependents to enter Britain
freely. Making no apology for returning to the subject, he said 'If I
discerned a threat to the future of the nation and did not speak out,
there could be no point in my remaining in political life'.[7] Towards
Heath the tone of the speech was almost conciliatory, if a little patronis-
ing for his belated support. There were however none of the lurid
examples and metaphors used in the April 1968 speech. Nonetheless
the speech drew a predictably fierce response, from the Labour side at
least. Mr Callaghan, the Home Secretary, urged Powell to rid himself of
the taint of racialism and realise that repatriation was nothing more than
a grandiose scheme with little hope of success.[8]

Powell followed up his speech with an address to the Bradford
Conservatives in July. In it he warned that the time would shortly come
when large cities and towns would become 20% to 25% coloured.
Again he spoke in terms of personal and local identification. He said
that 'you in Bradford have shared with us in Wolverhampton and with
the other people of certain other towns and cities what until recently
was a private grief'.[9] He also spoke of the impression 'ordinary people
like ourselves' have that the number of immigrants entering the country
was larger than official figures showed.[10] If the purpose of these two
immigration speeches in summer 1969 was to consolidate his popular
support, they were a success. After his Bradford speech Gallup found
the number of people agreeing with his views on immigration had

increased since November 1968 from 58% to 64% while those opposing him had slipped from 26% to 24%.[11]

The 'Powell phenomenon' in the polls was now well over a year old. He still made no move however to challenge Heath's leadership directly or even to organise back-bench supporters, much to the consternation of his admirers. In late September and early October 1969 a consortium of businessmen issued almost daily statements about the amount of money they were willing to offer Powell should he stand for the Tory leadership. The group first announced they would pay him £10,000 to stand against Heath. When the offer drew no reply they raised it to £20,000. At that point he issued a statement that the Conservatives already had a leader whom he supported. Undeterred, his would-be backers indicated that pledges of over £39,000 had been received. He still refused to stand against Heath.[12]

Such dramatically selfless pledges of loyalty to Heath put him in a strong position to continue opposing him on almost every issue. He continued to speak against the Market until the party conference in October when, however, he chose to speak on the economy and urged the Government to float the pound in the wake of the German Government's decision to expose the Deutschemark to the market.[13] Although Macleod replied to Powell in astringent terms, the latter's apparent statesmanship and almost disinterestedness probably made him more formidable to the leadership than any outright challenge on the E.E.C. or immigration. In fact there was only a 395-vote majority for a resolution which stated that the Conservative party policy was the only one likely to be successful in controlling immigration. The substantial negative vote was a clear demonstration of Powell's effect inside the constituency associations.

The polls moreover showed that the erosion of his popular support had stopped. Indeed, as Figs 3.1 and 3.2 show, his standing actually began to improve again after the party conference in October 1969.

The public's unfavourable comparison of Powell with Heath as a leader did not apparently rest on any conviction that he was less sincere or weaker in his beliefs than Heath; rather the reverse, as Table 3.1 shows. Despite (or perhaps because of) his weaker ratings on these criteria, Heath was held more likely than Powell to solve the country's problems.

Having now 'pulled' Heath near his own position on immigration, Powell opened up a further gap by taking an even tougher line in a January 1970 speech to the Young Conservatives at Scarborough, arguing that repatriation was the first-priority solution for the social problem areas of high immigrant concentration. Special social welfare expenditures on such areas only spread the illusion that the problem could be alleviated. Such spending should in fact be cut out almost entirely:[14]

Except in connection with and as an integral part of a policy of voluntary repatriation, measures of finance and others to alleviate the problem of areas especially affected and, still more, measures to promote and facilitate the absorption or integration of that part of the coloured population which will eventually make a permanent home here and become a part of the national life, are worse than merely neutral. They are positively harmful in their net effect, because they encourage all concerned to deceive themselves for longer and longer as to the true magnitude and nature of the prospect and to squander these few remaining precious years when it might still be possible to avert disaster.

TABLE 3.1   The ratings of Heath and Powell on four leadership attributes, Oct 1969

	Most sincere %	Better leader %	Stronger in beliefs %	More likely to solve the country's problems %
Heath	36	47	24	44
Powell	40	35	60	30
Don't know	24	18	16	26
	100	100	100	100

Source: N.O.P. Political Bulletin, Oct 1969.

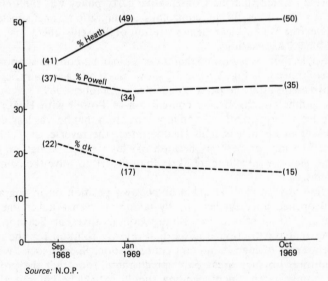

Source: N.O.P.

Fig. 3.1   Heath or Powell for prime minister 1968–69

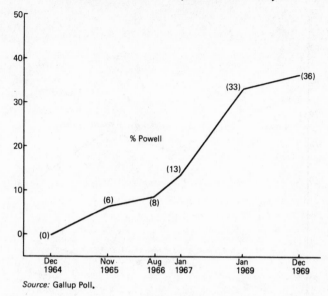

Source: Gallup Poll.

Fig. 3.2   First three men for Conservative government 1964–69

Heath interpreted the speech to mean that depriving areas of aid might solve the problem by creating conditions so deplorable that immigrants would leave of their own accord. Based on this interpretation, Heath labelled Powell's views 'unchristian' and said they were an example of 'man's inhumanity to man'.[15] This exchange widened the rift between the two men even farther and the Chief Whip, William Whitelaw, tried to arrange an exchange of letters between the men so that the dispute could be calmed down. However, the reconciliation attempt failed when Heath not only refused to concede that his interpretation of Powell's remarks merited any changes, but went further still – Powell's views, he said, were at variance with those of the Shadow Cabinet on almost every issue. He also pledged that Powell would not become a member of his government if the Conservatives won the next general election.[16]

Powell's ostracism was now complete. Heath had in effect announced that Powell was a politician without a future, a voice to cry permanently in the wilderness. This, together with fierce and renewed criticism of Powell from almost all points of the political compass, probably helped reduce support for his immigration views which, as Fig. 3.3. shows, diminished sharply after his Scarborough speech. Nonetheless his views still very easily commanded majority support among those with opinions about them.[17]

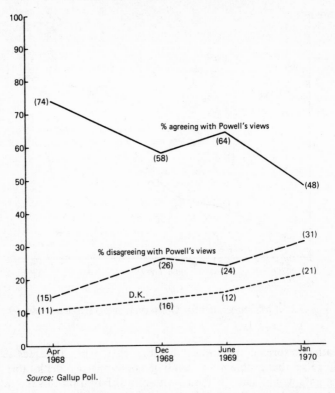

Source: Gallup Poll.

Fig. 3.3   Attitude to Powell's immigration views 1968–70

Yet just at the point that Powell's exclusion from any future Conservative government was being stated publicly, his influence on his party's leadership could be seen most dramatically. The Tory Shadow Cabinet convened for a weekend retreat at the end of January 1970 and the policy statement that came out of their Selsdon Park conference was very similar to the line Powell had been articulating for the past five years. They took a strong stand on law and order and crime in the streets after being shown television commercials from the 1969 New York City mayoral election. More to the point, they recommended that immigrants be treated in the same manner as aliens. On economics they came close to adopting an openly Powellite posture. Their recommendations for lower direct taxation, an end to Selective Employment Tax, greater competition in industry and fewer investment and development grants marked the seemingly final turn of the party away from the Butskellism of the post-war period.[18] Powell did not attend the gathering and subsequently refused to take credit for the policy document the conference produced. But he called the gathering a splendid public relations exercise and indicated that the party now recognised that events of the 1960s proved that much of what he had been saying during that period was right.[19]

Meanwhile he continued to deliver broadsides on the immigration issue, claiming (this time with the reluctant agreement of such groups as the Runnymede Trust) that his earlier predictions on entry statistics were being borne out.[20] He also launched a series of attacks against his most extreme and unruly opponents, student demonstrators. Echoing widespread anti-student feeling, he declared that student unionisation was 'a dangerous vehicle of anarchy and disorder'.[21]

The *Sun* took a poll of its readers (80% of whom are manual workers[22]) in March 1970 to ascertain whether they were aware of Powell's specific views on immigration.[23] While the *Sun* survey was not a random sample, they did receive replies from 20,000 readers. Overall 65% agreed with Powell's views and 35% disagreed. Interestingly, the *Sun* readers seemed inclined to believe that his views were more extreme than they actually were. Two-thirds believed that he had advocated issuing coloured immigrants with identity cards while another two-thirds said that he supported compulsory repatriation of any immigrant who had not lived in Britain for five years. At no point has he ever advocated either of these measures.

By this time a general election was clearly in the offing. The Conservative lead in the opinion polls, which reached its highest point (28%) just at the time Powell was making his Birmingham speech,[24] steadily dropped and by May 1970 the Gallup Poll showed a 7·5% Labour lead. Taking his cue from this and from favourable local election results, Mr Wilson-decided on a June election. Clearly Powell was going to be a major problem in the election, both for Labour because of his popularity with working-class voters, and for the Conservative leadership because of their disputes with him. Preserving all possible distance from him, Heath refused to exploit the immigration issue for political gain and tried to fight the election as if Powell did not exist. The public, of course, was very well aware that he did – in late May a *Sunday Times* poll showed that he was considered by half the electorate to be the leading Conservative after Heath. A similar *Sunday Times* poll in October 1968, had placed him fourth behind Heath, Sir Alec Douglas-Home and Reginald Maudling.[25]

The Conservatives' 1970 election manifesto was very much like the sort of document Powell would have produced before 1968. They advocated cuts in government spending and taxation, less government interference in business and industry, no compulsory wage controls, and a general strengthening of the competitive free enterprise system.[26] Powell also advocated these policies but gave far greater emphasis to immigration and the E.E.C. in his own election address. On immigration he called for a complete halt to all entry, a new citizenship law to distinguish between people who belong to the U.K. and the rest of the world, and voluntary repatriation. Unless these steps were taken the immigration problem could bring 'a threat of division, violence and bloodshed of American dimensions' and would thus add 'a powerful weapon to the armoury of anarchy'.

On the Common Market Powell avowed quite clearly his intention to force the Conservative party into opposing entry into Europe. While in his 1966 manifesto he had advertised his party's 'determination to get rid of the barriers between this country and its natural market in Western Europe', he wrote in 1970: 'The Conservative party is not yet committed to Britain entering the Common Market. I shall do my utmost to make sure we never do.'[27] The Conservative leadership attempted to ignore the manifesto, a difficult feat since it had been successfully timed to win treatment in the Sunday nationals. In answer to questions both Heath and Maudling played it down, suggesting that it contained nothing new.[28] Except for an attack from Quintin Hogg, Powell received little attention and it seemed that the tactic of ignoring Powell might succeed – until June 3 when Anthony Wedgwood Benn lashed out at him. Benn suggested that Powell had 'hoisted the flag of racialism' over Wolverhampton, a flag which was 'beginning to look suspiciously like the one that fluttered over Dachau and Belsen'. Powell's comments about immigrants were, Benn said, 'evil, filthy and obscene'. His colleagues in the Labour party immediately recognised the intemperate and politically damaging nature of his remarks. Harold Wilson was privately outraged by Benn's speech but said publicly only that he was not Benn's speech-writer but would not have used such language himself. For his part Powell responded by saying that he had returned from Australia in 1939 to fight the Nazis and would do the same now if the situation presented itself.[29]

Benn's outburst received huge publicity and put Powell in the centre of the election stage. Moreover Benn had effectively given the Tory leader a chance to defend Powell (and indirectly court his large working-class constituency) without specifically endorsing his views. Heath's personal animosity for Powell was such, however, that he could not bring himself to follow this course of action. Instead he went out of his way to dissociate himself from Powell's racial views, while attacking Benn for trying to smear the whole Tory party with Nazism. The inference appeared to be that Heath did not disapprove of Benn's language if it applied only to Powell.[30]

Apart from his election manifesto, and a speech on the balance of payments, Powell's first major speech came on June 11 in the midst of the national newspaper strike. Addressing his Wolverhampton constituents, Powell dwelt on the number of immigrants being let into the country and the lack of public recognition of how fast that population was growing.[31] In a truly sensational allegation he suggested that the public had been misled about the number of immigrants entering each year to the point 'where one begins to wonder if the Foreign Office was the only Department of State into which enemies of this country were infiltrated'.[32] There were numerous brawls at the speech between supporters and opponents of Powell so that the newspapers still appearing had near-riots to report, as well as allegations about treason plots.

Heath again felt compelled to rebut Powell directly. At his next morning's press conference, he attacked his views on the rights of dependents of coloured immigrants to enter and emphasised the need for special help to be given to areas with large concentrations of immigrants.[33] As for Powell's charge about spies infiltrating the Foreign Office, Heath coldly suggested that Powell place any evidence he had in front of the Home Secretary. This fierce attack on Powell led to more questions about the Conservative party's attitude towards him, and whether he and his colleagues still supported him as an official party candidate. Heath gave a begrudging 'yes' to the question and tried without success to turn the discussion to economics. A major part of the next day's press conference (June 13) was spent with Heath trying to persuade the press to shift its attention away from Powell to more important issues. He had little success, however, especially as Powell was scheduled to make another major address that day.

This June 13 speech came at the tail-end of the newspaper strike and proved to be highly controversial and emotive. Britain, Powell said, was under siege from 'the enemy within'.[34] The enemy – more sinister than the Nazis or the communists – was invisible and aimed to destroy society. Powell's 'enemy' included protestors (both student demonstrators and mobs in the street), militant Catholics in Northern Ireland and coloured immigrants. The great danger was that the British people would fail to recognise the danger before it was too late. There was almost no overtone of partisan politics in the speech and the peroration included only an indirect reference to supporting the Conservative party. In fact the strongest implication appeared to be that politicians of all parties had failed to understand the problem Britain faced. Heath again felt compelled to criticise the speech. He charged Powell with dividing the country and doing great damage.[35]

The speech drew headlines in the Sunday papers, the *Sunday Mirror*, the *Sunday People* and the *News of the World* all leading with it.[36] A Conservative party private poll showed that 48% of the electorate had heard about the speech and 67% said that Powell had 'made sense', (though 80% of those who had heard about the speech said it would probably damage the Tory's chances). At his Monday press conference (June 15) Heath refused to be drawn into another discussion of Powell.

Powell made another speech that Monday on the Common Market, suggesting that all candidates standing in the election should make their position clear on the issue. Powell opposed a referendum on the subject: a government would be unable to continue if the people chose a course of action in a referendum opposite to one the government had recommended. In such a situation it would be highly irresponsible for a government to try to continue ruling.[37] This made it all the more critical for M.P.s to be aware of the people's feelings. The speech again contained no direct plea for the electorate to vote Conservative.

Having now stated an almost alternative programme on the E.E.C. and immigration, Powell made a determined effort to transform his personal support into Tory support.[38] He said that the election was not about him personally but concerned a set of principles both he and the Conservative party believed in. While he indicated that he felt unjustly treated by his party's leaders, who had not rebutted the unfair charges, insults and obscenities that had been used against him, he told his followers that the Conservatives still deserved to be supported because of their commitment to economic and political freedom.

It is hard to come to a clear understanding of what he was trying to do in the 1970 election campaign. The only time he ever explicitly appealed to his audience to vote Tory was in his final election address. And even in that speech he prefaced his 'vote Conservative' plea with his own account of how he had been mistreated by his colleagues. A number of interpretations are possible. It could be that he wanted to make it clear he could disagree totally with Heath yet remain a loyal Conservative (as defined in his terms). It is also possible that he sought to emphasise his distance from the Tory leadership so that he would be given the credit in the event of a Conservative victory. He could have been trying to lay the groundwork for the case he eventually made – namely that he alone was responsible for the election upset. There is also a more Machiavellian interpretation which can be given to his actions. Powell, like many observers, could have become convinced during the election campaign that he was fighting for a lost cause. If that were the case, he could have been using the election campaign as a means of pressing his claim for the leadership. Heath had been running far behind Wilson in the polls and another election loss would most likely have been blamed on their leader. His own line during the campaign was so different from that of the leadership that he may have hoped to argue after a defeat that the party would have won more support had it stood on his manifesto.

But of course there was never a chance for Powell to implement the last strategy. The election result, a Conservative gain of seventy-seven seats giving them a comfortable overall majority of forty-three, was a bombshell. An elated and triumphant Mr Heath moved into No. 10 amidst the stunned silence of his opponents. Within the Tory party all thoughts of a leadership contest vanished in a tide of euphoric

gratitude to their leader, who had remained almost alone in his stead-
fast predictions of victory. It was the greatest electoral upset since the
end of the war.

A fever of controversy erupted over the result. Had Labour over-
confidence led their traditional supporters into abstention? Had they
been demoralised by England's exit from the World Cup shortly before
the vote? Had the polls been technically faulty or had there been large-
scale swings of opinion over the last month? Controversy was fiercest
of all over the effect of Powell, with many Labour politicians bitterly
complaining that they owed their defeat to racialism. Many Conservatives, probably at least, wondered guiltily whether this might not be
correct, but Mr Heath and the party leadership indignantly dismissed
such attempts to expropriate the credit for their victory. Many liberals
(in all parties) felt that, whatever the truth of such suggestions, it was
important to deny any credit to Powell in order to minimise the public
credence given to his views. Both the Institute of Race Relations and
Michael Steed, a prominent Liberal whose position as statistical analyst
for the Nuffield election studies provides him with the position virtually
of official chronicler, concluded negatively that there was no consistent
evidence to suggest that Powell's impact had swayed the result. True,
there had been an above average swing to the Tories in the West
Midlands. In Wolverhampton South West there was an 8·7% swing to
the Tories, which was 3·6% more than the overall English swing. Also,
a number of constituencies around Powell's (such as the neighbouring
Wolverhampton North East, Cannock and Brierley Hill) then showed
above average swings to the Conservatives. But both Steed and the
I.R.R. concluded there was no relationship between above average
swings to the Tories and candidates who took Powellite positions.[39]
Neither survey found any consistent relationship between constituencies
with large immigrant populations and swings to the Tories. While there
did appear to have been a slight 'Powell effect' in the West Midlands
which possibly cost Labour a seat or two,[40] a number of seats in London
and Birmingham with high immigrant concentrations had swung to the
Tories by less than the national average.[41]

Both the I.R.R. and Steed reported that immigrant turnout was much
higher than expected and it was possible that Powell's impact in
constituencies with large numbers of immigrants had been offset by a
large coloured vote for Labour. This was merely a speculative point
however, and, as Steed noted, there was no way to use election statistics
to test the hypothesis that Powell brought the Conservatives votes
nationally.[42]

It is possible to take the argument somewhat further. Examination
of aggregate election data, apart from suggesting a regional 'Powell
effect' in the West Midlands (irrespective of whether Tory candidates
were Powellite or not), leads to no clear conclusion. It is however

reasonable to assume that immigration was a national issue and that the 'Powell effect' would have had some impact across the board and nationally, not merely regionally and in constituencies with high immigrant concentrations.

There is certainly no doubt that Powell had every chance to make such a national impact, for he received a quite extraordinary amount of national press attention during the campaign (as Table 3.2 shows) – so much so that he equalled or outdid each of the three major party leaders. In this respect it was a virtual four-party election, except perhaps in the eyes of the furiously anti-Powell *Guardian* and the solidly Labour *Mirror*.

TABLE 3.2   Percentage of column-inches of election coverage devoted to Powell, 1970

Times %	Sketch %	Express %	Sun %	Mail %	Telegraph %	Mirror %	Guardian %
20	17	16	14	13	12	10	5

Source: Butler and Pinto-Duschinsky, *The British General Election of 1970*, p. 233.

There is also no doubt of his decisive impact on the election if one takes account of the enormous number of positive letters he received during the campaign and the reports which appeared of interviews with politicians after the election. Three of the major polling organisations – Harris, Gallup and N.O.P. – all concluded that Powell had made a considerable impact. The Harris Poll concluded that Benn had committed the biggest blunder of the campaign by attacking Powell for his immigration statements. Immigration was virtually the only policy area where the Tories had a better rating than Labour, and Powell, in their surveys, came across better on television than almost any other politician and had strongest appeal with working-class voters who had just been won back to Labour. Fifty-five per cent of Harris' respondents obtained favourable impressions of Powell on T.V. while 25% obtained bad impressions. Moreover Harris found it would probably have cost the Tories support had Heath taken action against Powell. Asked if they would respect Heath more or less if he expelled Powell from the Tory party, 18% of the sample said they would respect him more and 28% said they would respect him less.[43] Gallup agreed with Harris's conclusion about Powell's impact, pointing out that 23% of their post-election sample said his speeches had made them more inclined to vote Tory while only 11% said they had made them less inclined to do so.

Respondents were also emphatic (by a 50%–10% majority) in their belief that his speeches helped the Tories.[44] National Opinion Polls provided fuller and more persuasive evidence for the same conclusion in their post-election survey, which compared respondents' views of how they had intended to vote (when polled during the campaign) and how they actually voted. Overall, 42% of their sample said Powell had an influence on the election. Of that group no less than 60% admitted to having been influenced positively or negatively by him, as Table 3.3 shows. Among both potential and actual Tory voters who mentioned him, almost half were encouraged to vote Conservative while only a correspondingly small number were negatively influenced. His influence extended even wider on the Labour side; fully two-thirds of Labour intenders and voters who said he influenced the campaign acknowledged that he had some impact on how they voted. Perhaps most importantly, roughly one in five Labour intenders and voters were influenced towards the Tories by him. Finally, his influence was found to have been overwhelmingly influential among non-voters; 65% of this group admitted to having been influenced in their opinions by Powell, no less than seven out of every eight in a pro-Tory direction. The inference is very plain that such non-voters were heavily made up of normally Labour voters cross-pressured into abstention by Powell.

TABLE 3.3   Powell's effect on partisan choice, 1970*

	All %	Non-voters %	Conservatives		Labour	
			voters %	intenders %	voters %	intenders %
More likely to vote Tory	37	57	47	47	18	22
Less likely to vote Tory	23	8	6	7	51	45
Neither	40	35	47	46	30	33
Don't know	—	—	—	—	1	—
	100	100	100	100	100	100

* The question was only asked of the 42% of all respondents who indicated in a prior question that Powell had played a role in the national campaign.

Source: *N.O.P. Political Bulletin*, June/July 1970, 11.

The Butler-Stokes panel study provides an indirect indication of Powell's effect in 1970 through their examination of the electoral impact of the immigration issue. For an issue to affect voting behaviour it must meet a number of conditions.[45] First, the issue must be salient to a large number of voters – they must know and care about it. Second, the issue is most likely to have an impact upon voting behaviour if opinion on the question is skewed heavily in one direction. If a population is evenly divided there is little for parties to gain by advocating either side of a question too strongly. The third condition is that the public must associate different positions on the issue with the various parties. People can feel passionately about a question, but unless they perceive clear differences between the parties the issue has no impact on their partisan choice.

In the case of immigration the Butler-Stokes panel study found that while the first two conditions were met in 1964 and 1966, the third was not. That is, people had strong opinions about coloured immigration and uniformly wanted tighter controls. But in both years the Conservatives were perceived as being only marginally more in support of tighter controls than the Labour party and then only by voters in areas of large immigration concentrations.[46] However in 1969 and 1970 the public came to associate restrictive immigration policies with the Conservative party. These differences between the parties moreover were perceived nationally and not just in areas with large concentrations of coloured immigrants.[47] By 1970, voters in constituencies with a strident anti-immigration Tory candidate were no more likely than the rest of the electorate in 1970 to say that the Conservatives had the most restrictive policy.[48] Local party activity or the presence of large numbers of coloured immigrants had little to do with the perception of the Conservatives as the more restrictive party in 1970. How can this be explained?

This fundamental change in the structure of national attitudes opened the way to the exploitation of the immigration issue as one of major national impact in 1970 in a way that it had not been in 1964 or 1966. It seems overwhelmingly likely that Powell himself was responsible for this change of attitudes and that it was his speeches between 1968 and the 1970 election which gave the Tories a national reputation as the party most against coloured immigration. No other political figure did remotely as much to bring the issue to the fore. The impact of his speeches, as we have seen, was quite explosive; and he was almost universally successful in reaching the public with his message. As Studlar has noted:[49]

> ... one is led to the conclusion that Powell was the major influence in differentiating the party policies in the mind of the voters. Most of the electorate had heard of Powell, knew generally what his proposals on immigration were and were closer in their own positions to Powell than to the actual positions of the Labour and Conservative parties. The events of the parliamentary campaign in 1970 worked to associate Powell's position with the Conservative party, however much the party may have baulked at the notion.

Butler and Stokes reached a similar conclusion from their own analysis of the data. They found that 75% of the electorate knew of Powell's immigration proposals and 78% said they were glad he spoke out during the campaign. Thus, they noted that: 'Even if Mr Powell was far from being the spokesman of the party, it is hard to doubt that he had succeeded in associating the Conservatives with opposition to immigration in the public mind.'[50]

Butler and Stokes present evidence to show that 1966 Labour voters were more likely to vote Tory in 1970 if they perceived that the Conservatives were more likely to keep immigrants out. Among 1966 Labour supporters 21% of those who felt the Conservatives were more likely to keep immigrants out voted Tory, while only 11% of 1966 Labour voters who felt that there was either no difference between the parties or that Labour was more likely to keep immigrants out voted Conservative. They concluded, 'Here is strong prima facie evidence of an issue affecting party strength.'[51]

Using a multivariate statistical technique, Studlar similarly found that the Tories profited substantially from the immigration issue to the tune of 6·7% of the vote,[52] a high level of issue voting which dramatically equalled the effect of economic issues in the 1964 and 1966 elections. Indeed as Studlar noted, 'This is the first indication that a social issue could have the same impact on the British electorate that economic and class issues do.'[53]

The 1970 wave of the Butler-Stokes panel study also provides more direct evidence of Powell's impact. Nationally there was a 4·7% swing to the Conservatives between 1966 and 1970, with the panel revealing a smaller 3·6% swing. For the sake of clarity those respondents who did not vote in 1966 or could not recall their choice and also the one-quarter of the 1843 respondents who were not asked to evaluate Powell were ignored. Those who said they did not know how they voted or indicated they had not cast ballots in 1970 were included, since it is possible that one of Powell's effects in 1970 was to produce uncertainty or abstention among traditional Tory or Labour voters. With the sample thus reduced a smaller universe is left with which to judge Powell's impact on voters who switched between 1966 and 1970.

Because of the small number of respondents available, the sample could only be broken into two categories: those who gave Powell 0–54 ratings ('anti') and those who gave him 55–100 ratings ('pro').[54] Overall, 36% were anti-Powell and 64% were pro-Powell. As Table 3.4. shows, among the anti-Powellites there was a small (1·8%) net movement to the Conservatives between the two elections while among the Powellites there was a 4·6% swing. Again because of the small number of respondents involved only two voting choices were recorded, Conservative and non-Conservative (including in the later category the 1970 non-voters).

TABLE 3.4 Pattern of the vote 1966–70 by attitude to Powell

	Anti-Powell		
	1966 %	1970 %	% change
Conservative	25·0	26·8	+1·8
Non-Conservative	75·0	73·2	−1·8
	100	100	
	(284)	(284)	
	Pro-Powell		
	1966 %	1970 %	% change
Conservative	56·3	60·9	+4·6
Non-Conservative	43·7	39·1	−4·6
	100	100	
	(499)	(499)	

Source: Butler-Stokes Panel Study, 1970.

Table 3.5 shows that among anti-Powell respondents there was twice as great a defection from Conservative ranks as movement towards them between 1966 and 1970. Among the Powellites the opposite appeared to be the case; they showed three times as much movement to the Tories as away from them. Yet these figures should not be taken to mean that Powell actually produced a counter-swing to Labour among the 36% of the sample that was hostile to him. Rather, as becomes clear from Table 3.6, anti-Powell respondents who changed their voting behaviour between the two years showed a net movement to the Conservatives; Powellite 'switchers' simply demonstrated a much more pronounced movement to the Conservatives. Thus Table 3.6 seems to suggest that Powell had a clear effect in influencing voters to switch to the Conservatives. The evidence shows that those who reacted negatively to him were not influenced to move in a Labour direction; but rather their rate of movement to the Tories was depressed slightly. Moreover if the entire electorate had behaved in the way anti-Powell 'switchers' did, then 1970 would have produced one of the most massive Tory landslides in history. Powell may have reduced the number of such switchers but did not appear to influence the direction of their movement.

In interpreting the figures in Table 3.6, two points should be kept in mind. First, respondents who were not 21 were not included in the analysis. By 1970 18-year-olds could vote and any possible anti-Conservative movement that was produced among them by anti-Powell sentiment would not be discovered through our data.[55] Also, because British elections are decided by a small number of voters changing parties, it is difficult to get enough switchers in a 2000-case survey to do multivariate analysis. In this case there were only 76 people who changed parties and, while the trends reported below are suggestive of a clear Powell influence, they do not meet tests of statistical significance.

It is of course possible that attitudes to Powell were not a major independent explanatory variable explaining the shift in voting behaviour

TABLE 3.5   Flow of the vote 1966–70 by attitude to Powell

| | *Anti-Powell* | |
| | *1966* | |
1970	*Conservative* %	*Non-Conservative* %
Conservative	89	6
Non-Conservative	11	94
	100	100
	(71)	(213)

| | *Pro-Powell* | |
| | *1966* | |
1970	*Conservative* %	*Non-Conservative* %
Conservative	94	18
Non-Conservative	6	82
	100	100
	(281)	(218)

Source: Butler-Stokes Panel Study, 1970.

TABLE 3.6   Party choice of those who changed their voting behaviour between 1966–70 by attitude to Powell

	Anti-Powell %	*Pro-Powell* %
Switch to Conservatives	60	71
Switch from Conservatives	40	29
	100	100
	(20)	(56)

Source: Butler-Stokes Panel Study, 1970.

between the two elections. If that were the case it would be necessary to offer other explanations of why respondents swung to the Tories and see whether these other possibilities would erase what seems to be a rather pronounced Powell effect. In the 1970 election two of the most obvious issues were economics and race. To test the effect of race on party choice, the sample was divided into two groups: those who took conservative positions on race and those who were relatively liberal.[56] To test the impact of economic issues, the sample was again divided into two groups: those who were dissatisfied with Labour's handling of the economy and felt the Tories would do better and those who did not feel this way. Thus we can test whether attitudes to Powell actually masked the impact of economic or racial issues.

The data in Table 3.7 and 3.8 show that among racial liberals and racial conservatives, as well as among voters who perceived a clear Conservative advantage on economic issues and those who did not, pro-Powell respondents were consistently more likely to have swung to the Tories than anti-Powell respondents. While the cell sizes are very small, the fact that the differences between the pro- and anti-Powell respondents did not disappear suggests that he did have an impact on the Tory victory.

The evidence also supports the hypothesis that Powell made his greatest impact on the working class. Among middle-class respondents attitudes to Powell were of no importance in influencing people to

TABLE 3.7   Party choice of those who changed their voting behaviour between 1966–70 by attitude to Powell, controlling attitudes to immigrants

| | Racial liberals | |
	Anti-Powell %	Pro-Powell %
Switch to Conservatives	58	68
Switch from Conservatives	42	32
	100	100
	(12)	(19)
	Racial conservatives	
	Anti-Powell %	Pro-Powell %
Switch to Conservatives	63	73
Switch from Conservatives	37	27
	100	100
	(8)	(37)

Source: Butler-Stokes Panel Study, 1970.

TABLE 3.8 Party choice of those who changed their voting behaviour between 1966–70 by attitude to Powell, controlling attitude to economic differences between Conservatives and Labour

| | *No Tory advantage on economic issues* | |
	Anti-Powell %	*Pro-Powell* %
Switch to Conservatives	63	70
Switch from Conservatives	37	30
	100	100
	(16)	(43)
	Tory advantage on economic issues	
	Anti-Powell %	*Pro-Powell* %
Switch to Conservatives	50	77
Switch from Conservatives	50	23
	100	100
	(4)	(13)

Source: Butler-Stokes Panel Study, 1970.

switch to the Tories. Working-class switchers behaved very differently. Among the relatively small number of working-class switchers who were anti-Powell (12% of all switchers), there was a slight movement to the Labour party. But among working-class switchers who were pro-Powell (50% of all switchers) there was more than a 2–1 movement to the Conservatives.

TABLE 3.9 Party choice of those who changed their voting behaviour between 1966–70 by attitude to Powell, controlling class

| | *Middle class* | |
	Anti-Powell %	*Pro-Powell* %
Switch to Conservatives	73	72
Switch from Conservatives	27	28
	100	100
	(11)	(18)
	Working class	
	Anti-Powell %	*Pro-Powell* %
Switch to Conservatives	44	71
Switch from Conservatives	56	29
	100	100
	(9)	(38)

Source: Butler-Stokes Panel Study, 1970.

While the cell sizes are again very small (and thus should be treated as suggestive rather than conclusive evidence), the data seem to show that Powell had his greatest impact in the North and Midlands and among respondants over 45. He appears to have had virtually no impact in Scotland and Wales or with voters under 45 and to have had a similar impact on men and women.

TABLE 3.10   Party choice of those who changed their voting behaviour between 1966–70 by attitude to Powell, controlling region

	Scotland & Wales		North of England & Midlands		London & South	
	Anti-Powell %	Pro-Powell %	Anti-Powell %	Pro-Powell %	Anti-Powell %	Pro-Powell %
Switch to Conservatives	60	42	67	92	56	61
Switch from Conservatives	40	58	33	8	44	39
	100	100	100	100	100	100
	(5)	(12)	(6)	(26)	(9)	(18)

Source: Butler-Stokes Panel Study, 1970.

TABLE 3.11   Party choice of those who changed their voting behaviour between 1966–70 by attitude to Powell, controlling sex

	Female		Male	
	Anti-Powell %	Pro-Powell %	Anti-Powell %	Pro-Powell %
Switch to Conservatives	46	59	78	88
Switch from Conservatives	54	41	22	12
	100	100	100	100
	(11)	(32)	(9)	(24)

Source: Butler-Stokes Panel Study, 1970.

There is additional evidence from the M.O.R.I. panel study that Powellites provided the bulk of the movement to the Tories between 1966 and 1970. It should be noted at the outset that there are difficulties in using the M.O.R.I. data to draw definite conclusions about the flow of the vote between 1966 and 1970. For one thing the initial wave of the panel study was conducted in late 1972 and early 1973 – two and a half

TABLE 3.12 Party choice of those who changed their voting behaviour between 1966–70 by attitude to Powell, controlling age

	44 and under		45 and over	
	Anti-Powell %	Pro-Powell %	Anti-Powell %	Pro-Powell %
Switch to Conservatives	63	60	58	78
Switch from Conservatives	37	40	42	22
	100	100	100	100
	(8)	(20)	(12)	(36)

Source: Butler-Stokes Panel Study, 1970.

years after the 1970 election. Secondly, people who identified as Powellites in 1973 need not have taken this position in 1970. Finally, the sample at this time was biased heavily to Labour so that the data show Labour actually having won the 1970 poll.

This bias can be ignored however because we are most concerned with relative rates of movement to the Tories; the sample's Labour bias would thus only make any pronounced movement to the Tories more noticeable.

Powellites were here identified as that proportion of the sample (25%) who said that Powell was the M.P. who best represented their views. The evidence in Table 3.13 shows that non-Powellites showed a net swing of 1·85% to the Conservatives between 1966 and 1970 while the Powellites showed a swing of 7·2%.

TABLE 3.13 Voting behaviour of 1973 Powellites and non-Powellites, 1966–70

	Powellites			Non-Powellites		
	1966 %	1970 %	Change 1966–1970	1966 %	1970 %	Change 1966–1970
Conservative	48·5	55·4	+6·9	38·1	39·8	+1·7
Labour	44·0	36·5	−7·5	55·5	53·5	−2·0
Liberal/other	7·5	8·1	−0·6	6·4	6·7	−0·3
	100	100		100	100	
	(334)	(334)		(973)	(973)	

Source: M.O.R.I. Panel Study, 1973.

Table 3.14 shows that in terms of actual movement between the two major parties the Powellites showed three times more straight conversions from Labour to the Tories than did the non-Powellites. Moreover Liberals who identified with Powell in 1966 were 50% more likely to vote Tory in 1970 than non-Powellites. The '1966' Conservatives were also slightly more likely to have continued to vote Tory if they identified with Powell.

TABLE 3.14   Flow of the vote 1966–70 among Powellites and non–Powellites

	Powellites 1966			Non-Powellites 1966		
1970	Con.	Lab.	Liberal/ Other	Con.	Lab.	Liberal/ Other
	%	%	%	%	%	%
Conservative	94	18	24	93	6	16
Labour	1	79	16	4	92	18
Liberal/other	5	3	60	3	2	66
	100	100	100	100	100	100
	(162)	(147)	(25)	(371)	(540)	(62)

Source: M.O.R.I. Panel Study, 1973.

Extrapolating from Table 3.14 above, we find that while Powellites were only 25% of the 1973 sample, they made up 45% of the respondents who shifted from Labour to the Tories between 1966 and 1970. They also made up 38% of the '1966' Liberals who moved to the Tories between the two years. Our data have very clear limitations of both size and time. Nonetheless the 'Powell effect' emerges so clearly and strongly, however much we allow all other possible variables, that the resulting impression, however suggestive, is very powerful. Powell fairly certainly had a significant effect in 1970 and his role was quite possibly decisive in the Tories' election triumph.

THE VICTORIOUS MR HEATH AND THE DEFEATED MR POWELL
However much Powell had swayed the electorate, the triumphant victor was unambiguously Mr Heath. Powell had helped achieve the most dubious success of putting his most bitter opponent into 10 Downing Street, his authority within the Tory party highly strengthened while Powell was as isolated as ever on the back-benches. A *Times* analysis in the aftermath of the campaign suggested that he spoke for no more than 30 Conservative M.P.s.[57] A *Sunday Times* poll of the 110 newly elected Conservative members of the House showed that only 35 supported Powellite positions on immigration.[58] They also found that there was little correlation between admiration for Powell and concern

about coloured immigration. Some racial moderates had great respect for Powell, while other hard-liners held him in low regard. While suggesting that the new members might be more open to persuasion than the returning Tories, the *Sunday Times* was careful to note that they were by no means monolithically committed either to Powell personally or Powellism (here taken to be his racial and economic views). The public – as Table 3.15 shows – were also increasingly likely to feel, however much they admired him, that he would not make a good party leader or prime minister.

TABLE 3.15   Electorate's attitude towards Powell, June 1970

	Agree %	*Disagree* %	*Don't know*
Has great courage and sincerity	78	11	11% = 100%
Make a good M.P.	27	43	30% = 100%
Only politician I admire	36	52	12% = 100%
Conservatives better off with Powell as leader	19	63	18% = 100%
Stirred up racial feeling	63	24	13% = 100%
Fanatical and dangerous	26	63	11% = 100%
Damage Tory election chances with attacks on Heath	18	63	19% = 100%

Source: O.R.C., *Sunday Times*, 21 June 1970.

Moreover, Heath's standing with the public was greatly enhanced by his election victory, as Table 3.16 shows, so that he moved further ahead of Powell and even outran Wilson in the polls.

TABLE 3.16   Choice for prime minister for the next five years, 1970

	June 1970 (*post-election*) %	*Sep 1970* %
Heath	25	30
Wilson	30	25
Powell	11	9
Don't know/others	34	36
	100	100

Source: *N.O.P. Political Bulletin*, June/July 1970 and Sep/Oct 1970.

Powell's own behaviour did little to dispel the impression that he regarded the election result as a personal setback, absenting himself from the House for almost the entire summer and making it clear that he would not attend the October party conference (which, it was clear, would be mainly occupied in lauding the victorious Heath). The Powells made plans to go on holiday during the conference but were forced to cancel their vacation after a dock strike. However, he still decided not to attend.[59]

Powell's new behaviour as a political recluse led some commentators to suggest that he might seek to play in Britain the role played in France by de Gaulle – waiting for the unmanageable national crisis which would lead to his assumption of power.[60] In fact, whatever Powell's own view was of such grandiose melodrama, he soon made it clear that he would enjoy his loneliness at Westminster rather than at any Colombey-les deux-églises. Indeed, in announcing that he would not go to the conference, a tone of resignation crept into his voice. He said he recognised that his days in the ranks of the leadership of his party were over.[61] He conceded that he had almost no chance of ever holding government office again, but said he would continue to speak out from the back-benches. Until Conservative party policy changed he would speak out on immigration, the E.E.C., and the prices and incomes policy.

Powell had of course campaigned for a Tory victory and could hardly show any public displeasure at the result. Yet it was quite clear that the result was a disaster for his career. Mr Heath now headed the Government, enjoyed a total ascendency in the party and the Cabinet as well as a higher standing in the country. He had stolen at least some of Powell's clothes not only on immigration but on economic issues too, and was now going to use his victory to make a determined effort at E.E.C. entry, so bitterly opposed by Powell. This last objective was more likely to be realised now that Pompidou had replaced de Gaulle but was also one which would increase Powell's isolation within the party. Moreover Heath, whose dislike and resentment of Powell were hardly a secret, quickly made it clear that there was no question of a reconciliation, let alone a Cabinet position. Naturally Heath firmly denied the suggestion that Powell had had any significant effect on the election result – victory was his. And this clearly was the political if not the psephological reality.

4 Continuing the Struggle for British Nationhood: the Battle against the E.E.C. and the Ugandan Asians

The aftermath of the 1970 election left Powell's fortunes at a low ebb not simply because it was his arch-opponent Mr Heath who sat in Downing Street, but because Powell appeared to have 'lost' his two key causes. The Tory M.P.s who had once been impressed by his economic views had no further need to look to him now that Heath himself was committed against an incomes policy and resolutely for the free market and a radical reduction in Government intervention even to help 'lame ducks'. The electorate as a whole, it seemed, had less need to look to Powell's leadership on immigration now that the new Government was committed to a major tightening of controls. The Common Market issue was now the great dividing issue between the two men and public feeling on this issue, though generally hostile to the E.E.C., was volatile, shallow and often confused, and heavily linked in the public mind with Labour's divided discontents; it was not, in a word, a promising issue for Powell. His position seemed almost beyond salvage. The only way back lay in the hope that the Heath Government would renege on its economic policy and allow large-scale coloured immigration to recommence. Within two years the twin miracle had happened.

The first portent of what was to follow came as early as November 1970, when the embarrassed Heath Government was forced to the discovery that Rolls-Royce was a lame duck and needed £42 million to enable it to complete the construction of the RB-211-22 aero-engine. Powell quickly broke the silence which he had maintained since the June election to attack the rescue operation. Very simply, the government should have let Rolls-Royce go bust. Indeed Powell went further, demanding a policy of active denationalisation. The real cause of inflation, he argued, was not wage increases – mere symbols, not causes – but the need to print money to finance just such rescue operations as this.[1]

Powell also sought to elaborate the themes he had first developed during the campaign into a more general Conservative philosophy of 'law and order'.[2] He was greatly handicapped however by his studied refusal either to make any explicit link between the crime rate and racial problems (in the manner then successfully being employed by many American conservatives) or to go beyond the advocacy of more funds being appropriated for law enforcement.[3] He emphasised indeed that he favoured penal reform and opposed the death penalty. This was no way to endear himself to the Tory right. Moreover, while he joined twenty-three other Tory back-benchers in opposing the Government's continuation of Rhodesian sanctions, he made no strong attempt to build support on this other issue so dear to his party's right.

RETURNING TO IMMIGRATION

In November 1970 Reginald Maudling, the Home Secretary, introduced the Bill which was to become the 1971 Commonwealth Immigrants Act and went a long way towards meeting Powell's proposals. The 1971 Act sought to eliminate the distinction between aliens and New Commonwealth citizens, and also to tie future immigration to economic criteria. Immigrants were no longer to be considered permanent settlers as soon as they arrived. To stay in Britain they would now need to hold jobs which the Home Office considered worthwhile. The Bill also included a repatriation provision. Publicly the Conservative party announced that the Bill was designed to fulfil their manifesto pledge that there would be no further 'large-scale permanent immigration'. Privately they doubtless hoped that the legislation would neutralise immigration as a political issue, robbing Powell of his thunder. Maudling, most likely wishing to mask how completely the Act conceded to Powell's views, added insult to injury by including in his announcement of the Bill strong criticism of Powell for offering highly suspect figures on the number of immigrants entering and living in Britain.[4]

Powell responded at this time merely by asserting that his figures on the number of coloured immigrants entering Britain were correct. But when he returned to the subject in February 1971 he stressed that in large part the damage had already been done, for immigration was only one way in which the coloured population might grow. The last Labour Government, he averred, had grossly underestimated – by up to 80% – the number of coloured births in Britain during the 1960s. Again, Powell suggested that such continual 'mistakes' could hardly be accidental.[5]

> The Government and public could not have been misled so persistently and gravely without a certain determination in some quarters to leave facts unascertained or to play down those that are known so that the situation is irreversible.

In a clear evocation of his 'rivers of blood' speech Powell warned that the nation had never known a greater danger and prophesied that 'the explosion which will blow us asunder is here and the fuse is burning, but the fuse is shorter than had been suspected'.[6] The only answer to the problem was 'massive, albeit voluntary' repatriation. He argued that significant numbers of immigrants were still citizens of their country of origin and had a strong desire to return. The Conservative Government should take additional steps to implement their election pledge to aid those immigrants who wanted to return to their native lands.

The speech was greeted with enormous publicity, angry civil service rebuttals and a torrent of denunciation. *The Times* Home Affairs correspondent Peter Evans interestingly suggested that Powell had no way of explaining his silence on immigration during the early and middle 1960s unless he could claim to have been misled as to the true magnitude of the danger.[7] The rest of the press reaction is reflected in their headlines: 'The Explosion Which Will Blow Us Asunder' (the *Sun*); 'Enoch's Nightmare' (the *Sketch*); 'Powell: Race Fuse is Burning Still Shorter' (*Daily Mail*); and 'Race Bomb Will Blow Us Apart – Powell' (*Daily Mirror*).[8] Heath once again felt compelled to dissociate himself publicly from Powell,[9] a move he could now make with a strong following even from the popular (and not just the quality) press. The *Sketch* called him 'blindly dangerous', while the *Sun* in a front page editorial headed simply 'This man is dangerous', argued that Powell was more dangerous than the immigrants because he had attitudes similar to those which led the Nazis to persecute the Jews in Germany.[10]

Powell gave two further immigration speeches in March, outlining the threat that Indian and Pakistani immigrants (whom he insisted on terming 'aliens') posed to the British way of life, and attacked the Maudling immigration Bill's patrial clause.[11] This section of the legislation allowed the free right of entry to Commonwealth citizens with a parent or grandparent born in Great Britain. The only aspect of the Bill Powell was satisfied with, indeed, was the section dealing with repatriation. Even here he supported higher levels of payment for immigrants willing to return to their native lands than the Government was willing to allow. He also suggested that the Government increase the period in which they were free to deport immigrants. Despite the fact that the Bill was largely inspired by Powell's own thinking, he had now again opened up a considerable gap between himself and official Conservative policy on race and immigration. Before passage, the Bill went through a lengthy set of committee hearings in Parliament. Powell was appointed to the committee and played a major role in efforts to make the Bill more palatable to the Tory right. In committee, Powell, Sir George Sinclar (Conservative), David Steel (Liberal) and sixteen Opposition members joined to defeat the patrial clause.[12] The alliance between Powell and Labour was a curious one. He opposed the measure because he was afraid it would allow large numbers of new Commonwealth citizens to enter Britain. Labour M.P.s opposed the Bill because they felt it was racialist; an implicit line was being drawn, they feared, between 'old' (white) Commonwealth immigrants and 'new' (coloured) Commonwealth immigrants.

He also clashed with the Home Secretary while the Bill was still in the committee stage. Maudling, attempting to guard his flank, argued that the repatriation clause in the legislation was designed to help any resident who did not fit into life in Britain to return home. Powell disagreed, maintaining that the clause was designed specifically for the repatriation of coloured immigrants.[13] He embarrassed Maudling further by pointing out in an article for *The Times* that the Government had left an unintended loophole in the 1962 legislation which allowed Kenyan Asians to enter Britain freely.[14] The Government took no action, only discovering their error with the passage of the Kenyan Independence Act in 1963. Powell also went on the B.B.C. to warn that unless there was a drastic cut in the number of immigrants allowed in the country, there would be racial warfare in fifteen years.[15]

As it was, Powell's campaign had scored a clear success. He was very pleased with the Government's compromise measure on the patrial clause – which was drafted after the committee defeat – restricting the right of patriality to anyone who had British nationality status at the time of their birth. However a Powell amendment giving the Government ten years to deport immigrants without appeal was rejected in committee.[16]

He continued to suggest in his speeches that the Conservative Government had still not grasped the full magnitude of the immigrant influx.[17] Since June 1970, he claimed, the influx had actually increased by 17%. He somewhat provocatively expressed his hope that the new legislation would help stem the flow and that the repatriation clause would be forcefully implemented by the Government.

In November, speaking to the Southall Chamber of Commerce, Powell again warned that while the immigrant flow from the West Indies had lessened, Asia remained a limitless immigrant source:[18]

> It is by 'black power' that the headlines are caught, and under the shape of the negro that the consequences for Britain of immigration and what is miscalled 'race' are popularly depicted. Yet it is more truly when he looks into the eyes of Asia that the Englishman comes face to face with those who will dispute with him possession of his native land.

Moreover he now openly stated his dissatisfaction with the implementation of the 1971 Act, accusing the Government of having 'sabotaged' its repatriation sections. He had several complaints. First, that the Government leaflet on the status of immigrants in Britain did not properly emphasise repatriation; second, the Government imposed a means test on immigrants wishing to return to their native land. (An interesting point in the light of his support for means-tested social services. Clearly immigration control was an issue exempted by Powell from the operation of market criteria.)

He also objected to a House of Lords amendment to the Act which limited payment for repatriation to those immigrants whom the authorities deemed unsuited to life in Britain. As he stated during his clash with Maudling, Powell believed any immigrant who wanted to leave Britain should be entitled to these payments, regardless of adaptability to British life or financial status. His bitterest criticism was reserved for the Government's decision to entrust administration of the repatriation programme to the International Social Services of Great Britain, an agency not competent to process the massive number of applications he felt would have to be handled.

Powell followed up this speech by sending the Home Secretary the names of 300 immigrants who had written to him asking to be repatriated, thus emphasising that he held Maudling and not the I.S.S.G.B. responsible for handling repatriation requests. Maudling played down Powell's public demonstration, simply turning the requests over to the agency for processing.[19] Powell did not give up, writing an article in December for the *Sunday Express* headlined 'Will Our Children Condemn Us?', repeating his arguments and castigating the Government for underestimating the problem.[20]

His immigration speeches had won him a substantial, if still only partial, recovery from his post-election limbo. While few were in doubt

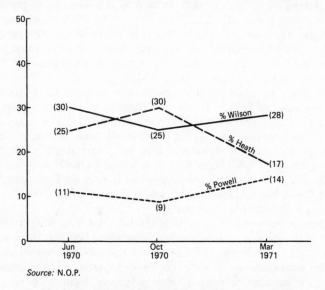

Source: N.O.P.

Fig. 4.1   Best prime minister for next five years 1970–71

that the 1971 Act was very much his child, he had notwithstanding managed simultaneously to take credit for the Act, have it amended, and yet also establish himself as a continuing focus of discontent on the race and immigration issues. N.O.P.'s poll on public preferences for prime minister, taken just after Powell's March 1971 speech, showed a clear recovery in his public standing at the same time that Heath's personal support was slipping precipitously.

THE FIGHT TO PROTECT PARLIAMENTARY SOVEREIGNTY
Meanwhile Powell had begun to shift his major theme of attack away from immigration and towards the E.E.C. issue which was to preoccupy him continuously until the 1975 E.E.C. referendum and indeed after that as well. The first phase of this campaign was concluded with the passage of the European Communities Bill in July 1972.

Powell's emergence as the leading advocate of the anti-Market cause occasioned some surprise and bitterness among his erstwhile front-bench colleagues who pointed out that he had not dissented on this issue in the early 1960s any more than he had on immigration. They did not hide their suspicion that he could simply not resist attacking the front-bench bipartisan consensus at this point as on others. On the other hand his conversion to the anti-Market cause was hardly surprising, given his conception of British nationalism and the stress on the centrality of parliamentary sovereignty to that nationhood.

According to Roth, Powell was sceptical of membership in the E.E.C. even during the 1950s. As early as 1956 'Cross-Bencher' in the *Sunday Express* noted Powell's hostility to the idea of Britain's joining a European free trade area and his 'lively suspicion of European entanglements'.[21] Powell remained unenthusiastic when the subject first became a live political issue but did not oppose membership for fear of offending the Prime Minister, Harold Macmillan, whose Cabinet he had joined at a time when the first negotiations to enter the Market were showing signs of failure. In the introduction to his first collection of speeches on the Common Market (published in 1971), Powell wrote that he had been prepared to accept membership then 'on the grounds of trade, as the lesser evil, compared with being excluded'.[22] Nonetheless in 1965, along with Nicholas Ridley, he wrote a One Nation pamphlet, *One Europe*, advocating the creation of a Ministry for European Affairs in the Conservative Government, and in May 1967 he voted for entry during the Wilson-Brown initiative.

When he delivered his first anti-Market speech in March 1969, he spoke of the state of national morale, somewhere between 'dejection and desperation', which was the heritage of the loss of Empire, the Suez disaster, the experience of being economically surpassed by neighbouring countries, and a humiliating and perpetual balance of payments deficit.[23] The case for rejecting entry rested on the need to instill national self-confidence – politically by protecting parliamentary sovereignty, and economically by asserting a self-sufficient capability. Powell began with a 'unilateral declaration of independence' and asserted boldly, 'We do not need to be tied up with anybody'.[24] The British people would achieve self-sufficiency, were not dependent on foreign nations for natural resources, and did not have to trade from a position of weakness. Failure to join the E.E.C. did not mean that trade with Western European nations would suffer – it had increased, not declined, since de Gaulle's 1963 veto. The country's internal economic problems, such as inflation, had nothing to do with failure to be accepted into the Market: France, after all, also suffered high inflation rates.

He was, he stressed, not against all forms of European unity – he had kind words for the European Free Trade Agreement and, more provocatively, for de Gaulle's *Europe des patries* under which Britain would be able to maintain parliamentary sovereignty. Indeed he seemed concerned in this first speech to keep open the possibility of reconciliation with Heath's European policy; even the E.E.C. was not a static body, he noted, and might perhaps evolve into the sort of institution he could accept membership in:

> There is indeed a point at which the development of supra-national, not to say federal, institutions and authority either in the E.E.C. or elsewhere in Western Europe, is likely to be arrested, and that the 'Europe of nations' is much the most probable form of the future face of Europe, as well as that in which Britain could most easily enter into the closer relations that she ought to have with all the various nations of the adjacent continent.[25]

It was of course quite clear by 1969 that neither Wilson nor Heath had been negotiating towards this sort of Europe but, while the speech may have given notice of a U.D.I. by Powell, it was still a declaration in muted, moderate tones.

A much sharper note was evident in Powell's next E.E.C. speech, delivered after General de Gaulle's retirement in May 1969, an event which simultaneously removed a major obstacle to British entry and any remaining prospect of a *Europe des patries*.[26] Powell, speaking at Market Drayton, urged the British people to accept that efforts to enter Europe were concluding, not beginning. He also attacked proposals for an Anglo-French nuclear deterrent; the very idea of having to accept responsibility for another nation's use of nuclear weapons (or their veto of one's own use of them) was a grotesque affront to national sovereignty as well as being tactically awkward.

The proposed creation of a European Parliament raised similar problems. An elected Parliament could not work unless the electorate regarded themselves as being part of a single nation, with their separate interests secondary to the interests of the whole. Unless this was the case 'the attempt to create an elective assembly or Parliament would be foredoomed not merely to disappointment but to ridicule and mutual recrimination'.[27] The speech contained no discussion of the economic consequences of E.E.C. membership. By shifting his position to the purely political questions Powell significantly hardened his position: one could either preserve or not preserve sovereignty – there was no room for compromise.

Such arguments did not fall on entirely unreceptive ears. In mid-July 1969 when an anti-Market motion in the Commons was supported by ten Conservative M.P.s who had voted for entry in May 1967, *The Times* political correspondent noted that these ten 'have now been reinforced as anti-Marketeers by the Tory nationalists who draw their inspiration from Mr Enoch Powell and a mixed group of economists'.[28]

Encouraged by signs of a swing in public opinion against the Market, Powell's tone hardened further. People would not, he warned, pliantly accept entry, just as they no longer pliantly accepted liberal immigration policies.[29] As yet (September 1969) the British people had not turned as decisively against the E.E.C. as they had against the free entry of Commonwealth citizens, but:[30]

the fact remains that this year the people of Britain addressed them-selves quite suddenly and intently to the questions of *oui* or *non* as viewed from their side. It would be premature to say that they have answered *non*; but there is no mistaking the change in mood since 1961 and 1962. The mood is different now. It is to demand that a clear, definite and cast-iron case be made out before Britain is again committed to accede to the Treaty of Rome.

Broadening his attack, he criticised the E.E.C.'s Common Agricultural Policy, was scathing of the suggestion that Britain could exercise greater international influence acting from within the E.E.C., and voiced strong doubts whether a united Europe would be able to construct workable democratic or representative institutions for itself.

It was a delicately balanced performance which was careful to avoid direct confrontation on the issue with the Tory leadership. Indeed Powell had introduced his remarks by quoting Heath's recent suggestion that the British people might want a major reassessment of Britain's European policy, a suggestion he warmly applauded. Heath, Powell said, 'never more accurately hit off the instinctive feeling of the great majority of his fellow-countryman than in those words'.[31] He had then gone on to pose the E.E.C. question as an all-or-nothing logical problem: either a democratic European union could be achieved because it was the case that the public was happy to surrender all claim to its separate sover-eignty (a condition whose existence Powell implicity doubted); or union could only be achieved undemocratically (in which case one should have nothing to do with it). By leaving open the improbable first alternative, he managed to maintain a conciliatory stance towards the leadership – while quietly setting up an insurmountable obstacle before them. Keith Renshaw, of the *Sunday Express*, made the shrewd observation that while Powell 'appears to have pointed a pistol at Mr Heath's head', he had done it 'in the nicest, politest way imaginable', adding that 'Senior politicians, not all of whom are warm to Mr Powell, believe that he has conducted a shrewd policy coup that will broaden his undoubted support among the Tory rank and file in the country'.[32]

At the Tory party's 1969 Brighton conference Powell maintained this delicate stance. He made clear his open opposition to the E.E.C. (he gave another speech opposing entry three days before the conference's E.E.C. debate). But he did not confront the leadership, refraining from participating in the debate itself, remaining silent while the conference approved the leadership's motion endorsing E.E.C. entry by a large margin.[33] It was clear nonetheless that his silence did not betoken impotence – he had supporters present, as became clear in the conference vote on the platform's immigration resolution. The resolution, stating that the Conservative policy on immigration was the only one likely to be successful, received only lukewarm endorsement and a substantial minority dissented altogether. The dissident vote was clearly a tribute to Powell's influence, though here too he refused to lead his followers against the platform.

While it was clear to the *cognoscenti* that Powell had, with his anti-Market speeches, begun to open a major second front against the Tory leadership, there was little sign that the public had noticed or reacted. N.O.P.'s polls of January and October 1969 allow us to make a before-and-after comparison of the initial effects of Powell's emergence as an opponent of the E.E.C.

TABLE 4.1   Heath or Powell choice for prime minister, 1969

	Jan 1969 %	Oct 1969 %
Heath	49	50
Powell	34	35
Don't know	17	15
	100	100

Source: *N.O.P. Political Bulletin*, Jan and Oct 1969.

Public predictions by the President of the E.E.C. Commission of a common currency and an elected Parliament in Western Europe by 1980 provided Powell with obvious material for a further E.E.C. speech in January 1970.[34] Starting from the premise that control of the money supply was the key to control of inflation, Powell argued that the creation of a common currency necessarily implied a central bank of Europe and uniform economic policies for all participating nations. To develop common economic policies, there would have by definition to be a common government to exercise control over public expenditure and employment. A common currency thus implied a common economic policy and the creation of a central E.E.C. government with sovereign power. The demand for direct elections was a mere corollary – it was unimaginable that one could have such a government unless it were elected by Europe-wide suffrage. There was thus no way that the all-important sovereignty issue could be side-stepped by talking of the E.E.C. as an economic proposition. In fact the economic problems stemmed directly from the political questions:[35]

> It is good that the centre of the debate in this country about Britain and the Common Market seems to be moving on from the economic to the political sphere, because as we have seen, the economic presupposes the political and is meaningless without it.

For the British to enter the E.E.C. while ignoring these fundamental implications 'is to court humiliation and perhaps disaster'.[36]

Powell was again careful to avoid direct criticism of his party's leadership, again approvingly quoting Heath, this time to the effect that it would be a mistake for the British to enter the E.E.C. without realising the full implications of a European policy. Having made his position clear to those who wished to note it, he left the E.E.C. issue aside in favour of the more explosive issue of immigration.

Amidst the furore of the 1970 election he delivered only one major speech on the E.E.C., lamenting the failure of the parties to present clearly defined positions on the issue.[37] It was, he felt, this vagueness of the parties that had led many to support a referendum on the E.E.C., a proposal he did not favour: it would be irresponsible for a government to continue in office if its proposals on the E.E.C. were rejected by a referendum, and in any case it was impossible to have a referendum on the general question of membership until terms were negotiated. In the first case a party would have to fight an election on the E.E.C. after a referendum; or if it had negotiated terms, it would have to ask for a mandate for them at an election. In either case there would have to be an election and the parties would have to make up their minds.

The 1970 election, he suggested, might be the last election where the British people could affect Government policies. Powell therefore urged each candidate standing for election to give the people his views on the subject. If candidates were unconditionally for or against entry that should be made clear. If their support for entry was conditional upon the terms negotitated, such candidates had a duty to make it clear what terms were acceptable. For himself – as he went on to make clear – he could not countenance such a surrender of national and parliamentary sovereignty, whose far-reaching implications for every field of policy he went on to spell out.

The speech was, in part, significant for what he did not say. He did not in any way attempt to pit himself against Heath on the issue or to chastise the party leadership for not taking an anti-Market stance. However the speech included no implicit or explicit endorsement of the Conservative party, nor did it mention that the Tory election manifesto included a provision for entry into Europe if the correct terms could be negotiated. He later indicated that the E.E.C. was not an election issue because the Conservatives' only direct commitment to the people was to negotiate new terms of entry. There had been no question of the Conservative party seeking a mandate for E.E.C. entry in the 1970 election. Yet he had indicated in his election speech on Europe that candidates should define as clearly as possible their positions on what terms would be acceptable. The speech had fired a number of warning shots across Heath's bow, but his confrontation with his party's leadership over immigration was probably all the controversy he needed.

After the election things moved fast. On the one hand, the Heath Government launched into negotiations in Brussels on presumptions clearly favourable to entry, acting very much on the mandate to do so. On the other hand public opinion began to swing massively against the Market. By the beginning of 1971 between 60% and 65% of the electorate were against entry and only 20% to 25% were in favour.[38]

There were moreover clear signs of a resentful public belief that an élite consensus had already decided the question without giving the people a chance to vent their feelings – feelings, it should be added, which at that time were diametrically opposed to those of the political leaderships. An O.R.C. summary of a poll conducted in February and March 1971 summed up these feelings:[39]

> ... there is a conspiracy on the part of politicians, media owners and big business to commit Britain to joining the Common Market before the public has had a chance to appraise the pros and cons or to know precisely what is happening. They are confronted with an unusual agreement between all three political parties that Britain should join, so normal political allegiances give them no guidance. They tend to feel that they are fed only the information that is favourable to Britain's joining.

Much the same élite-mass gap had existed – and been resented – over the immigration issue. Yet there were profound differences between the way the two issues affected the public. Immigration was a highly emotional issue which excited (and scared) many people. It was most salient at the mass level, and agitation from the electorate at large had forced the élite to deal with the question. The Common Market on the other hand was most salient at the élite level. Only after Britain was rejected for the second time in 1967, with both parties in general retaining their commitment to entry, did the public become distrustful. But as soon as terms were agreed in 1971, public support for entry increased dramatically.[40] The Common Market for a time produced the same sort of reaction as immigration did in the mass electorate, though the feelings were much less intense because the question was more remote from peoples' lives. Moreover, as soon as the question was favourably resolved, support for the élite consensus position rose steadily.

THE BATTLE IN THE COUNTRY AND PARLIAMENT

But the new situation made a clash between Powell and the Heath Government over the E.E.C. inevitable. Heath's clear determination to achieve British membership as quickly as possible meant the issue had to be dealt with. Moreover, with the passage of the new Immigration Act, Powell was free – some would have said hungry – for another issue. The clear change in public opinion over the E.E.C. seemed to have produced a situation tailor-made for him. Just as he had championed the silent majority against the bipartisan unity of the political élite over immigration, so now again Powell tried to portray himself as the people's voice against the élite consensus on the E.E.C. One is probably not attributing too great a degree of prescience to Powell in suggesting that he had foreseen in all probability something very like this situation in June 1970. Certainly his declaration then of the limited presumptive mandate any government could honourably claim over the E.E.C. allowed him now to charge Heath with duplicity and even betrayal.

He launched his initial attack in a speech given in County Down, Northern Ireland, claiming that during the election both parties had taken the attitude that they would see what terms would be obtained and then put them before the electorate. The basic question of principle was apparently left open. But after the Conservative victory 'the issue of principle was treated as settled', with popular assent simply assumed, subject only to the tidying up of a few details.[41]

His own criticisms of the E.E.C. now significantly included the claim that membership would bring higher food prices – electorally a far more powerful point than any argument about sovereignty.

Nonetheless he continued to give greater prominence to the sovereignty argument than was at all common amongst the normal run of anti-E.E.C. speaker, always concluding that the central point was the British people's concept of nationhood.[42]

The question of membership resolves itself, not ultimately but immediately and *in limine*, into the most basic of all possible questions which can be addressed to the people of any nation: can they, and will they, so merge themselves with others that, in face of the external world, there is no longer 'we and they' but only 'we'; that the interests of the whole are instinctively seen as over-riding those of any part; that a single political will and authority which must be that of the majority, is unconditionally accepted as binding upon all? That is the question. That is what the real debate is about. In this each must speak for himself. For myself, I say that to me it is inconceivable that the people of this nation could or would identify themselves politically with the peoples of the continent of Western Europe to form with them one entity and in effect one nation.

Powell's attack on Heath became more pointed still in April at Wolverhampton.[43] The Conservative party and Mr Heath had 'misled' the electorate by acceding to the Community after having pledged in their election manifesto to join only if negotiations were successful. In fact, the Government had 'accepted the Community, and its rules and principles exactly as they stand' and sought only to negotiate about what would happen in the transitional period.[44] The British people would never 'submit to becoming part of the Community as the result of a trick, and they will never forgive any person or party who they feel has got them there by sleight of hand'.[45]

Clearly encouraged by the swing of opinion shown by the polls, he reminded Heath of his election pledge that Britain could not enter until the decision had the support of the British Parliament and people. Now, he noted, 'there can be no doubt or dispute that a majority of the electorate, let alone, in Mr Heath's words, the British people, do not support entry. The Government is negotiating at Brussels over the details of the transitional period when they know that the people here at home are against membership.'[46]

In almost the same tones he had used over the immigration issue Powell warned the Government of the popular wrath to come if they persisted in their course:[47]

On other subjects, governments may well act in the light of their own beliefs and insight as to what is right. Not so on this. Only the nation itself can say what it is and feels itself to be. The people of this country have had a bitter experience in the last twenty years, when their politicians, by intention or default, brought about a profound alteration in the identity of the nation, and then asserted that it was too late to argue about. They are in no frame of mind to see a repetition.

Mr Heath did not himself deign to reply to this onslaught, instead leaving the task to his chief negotiator in Brussels, Geoffrey Rippon. Rippon did not deal with the substance of Powell's criticisms of the Heath Government, but simply counter-attacked by suggesting that Powell's own career was littered with dramatic reversals of attitude –

over the question of whether nurses should be exempt from the provisions of Selwyn Lloyd's 1962 pay pause; on Concorde; and finally his
reversal on the E.E.C.[48] Rippon thus set the keynote for the subsequent
tactics of the whole Conservative Government towards Powell; he was
not to be answered directly but was to be dismissed as an irresponsible
politician who could no longer be taken seriously.

In the spring of 1971 Powell set off on a wide-ranging speaking tour
of Western Europe, travelling to France, Italy, Germany and the
Netherlands to speak on the subject of British entry to the E.E.C. While
it would be foolish to ignore the probability that these trips were made
out of a high-minded seriousness, one may well wonder what political
objective he believed himself to be pursuing by absenting himself for
long periods from the British political scene. For though reports of the
speeches duly appeared in the British press, their impact could only have
been extremely limited. Ostensibly the reasons for this tour were to
explore the attitudes of foreign leaders and their electorates to British
entry, and to attempt to explain his own views on the E.E.C. to them. At
times he sounded almost as if he wished to warn the Europeans as to the
far-reaching nature of the enterprise they had embarked upon – as when
he told his audience in Lyons that British E.E.C. membership would
fundamentally alter the political structure of Western Europe. It
meant that 'a connection is to be formed which is not intended again to
be dissolved, but which is to result in all the peoples of the Community
coming to form in effect one electorate'.[49] The implications of British
membership both for British sovereignty and that of other Western
European governments were such that the people as well as the politicians
of these countries had to make their feelings clear. The position in
Britain, he informed them, was that 'the greater part of the people of
Britain are profoundly opposed to British accession to the Community'.[50]

There was more than a hint that his audience might well be wise
themselves to oppose British entry. He was at pains to point out that
Europeans had to understand the peculiarly strong English attachment
to parliamentary sovereignty and that a decision against British entry
would in no way imply a lessening of Britain's military commitment on
the Continent. He could not, he concluded, believe the people of the
Community wanted unwilling partners. At such times Powell appears to
have been courting the possibility of another '*non*' to keep Britain out,
while simultaneously wishing to engage the sympathies of his audiences
for a possible British refusal to enter even if they *were* welcome, a
refusal which would bear no penalty for Europe. In Frankfurt-am-Main
he treated his audience to a contemptuously *realpolitik* analysis of the
Brussels negotiations.[51] These were, he suggested, largely irrelevant
because the fundamental nature of the Community and the Treaty of
Rome in particular was not under negotiation. They concerned merely
the stages of transition through which Britain would join, and thus

avoided the basic issue of whether or not the country should join. For the first time Powell also set out his own conditions for acceptance of British entry. First, there would have to be a 'massive majority' of M.P.s in both parties for entry. Second, irrespective of what happened at Westminster, a majority of the British people had to support entry. He was pessimistic about either of these conditions being met.

Speaking at The Hague,[52] Powell entered into long arguments to suggest that the Dutch could favour British entry only if they were confident that their interests coincided exactly with Britain's – something he frankly doubted. He was no doubt conscious that he was speaking in a country with its own uncomfortable experience of the post-imperial legacy of a large immigrant population from the ex-colonies. After the speech – which had been singularly lacking in mention of potential benefits accruing from British E.E.C. entry – he was asked if he could think of anything good which would result from British membership. He thought for a moment and replied that membership would allow the free movement of Britain's immigrants into other E.E.C. nations. . . .

Meanwhile the 'Great Debate' on the E.E.C. in Britain went tepidly on. Returning to the more nearly native soil of Doncaster in June Powell again sought, almost desperately, to raise the temperature.[53] The British people had, he said, become aroused by the prospects of entry into Europe: something 'very big and very deep' had happened to them during the first part of 1971. Old England, indeed Olde Englande, was awakening, Arthur stirring in his grave:[54]

Like a heavy sleeper roused at last by an insistent alarm bell . . . . They have rubbed their eyes and cleared their throats and got ready to speak, to give their answer. It is as though with one accord, they had said to one another: 'This is not a little thing, but a great business. We will decide it – no one else.' There is something almost uncanny, something which makes the pulse beat a little quicker, in watching a whole nation instinctively cut through and thrust aside details, pretences, trivialities, and go to the heart of the matter. Untutored, uninvited, and indeed unwelcomed, they have insisted upon discerning the simple, overwhelming important question: to be or not to be, to be ourselves or not ourselves.

Powell had, it was clear, miscalculated. True, as negotiations at Brussels continued, the polls showed a rising public awareness of the E.E.C. issue but this increase in interest was correlated with a swing in support for Europe, not against. Moreover there was no support for his contention that sovereignty was the key issue in people's opposition to E.E.C. entry. National opinion polls conducted in 1970 and 1971 showed that never more than 4 % of the electorate mentioned sovereignty as one of the reasons why Britain should not join. The major public concern about membership centred on its effect on the cost of living. It became increasingly clear that the wild swings for and against entry in the 1969–1971 period were symptomatic mainly of the very shallow public penetration of the issue: opinion was malleable largely because people were not passionately concerned about it. One study of British public opinion has concluded that the E.E.C. was only of 'marginal political influence' during this period. It had no effect on people's attitudes towards the Government and no likely effect on people's partisan choices in future elections.[55]

There are unfortunately no survey data on which to base a judgement of how Powell's anti-E.E.C. activities affected his public standing in this period. There was certainly little evidence that he had made any particular impact on the Tory back-benches, where he became more isolated than ever. To embrace Powell now was to accept a whole programme – not only on the E.E.C. but on incomes policy, immigration and even Northern Ireland. It was also to identify oneself with a bitter opponent of the party's leadership. Powell was dismissed by some, ignored by many and in some quarters regarded as a disloyal pariah. Little wonder that those who found themselves sharing his opinions on a single issue were often almost hasty in their eagerness to dissociate themselves from him on any wider front. Such was the situation on the eve of the major parliamentary battle over the principle of British E.E.C. membership.

By June the Cabinet decided to hold off a vote in Parliament until the autumn in the hope that public opinion would consolidate in favour of entry and to give the party conference a chance to pass judgement on the question. By waiting, moreover, the Cabinet could hope to avoid accusations by anti-Marketeers like Powell that they were ignoring the public and party organisations in taking the decision to enter the Market.[56]

Powell threw himself into the fray. Between July and the October 28 vote on entry he delivered at least ten speeches across the country, restating the anti-Market case, leaving the cultivation of back-bench opposition at Westminster to more 'clubable' men such as Neil Marten. There was now very little left for Powell to say on the issue. He was tireless nonetheless in his reprise of every possible argument against the E.E.C., endlessly stressing that this was a question so fundamental that concern for country had to over-ride concern for party, and reminding Heath of his pledge of a free vote on the Market during the 1970 election.[57] (In June Heath had given some indication that he planned to enforce a three-line whip.)

In mid-September Powell flatly predicted that Britain would never actually enter the Market.[58] Nearly a month later he delivered a highly emotional speech at the Conservative conference.[59]

I do not believe this nation, which has maintained and defended its independence for a thousand years, will now submit to see it merged or lost, nor did I become a member of our sovereign Parliament in order to consent to that sovereignty being abated or transferred. Come what may, I cannot and I will not.

About a week before the House of Commons vote, Powell predicted in a speech at Newport that the Conservative Government would destroy itself by seeking entry into the Community.[60] The gap between the leaders and the led had simply become too wide for the Government to continue to function effectively. People felt neither consulted nor represented in places of power when decisions affecting their lives were taken.

There is again no indication that Powell's speeches had any effect on the Tory rank and file. At the conference, delegates approved by 2474 to 324 a resolution supporting membership.[61] Among the Tory back-benchers the tide was falling away too. The Conservative Group for Europe had estimated in early 1971 that there were 62 likely Tory votes against the Government in a division on the E.E.C. By 1 August that estimate had dropped to 41. Between the C.G.E. estimate in May 1971 and their last prediction on 1 August the predicted number of Tory M.P.s supporting the Government rose by 67, from 217 to 284. In the event, the C.G.E.'s estimate proved to be remarkably accurate. Overall, 282 Tories and Ulster Unionists supported the Government, 39 (including Powell) opposed it and 2 abstained. By the day of the vote the Conservative leadership was sure enough of its support to decide it did not need a three-line whip; it was hardly worth dragooning in an extra two or three votes (all their estimates revealed) at the cost of uniting the anti-Marketeers as a hounded band of patriotic martyrs. With Labour defections against their party's whip, the Conservative motion was passed by 356 to 244 votes, a majority of 112.[62]

The vote was clearly a defeat for Powell, but if anything it only served to make his attacks on the Heath Government sharper. In a speech at Rugby in late November, he took up the themes of his earlier Newport speech.[63] In all the letters he had been getting from voters the view was, he said, that the ordinary person counted for nothing with the political parties and the Government. Many felt totally unrepresented, and believed that there was a conspiracy of the 'top' people in Parliament and the media to ensure that what ordinary people believe should be ignored. The situation was, he warned, fraught with almost apocalyptic dangers:[64]

Comparisons cannot be proved or quantified but I do not believe that there has been anything on the same scale in British politics since manhood franchise and quite possibly not for long before.

The formerly normal phenomenon of the suppressed and disregarded minority has been inverted. People have settled down to a dazed and irritated acceptance that they are living in an age when the majority is always wrong.

In the aftermath of the E.E.C. vote, Powell also turned back to a subject he had ignored through most of 1971 – economic policy. He had been too preoccupied with the E.E.C. to comment on the Government's indecision about whether it should subsidise the Upper Clyde shipyard. But after Mr Barber, the Chancellor, announced that the Government had approved a general policy of fostering capital expenditures by nationalised industries to cut unemployment, Powell broke his silence. The Government, he warned, would face a fierce attack if it reversed its 'lame duck' policy. The Post Office's Giro service should have been allowed to go bust. If there was substantial public interest in this service, private enterprise would pick it up. It was ominous that the Government had decided to bail out the Giro service. If they could make this decision once, they could make it a hundred times. In retrospect, the prediction he made in autumn 1971 proved to be extraordinarily accurate: 'from this egg a whole family of lame ducks will speedily be hatched'.[65]

DEFEATED BUT NOT VANQUISHED

The E.E.C. vote of 28 October 1971 was however a vote of principle without legal effect, merely affirming 'That this House approves Her Majesty's Government's decision to join the European Communities on the basis of the arrangements which have been negotiated.'[66] The vote came before the Treaty of Accession had been written and before all minor matters pertaining to entry had been clarified. As Kitzinger noted, 'A vote of principle on a declaratory motion was one thing: the passage through the House of Commons of all the enactments that were the prerequisites of full legal membership was quite another thing.'[67] The anti-Marketeers' cause was not yet conclusively defeated and their relative optimism was not entirely groundless. The first poll conducted after the vote showed the public still opposed to entry.[68] It was moreover hard to imagine that the sixty-nine Labour pro-Marketeers of 28 October would continue to defy their party's whip and vote with the Government on every division of the legislation taking Britain into the E.E.C. Perhaps because he became embroiled in the controversy over repatriation with Reginald Maudling in late 1971, Powell waited until early January to speak out.[69] Publicly, at least, he continued to be optimistic about his cause. The 112-vote majority he termed 'utterly deceptive'. Powell predicted that the Government's margin on the literally hundreds of divisions over the European Communities Bill would slip significantly with the return of Labour M.P.s to their party whips. A clear possibility of a Government defeat remained. Moreover he doubted whether a vote on general principle had much meaning in the Westminster context:[70]

> The House of Commons is never at ease with general policies; it is most like itself when it turns its attention to the specific, the concrete and often the apparently trivial. The protracted debate of last year was no more than the overture; the real play or opera begins next week.

Nonetheless there was little that Powell or any anti-Market M.P. could do in January 1972 when Heath went to Brussels to sign the Treaty of Accession. But two days after it was signed Powell also travelled to Brussels to criticise Heath's action.[71] The event was 'uniquely unreal' because the Government did not have the support of Parliament or the people in taking the action.[72] The House was divided down the middle on the issue and still less than 50% of the British people supported entry.

Immediately after the signing of the Treaty of Accession the Government laid before Parliament its European Communities Bill. The first part dealt with constitutional and financial problems while the second touched on aspects of British Law which had to be changed when Britain entered the Market. This second part gave legal authority to present and future Community laws which were self-executing under the treaties, and also dealt with specific sections of Community law which needed specific enactment by each member nation to make way for implementation. The third and final part dealt with Britain's monetary obligation to the E.E.C. Bipartisanship over the Market collapsed with the publication of the Bill. The Labour Opposition was angered, protesting that by accepting part of the Bill, Parliament was accepting pre-existing Community legislation they had barely had time to consider and which had been passed without their consent. Mr Rippon's assurance that Brussels would not act on major matters of policy without the consent of the House did little to mollify the Labour party. Moreover the stated refusal to accept any amendments to the Bill helped widen the distance between pro- and anti-Marketeers.[73]

With Labour's turn against the Market, the key group became the 41 Conservative and Ulster Unionist M.P.s who opposed the Government's motion in October. If all of them decided to maintain their position the Government might conceivably be defeated. It was at this point that the weakness of Powell and other Tory anti-Marketeers within the parliamentary party became both critical and glaring. As pressure from the front-benches increased, their support began simply to melt away. Following the signing of the Treaty of Accession in January, only seventeen of the thirty-nine Conservative and Ulster Unionist M.P.s who opposed entry in October attended an anti-Market caucus.[74] On the first reading of the measure in late January only four Tories (including

Powell) opposed the Government.[75] Nevertheless, with almost uniform Labour opposition the Government's majority slipped to twenty-one. The vote on the second reading was even closer. Despite the direct personal intervention of Heath and the Tory whips – who emphasised that the Government would resign if defeated – the majority slipped to eight as fifteen Conservative and Ulster Unionists opposed the Bill.[76] If the Tory anti-Marketeers had been able to hold on to just twenty-four of their original forty-one supporters, it would have been enough. Even before the vote Powell had bitterly acknowledged the collapse of the anti-Market forces, accusing the Government of having put 'immoral' pressure on Tory and Ulster Unionist M.P.s to support the Market.[77] The Government, he said, had gone as far as to threaten the Ulster Unionists with loss of Westminster support if they failed to support Heath's position. In an attempt to salvage something from the defeat, Powell offered an amendment to the Bill providing that future regulations promulgated in Brussels should not be binding on the U.K., though he acknowledged that existing regulations dealing with U.K. tariffs, the Common Agricultural Policy and sugar prices would remain binding.[78] Despite almost unanimous Labour support, the Powell amendment was defeated in March by a 213–202 margin.[79]

Powell showed anger and even bitterness over the defeat. The great assertion of national popular resistance to the E.E.C. that he had predicted had simply failed to materialise. This he acknowledged in January 1972 in the tones of a tribune betrayed by his followers.[80] The people, he said, had the power to protect their form of self-government but:[81] 'I do not presume to know if they will exert their power to decide. It is not for me to fathom whether they care at all or know how deeply they care.'

If the Government did not have the support of the people in entering the E.E.C. and still managed to take that action without arousing any public outcry, then it was the people in the end who deserved the blame. Should this happen:[82]

> Do not blame the whips; do not blame the Members; do not blame the patronage machines; do not blame the pressures, the threats, the promises, the bribes. It is the nation itself that will have judged itself. When it could have spoken, it will have stayed dumb; when it could have acted it will have remained idle.

Nonetheless, after the second reading, the main brunt of Powell's attack was directed against the Heath Government for acting without the full-hearted consent of either the people or Parliament. No advocate of membership had tried to argue that the people supported the Government in its action. Even in the House the majorities achieved were too marginal for any claim to whole-hearted support to be countenanced. The second reading was only carried because 'no device of political pressure and thuggery' was resisted in the effort to win Conservative votes for membership.[83]

By April he no longer saw an apathetic public. Rather the Government and the country 'were on a collision course' over the E.E.C. If the Government persisted in trying to take Britain into Europe there would, he warned, be dire political consequences for the Tory party and its Leader:[84] 'The disaster would be mortal to our party as we know it, and in a special and quite peculiar sense to our leader, the Prime Minister, because of his personal identification with the decision.'

He had now ceased to avoid direct criticisms of Heath. Should he take the country into the Market, Powell said, Heath 'would go down to history bearing with him the indelible brand of broken faith and trust betrayed'.[85] This speech, containing the attack against Heath, was not released through Conservative Central Office, nor did Heath respond to it.

At this point Powell's criticism of the Heath Government again extended past the E.E.C. The Government's movement towards an interventionist economic policy gave him another front on which to attack the Prime Minister. After the Coal Board granted the striking miners a 21% increase in February 1972, Powell termed the settlement 'unconditional surrender' and indicated there were two things the Government could learn from the dispute. The first and more general point was that national ownership was an intolerable form of management in a free society. The second lesson was that the Heath Government's doctrine that in the fight against inflation the public sector must set the way for the private sector was actually the reverse of the truth.[86] The Government's decision to spend £35m. to create three yards at Upper Clyde (thus providing assured employment for 4300 people) brought an even fiercer attack. Speaking at Edgbaston Powell said that nothing served to undermine a government more than to be thought to have abandoned the principles on which it was elected:[87]

> The exceptions are beginning to replace the rules and the practice to contradict the principle. The nationalisation of Rolls-Royce Aviation is no longer isolated when it has been followed by the rescue of the Mersey Docks and Harbours and the massive infusion of public money into the shipyards of the Upper Clyde. The increase and no longer reduction of government expenditure has become an accepted element of policy.

But the Common Market still remained Powell's main area of attention. Labour anti-Marketeers in April attempted to force the Government into some sort of confrontation at the polls before E.E.C. entry was accepted. The official Labour position was, unsurprisingly, a preference for a general election which, given the polls, seemed likely to place a Labour Government in power. Powell was, significantly, the only Conservative M.P. to support this motion.[88] A section of the Labour party also put forward a motion calling for a popular referendum on E.E.C. entry. Despite his long-standing and clearly defined opposition to such a constitutional innovation, Powell was one of thirteen Tories to support this motion too. (Fourteen other Conservatives abstained, but Labour defections gave the Government an easy majority of forty-nine against the proposal.)[89] Powell made clear his continuing repugnance in principle to the referendum idea but supported it as a tactical gesture, arguing that Parliament if it passed such a proposal would be tacitly acknowledging that it did not have the consent of the British people to enter the Market.

His opposition to the Government continued through every division on the European Communities Bill. Indeed, analysis of the voting on each of the 104 divisions on the Bill showed that he opposed the Government more times (81) than any other Conservative M.P. John Biffen was right behind (78) followed by Roger Moate (71) and Neil Marten (69). There were several close scrapes for the Government – including majorities of only five votes on two amendments moved by Powell – but in the end Heath's majority always just held. Finally, in July 1972 the Bill passed into law with a still narrow seventeen-vote majority. The great parliamentary battle was over.[90]

The defeat led Powell to issue dire warnings about the effect of E.E.C. entry on the Tory party. In late September 1972 he travelled to Brussels and spoke about the attitude of the British people towards membership.[91] The mood in Britain then was one of 'cold anger' because Government decisions no longer reflected the will of the people. Britain would not remain a member of the Community because public opinion would not stand for it.[92]

> These resentments (over sovereignty) will intertwine themselves with all the raw issues of British politics: inflation, unemployment, balance of payments, the regions, even immigration, even Northern Ireland; and every one of these issues will be sharpened to the discomfiture of the European party.

His bitterness against the Conservative party also led him to offer indirect praise for the Opposition. It was no doubt surprising for the audience in Brussels to hear Powell reporting that Labour now enjoyed more popular support than the Conservatives and to hear him note that they had only narrowly lost the 1970 election. A month later in Yarmouth, he suggested that the Tories' 'broken pledge' over the E.E.C. foreshadowed a blank future for the party:[93] 'No statesman, no government, no party will survive if the essential compact with the people which is entered into as the price of office is wilfully or recklessly or deceitfully broken.'

It was thus a major and bitter personal defeat for him, fulfilling all his darkest fears of June 1970. The battle had completely isolated him within the Conservative party, both at the mass and élite levels. His personal anger with the Government was such that he could no longer avoid taking a jab at the leadership even when they adopted policies he approved of. Thus when Heath finally decided to float the pound in June 1972 – a policy Powell had long advocated – the action was greeted with derision. The decision, Powell said, marked 'a fitful gleam of the recovery of sanity' and was clear recognition that inflation could only be controlled 'by throwing in the sponge and doing what Enoch said'.[94]

The Government's success in passing the European Communities Bill for the first time raised the question of whether Powell would actually remain in the Conservative party. He had continually emphasised that the issue of E.E.C. entry was more important than party and had even lent his support to the Opposition's attempt to use the issue to install a Labour Government in power. He clearly now had either to persuade the party to reverse its position; or to reverse his own attitude; or to leave the party altogether. The first alternative seemed hardly likely to be realised – the parliamentary struggle had proved only how little support there was for his position in his party; the second was hardly thinkable. He naturally determined to work for the first alternative but, from July 1972 on, the hitherto unimaginable third alternative – quitting the Tory party – had perforce to enter the reckoning. Not surprisingly, many shared the conclusion of the *Economist* at this point – that he was 'a dead duck' in British politics.[95] It was at this point that his fortunes found the most unlikely of saviours – President Idi Amin of Uganda.

THE UGANDAN ASIANS

The Ugandan Asian controversy had been in prospect for some time. It was, pretty clearly, only a matter of time before a Ugandan government followed the example of their Kenyan counterparts towards the unfortunate Asians in their midst. As Amin's attitude hardened towards the eventual expulsion order, attention centred on the 50,000 of his victims who held British passports. Powell warned in a *Times* article that this did not necessarily entitle them to enter Britain.[96] The humanitarian need to offer refuge to the Ugandan Asians was a responsibility for the entire world community, a responsibility of which Britain's share would be infinitely small. He again warned of the potential this situation held for racial violence, citing particular incidents which had recently occurred in Liverpool. When the eventual expulsion order came however in 1972, the Government quickly made it clear that the 50,000 would be allowed to enter the country.[97] Heath was clearly furious at Amin's action – the more so since he had hardly hidden his pleasure at Amin's original overthrow of the Obote regime, and now felt let down as well as domestically embarrassed. For it was already clear

that while public opinion was loudly condemnatory of Amin and sympathetic to his victims, there was considerable resistance to the idea of
Britain opening its doors to the flood of refugees. A number of local
authorities indeed made no bones about their reluctance to act as hosts.
It was of little moment for the Government to point out that 50,000
was a relatively small number, even in one year's immigration statistics.
The image of a large new wave of coloured immigrants was well
established in the public's mind and all the earlier fears of the 1960s
were swiftly reawakened. Eager to dispel any impression that it was
willing to affront the feelings of its own citizenry simply out of largeness
of heart towards foreigners, however maltreated, the Government
sought to argue that it had at least a quasi-legal obligation to the
refugees. This was precisely the point most hotly contested by Powell.

When Peter Rawlinson, the Attorney General, declared that under
international law a person with nowhere to go should be permitted to
reside in the nation whose passport he holds, Powell attacked him
bitterly, accusing him of having 'prostituted' his office.[98] Powell argued
that ever since the Commonwealth Immigrants Act of 1962 citizens of
the Commonwealth had ceased to have any automatic right to British
citizenship. East African Asians were, he pointed out, denied free
movement between E.E.C. nations precisely because they were not
British nationals. His continued and angry criticism hit too raw a
nerve to go unanswered and he drew a stern, semi-judicial rebuke from
Lord Hailsham, the Lord Chancellor, for questioning the Attorney
General's integrity.[99] Powell, doubtless realising that the tactic of the
party's leaders was to ignore and dismiss him, made it impossible for
them to continue in this course by challenging them directly at the
Tory conference in October. Acting in his capacity as president of the
Hackney South and Shoreditch constituency association, he presented
a resolution on immigration.[100] The party managers had not initially
planned to debate immigration at the conference and the Powell resolution had to be voted on to the agenda by ballot of the constituency
delegates – which it was, by the highest vote of any resolution under
consideration. In fact the resolution received the highest vote of any
balloted proposal since World War II. It was not of itself particularly
controversial, stating with wicked simplicity that Conference believed
the Conservatives' declared policy on immigration (the one developed by
Heath before the 1970 election) to be the only approach likely to be
successful. It was difficult to see how the leadership – or any delegate –
could oppose this. However, in his speech Powell made it clear that a
reaffirmation of past Tory policy would in his view mean that the
Ugandan Asians could not enter. Broadening his attack he again argued
that the rapid (100,000 per annum) growth of the coloured population
would have a drastic and disastrous impact on the British way of life,
decisively altering the character of the larger cities. The only solution

was to end immigration completely and to offer assistance for repatriation. Failure to do this would, he warned, lead to almost certain electoral defeat.

His likely tactics had been clear enough. On the eve of the conference, Heath, clearly anticipating Powell's speech, declared that the British had an obligation to the Ugandan Asians which the party must not back away from.[101] At the conference debate however he sat grim-faced and silent as Powell stalked to the platform in an atmosphere of high tension and with considerable barracking from the Young Conservatives in the galleries. The scene of open division and major challenge to the leadership was quite unprecedented at a Tory conference. In the circumstances Powell's speech – brief and moderately phrased – produced a feeling of some anti-climax. There was no personal attack on Heath or anyone else, no Roman watching the Tiber, no rivers foaming with blood. Powell stalked back to his seat amidst considerable applause, mixed with boos, and sat impassive through the rest of the debate. The leadership recognised that Powell's amendment had a chance to pass overwhelmingly because of its uncontroversial nature. If this happened they were afraid that he would take to stumping the country, claiming that the Tory conference had ratified his line on immigration. To prevent this from happening the leadership persuaded the Young Conservatives to propose an amendment to Powell's motion congratulating the Government for its swift action in accepting responsibility for the fate of the Ugandan Asians. Powell was followed to the platform by David Hunt, the Y.C. chairman, whose speech, frequently interrupted by the noisy cheers of his supporters in the gallery, launched a fairly unrestrained series of attacks on Powell and concentrated mainly on a vehement denunciation of racialism. This left Robert Carr, the Home Secretary, to reply to the debate. Carr, a well-known liberal on this and other issues, was widely expected to denounce the Powellite position in ringing tones of principle – this, at least, was what the media had forecast in the tremendous build-up to the debate. They were disappointed, for Carr was bending with the wind – he could afford to after Heath's speech. The Conservative Government, he emphasised, had indeed already taken a hard line on immigration, in fulfilment of their election pledges. He made considerable play with the voluntary repatriation scheme and the twenty-four hour a day monitoring of illegal immigrants provided for in the 1971 Act and, on the Ugandan issue, stressed that only holders of British passports were to be allowed admission. Having thus covered his right flank he was then able to end his speech with a ringing – if routine – declaration that the Tory party would not embrace racialism. He was received with rapturous applause, as well as scattered boos and hisses from the Powell supporters. The Y.C.s' motion was carried by 1721 to 736, a majority of 985.

The media had in the weeks before the conference built up the immigration debate to a point where anything less than a full-scale gladitorial clash between Heath and Powell was an anti-climax and where anything less than an outright numerical victory for Powell was seen as a resounding defeat. After the conference, there was accordingly no shortage of commentary to the effect that Powell had been utterly vanquished, his career set back.[102] Ronald Butt (of *The Times*) wrote that he had weakened his general influence within the party by choosing to debate immigration – an argument based on an apparent assumption that his influence in other policy areas was greater even than in the field of immigration.[103]

It was left to David Wood, *The Times*'s political correspondent, and Patrick Cosgrave, the *Spectator* columnist, to argue the more obvious case that Powell had achieved a significant show of strength against the Tory leadership.[104] In Wood's report of the conference he indicated that senior Tories were surprised that his motion had been defeated only by a 2–1 margin. A 5–1 victory had been expected. Cosgrave similarly indicated that before the vote Tory front-benchers expected Powell to get only 200 to 300 votes. Even before the vote Cosgrave had written a column implying that this was a serious underestimate of Powell's support.[105] His hunch confirmed by the balloting at the conference, Cosgrave pointed out that these same ministers had fundamentally misjudged Powell's impact, demonstrating 'how far in recent years the leadership had got out of touch with what was going on in the constituencies'.[106]

In fact Cosgrave, if anything, understated his case. Only a few months before, after all, Powell had been the only Tory M.P. to vote for a motion which threatened to install a Labour government. He was almost totally isolated on the back-benches. In a party which values loyalty to its leadership above all other virtues he had repeatedly and bitterly deserted party ranks to level angry and direct accusation against its leader. Shortly before the conference he had gone further in his attack on Rawlinson, and had been roundly rebutted by the Lord Chancellor, no less. The party leader himself had found occasion to make a special speech in advance attacking Powell indirectly. In the debate itself there had been considerable manoeuvring for support against Powell – the whole stratagem involving the Young Conservatives was fairly plain. No member of the party leadership had engaged Powell as directly as Hunt, enjoying the licence of youth, had dared to. It is unthinkable that the Young Conservatives could have packed the galleries, replete with cheer-leaders and prepared placards, without at least the implicit approval of the leadership. The media had been universally and strongly against the Powell motion for days before the conference. Carr, an already popular minister, had offered an official alternative to Powell which lacked nothing in its advocacy of a severely restrictive immigration policy. It is little wonder that senior Conservatives should have been so confident of routing Powell; the stage appeared to be set for a complete débâcle.

In the face of all this, Powell had shown very considerable (and apparently entirely unorganised) strength. This had been immediately evident in the pre-conference balloting for resolutions as well as in the actual vote, where he had carried no less than 30% of the delegates with him. There was no precedent for such a large-scale Tory conference rebellion against a united and determined leadership enjoying the advantages of governmental office.

Powell's strength also showed up clearly in a poll of several hundred conference delegates by the *Spectator*.[107] The delegates were first asked who, in their opinion, had dominated the conference? Thirty-eight per cent said the Young Conservatives had, 30% said Carr, 23% Powell and 8% Heath. Forty-six per cent thought Carr had given the best speech, 23% thought Powell had, and 19% named David Hunt of the Young Conservatives. As choices for the Conservative leadership, should Heath resign, Carr was named by 38%, Powell by 37%. Perhaps the most striking aspect of the poll – apart from the support it revealed for Powell – was the sheer dominance of the immigration debate in the minds of respondents, who answered very largely as if the conference had consisted of that and nothing more. Powell received the support he did on the basis of a single conference speech of under ten minutes. During the week every leading Minister had spoken, all of them benefiting from the right to sum up debates on their subjects. Such summings-up enjoy a longer time allowance than other speeches and provide the opportunity for measured, magisterial performances. Nonetheless both the second and third 'best speeches' were thought to come from non-Ministers, the last indeed from a non-M.P. whom probably few could have named before the conference.

The Government certainly reacted sharply to the conference debate, almost immediately afterwards promulgating new immigration rules which restricted the entry rights of Commonwealth citizens and allowed freer entry for citizens of E.E.C. nations.[108] The Government maintained its position over the Ugandan Asians but otherwise the move was a further and clear concession to Powell – who was however hardly satisfied. When the new rules came before the House there emerged the same, though now strengthened, coalition which had forced the amendment to the 1971 Act. The coalition included hard-line opponents of any immigration (including Powell), anti-E.E.C. Tories who felt the new rules gave unfair preference to Common Market nations, pro-Commonwealth Conservatives who felt the new rules slighted New Zealand and Australia, and civil-libertarian Labour M.P.s who felt the new rules were too strict. In all, six Tories including Powell voted against the measure while forty other Conservatives abstained. The result was a resounding – and embarrassing – Government defeat by thirty-five votes. During late

1972 Powell also pressed for a new code of nationality to provide the Government with a permanent legal distinction between Commonwealth and U.K. citizens,[109] arguing that much of the immigration controversy was due to the lack of this clear dividing line. He also began campaigning to have the franchise taken away from Pakistanis living in Britain,[110] a move implied, he suggested, by Pakistan's withdrawal from the Commonwealth in December 1972.

The whole Ugandan Asian controversy finally tapered off in early 1973 when the Government introduced its revised immigration rules limiting entry to those who had a grandfather born in the country.[111] All others seeking entry were required to have work permits. These new rules, benefiting white Commonwealth residents to the exclusion of most non-whites and residents of E.E.C. nations, seemed designed to prevent the possibility of any repetition of controversies such as those over the Kenyan and Ugandan Asians. The concession to Powell was quite clear for all to see. This was now the fourth time in five years he had forced major changes in immigration policy on successive Governments.

On economic affairs the Government continued its U-turn away from the free-market policies Powell had long advocated. After Heath announced a Government proposal for a voluntary £2 limit on wage increases and a 5% freeze in retail prices in late September, Powell attacked fiercely. Just before Heath released his proposals, Powell – in a speech not released by Central Office – once again set out the reasons why a prices and incomes policy was harmful.[112] After the details of the Heath proposal became known, Powell made the accusation that the main portions of Conservative policy 'have been demolished by their builders' and said the package had been 'so suddenly assembled and so ill-digested that it has taken his own Cabinet colleagues utterly by surprise'.[113] When the Government failed to agree with the C.B.I. and the T.U.C. on a voluntary programme of controls, Heath reluctantly turned to a statutory measure. The announcement of the Tories' ninety-day standstill on wages, prices and rents led Powell to ask whether Heath had taken leave of his senses:[114]

Does he know that it is fatal for any government, party or person to seek to govern in direct opposition to the principles on which they are entrusted with the right to govern? In introducing a compulsory control on wages and prices in contravention of the deepest commitments of this party, has he taken leave of his senses?

Later in December Powell spoke of the 'insidious corrupting power' of the freeze after the Government requested food retailers to sign monthly statements that they were adhering to it. Citizens in a democratic society should not have to sign statements that they are obeying the law. The freeze, he said, was also proving to be insidious because Heath was using it to undermine the sovereignty of Parliament. The Prime Minister had told the General and Municipal Workers Union (G.M.W.U.) that they could not ask the Gas Council for a wage increase until the Government issued new guide-lines. Heath's action shocked Powell. Did the Prime Minister believe that a letter from him carried the force of law? He contended that Parliament, and not the Government, had the sole power to issue new wage and price guidelines, if they were to be promulgated at all.[115]

Examination of the poll data collected during the Ugandan Asian controversy and during the battle over an incomes policy demonstrated that Powell probably reached a peak in personal popularity at the time. Gallup asked respondents just after the Tory conference in October 1972, and again in April 1973, which Tory politicians were assets to their party. The results (see Table 4.2) show that Powell, already well entrenched after the conference, was the only figure to maintain his support in the months that followed, thus emerging ahead of all contenders.

TABLE 4.2   Conservative politicians as assets to their party 1972–73

	Oct 1972 %	Apr 1973 %
Douglas-Home	42	36
Powell	41	41
Barber	39	37
Carr	39	28
Heath	36	34

Source: Gallup Political Index, Oct 1972 and Apr 1973.

After the conference O.R.C. repeated a number of the questions they had asked immediately after the 1970 general election to see how attitudes towards Powell had changed. Their results too show a strong improvement in Powell's position (see Table 4.3).

TABLE 4.3   Electorate's attitude towards Powell, 1970–72

	June 1970 %	Oct 1972 %	Change
Powell is the only politician I admire			
Agree	36	40	(+4)
Conservatives better off with Powell as leader/prime minister			
Agree	19	39	(+20)
Powell has stirred up racial feeling			
Agree	63	60	(−3)

Source: O.R.C., Sunday Times, 21 June 1970 and *The Times*, 16 Oct 1972.

Similarly an N.O.P. poll released in December 1972 showed that Powell (with 29 %) easily topped all other politicians in their respondents' estimation of the 'M.P. who best understood the problems facing the country'.[116] The three major party leaders – Wilson (18 %), Heath (14 %) and Thorpe (12 %) – all trailed for behind him. A Man of the Year poll for the B.B.C.'s *World at One* showed Powell the victor with twice as many votes as Heath even though 1972 had been the year of Heath's final triumph over the E.E.C.[117]

Thus by the end of 1972 Powell had staged a public recovery which had seemed hardly predictable in June 1970 or even July 1972. He had fought an initial and bitter battle against the E.E.C. which had not only ended in complete failure but which, by the end, had clearly placed a question mark over his entire future career within Conservative ranks.

Two factors accounted for his rescue. First, the staggering defeat of the Heath Government in the 1971–72 miners' strike had forced a complete U-turn in Government economic policy. As the full proportions of the defeat became clear, the standing of both the Heath Government and of Heath himself within the Tory party fell sharply. Many Conservatives felt humiliated by the triumphant miners and dockers and hankered after the free-market policies advocated by Powell but now abandoned by Heath. Heath, it was true, had brought to fruition a personal struggle of more than a decade to secure British membership in the E.E.C. The triumph however was not reflected in popular feeling towards the E.E.C. and indeed suffered from the same fatal handicap that had brought about Powell's defeat on the issue: the public simply did not care enough about the Market either to reward Heath or punish Powell. The result was that Powell's protracted battle over the E.E.C., no matter how ineffectual and unsuccessful, had not prevented him from gaining from the failures and lapses of the Heath Government.

Secondly, and more importantly, the immigration issue had appeared yet again, this time in the shape of the hapless Ugandan Asians. Powell had not received a major accession of support – he was by now a quite automatic rallying point on the issue – but had again forced a major change in Government policy on the subject. Moreover he had used the issue to take the fatal step he had always thus far resisted – an open challenge to the leadership at the Tory conference. Here he had been defeated, as he doubtless expected to be. The point was that he had made the challenge at all and that he had gained the support he had. It seems likely that the roots of this challenge lay not in Uganda but in Powell's E.E.C. defeat. The outcome of the E.E.C. battle had left him with little alternative, as we have argued, between changing his position, leaving the party or launching an open bid within it to challenge the leadership and win it to his side. He had done enough to establish that he enjoyed considerable support both within the party and beyond it with a wider public. It was clearly not yet enough, for the E.E.C. issue had not yet been finally disposed of – but remained to pose a threat to his continued presence within Conservative ranks. By this time however Powell had become deeply embroiled in yet a further issue of major importance, that great graveyard of English politicians – the Irish problem.

5 Enoch Powell and Ulster, 1968-73

In the 1960s, as we have seen, Enoch Powell's emergence as the most powerful dissenting voice in British politics was tied to three great issues in particular – free-market economics, immigration and hostility to British entry to the E.E.C. In the 1970s a fourth theme, Northern Ireland, came to occupy an increasing, even predominant role in his political career.

His increasing involvement in the tragic and turbulent affairs of Northern Ireland, which most English politicians were only too keen to leave well enough alone, surprised many of his supporters and opponents alike. The opposite reaction might have been more appropriate, for it is difficult to see how Powell, with his strong conception of British nationhood, so central to all his thought, could leave alone the set of problems Northern Ireland presented for the future of the United Kingdom. He gave little mention to Northern Ireland's problems following the outbreak of hostilities during the Catholic civil rights campaign of 1968 and 1969. His career during this period was of course dominated by the immigration issue and his conversion to the anti-Market cause. These issues – doubtless preoccupying enough – formed the basis of his challenge to the Tory leadership. It was only after the 1970 election that he turned to Northern Ireland, at a time when he was ready to acknowledge that his chances of a Cabinet position or the party leadership were very slim. The 1970 election result served greatly to heighten the confrontation between Powell and the Heath leadership, in good part for the paradoxical reason that Heath seemed to have stolen Powell's political clothes on immigration and economic issues. The E.E.C. issue, however important, lacked political punch and might continue to lie in the doldrums a long time if the Brussels negotiations were protracted. Powell, in a word, could not only afford but perhaps also *needed* another issue; and Northern Ireland, given his particular intellectual bent, was the obvious choice.

*　　*　　*

The most useful way to begin a consideration of Powell's views on Northern Ireland is to turn to a speech he delivered in 1968 in Wales.

The speech was reported the next day as a statement of his position on devolution in Scotland and Wales, but in fact the major part of the speech dealt with Northern Ireland.[1] The speech was delivered at a high level of abstraction and did not touch in any substantial measure on the practicalities of coping with civil rights campaigns.[2]

For Powell it was important that the political parties should begin speaking about the position of Northern Ireland in the United Kingdom during the late 1960s because for the first time since the 1920s the definition of British nationhood, and with it the unity of the realm, was in question. As a Conservative he had particularly to be concerned, for:[3] '[It is] the business of the Tory party above all to think and to speak out about the future of the United Kingdom because nationhood, with all that word implies, is what the Tory party is ultimately about.'

As we have seen, nationhood is a wholly subjective idea to Powell. A people are a nation because they conceive of themselves as such. All other concerns are secondary to a people's self-perception. Hence in his view the struggles of the previous century to keep Ireland in the Union were mistaken – nationhood cannot be enforced. If a people, in a settled and preponderant majority, wish to break away from a nation to form their own – and the argument applied to the Welsh and Scots, not just the Irish – they should be allowed to do so. He was however firmly opposed to any form of limited devolution of power to the outlying areas of the U.K., an attitude largely explicable by his belief that 'nationhood is an absolute'.[4] A country could not have partial nationhood. If a people truly wanted to proclaim themselves a nation they would be unwilling to accept anything short of complete independence. Thus, when Britain withdrew from its overseas dependencies, the action was not taken with the idea of seeing whether these areas wanted to become nations, but rather as a series of gradual moves towards complete independence.

In the case of Northern Ireland it had been quite clear, ever since the six counties were separated from Ireland in 1921, that the great majority of its people wanted to remain part of the U.K. The loyalists, in Powell's view, did not really want any form of self-government. Rather, they accepted self-government as a necessary part of the settlement separating the Republic from the U.K. What was unambiguous was their wish to belong – and the reality of their belonging – within the U.K.

As for Scotland and Wales, if their people wished to be totally independent of England, their wishes too should not be resisted. But, Powell felt, it was important that they should be aware of what nationhood entailed. Should Scotland and Wales become independent they must have their own government, currency, central bank, parliament, internal and external security forces: they could not rely on others for their political and economic sustenance. Until this question of Scottish and Welsh nationhood had been made entirely clear (through preponderant nationalist electoral majorities), no devolution of power should be considered. To Powell the creation of separate parliamentary institutions would be a declaration that the people of these realms no longer considered that Parliament at Westminster adequately represented their interests. The creation of separate Parliaments:[5] 'would be the watershed, the parting of the ways, the saying that a separate nation had been consciously, deliberately, and once and for all admitted to be there'.

The implications of Powell's views on Wales and Scotland for Northern Ireland were clear. Under no conditions could he sympathise with the willingness of some Protestant extremists to consider the possibility of a Unilateral Declaration of Independence on the Rhodesian model should the British Government make any attempt to rule Northern Ireland directly.[6] Within the Northern Ireland context this placed Powell closest to the position of the Rev. Ian Paisley who, during most of the 1970s, favoured the total integration of Ulster into the U.K. should there be any alteration in the province's position.

With the exception of this 1968 speech Powell devoted little attention to Northern Ireland over the next two years, a few other isolated remarks apart.

He did not return to the Northern Ireland question until early 1970 when he addressed an Ulster Unionist rally. Again he emphasised that the central issue in Northern Ireland is 'belonging or not belonging. The belonging of Northern Ireland, and the not belonging of the Republic, are at present obscured by the condition of the law.'[7] This latter reference was to the Ireland Act of 1949 which gave Irish citizens privileges of entry, residence and settlement not enjoyed by other foreigners. Powell also offered his solution to the controversy raging in Northern Ireland, albeit in a vague and general way:[8]

Nothing, in my judgement, would conduce so much to banish strife and disorder as the plain and open assertion, in legal and constitutional terms, that the people of these countries belong, uniquely and solely, to the United Kingdom and are part and parcel of this nation, which is in the process of defining and recognising itself anew.

The next mention of Northern Ireland came in the June 1970 general election campaign. His references here to Northern Ireland were brief and were made in the context of his 'enemy within' speech,[9] a category including immigrants and university students as well as Catholic extremists in Northern Ireland. In the speech he explicitly adopted the position of the Protestant loyalists in Northern Ireland – that the civil rights campaign was nothing more than an attempt to destroy the civil Government. Civil rights and even religion were secondary issues.

The 'enemy' in Northern Ireland was trying to undermine the civil Government by using the civil rights campaign and religious issues.

His decision to involve himself more deeply in Ulster appears to have been taken towards the end of 1970. He began 1971 by making his first major speaking tour through the province, where he had previously spent little time.[10] The speeches did not touch on the two pressing concerns of the Northern Ireland Government at the time – ending the rioting in Ballymurphy (Belfast) and supplying more troops to the Chichester-Clark Government[11] – but dealt instead with the more abstract problem of the relationship between Northern Ireland and the U.K. His speech to the Young Unionists in Londonderry summarised his views, with a very consistent echo of his 1968 Welsh speech.

Once again Powell started from the premise that the central issue in the controversy was whether Northern Ireland was part of the United Kingdom or whether it was part of the Irish Republic. Humanitarian concerns about the need for people of different religions to get along obscured this basic concern. There could not be two answers to this fundamental question. Northern Ireland should be considered part of the United Kingdom because the Protestant majority 'consider and assert themselves to be not a separate nation but, if I understand aright, a part of the nation which inhabits Great Britain. It is not an issue on which both sides can be satisfied; one or the other must prevail.'[12]

Powell felt the situation in Northern Ireland was particularly dangerous because the Catholic minority – as a result of events which surrounded the creation of the Irish Republic – had maintained the hope that Northern Ireland could be detached from the U.K. The prospect of detachment gave rise to the possibility that violence and civil war would possibly achieve success. If it did not wish to encourage terrorism, Westminster must at all costs not 'indulge in the common human weakness of trying to have it both ways at once'.[13]

It was, he declared, essential for the British to assert their nationhood, and hence it was incumbent on the people of England to rally to the Unionist cause. But part of the problem in redefining British nationhood lay in the citizenship laws. Because the only citizenship status known in law was 'Commonwealth citizen' the country had been going through a long crisis concerning the right of Commonwealth residents to enter Britain freely. The important issue was for the British to have the courage 'to declare that we too are a nation, and have a right as good as any other to be recognised, and to recognise ourselves as distinct and unique'.[14]

It was easy for Powell to speak about the problems of Northern Ireland while touring the province. Making the case for an English politician to take up the controversy in England was however quite another thing. This was the task he set for himself in his next major address on Northern Ireland to the South Buckinghamshire Conservative

women in March 1971.[15] He told his audience that they, just as
much as the people of County Down, had cause to be concerned about
the problems for 'when one part of the nation is under attack, the
whole is under attack'.[16]

Those Catholics in Northern Ireland who participated in demonstrations and terrorist activities were not, he declared, common criminals.
Common criminals did not question the legitimacy of a régime and were
not, in that sense, 'enemies' of the nation. But in Northern Ireland large
sections of the Catholic community were 'enemies' of the United
Kingdom, because they sought to use violence as a means of detaching
part of the U.K. to transfer it to another nation. By inference, then,
the Protestant 'ultras' were not enemies of the state in the way the
Catholic Republicans were, even if those Protestants engaged in activities as violent as those of the I.R.A. Powell thus explicitly rejected the
view that the Army could be an impartial force, restraining two groups
who were equally guilty of breaking the law. Rather, the situation in
Northern Ireland pitted an aggressor against the aggressed; the
Protestants were 'friends' and 'loyal' while the Catholics were disloyal.
The Army's function in Northern Ireland was to put down an avowed
enemy of the nation which was attacking loyal citizens.

Given this view of the situation it is not surprising that Powell
reacted with horror to the fact that there were certain sections of
Londonderry (the Bogside, for example) and Belfast that the Army
would not patrol – the so called 'no go' areas, policed by groups such
as the Catholics Derry Citizens Defence Committee which were not
accountable to civil authorities.[17] For a time the Government at
Westminster tried to deny that there were in fact such areas, but by the
time of Powell's address, there was little disagreement that such districts
did indeed exist.[18] Naturally Powell viewed them as pockets of enemy
territory which the Government had abandoned. Refraining from trying
to re-establish the Government's authority in these areas was 'as wise as
it would be to leave enemy posts undisturbed behind one's lines'.[19]

Powell's speech elicited only a small and negative response from the
Government. Two days after his speech Mr Maudling, the Home
Secretary, announced on television that any decision to enter the 'no go'
areas would be taken by military officials and not by politicians.[20] He
thus effectively disclaimed responsiblity for the 'no go' areas, leaving it
as a military problem. To Powell, of course, their significance lay in their
symbolic political importance.

Powell did not speak again on Northern Ireland until autumn 1971
when he addressed a Unionist rally in County Tyrone.[21] Again,
stressing how essential it was to emphasise that Northern Ireland was
part of the United Kingdom and not a separate nation, he obliquely
dissociated himself from support of a prime Unionist objective, the
continued existence of Stormont. The existence of three separate

Governments at Dublin, Westminster and Belfast did help to create the feeling that three separate states existed. This, by clear implication, he found regrettable, though equally clearly his objection was not to the existence of separate Governments in Dublin and Westminster. Few bothered to read between the lines, for the main brunt of the speech fell on the Heath Government, the first time Powell had explicitly attacked the Government on Northern Ireland. It should be the object of the Heath Government to discourage such feeling and to encourage the identification of Northern Ireland with the rest of the U.K.; instead, he asserted, they work from the assumption that the majority in Northern Ireland was wrong. The Government should be standing up directly for the Protestant majority, not deepening its fears and gladdening its enemies by the recent holding of talks between Mr Heath and Mr Lynch, the Eire Prime Minister. Mr Heath should never have lent himself to such an exercise.[22]

Following through this hard line, Powell argued that both the present Conservative and past Labour Governments were guilty of 'disastrous innocence' for assuming that problems in Northern Ireland could be ameliorated through reforms. The only reform that would satisfy the Catholics was separation from the U.K. Citizens of Eire should be treated as aliens, with controls on their right of entry to Britain and their participation in its electoral system.

Powell's strong sense of British nativism, so apparent over the immigration issue, was now thus nicely wielded to provide the guiding principle for a Northern Ireland settlement. It only remained for him to bring in that other major threat to British nationhood, entry into the E.E.C., this time with a special twist:[23]

I do not see how any Unionist Member of Parliament representing an Ulster seat can vote for British entry. A vote for British entry is a vote for the political unification of Ulster and the Republic, and only a dangerously innocent or dangerously subtle politician would quibble that it means association with the Republic without dissociation from the United Kingdom. For Ulster unification with the Republic is dissociation from the United Kingdom: that is what Unionism for Northern Ireland has always been about.

He also placed the blame for violence in Northern Ireland on Westminster. If the Government made it clear that there was no hope of the separation of Northern Ireland from the U.K., Republicans would lose all hope. However, by offering piecemeal reform the British Government was in effect telling the terrorists that if they kept on agitating they would reach their objectives. Thus the only effective policy was a consistent pro-Unionist position.

Powell was speaking in something of a vacuum. His highly abstract analysis of the Northern Ireland problem was made against a background of continual and confused political violence in the province, a situation in which Westminster policy staggered uneasily from one immediate crisis to another. This same situation had destabilised the old game of Northern Ireland politics, producing a great wave of Protestant reaction. This reaction thrust aside the old-established Unionist élite and placed a premium on politicians with strong gut-reactions and grassroots connections – hardly a description of Powell's position in Northern Ireland.

Nor was the Tory party more receptive terrain for Powell. The party, as uncertain as any other section of British opinion, tended to support the Government's policy initiatives fairly blindly. The old Unionist connection no longer had its former force – indeed if anything it produced tremors of guilt and a corresponding wish to dissociate from the extremism. Public opinion as a whole was shocked by the ferocity of events in Northern Ireland and receptive to any solution which promised to rid Britain of a nagging problem which, in the last analysis, had little to do with life on the British mainland. A September 1971 N.O.P. poll showed that 32% of respondents wanted the province to be joined with Eire, while only a plurality (42%) favoured the *status quo* of keeping it in the U.K. Powell was hardly on strong ground when far less than a majority were willing to support the continuing integrity of the U.K. Moreover respondents considered Northern Ireland only the fourth most important national problem, after the cost of living, unemployment and the Common Market.[24]

In March 1972 Mr Heath announced the imposition of direct rule, thus abrogating Stormont's jurisdiction. Convinced that the Northern Ireland Prime Minister Brian Faulkner could no longer keep the peace, Heath also announced that, along with direct rule, Westminster would also take complete responsibility for maintaining law and order. Actually the decision to transfer responsibility for keeping the peace was made first. The Faulkner Government announced it could not continue to serve on these terms, thus necessitating the imposition of direct rule. In addition Heath announced that there would be periodic plebiscites on the question of Northern Ireland's status as part of the U.K. and that internment would be phased out. He also designated William Whitelaw as Secretary of State for Northern Ireland. Not surprisingly these decisions were unpopular with Ulster's Protestants, drawing sharp criticism from Unionist members of Stormont. Some 190,000 Protestant workers also came out on a two-day work stoppage in protest against the action.[25]

Powell bitterly criticised the imposition of direct rule as soon as Heath's policy was announced,[26] suggesting that the Government had only given the 'enemy' hope that it could break the six counties away from the U.K. Direct rule served only to emphasise the differences between Northern Ireland and the rest of the U.K. He also continued to press his suggestion that the Government should control all movement between the Irish Republic and the U.K. All Irish citizens should be required to carry passports whenever they travelled in Great Britain. Finally Powell also again recommended that the Army should patrol all the territory in Northern Ireland, and not by-pass the 'no go' areas. In another speech five days later he suggested that the citizens of Ulster should carry identity cards and that Southern Ireland should be recognised as a foreign country.[27]

His views were, again, hardly universally shared. He was only one of eight British M.P.s to vote against the second reading of the Government's Northern Ireland (Temporary Provisions) Bill which gave them authority for the implementation of direct rule.

The eighteen opponents of the measure consisted of nine Ulster Unionists, Bernadette Devlin, Powell and seven other Conservatives.[28] Mr Whitelaw, the newly appointed Secretary of State for Northern Ireland, quickly issued a statement indicating that he would not order Government troops to occupy the 'no go' areas and specifically indicated that Powell's hard-line pro-Unionist position was unacceptable to the Government.[29] Powell angrily accused Whitelaw and Heath of being interested only in maintaining a temporary peace in Northern Ireland, without concern as to whether it stayed in the U.K.[30] Public opinion showed no signs of listening to him on the issue at all. After the imposition of direct rule, N.O.P. found that the percentage of respondents favouring the unification of Northern and Southern Ireland increased from 32% to 36%, while those favouring keeping Ulster in the U.K. remained stable at 42%. A narrow 40%–38% plurality of Labour voters favoured unification, while a more substantial 49%–32% plurality of Conservatives were for keeping Ulster in the U.K.[31]

Powell spoke on Northern Ireland periodically during the spring of 1972, following the imposition of direct rule,[32] but it was not until June 1972 that he shared a platform with other Ulster Unionist politicians.[33] At a Unionist rally in Banbridge, County Down, Powell staged a minor but significant coup by bringing together on the platform with him the two leaders of the opposing wings of the Unionist Party, Brian Faulkner and William Craig. Powell's own speech was studiously diplomatic, urging Unionists that the way to reach the Heath Government was through professions of loyalty to the U.K., not through acts of violence which merely had the effect of undermining any sympathy their position might arouse.

His criticisms of Westminster's policies in Northern Ireland continued through the summer of 1972. He particularly criticised Whitelaw's decision to meet members of the I.R.A. and subsequently to transmit their demands for a cease-fire to Heath.[34] Noting the secrecy that surrounded the meetings, Powell also asked whether the Secretary had signed any secret agreements with the I.R.A.[35] Whitelaw's policy, he declared in the Commons, had the effect of driving Northern Ireland further into civil war. Whitelaw replied that he saw no alternative to trying to negotiate peacefully with both sides. In a later written reply to Powell, Whitelaw indicated that he had signed no written agreement with the I.R.A.[36] In fact, Whitelaw had trespassed almost beyond the bounds of the publicly acceptable by sitting down with men universally reviled for their atrocities. He appeared somewhat shaken by the criticisms his initiative received and almost immediately thereafter began to stress that there was no question of any further such meetings.

His initiative having failed, the Government invaded the 'no go' areas in an effort to reduce the level of terrorist activity. The military's effort was carried out smoothly with only a minimum of violence.[37] Nevertheless this action was unpopular with the British electorate; a 42%–31% plurality opposed the action.[38] The Government made deliberate efforts to ensure that Powell was not given credit for this decision, with Whitelaw's sharpest attack on Powell's policies coming just a week before the 'no go' areas were reoccupied. Powell doubtless recognised the ploy and deliberately did not applaud the Government's decision. Rather he asked publicly what long-term steps the Government planned to take to avert future I.R.A. terrorist activities. Hugh Macpherson, in his analysis of Powell's speeches on Northern Ireland, suggested that his influence at Westminster had shrunk, and not grown, through his activities in the six counties:[39]

> The Ulster crisis presented a golden opportunity for the Wolverhampton prophet to gain a following among members of the House. He has not proved so far capable of gaining that following. One of the small band of genuine Powellites remarked to me that he thought Mr Whitelaw had just about judged this correctly by going as far as he did with the Provos.

> Perhaps Mr Powell has gained the affection of the Ulster Unionists and a few military irregulars. But he has also alienated so many of his own party by his opportunism that the call from a grateful nation seems more remote.

If he won no additional British support, Powell certainly was gaining increasing recognition from Protestant ultras. In late August 1972 the extreme Loyalist Association of Workers announced that they had invited Powell to chair a conference of theirs in September and then address a rally the next day. For the first time he was faced with a major political choice as to his alignments within the maelstrom of Northern Ireland politics. For the L.A.W. – with its undeniable grassroots strengths – had talked of the possibility of actually fighting the British should the Unionist cause be abandoned. The leader of the L.A.W. – as well as his lieutenant – had been quoted as saying, 'If we're sold down the drain, there wouldn't be civil war. There would be armed rebellion against the Government of Britain.'[40] The L.A.W. was also part of the Ulster Vanguard, a coalition of Protestant extremist groups which was set up by William Craig as an umbrella organisation for loyalists.

Powell was wary, conscious of the basic philosophical differences between the L.A.W., Craig and himself. Craig after all had been sacked from his position as Minister of Home Affairs by the then Ulster Prime Minister, Terence O'Neill, in 1968 because he had questioned section 75 of the Government of Northern Ireland Act (1920), which gave absolute sovereignty over Ulster to Westminster, notwithstanding the establishment of a Parliament at Stormont.[41] At a Unionist rally in December 1968 Craig had said that he would resist any effort by the British Government to interfere with the government of the province. The power to intervene was in his view reserved only for emergency situations where the Northern Ireland Government requested British assistance.[42] Craig's views and the views of Billy Hull, leader of the L.A.W., were distinctly at variance with those of Powell, in whose ideal world a separate Parliament would not even exist in a Northern Ireland which would be indistinguishable from the rest of the U.K. For all the political temptation the L.A.W. invitation may have offered, Powell turned it down.[43] At the rally Craig told a crowd of 15,000 people that if the Protestant majority were not granted its rights it would set up its own parliament and government. Hull pointedly said that those who had not attended the rally should not call on loyalists for support in the future. The Stormont rally was attended by three Unionist M.P.s as well as the chairman and vice-chairman of the parliamentary Ulster Defence Association, another extreme group aligned closely with Craig.

Joining Powell in turning down invitations to the rally were Ian Paisley and the former Prime Minister, Brian Faulkner. While Faulkner and Paisley represented different strands of Unionist opinion, they were both opposed to any U.D.I. by the Northern Ireland Protestants. Faulkner moved away from his former position on the right wing of the Unionist party towards a more conciliatory position with regard to the Conservative Government. In doing so, he slowly but inexorably began losing support inside the Unionist party. Paisley had called any talk of an independent Ulster 'stupid and utter balderdash' and had indicated that he favoured the integration of Ulster into the U.K.[44] Powell shared Paisley's position and, apparently in order to demonstrate his differences with Craig and the Ulster Vanguard, he accepted another speaking engagement at the same time as the mass rally at Stormont was taking place. Speaking in Ballymena, County Antrim, Powell reiterated his established position, indicating that he preferred total integration of Northern Ireland into the U.K. when direct rule ended.[45] Although he effectively repeated this speech a fortnight later in Belfast,[46] he fell virtually silent on Ulster affairs for six months, perhaps somewhat taken aback at the apparent impasse that had been reached.

Powell's next major speech on Ulster was not until after the publication of the Government's White Paper on Northern Ireland in March 1973. The White Paper called for the creation of an Assembly elected by proportional representation to ensure adequate Catholic membership; continuation both of the office of Secretary of State for Northern Ireland and of control over the province's security from Westminster; and the creation of a Council of Ireland so that representatives of the North and South could discuss common interests. According to the White Paper the Assembly would have committees whose chairmen would form the Executive. The White Paper also included the provision that Northern Ireland would remain part of the United Kingdom as long as a majority of the people wanted it to do so.[47]

By calling for P.R. the White Paper was creating a situation which would require a substantial degree of power-sharing between Protestants and Catholics. Powell jumped on this section of the White Paper and said that power-sharing was a 'built-in contradiction' and an 'absurdity'.[48] The solution to the problem was to place Northern Ireland in a situation similar to Scotland and give it a Westminster delegation as large as the Scots. If the Government at Westminster was insistent on developing power, it should clearly map out how much power the Assembly would have before, and not after, the elections. He was also critical of the Northern Ireland Constitution Bill which put into legislative form the proposals embodied in the White Paper.[49]

The Northern Ireland Constitution Bill provided for a seventy-eight-member Assembly with a power-sharing Executive of twelve people. The Executive would only be given power when the Secretary of State was satisfied that it had gained wide acceptance in the community. In addition the Secretary of State retained the power to appoint two people to the Executive who were not members of the Assembly. The Bill also gave the Executive power to enter into agreements with the Republic of Ireland on matters that fell within its authority.

Following the publication of the legislation, Powell alleged that this arrangement did not provide for a responsible Executive or Assembly.[50] The idea of trying to bring Protestants and Catholics together was doomed to fail because the Catholics wanted to break away from the U.K. Moreover the Northern Ireland Constitution Bill avoided the issue of whether Northern Ireland was part of the United Kingdom or a separate entity. Powell also later indicated his opposition to another section of the legislation which provided for periodic plebiscites in Northern Ireland on whether it should remain part of the United Kingdom.[51] In the report stage of the Bill at Westminster, Powell and the Ulster Unionist members voted for a Labour motion removing the section of the Bill calling for a referendum on the status of Northern

Ireland every ten years. The amendment was defeated by a Government majority of six in a 264–258 vote.[52] While Powell had allied himself with Labour on this amendment no such coalition could be constructed to oppose the measure on its second reading. There were only seven votes against the measure and 230 in favour. Only one other Conservative M.P., Harold Soref, joined Powell in opposing the measure. Four Ulster Unionists and one Labour member were the only other opponents of the Bill.[53]

Powell adopted a low profile on Ulster for the rest of 1973. He did deliver two speeches in the autumn calling for the integration of Ulster into the U.K., but devoted most of his attention to British domestic economic woes instead. But it was in one of the speeches to the Londonderry Imperial Unionist Association that he indicated that Stormont could never be propped up. He also pointed out that separatism was antithetical to true Unionism:[54]

> The true patriotism of Northern Ireland is not a separatist patriotism; it is a Unionist patriotism, a British˙ patriotism ... only incomprehension, ambivalence (or worse, rejection) could succeed in turning Unionism into that denial of itself: isolationism. ...
>
> There is only one side that can be taken, and there is only one form the decision can take. We cannot retrace our steps to 1969 and before; *the mould of Stormont is broken and, like it or not, cannot be put together*. There is only one way in which the determination of the majority in this province not to form part of any other state can be expressed. That is the way in which the determination of every other part of the United Kingdom is expressed; full, and exclusive, representation in the Parliament of the United Kingdom.

But with the exception of these two speeches he was generally silent on the issue. For example he made no public comment in early December when Heath held tripartite talks with Liam Cosgrave of the Republic and members of the Northern Ireland Executive designate.

Again, public opinion poll data showed that only a small fraction of the British electorate agreed with Powell's solution to the Northern Ireland controversy. Only 24% of an O.R.C. sample favoured direct integration, 34% advocated the unification of Ireland and 23% supported the resurrection of a provincial government subordinate to Westminster.[55]

The tripartite talks were significant for Powell only indirectly in that they hastened the break-up of the Unionist party, weakening the hand of moderates like Faulkner and strengthening the right of the party. Because Faulkner accepted the White Paper conditionally, subsequently co-operated with the Heath Government and participated in the talks, he lost a good deal of support inside the Unionist party. Even before the talks began, members of the Unionist party who had stood in the

Assembly elections on a policy of opposing the Heath Government's White Paper had begun working to undercut Faulkner's position. Harry West, Assembly member for Fermanagh and South Tyrone and leader of the ten unpledged (that is, anti-Faulkner and anti-White Paper) Unionists had called for Faulkner's resignation in October and narrowly failed to carry a resolution in the Unionist party's standing committee condemning his participation in the talks.[56] Faulkner's position was further eroded just before the Sunningdale talks opened when West organised a new party consisting of the ten unpledged Unionists in the Assembly and five of the seven Unionist M.P.s at Westminster.[57] Early in January 1974 Faulkner's credibility was destroyed when he was given a vote of no confidence by his party, occasioning his resignation as leader.

As part of the effort to build support for his group, West sought out Powell on at least two occasions to ask him to assume the leadership of his new group. While West was on the right wing of the Unionist party, he did not take as extreme a position as William Craig did. True, West had been expelled from the Unionist party in 1970 along with Craig, but thereafter a perceptible distance had separated the two men. In 1973 West specifically dissociated himself from Craig's call at a Unionist rally for open opposition to the British Government should they abandon the Unionist cause.[58] West's first approach to Powell came during the 1973 Conservative conference, indicating that his faction was upset by Faulkner's willingness to support power-sharing and that he felt his group needed a strong leader. Powell evidently did not take the offer seriously then and indeed publicly stated that no approach had been made.[59]

Thus by the end of 1973 his involvement with the Northern Ireland issue had placed him at a major crossroads. He is a man deeply versed in English history and has not infrequently shown himself to be properly conscious of the possible parallels between his own career and that of that other great popular tribune of the Midlands, Joseph Chamberlain.

But if in taking up the Northern Ireland issue Powell had sought to launch a great popular campaign for the preservation of the Union in the manner of Chamberlain, leading the Liberal Unionists in opposition to Irish Home Rule, he had fallen far short of achieving Chamberlain's impact within the politics of the British mainland. The Conservative Government had perhaps been irritated and occasionally embarrassed by Powell's rhetoric as they strove to deal with the Irish problem yet again – but no more. As far as British public opinion as a whole was concerned, Powell's words on Northern Ireland had fallen on deaf, ignoring ears. If anything his political isolation has increased. To many indeed the very fierceness of his abstract concern seemed wild and unreal, the behaviour of a politician now wandering in a wilderness increasingly remote from popular feelings and realities.

On the other hand his involvement with the Northern Ireland question had won him the possibly unexpected reward of a whole new popular following in the province itself. As the Northern Ireland crisis dragged on and the limitations of gut-reaction political responses became increasingly clear to Protestant politicians, so Powell's powerful and coherent analysis, his unyieldingly hard line against Catholic agitation and his sheer status as a major political figure, all exercised an increasing attraction.

However flattering the approaches to him from the L.A.W. and later from West, they also posed a major problem for Powell. He had now achieved a new political base, a clear alternative on which to fall back if his position within the Tory party became untenable. To that extent he could now face with some confidence and security his show-down with the Heath leadership which had threatened for so long and which the E.E.C. issue had made all but inevitable. But his very identification with this new potential constituency was simultaneously weakening his position within Conservative ranks.

His refusal of West's offer made it clear that he was not going to make that identification final and irreversible unless he had to. He was not in a word going to jump, at least until he could make it publicly clear that he had been pushed.

6 The Final Break with the Tories

By the close of 1972 Powell clearly stood at another cross-roads. Whatever other defeats it had sustained, the Heath Government had succeeded in one respect – it had finally achieved British entry into the E.E.C. But Powell could not accept that decision. He avowed his clear intention of continuing to fight for its reversal, even if this could only be achieved at the expense of the Conservative party and Government.

Moreover he was now at complete odds with the Government's economic policies. Indeed his reaction to the Government's introduction of a ninety-day wage and price freeze was to question, in November 1972, whether Mr Heath had entirely lost his senses. The attack was so frontal and gained such enormous publicity that it seemed to some that Powell had already surrendered all hope of ever making his peace not only with Heath but with the Conservative party as a whole. The fact was however that in the wake of the 1971–72 miners' strike a mood of muffled disgust had been growing among Tory back-benchers. This mood was deepened by the U-turn and although Powell was the only Tory M.P. to vote against the Government in November, three others spoke on his side of the issue and even they clearly represented only the tip of the iceberg.

Powell's attacks on the Government's economic policy continued into 1973. He criticised the Prime Minister and Cabinet for acting outside the law in intervening in a dispute between the unions and the British Gas Corporation.[1] They had no authority to intervene, he maintained, unless they had explicit parliamentary approval. When the Government announced their phase 2 wage controls in mid-January, Powell again attacked them for trying to control inflation with a £1 plus 4% wage freeze:[2] 'The country has twice before been through this cycle and knows perfectly well how it inevitably ends in failure and ridicule. It is tragic that we have to go around again.'

Surprisingly Powell and his monetarist colleagues on the Tory back-benches made no effort to debate this subject with the Chancellor, Mr Barber, at the meeting of the 1922 Committee held before the measure's second reading.[3] In the parliamentary debate Powell expressed his anger that neither party was speaking against the concept of an incomes policy.[4] Powell was again the only Tory M.P. to oppose the Government.

That no major interest in Britain was speaking against the incomes policy was a continuing source of anguish to Powell. 'Somehow common purpose and understanding has to be regained and the chain of fatality broken which is leading to a catastrophe', he asserted in February.[5] There was no point in hoping for a lead from the trade unions, who could not 'remain in the channels of free collective bargaining without renouncing their attachment to an economic and political theory, call it socialist or Marxist, with which free collective bargaining is incompatible'. Government Ministers were 'prisoners on a madly hurtling projectile, like Mazeppa on the back of a wild horse'.[6] The Government could not effectively deal with inflation unless they accepted responsibility for it and refrained from shifting the burden to others. He was no more charitable to the Labour party: 'The Opposition sits gagged and in chains, imprisoned by its own past, opposing on any old pretext, and silent when it comes to uttering the arguments which the nation needs to hear.'[7] Powell may have felt himself to be an entirely isolated lone voice but, as Ronald Butt wrote in early March, his analysis of the economic situation 'coincides with the instincts of many (Tory) backbench M.P.s to a greater extent than any other time since the party came to power'.[8] Powell's opposition was not merely to incomes policy pure and simple. While statutory policies governing prices and incomes he opposed as the unacceptable face of the corporate state, 'voluntary' policies were no better. Thus Powell spoke out again in June 1973 when the Government indicated that their phase-3 controls might take the form of voluntary controls, with statutory power kept in reserve. A decision to act in this way, Powell said, 'has all the characteristics and consequences of government without law. It is arbitrary, it is capricious, it is uncertain, it is covert, it is unappealable. When we find that, with the best of intentions, we are being carried towards that goal, it is time to stop and think. Above all it is time for the individual to do so for, in the last resort, the defence of liberty under the rule of law lies in his hands.'[9]

In this first half of 1973 Powell stood poised apart from both major parties. He also stood poised on the very peak of his popularity with the public. In the wake of the Ugandan Asian controversy he had actually overtaken Heath in the polls as a popular choice for prime minister and was not far behind Wilson, as Fig. 6.1 shows. Moreover when M.O.R.I. in February 1973 asked respondents to omit the practical considerations imposed in choosing a premier by simply asking who best represented their views, Powell did even better, with 25 % choosing him, against 28 % for Wilson and 19 % for Heath. By June 1973 Powell was in a virtual dead-heat with the two leaders even on the 'choice of prime minister' question, as Fig. 6.1. shows.

Powell's future hung in the balance, frustratingly for his followers. He had broken with both parties over immigration, Northern Ireland

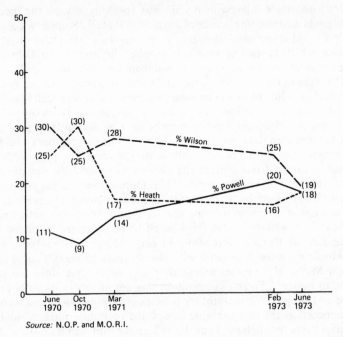

Source: N.O.P. and M.O.R.I.

Fig. 6.1 Electorate's choice for prime minister for the next five years 1970–73

and economic policy, though on all three issues – especially the last – a significant section of Tory opinion sympathised with him. But he was irrevocably opposed to the Tory leadership over the E.E.C. question. While he had his Tory sympathisers on this issue too, there was no doubt that his stance brought him closer to a substantial body of Labour opinion, not only in the country but in Parliament as well.

It was clear that he thus faced a very fundamental choice, and one that he would have to make while running at the head of an enormous body of mass support. If the February 1973 M.O.R.I. poll was a fair reflection, about 10 million voters saw him as the man best representing their views, giving him a following of Gaullist proportions.

His followers were in part frustrated by his refusal to countenance their adventurist proposals, in part by the fact that he had put himself beyond the pale of political respectability over immigration. This situation was highlighted at the beginning of 1973 when a group of millionaire businessmen attempted to mount a campaign to keep Powell in the Conservative party and eventually make him its leader.[10] The millionaires persuaded the chairman of the Brent constituency association to mail copies of Powell's speeches to chairmen of other constituency parties. Their letter in support of him dealt almost exclusively with his economic views, making no mention of immigration save for an oblique reference to his strong working-class support. Powell remained aloof from the group and refused to encourage its activities, saying that the party already had a leader, making the campaign for him irrelevant. His refusal to get involved with an organised effort to make him party leader was of course entirely consistent with his refusal to get involved with the similar effort of 1969.

While his supporters might soft-pedal the immigration issue, there seemed little doubt that Powell owed much of his popularity to it – though after the revised immigration rules were adopted he had very little to say on the subject, restricting himself to one speech of criticism in April against the Department of Education for publishing what he considered to be a grave underestimate of the number of coloured children in London schools.[11] Perhaps mindful of the initiative mentioned above he made special reference to the statistics for Brent. By this stage however he had so thoroughly established himself as a lightning conductor on the immigration issue that he hardly needed to say much more to attract support from it. Indeed he seemed able to exercise influence even by refusing to talk about it. In a May 1973 by-election he announced that because of his disagreement with the Tory candidate on the E.E.C. and immigration issues he could not in good conscience campaign for him. Labour won the seat by an 8000-vote margin while a National Front candidate got a substantial protest vote of 4800.

It was against this background that Powell went to Stockport in June 1973 to deliver a momentous speech. Taking up the E.E.C. question again, he warned that in some instances political principles were more important than party and that, in pursuit of these principles, some Tories might have to support their political enemies. In hinting that he might have to support Labour, Powell again explicitly conjured up the figure of Joseph Chamberlain and alluded to the latter's decision to leave the Liberal party over the issue of Irish Home Rule. The European issue, he declared, was simply one which allowed no room for compromise:[12]

> Independence, the freedom of a self-governing nation, is in my estimation the highest political good, for which any disadvantage, if need be, and any sacrifice, are a cheap price. It is worth living for; it is worth fighting for; and it is worth dying for.

In an interview after the speech, he reaffirmed that he would 'live and die a Tory' but said he might have to side with Labour over the issue of renegotiation of the terms of entry into the E.E.C.[13] He also made clear in the interview that he was willing to face Labour rule for the rest of his life if that was the price for preserving parliamentary sovereignty.[14] Harold Wilson quickly issued a statement that under no circumstances could he work with Powell. Heath indicated that Powell was 'a bitter and backward-looking man' who had turned to Labour as a last resort.[15]

The speech was a bombshell. True, Powell was not yet fully over the brink, but he had now shown how far he might go, and in which direction. The impact of the speech on his popular support did not at first seem to be very substantial. As Fig. 6.2 shows, those believing him to be a party asset did begin to slip from this point, as we have already seen (Fig. 6.1), and although Powell's support fell after the Stockport speech, so did that of Heath and Wilson, so that his relative standing actually improved.

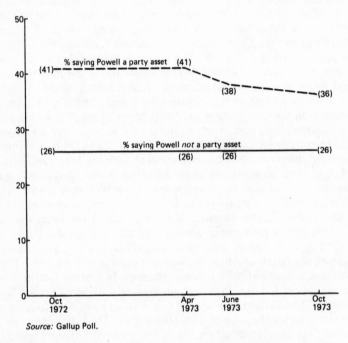

Source: Gallup Poll.

Fig. 6.2   Evaluation of Powell as party asset Oct 1972–Oct 1973

Moreover, as Table 6.1 shows, Powell out-ranked his rivals on almost every count in detailed popular assessment at this point.

The last rating in Table 6.1 is significant. For all their plaudits, the public did not actually find Powell very likeable. Indeed the ratings above were all the more impressive when viewed against the alleged British preference for moderation in all things. The polls found only 1% of their respondents regarding Powell as a moderate, while he was the man most widely (45%) regarded as extreme – far ahead of Michael Foot (12%) and Tony Benn (11%).

Media commentators tended to see Powell as being at his peak. In

TABLE 6.1 Popular assessments of personal attributes of Powell, Wilson and Heath, June 1973

	Powell	*Wilson*	*Heath*
In touch with people	41% (1st)	30%	17%
Good speaker	47% (1st)	36%	25%
Can believe everything he says	17% (1st)	9%	8%
Know where he stands on the issues	46% (1st)	16%	18%
Strong and forceful	56% (1st)	19%	13%
Sincere	32% (1st)	19%	21%
Says what he believes	52% (1st)	15%	14%
Presents ideas clearly	38% (1st)	19%	18%
Puts country ahead of politics	23% (1st)	10%	12%
Has prime ministerial qualities	22% (2nd)	23% (1st)	19%
Warm and friendly	5% (7th)	20% (1st)	10%
	(855)	(855)	(855)

NOTE: The position in parentheses refers to Powell's position relative to the other leading Tory and Labour politicians.

Source: Gallup Poll CQ855, 21–25 June 1973.

an editorial entitled 'Who's Afraid of Enoch Powell?' the *Economist* wrote: 'It is a rare Tory M.P. who doesn't have a Powell group of some real consequence in his local association. If any single man has the capacity to cause a political upheaval it is the member from South West Wolverhampton.'[16] The editorial went on to hypothesise – probably correctly – that he was trying to bring down the Conservative Government by his hints of support for Labour. After the series of strong Liberal showings in by-elections, the *Spectator* suggested that the protest vote would have been even larger had Powell run candidates against the major parties.[17] Nonetheless the fact was that his standing could hardly fail to suffer from his becoming more closely tied to the E.E.C. than to the (much more powerful and emotive) immigration question. Already he had lost a slight margin of Conservative support – which he was not to regain. June 1973 saw him at this peak – and over.

Powell attempted during the rest of 1973 to attack the Heath Government on as wide a front as possible – not only over the E.E.C. but repeatedly over its prices and incomes policy and on inflation. He attacked Heath frontally, saying the Prime Minister feared him because he could not really comprehend his approach to politics.[18] He took up the immigration issue again in the autumn, loudly applauding a report of the Commons Select Committee on Race Relations which confirmed his prognostications as to the growth of immigrant ghettoes and his criticisms of the Department of Education and Science for their figures on the number of immigrants in Britain's schools.[19] Powell also attacked the Tory leadership over immigration in early October, warning that the party was bound to lose votes on the issue because it had broken its promises to the electorate, most notably over its repatriation programme.

He chose however to speak on neither the E.E.C. nor immigration at the Tory conference, instead giving a fairly routine (for him) speech on economic questions with a plea mainly for restriction of the money supply and a more nearly balanced budget. His rhetoric was low-key and there was nothing out of the ordinary in the address. However, Mr Barber, the Chancellor, in a speech almost certainly conceived before the text of Powell's speech had been released, delivered a stinging personal attack. Powell, Barber said in one of the more quoted sections of the speech, 'has the moral conceit and all the intellectual arrogance of the fanatic'. Powell as if regarding Barber as a mere catspaw for Heath, made no reply.[20]

One reason for Barber's ferocity may well have been that it was by this stage clear to the Chancellor that he would shortly have to reverse his policies in exactly the way Powell had been advocating. Just as the Tory Government had covered its flank by attacking Powell while it tightened immigration controls, so Barber was doubtless keen to widen the gulf between Powell and himself before adopting the latter's fiscal policies. Only two months after his conference attack on Powell, Barber announced a budget for 1974 including both curbs on Government spending and higher taxes. These recommendations, as Ronald Butt and David McKie suggested, were precisely the course of action Powell had suggested.[21] As McKie noted:[22]

> For months he thundered out a message for a balanced budget, a disciplined money supply, a thinned down programme of public spending and a higher rate of taxation as the proper remedy for the progressive wasting of the economy. In recent weeks he has seen the government come round to most and more.

Barber's attack had however struck a new note. To many it seemed that the Tory Establishment felt that Powell's falling popularity made it safe to attack him. The *Economist*, in sharp contrast to its editorial of only a few months before, now noted that his support was pretty much limited to the electorate and constituency parties, and that even while the Government's standing went down, Powell's influence in the parliamentary party had not increased. It also observed a tendency, indeed, for Tory M.P.s to blame him at least in part for the Government's decline in public standing.[23]

Poll data collected after Conference suggested however that Powell's decline in standing with the public, though clear, was still slight. National Opinion Polls found that only 32% of their respondents agreed that he was a 'frustrated fanatic' while 59% disagreed.[24] Gallup found that only 36% now said that he was an asset to his party, a fall of 2% since June 1973 but still a rating which left him as the leading Tory politician with the electorate.[25]

While Powell might have exercised restraint at the conference, he held nothing back in the weeks after it. He attacked Mr Carr, the Home Secretary, for not speaking out firmly enough for tighter immigration controls.[26] Carr, he said, was 'out of touch' and 'a dangerous man'.[27] When Mr Whitelaw, the Secretary of State for Northern Ireland, criticised him (in a by-election speech) for allegedly advocating unemployment as a cure for inflation, Powell answered that temporarily high unemployment was indeed one of the necessary by-products of a successful fight against inflation, though it was by no means something he desired. He had, he reminded Whitelaw, made it clear in his conference speech that the Government would have his unflinching support if it found the nerve to take the necessarily tough and unpopular measures to combat inflation.[28]

By this stage the entire political scene was overlaid by the lengthening shadows of the second great struggle between the miners and the Government in two years. There was an almost visible hardening of Tory ranks and sensibilities as the climactic showdown drew nearer. In the atmosphere generated by the strike anything less than unstinting loyalty to the Government quickly became, among Tory sympathisers, unpardonable, even unthinkable. (When the Director-General of the C.B.I., Campbell Adamson, obliquely criticised the Government towards the end of the strike, he was quickly forced to a position of offering his resignation.) Powell, unabashed, took Heath to task for his criticisms of the miners. It was the Government, not the unions, which were responsible for inflation. Thus Heath's 'get tough' policy with the unions made no sense – high wages were an effect, not a cause, of inflation. The only way to control inflation was through Government control of the money supply.

When the Prime Minister accused the miners of defying the law by not accepting the Price Commission and Pay Board's offer, Powell retorted that this was nonsense: the Government's wage controls were not legally binding on the miners. In language reminiscent of that which he had employed a year earlier, he again questioned Heath's mental health:[29] 'One cannot but entertain fears for the mental and emotional stability of a head of Government to whom such language can appear rational.'

He went on to allege that 'more and more symptoms appear that the Government has withdrawn into a world of make-believe of its own, in which disasters are transmuted into successes'.[30] He also defended his comment of a year earlier that Heath appeared to have taken leave of his senses. Terming the statement 'a solicitous request', he said it had been justified because statutory controls were unsuccessful for Labour, had been denounced by the Tories in Opposition, and ruled out in the 1970 Conservative manifesto. The Counter-Inflation Bill had proved to be a disaster on two counts. First, inflation had risen rather than fallen since the Bill was passed. But also it created antagonism 'at once futile and disastrous' between the state and other interests in society. A day later in a radio interview he unrepentantly defended the terms of his attack on Heath and added that statutory controls had been implemented only because of the Government's 'brute force'.[31]

As soon as leading Conservatives began speaking about the possibility of holding an election over the miners' strike, Powell criticised the idea.[32] To hold an election over the miners' failure to abide by the incomes policy would be 'an act of total immorality'.[33] He argued that the 'supposed issue in the conflict which bids fair to divide the nation today is a wholly bogus issue, a figment of the fevered imagination of politicians in a tight corner of their own manufacture'.[24] But initially he did hold out the possibility that he might support Heath if the Tory leader's election principles were acceptable to him. It was impossible for these terms to be met – for he had already made it clear that one of the reasons he considered the election immoral was because he believed Heath planned to abandon phase-3 controls immediately after a Tory victory. To fight an election on a principle and then abandon it represented the height of irresponsibility. Also he reiterated his view that inflation would be made no better or worse whatever the settlement the miners reached with the National Coal Board.[35] Only through Government action to control the supply of money could inflation be controlled. Thus Heath was creating division where none need exist. The country had almost reached the point of a violent class struggle in a fight over unworkable policies.

Early in February 1974 Powell offered his own solution to the crisis: the Government should tell the N.C.B. that like other managements it had the job of determining at what prices it could hire labour.[36] At the same time the Government should warn the N.C.B. that it would not increase the Board's overdraft, so that coal prices would have to rise if the wage settlement proved to be too high, and second that the N.C.B. should aim to achieve higher output from the more productive and economic pits. He emphasised that the Government had no right to demand that the miners should handle their wage demands in any particular fashion because of patriotism. The miners were not defying the law and Parliament with their wage request; they were merely defying an arbitrary limit which the Government had placed on wages.

After the announcement of the election, Powell made it clear he would not stand as a Tory candidate.[37] In a letter to the chairman of his constituency association, he wrote:

I consider it an act of gross irresponsibility that this general election has been called in the face of the current and impending situation. The election will in any case be fraudulent, for the object of those who called it is to secure the electorate's approval for a position which the Government itself knows to be untenable in order to make it easier to abandon that position subsequently. It is unworthy of British politics and Government to try to steal success by telling the public one thing during an election and doing the opposite afterwards.[38]

He also added that he could not ask the voters of Wolverhampton South West to support policies which were in direct opposition to those he had asked them to support in 1970. Heath immediately issued a statement indicating that the Conservative party was not worried about Powell's decision.[39] Very soon after his decision to withdraw, the United Ulster Unionists approached him and asked him to take a nomination in Northern Ireland.[40] While he had championed the cause of the Ulster Protestants for four years, he was unwilling to take himself out of English politics and refused the offer. There was after all still so much to play for. Were the Conservatives to be badly beaten in the election the party might at last turn to him – he could hardly afford to be in the ranks of the Ulster Unionists if he was to keep that hope alive.

THE ELECTION IN WOLVERHAMPTON SOUTH WEST

Powell's announcement that he would not stand in February 1974 was a sensation, but hardly a surprise. In his own constituency an increasingly troubled and feverish atmosphere of anticipation was already many months old.[41]

His June 1973 speech at Stockport had naturally raised questions for the officers of the Wolverhampton South West Conservative association as to whether he would be their parliamentary candidate in the next general election. Powell had after all said he was prepared to have a Labour Government for the rest of his life if it meant Britain would stay out of the Common Market. The statement generated particular resentment from two sections of the association. The first group consisted of loyal party workers who had been in the association since the early 1950s and who felt that socialism, and not the Common Market, was their main enemy. These people had known Powell well before his immigration speeches and took an almost paternalistic attitude towards him, believing they had helped prepare and train him to become a major force in national politics. Accordingly they made no public outcry after the Stockport speech, but in a series of formal and informal meetings during the summer and autumn of 1973 sought to determine whether he would stand in the next election. The other group was more vocal, primarily because their ties to Powell were weaker and they were stronger supporters of British entry into the E.E.C. They were concentrated mostly in Tettenhall, an upper middle-class suburb of Wolverhampton, which had been taken from the Brierley Hill constituency and added to Wolverhampton South West in 1972. Tettenhall is a staunchly Conservative area, populated mostly by long-established Midland business families and an increasing number of middle-level management personnel of national companies with branches in the Wolverhampton area. Tettenhall residents – of both types – were strong E.E.C. supporters and made their feelings known to Powell at a series of household meetings which were held after the 1972 redistribution. Initially the less affluent Conservatives living in the town proper resented the more affluent and less active additions to the constituency, but an accommodation was reached when Peter Wesson, a ward committee chairman in Tettenhall, was made a vice-chairman of the South West association.

The question of Powell's position came to a head at the association's annual general meeting in December 1973. Before the meeting, the association's president, Peter Farmer, and its chairman, George Wilkes, met Powell privately and implored him to let the people know what he would do if a general election were called in the next couple of months. Farmer and Wilkes came away with the impression that he would answer the question directly, but when questioned at the meeting he stated he would not fall into the trap of answering hypothetical questions. For the first time the resentment of the Tettenhall group was expressed publicly when Wesson, in the course of announcing his resignation as vice-chairman, criticised Powell and urged him to 'turn aside from the flames of martyrdom'. While Wesson's speech did reflect the views of many Tories in Tettenhall, he was acting individually. No censure motion was introduced nor was their any organised show of strength against Powell. The meeting ended with his being readopted and given a vote of thanks by the association members.

Despite the show of harmony, a number of his closest friends in Wolverhampton were worried about his behaviour that night. One long-time friend recalled that Powell 'wasn't himself'. 'I got the impression he really wasn't with us', she commented. After the meeting, he tried to slip out early to avoid any direct confrontations over the E.E.C. with the membership but the officers forced him to stay and greet association members.

While Powell did say subsequently that if Heath were to call an election over the miners' strike, it would be a 'fraudulent' election and an 'act of immorality', he took pains to emphasise to the association that he still considered himself a loyal Conservative. Addressing the Penn ward committee annual dinner two weeks after his comments on the calling of a general election he pledged loyalty to the Conservative party, and, to underscore the point, said he supported Mr Barber's December Budget.

Despite Powell's show of loyalty, Wilkes, the association chairman, became convinced that he would not be the parliamentary candidate if a general election were to be called shortly. He informally mentioned to other officers that they would have to assemble a selection committee shortly, but the vast majority of the membership and officers refused to believe that they would soon have to choose a new candidate.

If Wilkes was not surprised by his ultimate decision not to stand, he was angered and hurt by the way he chose to make his feelings known. When Heath announced on 7 February that there would be a general election three weeks hence, Powell sent the letter quoted on pp. 122–3 to Wilkes, with a copy to his agent, Robin Pollard, at the association's office. But he also gave the letter to the press with a midnight embargo, theoretically giving the association time to digest the information before the public was informed. But owing to some misunderstanding, the embargo was broken and Wilkes heard the announcement on his car radio. The fact that the press and thus the public knew of his decision before the association deeply offended Wilkes and the other association officers.

Nevertheless, Wilkes, having expected the decision, knew that the association had to move quickly to select a new candidate. There was a meeting that night at association headquarters and Wilkes took the attitude that their first duty was to hold the seat for the Tory party, and not light candles for Enoch Powell. Accordingly he brushed aside the wishes of some members who wanted to approach Powell to ask him to reconsider. He also persuaded the association to dismiss out of hand any move to select an interim candidate to hold the seat until Powell decided to return.

There was one group in the association that did want to keep the seat open for him. This section of the membership was willing to do practically anything to keep him in Parliament, including supporting him as an independent or independent Conservative, or putting up an interim candidate until he decided to return to Parliament. The 'resurrection brigade' – as they came to be known – was never a tightly organised faction, but was rather a loose collection of people whose political careers had begun at the time Powell was just achieving national prominence. They had not known him before his emergence as a national figure and they tended to regard him with more awe and deference than older members of the association. In effect, they were Powellites first and Tories second whereas the older members of the association prided themselves on being loyal Conservatives first and last.

When it became clear that the association would not put up an interim candidate, two people who felt very close to Powell, his agent, Robin Pollard and the vice-chairman of the association, William Clark, decided to present themselves as candidates before the selection committee which Wilkes was chairing. To prevent any conflict over the selection of candidates, the committee unanimously agreed that no local people would be seriously considered for the nomination. First, there was fear that if a local person was selected he might be seen as a stalking horse for Powell. Also the selection committee was afraid that the cleavage between Tettenhall and the rest of the association would be heightened if a person from one of the two areas were selected.

Because Pollard had served the association faithfully for eleven years he was granted an interview, but neither he nor Clark were seriously considered. They selected Nicholas Budgen, a solicitor from a neighbouring town, as the candidate. In may ways Budgen was an ideal candidate for Wolverhampton South West. He regarded Powell as 'arguably one of the most brilliant political philosophers of our time' and shared his analysis of the cause and cure of inflation.[42] There were enough similarities between Budgen and Powell to appease the Powellites and enough difference to satisfy the loyal Conservatives and Tettenhall residents. On immigration Budgen shared Powell's support for strict controls, but opposed repatriation and felt that some dependents should be taken in. On the E.E.C. he supported entry but opposed direct elections to a European Parliament because of the potential effect on the sovereignty of the British Parliament. He agreed with Powell that a statutory prices and incomes policy was an affront to a free society, but took the attitude in the election campaign that the law of the realm had to be obeyed. Because he was so new to the association, Budgen stayed aloof from the local campaign machine and sought to fit himself in as inconspicuously as possible. He did emerge victorious, but with a greatly reduced majority. The constituency's swing of 17% to Labour actually underestimates the movement between the two elections because the addition of Tettenhall made Wolverhampton South West an even safer Tory seat. In the old part of the constituency it is likely that the swing to Labour was as high as 20%.

Apart from his letter to Wilkes, Powell made no effort to contact other members of the association until after the election campaign. He did not personally return to Wolverhampton to thank his associates – some of whom had helped him for twenty-five years. Instead, he sent out handwritten letters thanking people for their help. Despite his endorsement of Labour in the election campaign, Powell indicated that he still hoped he could restore the party to a position he could support. In fact in some letters he expressed the view that had the election come later in the year, it would have been conceivable that he would have been able to stand as a Tory. Presumably by then the miners' strike would have been resolved and statutory controls phased out. His failure to return to Wolverhampton to thank his supporters personally generated a great deal of resentment and bitterness which was still evident to an interviewer fully two years later. In some houses pictures of Powell were taken down from the walls and many of his past associates continued to speak of him in tones carrying more than mild anger. The expectation that he would return to Wolverhampton soon evaporated entirely and Budgen settled in comfortably as a popular M.P.

ENDORSING LABOUR

Following the announcement of his decision not to stand in Wolverhampton, Powell agreed to speak during the campaign for the 'Keep Out' movement – a group co-ordinating anti-Common Market activity. His decision to speak for the group sparked speculation that he would endorse Labour because the group had publicly indicated that Labour was the party most likely to take Britain out of Europe. Just three days before the election Powell told voters in Birmingham that a vote for Labour was the only way to have a say on the over-riding issue of the general election – the E.E.C.[43] The Conservatives were committed to staying in the Community and relatively unconcerned with what Parliament or the people felt. Powell said Heath had by-passed Parliament in his support for economic and monetary union of Europe by 1980. To Powell, Heath's action represented an irresponsible disregard of the people and Parliament, and was indeed close to being unlawful. But instead of recognising his own misdeeds, Heath 'on the basis of a few defaulting town councillors at Clay Cross and some foolish utterances by a trade union official is heard accusing his political opponents of lacking respect for the law'.[44] The election was about parties and issues, not personalities. Thus he felt he had to support Labour because the party was committed to renegotiation of Britain's terms of entry into Europe.

In another speech at Shipley Powell emphasised that he was born a Tory, still remained a Tory and would die a Tory.[45] But he again made it clear he felt Labour should win the election because of their commitment to renegotiation and a subsequent referendum. It is worth noting that in both his speeches for the Get Britain Out campaign, Powell never explicitly said 'Vote Labour'. He demonstrated no great enthusiasm for the party but instead made it clear that because of the importance of the European issue it was necessary for people to support Labour.

To Powell, none of the Labour policies he disagreed with were irreversible if they were implemented.[46] However, he was convinced that if the Tories won the election Britain would be committed to the Market without any chance of withdrawing in the forseeable future. In the Shipley speech he also emphasised the personal importance of the issue to himself:[47]

Here is a man who promised his electors in 1970 that he would do everything in his power to prevent British membership; who voted against it in every division, minor or major, which took place in the ensuing Parliament; who did so even when success would have precipitated a dissolution; who allied himself openly on the subject with his political opponents; who made no secret of his belief that its importance over-rode that of all others; and who warned that it was one of those issues on which men will put country before party.

Since he had never explicitly told an audience that they should vote Labour, there was still a bit of doubt before the poll about the specific nature of his endorsement. All questions were answered the day before the February election when Powell announced he had voted by postal ballot for the Labour candidate in Wolverhampton South West.

POWELL'S ELECTORAL IMPACT
Powell had in all probability, as we have seen, had a very major impact on the 1970 election result. How great was his influence in the opposite direction in February 1974? There seems little doubt that his influence and popularity were in sharp decline at this point from the peak of a year earlier – as both Figs. 6.3 and 6.4 show – though of course, Fig. 6.4's results leave room for some ambiguity. Given his stance it was very difficult to see how one could rationally believe he was a Conservative party asset in February 1974.

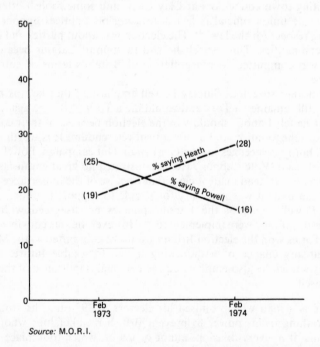

Source: M.O.R.I.

Fig. 6.3   Percentage of electorate saying Powell and Heath best
represent their views Feb 1973–Feb 1974

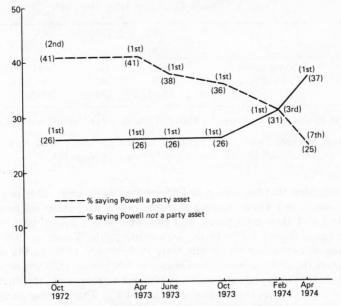

Note: The figure in parenthesis below the decimal point is Powell's absolute score on the question while the figure above the parenthesis is his position relative to other Conservative politicians.

Source: Gallup Poll.

Fig. 6.4   Per cent saying Powell a Conservative party asset 1972–74

As to Powell's impact on the actual electoral result it seems clear that, while his influence was most significant nationally in 1970, he made his greatest impact in February 1974 in the West Midlands. The 1970–74 swing to Labour in Powell's part of the West Midlands (known as the Black Country) was 7·5%.[48] In similar urban seats outside the West Midlands the swing was between 2% and 3%. The swing in the six constituencies around Wolverhampton was 10%, while in Powell's own seat, Wolverhampton South West, the swing to Labour was 17%. As Table 6.2 shows, the Black Country swung by equal margins to the party Powell backed in both 1970 and 1974.

Despite these results, Michael Steed has tended to play down Powell's influence on the February 1974 vote, arguing that his influence was at its peak in 1970 and that for a variety of reasons former Labour voters returned to their party in February 1974.[49] In his view Powell's Labour endorsement was only one of a number of possible explanations for the swing back to Labour.

Steed accounts for the high Labour swing in the Black Country in a number of ways. Since the turnout in these seats was lower than expected,

TABLE 6.2   Black Country results, 1966–74*

	1966 %	1970 %	1974 %
Conservative	44	56	44
Labour	56	44	56
	100%	100%	100%

* The results are percentaged without liberal or other minor party votes.

Source: Michael Steed, 'The Results Analysed', in Butler and Kavanagh, *The British General Election of February 1974*, p. 331.

he conceded that the swing to Labour may have been occasioned by cross-pressured Tories staying at home rather than choosing between Powell and their own party. But this was only a minor part of his argument. Steed pointed to the high swing to the Tories in 1970 as a means of explaining the results there in February 1974. In the Black Country the 1970 swing to the Tories was 2·5% more than the national average for urban seats and in the six Wolverhampton area constituencies the swing was twice the national average of 4·5%. Thus Steed argued that Powell's real effect may have come in 1970 when he won voters over to the Tories on immigration. After that issue was defused, these voters may have naturally returned to the Labour party. He also suggested that Powell's own movement away from the immigration issue and his attacks on the Tory leadership may have so confused 1970 Tory converts that they either stayed at home or swung back to Labour. Steed gave little credance to the notion that Powell's late speeches in February swung votes to Labour.

However there are a number of problems with Steed's analysis. First, in his 1970 analysis of the results he had failed to give Powell much credit for the West Midlands swing to the Tories.[50] Noting that a number of seats with large numbers of coloured immigrants showed below average swings to the Tories, he had then questioned the assumption that Powell had an effect on the vote. It is simply impossible for his analysis to be right for both 1970 and February 1974 – indeed, the only consistency in his arguments appears to be in his uniform resistance to attributing any significant electoral impact to Powell on either occasion.

We have already cause to find fault with Steed's 1970 analysis on two grounds. First, it has been argued that the immigration issue had a national rather than local effect. Second, in seats with large numbers of immigrants we have suggested that Powell may have mobilised white voters to support the Conservatives and counter-mobilised immigrants to vote Labour. Steed's analysis of February is similarly open to question. Some N.O.P. poll data helped to shed doubt on his assumption.

A Marplan poll in the Birmingham constituency of Perry Barr a week before Powell's endorsement of Labour showed a 13% Conservative lead. After the endorsement speech in Birmingham a follow-up poll showed that the Tory lead had become a 2% Labour advantage.[51] Further evidence of Powell's 1974 influence in the West Midlands comes from an N.O.P. survey in which respondents were asked whether Powell's intervention in the national campaign on behalf of Labour had influenced their actual vote.[52] Overall, 6% of all respondents (nationally), but 8% West Midlands respondents, said he made them more likely to vote Labour. Only 2% of the national sample said he made them more likely to vote Conservative, suggesting a massive 4% national margin attributable to Powell.

It is however true that the national data are by no means as clear as they were for 1970. Thus 44% could not recall without prompting the role he played in the campaign. Of the 56% who were aware that Powell had played a role in the campaign, only 23% (or slightly under 13% of the sample) mentioned that he had urged people to vote Labour.

TABLE 6.3   What people heard in Powell's election speeches, Feb 1974*

	What Powell said about election %
Vote Labour	23
Anti-E.E.C.	20
Won't stand	15
Immigration	6
Election immoral	2
Other	5
Don't know	5
	(2142)

* The base here is all those respondents (56% of those questioned) who heard about his election speeches. The percentages only added up to 80% in the original data source.

Source: *N.O.P. Political Bulletin*, Feb 1974, 38.

Powell's influence was greatest among Labour voters in the N.O.P. survey, as Table 6.4 shows. There are thus two possible explanations of his effect. First one could argue that his greatest effect was to stimulate turnout among Labour voters and people not intending to vote. Alternatively it could be assumed that among those 13% a significant number were former Conservatives whom Powell had already converted to Labour with his Birmingham and Shipley speeches or through his attacks against the Heath Government since mid-1973.

TABLE 6.4   Powell's impact on partisan choice, Feb 1974

	All %	Conservatives %	Labour %	Liberal %
No effect	87	92	84	87
Less likely to vote at all	—	—	—	—
More likely to vote Conservative	2	4	—	—
More likely to vote Labour	6	1	13	3
Other	—	—	—	1
Don't know	5	4	3	5
	(3792)			

Source: *N.O.P. Political Bulletin*, Feb 1974, 38.

A M.O.R.I. survey conducted immediately after Powell stood down provided even stronger evidence that his withdrawal helped Labour. Of those voters who said Powell's withdrawal would influence their vote, a 2:1 majority said he made them less likely to vote Conservative. A quarter of those who told M.O.R.I. they would be voting Conservative said that Powell's withdrawal made them less likely actually to do so on polling day. Also a M.O.R.I. survey of Labour candidates after the poll showed that 39% said his 'Vote Labour' speech helped them while only 1% said it hurt them. The remaining 60% said it had no effect or were unable to judge its impact. Also 49% of Labour candidates in the most marginal constituencies said it helped them while only 2% said it hurt them.

TABLE 6.5   The effect of Powell's withdrawal from the campaign on people's vote, Feb 1974

	All %	ABC1 %	C2DE %	Con. %	Lab. %	Lib. %
More likely to vote Conservative	14	10	16	9	13	12
Less likely to vote Conservative	28	27	29	25	28	27
Neither	53	58	49	65	57	56
Don't know	5	5	6	1	2	5
	100	100	100	100	100	100
	(523)	(194)	(329)	(171)	(166)	(103)

Source: M.O.R.I., 10 Feb 1974.

Further evidence of Powell's impact in February 1974 comes from the February 1974 wave of the Butler-Stokes panel study. Our first problem in using these data is that we are faced with '1970' Powellites (defined as respondents who gave him a 55 or higher score on a 0–100 scale) and with '1974' Powellites (defined as respondents who gave him a 6 or higher score on a 0–10 scale). These were by no means an identical group. Between 1970 and 1974 there was a noticeable drop in Powell's support and significant changes in respondents' attitude towards him. In 1970, 40% of the sample were unfavourable to him and 60% were favourable. In 1974, 56% were unfavourable and 44% were favourable. Moreover, over half the Powellites in 1970 were unfavourable to him by 1974 and 37% of those who were unfavourable in 1970 were favourable by February 1974. In terms of voting behaviour the two groups of Powellites also differed dramatically, as Table 6.6 shows.

TABLE 6.6   Voting behaviour of 1970 and 1974 Powellites

| | *1970 response* | | *1974 response* | |
	Anti-Powell %	*Pro-Powell* %	*Anti-Powell* %	*Pro-Powell* %
1970 vote				
Conservative	23·4	56·5	49·8	33·7
Labour	62·3	33·4	40·6	55·9
Liberal/other	14·3	10·1	9·6	10·4
	100	100	100	100
	(244)	(398)	(498)	(401)
1974 vote				
Conservative	20·2	47·7	48·7	22·9
Labour	55·5	33·7	35·0	54·3
Liberal/other	24·3	18·6	16·3	22·8
	100	100	100	100
	(272)	(430)	(540)	(442)

Source: Butler-Stokes Panel Study and British Election Study at Essex University, 1974.

Thus we find that among the 1970 anti-Powellites there was a 1·8% swing to the Tories and among the 1970 Powellites there was a 4·8% movement to Labour. Among the 1974 anti-Powellites there was a similar 2·3% swing to the Conservatives and a 4·6% movement to Labour among the Powellites. (Overall, the Butler-Stokes panel showed a 0·9% swing to Labour.)

But because the two groups of Powellites showed similar net directional movements between the two elections, we may not impute to them a similar – or indeed any – 'Powell effect'. As Table 6.7 shows, the

1970–74 movements between the two major parties were exactly the same for both the pro- and anti-Powellites of 1970 vintage. The really striking difference between the pro- and anti-groups was, rather, the latter's much greater propensity to defect to minor parties in 1974. On the other hand 1970 Powellites who had been outside the two-party framework in 1970 showed a marked pro-Conservative movement in 1974. For all Powell's pro-Labour appeal such voters were three times as likely to move towards the Tories as their minor party counterparts who were anti-Powellite in 1970. This entirely opaque result suggests that there is little to be gained by further analysis of 1970 Powellites in the wholly different context of 1974, by which time, as we have seen, the whole nature of Powellism had changed.

TABLE 6.7   The flow of the vote 1970–74 by 1970 attitude to Powell

| | 1970 pro-Powell 1970 vote | | | 1970 anti-Powell 1970 vote | | |
| | Con. | Labour | Liberal/ other | Con. | Labour | Liberal/ other |
1974 vote	%	%	%	%	%	%
Conservative	80	5	19	67	5	6
Labour	10	80	8	10	82	18
Liberal/other	10	15	73	23	13	76
	100	100	100	100	100	100
	(211)	(123)	(36)	(52)	(139)	(33)

Source: British Election study at Essex University, 1974.

When we turn to the '1974 vintage' Powellites however a very clear 'Powell effect' is evident as Table 6.8 shows. No matter how they had voted in 1970, Powellites were markedly more likely to move towards (or remain) Labour voters in February 1974 than their anti-Powellite counterparts. Indeed it is quite clear than had only anti-Powellites voted, February 1974 would have witnessed a Tory landslide. But, on the face of it at least, Powell appears to have more than countered this by the massive defections he apparently induced among 1970 Tory voters. No less than 35% of this group who were pro-Powell in February 1974 deserted their party (their reluctance to go the whole way to a Labour vote is apparently underscored by twice as high a rate of defection to minor parties among them as among Tory anti-Powellites).

The same points are clear when we isolate the 1970–74 vote switchers (Table 6.9) and clearer still when we confine ourselves to those moving only between the major parties (Table 6.10).

Moreover this strong 'Powell effect' is still visible when we control the effect of key election issues such as the E.E.C., the miners' strike,

TABLE 6.8   The flow of the vote 1970–74 by 1974 attitude to Powell

1974 vote	1974 pro-Powell 1970 vote			1974 anti-Powell 1970 vote		
	Con. %	Labour %	Liberal/ other %	Con. %	Labour %	Liberal/ other %
Conservative	65	4	5	84	11	23
Labour	17	83	15	7	77	9
Liberal/other	18	13	80	9	12	68
	100	100	100	100	100	100
	(121)	(212)	(39)	(238)	(186)	(44)

Source: British Election Study at Essex University, 1974.

TABLE 6.9   Voting behaviour of switchers by 1974 attitude to Powell

	1974 pro-Powell %	1974 anti-Powell %
Switch to Conservatives	12	32
Switch to Labour	31	22
Switch to Liberals/others	57	46
	100	100
	(86)	(94)

Source: British Election Study at Essex University, 1974.

TABLE 6.10   Voting behaviour of respondents who moved between Conservative and Labour parties by 1974 attitude to Powell

	1974 pro-Powell %	1974 anti-Powell %
Switch to Conservatives	27	59
Switch to Labour	73	41
	100	100
	(37)	(51)

Source: British Election Study at Essex University, 1974.

TABLE 6.11   The flow of the vote 1970–74 by 1974 attitude to Powell, controlling the effect of the E.E.C., Prices and immigration

| | No Labour advantage on E.E.C. | | | | | | Labour advantage on E.E.C. | | | | | |
| | Pro-Powell 1970 vote | | | Anti-Powell 1970 vote | | | Pro-Powell 1970 vote | | | Anti-Powell 1970 vote | | |
1970 vote	Con. %	Lab. %	Lib./ other %	Con. %	Lab. %	Lib./ other %	Con. %	Lab. %	Lib./ other %	Con. %	Lab. %	Lib./ other %
Conservative	79	7	3	86	14	24	39	1	10	71	2	0
Labour	9	81	17	6	73	5	34	85	10	16	87	67
Liberal/other	12	12	80	8	13	71	27	14	80	13	11	33
	100	100	100	100	100	100	100	100	100	100	100	100
	(80)	(106)	(29)	(207)	(132)	(41)	(41)	(106)	(10)	(31)	(54)	(3)

| | No Labour advantage on miners | | | | | | Labour advantage on miners | | | | | |
| | Pro-Powell 1970 vote | | | Anti-Powell 1970 vote | | | Pro-Powell 1970 vote | | | Anti-Powell 1970 vote | | |
1974 vote	Con. %	Lab. %	Lib./ other %	Con. %	Lab. %	Lib./ other %	Con. %	Lab. %	Lib./ other %	Con. %	Lab. %	Lib./ other %
Conservative	81	21	6	90	40	37	27	1	4	51	3	0
Labour	3	61	6	1	50	0	53	87	22	34	84	23
Liberal/other	16	18	88	9	10	63	20	12	74	15	13	77
	100	100	100	100	100	100	100	100	100	100	100	100
	(87)	(33)	(16)	(147)	(38)	(27)	(34)	(129)	(23)	(41)	(148)	(7)

Source: British Election Study at Essex University, 1974.

| 1974 vote | No Labour advantage on E.E.C. | | | | | | Labour advantage on E.E.C. | | | | | |
| | Pro-Powell 1970 vote | | | Anti-Powell 1970 vote | | | Pro-Powell 1970 vote | | | Anti-Powell 1970 vote | | |
	Con. %	Lab. %	Lib./other %	Con. %	Lab. %	Lib./other %	Con. %	Lab. %	Lib./other %	Con. %	Lab. %	Lib./other %
Conservative	74	6	9	88	26	28	20	3	0	29	3	0
Labour	8	72	18	2	59	11	65	88	12	71	87	0
Liberal/other	18	22	73	10	15	61	15	9	88	0	10	100
	100	100	100	100	100	100	100	100	100	100	100	100
	(101)	(64)	(22)	(221)	(85)	(36)	(20)	(148)	(17)	(17)	(121)	(8)

| 1974 vote | Non-racialists* | | | | | | Racialists* | | | | | |
| | Pro-Powell 1970 vote | | | Anti-Powell 1970 vote | | | Pro-Powell 1970 vote | | | Anti-Powell 1970 vote | | |
	Con. %	Lab. %	Lib./other %	Con. %	Lab. %	Lib./other %	Con. %	Lab. %	Lib./other %	Con. %	Lab. %	Lib./other %
Conservative	68	6	9	92	14	27	65	3	4	81	9	17
Labour	9	80	0	3	69	8	20	84	21	8	83	11
Liberal/other	23	14	91	5	17	65	15	13	75	11	8	72
	100	100	100	100	100	100	100	100	100	100	100	100
	(22)	(36)	(11)	(59)	(80)	(26)	(99)	(126)	(28)	(179)	(106)	(18)

* Racialists were defined here as those who gave affirmative answers to two of the following four questions. Are there too many immigrants in Britain? Do you feel very strongly about the problem? Do you feel immigration is a problem in your neighbourhood? Do you support repatriation? Non-racialists here gave 0 to 1 affirmative answers.

Source: British Election Study at Essex University, 1974.

prices and race (Table 6.11). Only among voters who perceived a clear Labour advantage on prices did there appear to be no substantial difference between the anti- and pro-Powell respondents in their rates of movement to Labour. Otherwise the 'Powell effect' remains strikingly clear no matter which issue or issue-public is selected. In some parts of the electorate the rate of defection from a 1970 Tory vote was quite staggering when a pro-Labour preference was combined with support for Powell, with defection rates of 60–80% being registered.

The Butler-Stokes data thus lend strong support to the view that Powell had a major impact on the pro-Labour swing of February 1974. It would seem though that this result – if such it was – was achieved only in the course of the campaign itself. There is no evidence that Powell had moved any votes towards Labour by his constant criticisms of the Tory Government from mid-1973 until the eve of the election. Indeed a M.O.R.I. panel study carried out just before the calling of the February election suggests a contrary movement, if anything, with Powellites (defined here as those saying he best represented their views) showing a differential tendency to move towards the Tories at the very time that Powell was becoming an increasingly strident opponent of his own party.

TABLE 6.12   Flow of the vote Feb 1973–Feb 1974 by 1974 attitude to Powell

	1974 pro-Powell			1974 non-Powellite		
	Feb 1973 preference					
	Con.	*Labour*	*Liberal/ other*	*Con.*	*Labour*	*Liberal/ other*
Feb 1974 preference	%	%	%	%	%	%
Conservative	84	11	29	91	6	23
Labour	4	71	18	4	86	11
Liberal/other	12	18	53	5	8	66
	100	100	100	100	100	100
	(57)	(55)	(28)	(341)	(421)	(141)

Source: M.O.R.I. Panel Study, 1974.

Such findings are not surprising when viewed in the overall context of the February 1974 campaign which, judging from other poll evidence, saw a large shift of support towards Labour (or possibly a large-scale revelation of submerged Labour support) very late in the campaign. It would appear that any 'Powell effect' was – like other pro-Labour partisan forces – only really marked in the closing stages of the election's remarkable course.

On balance it seems not imprudent to argue that Powell probably played a significant role in Labour's surprise victory of February 1974. Virtually all the poll data support such a conclusion, as do a host of straws in the wind such as the canvassed opinions of Labour candidates themselves. It is of course worth remembering that Powell's support in February 1974 was smaller than it had been in either February 1973 or in the 1970 Butler-Stokes survey. Still, his following remained substantial (15% told M.O.R.I. he best represented their views three weeks before the poll) and the fact that 56% of the electorate could spontaneously mention speeches by someone who was *not* standing as a candidate – at a time when they were being overwhelmed with speeches by those who were – is remarkable enough in its way.

Moreover the West Midlands data, both opinion polls and actual results, surely allow of little doubt that Powell had a very significant impact, locally at least – quite possibly great enough to rob the Tories of a crucial plurality in Parliament. It is certainly possible to argue that Powell may indeed have put Edward Heath into Downing Street in 1970 and evicted him in February 1974. Be that as it may, his own career had hardly survived undamaged. Had he merely stood down and not supported Labour his position within the Tory party would surely have been greatly enhanced in the wake of the result. As it was, Powell had cut the Gordian knot only to tie a tighter one. For his act of disloyalty made him a pariah to Conservatives at all levels of the party – a status he had long enjoyed and continued to enjoy with the Labour party on account of his racial and economic views. He had frequently sounded like a voice in the wilderness. Only now was he truly there.

7 Returning from the Wilderness: Standing in South Down

If Powell had hardly appeared pleased at the 1970 election result, his reaction to the February 1974 result seems to have been even stronger. Perhaps he had hoped for an even more crushing setback for Heath, or perhaps he was simply bitterly conscious of the high price he had paid. For the first time in nearly a quarter of a century the new Parliament assembled without him.

His first public appearance after the election was marked by considerable bitterness as he attacked the press for failing to document Heath's changes of position on issues between 1970–74.[1] There was even some speculation that Powell's bitterness was so intense that he might resign from the Tory party. The fact was that, for the moment at least, Heath had survived as Tory leader. There would have to be another election soon and, having survived the initial shock of defeat, Heath would now head the Tory party into it. A further defeat would doubtless settle his fate but Powell would now be in no position to influence the issue. He had used up all his ammunition and his arch-enemy was, gallingly, still not quite unseated.

Powell now betook himself to the Ulster Unionist convention at Portrush where, however, his emphasis on direct integration of Ulster into the U.K. was unequivocal, leaving little room open for the restoration of Stormont – an institution still dear to the heart of most Unionists. While Powell was not actually booed, there was a good deal of grumbling after he finished speaking, for the conference was to promulgate a policy statement calling for significant devolution of power within the context of a federal U.K. – positions which were anathema to Powell.[2] It is possible that he was already flirting with the idea of reviving the earlier offer of a Unionist parliamentary nomination. If so he was disappointed and he appeared to turn his sights back to England, where he attempted a reconciliation between himself and the Tory leadership, giving a major address to the Conservative Trident Group.[3]

The tone of the speech was conciliatory – he urged the party to look to the future and forget the past. However, he refused to concede that there was any room for discussion of the issues which had driven

him from the party. For example, he said the results of the Heath
Government's interventionist policies of 1972–74 now made it clear that
the 1970 Tory economic policies were correct. Moreover he remained
unequivocally against E.E.C. entry. Not surprisingly the speech got a
cool response from the Tory leadership.[4] David Wood suggested that
Powell was not really trying to make peace as much as give the Tory
leadership a graceful way of coming to him. By not conceding that he
had been wrong on the issues, he was probably trying to get those who
were dissatisfied with the Heath leadership to embrace him. A conciliatory tone was the only compromise he was willing to make. It is also
possible that the speech was an advertisement of his availability to
Conservative constituency associations looking for parliamentary
candidates. In a way Powell's speech may have been part of his continuing effort to bring down the Conservative leadership, though the
attempt was a bit more coy than his previous efforts.

His supporters made one final attempt to gain him an English
constituency nomination in June but he was turned down by the Batley
and Morley Conservative association.[5] This little-noticed initiative was
not, apparently, encouraged by Powell – who would not have allowed
his name to go forward without reconciliation with the party leadership.
For him to return to Parliament it was now Ulster or nothing.

Despite this state of affairs it is probably fair to say that his first wish
was to make peace with the Conservatives (but only on his own terms).
His primary loyalty was to the Tories, not to the Ulster Unionists, and
he no doubt recognised that the Unionists have always been on the
periphery of British politics. As Harbinson has documented quite
convincingly, Unionist politicians with the exception of Sir Edward
Carson have by and large had almost no impact on politics at Westminster.[6] Journalists writing in mid-1974 also recognised this point and
urged Powell to remain in England. The *Economist* published an editorial
suggesting that he had turned to Northern Ireland because he perceived
a grave national crisis there and wanted to be in a position to anticipate
the controversy.[7] Michael Harrington, a *Spectator* columnist, took a
probably more realistic view, urging Powell to pull himself out of the
'Northern Ireland quagmire' if he entertained any hope of reconciling
himself with the Conservative party. To Harrington, Powell's image
was tarnished by his associations with people like West, Craig and
Paisley:[8]

> No serious British politician would dream of making the Irish
> question the very centre of his political activity unless he held minister-
> ial responsibility and certainly not in the company of people who are
> regarded by most British politicians as bloodthirsty extremists.

Because Powell met with no Conservative response in the spring of
1974, it seemed clear that he had to keep his attention focused on

Northern Ireland if he wanted to retain any hope of returning to Westminster in the approaching election. The collapse of the power-sharing Executive in Ulster during May 1974 provided him with an issue around which he could rally support.[9] Following the fall of the Executive, he travelled to Belfast and told a Unionist meeting that he had warned Parliament in 1973 that the Heath-Robinson Constitution would not prove to be workable. He also delighted the crowd by telling them that he supported the reintroduction of the B Specials as well as the reinvigoration of the Royal Ulster Constabulary.[10] Protestant sentiment in favour of these institutions (whose demise had been brought about by the Hunt Report of 1969) still ran deep, and this was a major effort by Powell to court grassroots Orange opinion.

Not surprisingly this same speech was far better received than his April address to the Unionist conference had been. Powell also spoke at Enniskillen in June and seemed to indicate he could accept devolved local government in Ulster. While advocating the full representation of the province at Westminster, he said that such an adjustment 'no more prejudges or prejudices future arrangements which may be thought best for its administration than it does for Wales or Scotland'.[11] This too was a very great concession. In his apparent eagerness for a parliamentary seat he was much more willing to give ground to the Unionists in Ulster than to the Tories in England.

Speaking in County Armagh in August Powell gave the first public indication that he was interested in obtaining an Ulster seat.[12] He again suggested Ulster should be entitled to any form of devolution which might be introduced in Great Britain and also criticised the former Tory Government for its handling of the inflation problem. Despite his clear willingness to embrace the Unionist position, his interest in an Ulster seat raised problems for the Unionists' leadership. A Unionist M.P. would have to give up his seat to make way for him. He would be very obviously and unpopularly a carpet-bagger (even Carson had come to Ulster from Dublin, not England, and Carson had made Ulster his first priority, while the Unionists could not expect Powell to act similarly).

Moreover Powell's uncertain position on the question of devolution of power back to Stormont raised problems for a number of Unionist leaders, particularly William Craig. On the other hand he had much to offer the Unionists. He had embraced their cause fairly whole-heartedly; he was an unrivalled orator, parliamentarian and political strategist, a great national figure who would enhance their cause, particularly since he still had a vast following in England. The polls now showed that though his popularity had declined from February 1973 to February 1974, thereafter it remained fairly constant, as Tables 7.1 and 7.2 show. Perhaps most strikingly, O.R.C. found that of those voters who wanted Heath replaced, Powell was the leading candidate at 21 %, 2 % ahead of

Whitelaw. A disproportionate amount of his support did come from Labour voters, but still he was the second choice of Tories behind Whitelaw. It should be remembered that after his Birmingham speech in 1968 a similar percentage favoured him for the Tory leadership. Yet at that point he was constantly in the media, while by March 1974 he was considered to be a spent force.

TABLE 7.1   Choice for prime minister, 1973–74

	Feb 1973 %	June 1973 %	June 1974 %
Wilson	25	19	30
Powell	20	18	14
Heath	16	18	14
	(2073)		

Source: M.O.R.I. Panel Study; *N.O.P. Political Bulletin*, June 1973; and O.R.C. *The Times*, 14 June 1974, p. 2.

TABLE 7.2   Number saying Powell best represents their views 1973–74

	Feb 1973 %	Feb 1974 %	July 1974 %
Per cent saying Powell best represents their views	25	16	17
	(2073)	(1290)	(827)

Source: M.O.R.I. Panel Study, 1973–74.

The day after Powell's speech in County Armagh, Captain Lawrence Orr, the member for South Down, said that he would not stand for re-election and indicated that he wanted Powell to take his seat.[13] Orr's announcement drew cautious and tentative approval from William Craig. The Vanguard leader emphasised that he was amenable to having Powell join the Unionist team, but did not want him as its leader. The Ulster Defence Association, closely aligned with Craig, was less kind to him, issuing a statement saying that he was as much use to the province as the member for Land's End or John o' Groat's.[14] After Powell's adoption however the U.D.A. held a secret meeting with him and agreed to support his candidature.[15]

The October 1974 election was duly called. Powell ran a vigorous campaign in South Down, perhaps a more energetic campaign than most Unionists expected.[16] His campaign activities included door-to-door canvassing in the Protestant areas as well as making numerous speeches urging Britain not to allow Northern Ireland to withdraw from the U.K. In his election speeches he endorsed the provisions of the U.U.U.C. election manifesto giving Ulster full parliamentary representation, the same administration as other parts of the nation and the same manner of policing as the rest of the U.K.[17] He also repeated his opposition to power-sharing and advocated strengthening the indigenous police force. The B Specials in particular were singled out for praise.[18]

Any tension that might have existed between Powell and the members of the U.U.U.C. appeared to dissolve during the campaign. West, Powell, Craig and Paisley held a unity rally in Belfast which saw each man get an equally warm response from the crowd.[19] However a few days after the rally Powell did raise some questions in the Unionist ranks when he travelled to Bristol and Manchester to repeat his February endorsement of Labour for the benefit of English voters.[20] Until the imposition of direct rule in 1972, the Unionists in Northern Ireland had taken the Tory whip and there still remained some hope that those ties might be restored. Moreover Labour had less sympathy for the Unionist cause than the Tories had. The U.U.U.C. leader, Harry West, had specifically urged Powell not to endorse Labour.[21] Powell paid little attention – he was clearly determined not to relinquish the issues in England which drove him to Ulster.

Nor could he resist a personal tilt at Heath and the Tories' national unity campaign. He said he was 'staggered and astonished beyond measure at the sight of a party leader seeking election for his party and himself on the basis that after they are elected they will decide on what policies they would propose to govern on'.[22] Returning to Northern Ireland Powell ruffled more Unionist feathers by speaking against the Unionist plan to revitalise the shipyards of Belfast with state subsidies which would provide additional jobs for the Protestant working class. He simply could not accept state support of private industry under any circumstances and hardly improved the situation by predicting that the inevitable collapse of the yards would only be put off for a while should subsidies be given.[23]

Powell could little afford such sallies, for his position in South Down was hardly secure. The seat was safe but not, after all, a fief, particularly given that many local Protestants clearly did not want an Englishman representing them. Moreover Brian Faulkner, for many years the South Down member for Stormont, worked actively against him. He had greatly irked the former Ulster Prime Minister by criticisms of power-sharing. Faulkner, Powell indicated, had been foolish not to realise that his failure to support the general strike in May 1974, and his support of power-sharing under the 1973 Northern Ireland Constitution could eventually lead to a united Ireland. To retaliate, Faulkner and his supporters spread the word that Powell had, effectively, been guilty of evicting Lawrence Orr (long a popular M.P.) from the constituency.

Powell's intervention in the campaign brought a large increase in turnout, from 65% in February to 72% in October. In absolute terms Powell increased Orr's total February vote, but he got a smaller share of the popular vote. In February Orr had taken 52·1% of the vote and won a 9·4% victory over his S.D.L.P. opponent. Powell could only manage 50·8%, giving him a 5·4% margin.[24] Observers in South Down have estimated that Faulkner cost Powell between 2000 and 3000 votes.

Still, Powell was back at Westminster. There was no suggestion this time on any hand that he had had any effect on the overall result – and we have no data to test such a proposition. What polls we have suggest that while his foray into Northern Ireland had cost him some support, he had managed to retain his hard-core English supporters. A 55–37% majority of British respondents told N.O.P. early in September they wanted Powell to return to Westminster.[25]

An N.O.P. poll in London also showed that 14% of voters there picked Powell as their choice for prime minister, putting him 5% behind Wilson.[26] Heath trailed a bad fourth with 9%, 2% behind Jeremy Thorpe. An O.R.C. poll after the election asked who should replace Heath if the Tory leader resigned.[27] After the February election their data showed that 21% wanted Powell. In November Powell's support dropped to 17%. Surprisingly he maintained his Tory following and suffered his greatest losses among Labour and Liberal supporters. Gallup was the only poll to show a marked decline in support for Powell. After February they had found 14% wanted Powell to lead the Conservative party should Heath resign, while in November only 4% selected him.[28]

At the close of the election campaign, Powell offered his own assessment (in *The Times*) of the current state of British politics. Conflicts of conscience were arising which stretched party loyalties past their breaking point.[29] In the Tory party, monetarists like Sir Keith Joseph (who Powell said was merely making arguments he had advanced much earlier) were more disturbed about Heath's economic policies than about those which a Labour Government might enact. The strength of the E.E.C. issue in the election was demonstrated by the fact that only a Tory victory could have ensured that Roy Jenkins and Shirley Williams would definitely stay in the Labour leadership. (Both had said during the campaign that they would resign from any government which took Britain out of Europe.) After the election Powell told the Weekly Newspaper Advertising Bureau that the Tories were a 'hollow shell of a party' following their two defeats.[30] Parliamentary democracy needed strong opposition parties and Powell urged the Tories to reunite around the principles which brought them success in 1970. These points were made against the background of the Tory leadership contest and may perhaps be considered part of Powell's self-justification for endorsing Labour in the 1974 elections. While the Tories may have been 'a hollow shell of a party', they were selecting a new leader and Powell was effectively being excluded not only from candidacy but from the whole selection process. His bitterness towards the Conservatives seemed indeed to increase. He now maintained that all anti-Marketeers who stood under the Tory banner were 'corrupt' because they were part of a party which was committed to staying in Europe.[31] Powell expressed little sympathy for the potential candidates in the leadership election. Those who had remained loyal to Heath throughout 1970–74 did not deserve consideration because they had failed to resign in protest against the interventionist policies of 1972–74. Those who remained inside the Government but later acknowledged that it had pursued the wrong policies (Mrs Thatcher and Sir Keith Joseph) were also guilty because they too should have also resigned after the introduction of an incomes policy. The only candidate who seemingly would be acceptable to Enoch Powell was Enoch Powell.

Powell played a relatively minor role in the Conservative leadership contest. He took no apparent pleasure in the ultimate election of Mrs Thatcher, despite her espousal of views similar to his own on economic affairs, and the support she drew from the few Powellites on the Tory benches. It is probably fair to say that he laid the ideological basis for Mrs Thatcher's election with the development of his economic philosophy during the middle and late 1960s and with his subsequent attacks against Heath following the imposition of wage and price controls. But once again his political clothes had been stolen.

Many of the interpretations of Mrs Thatcher's victory centred on the reaction inside the party against the interventionist policies of the Heath leadership period – the very policies that Powell consistently condemned.[32]

Mrs Thatcher's election in this view represented a repudiation of the *noblesse oblige* brand of Toryism which had evolved over the last hundred years. Powell's greatest impact may in the long run have been to lead that process of repudiation. Martin Walker has pointed out the influence of Powell's thinking on the Tory party in the post-Heath period:[33]

Mr Powell has seen in the Conservative party he loves the downfall of his collectivist opponents Mr Heath, Mr Barber and Mr Peter Walker. He has seen his own monetarist theories being taken up by Sir Keith Joseph (Mrs Thatcher's leading advisor in the pre-election period). Mr Powell himself has hardly triumphed, but his ideas have not done at all badly.

Mrs Thatcher's political thinking – as elaborated for example in a *Daily Telegraph* article just before her election – does indeed often appear to be a less rigorous form of Powellism.[34] She clearly shares Powell's aversion to planning, to state direction of the economy, and to the technocratic approach to politics which Heath championed. Government had no role in business and should not encourage schemes like industrial democracy and co-partnership. An ardent opponent of nationalisation, she argued that 'if management is bad and does not adequately consult workers it deserves to fail'.[35]

It is clear then that at least a substantial portion of the party had accepted much of Powell's economic analysis and selected their new leader accordingly. There was indeed apparently some sentiment for Powell on the back-benches, according to David Wood:[36]

> Part of the truth is that the preferred candidate of the anti-Heath forces is in baulk. He is Mr Enoch Powell, now an Ulsterman by adoption and a supporter of the Labour ticket in two general elections. There is no way Mr Powell can yet manoeuvre himself back on to high ground. But a considerable part of the 1922 Committee, believing that he alone has it in him to swing between a million and two million votes to the Conservative party, hopes that he may be made available by events before it is too late.

Mrs Thatcher's election was thought by some to bring Powell's return to the Tory front-benches a step closer. Powell hardly seemed to hasten the event. During the selection procedure and immediately thereafter he denounced Mrs Thatcher in no uncertain terms for remaining in the Heath Government after 1972. He also accused her of having presented inaccurate figures on the number of coloured children in British schools while she was Secretary of State for Education.[37] Mrs Thatcher told interviewers after her election that Powell would not join her front-bench team; he had, after all, deserted the party twice in 1974. Since her election she has made no approaches to him, and her senior advisers have maintained that the initial approach must come from him. For his part he has made no move to effect a reconciliation. After Mrs Thatcher said publicly that he would not join her front bench, he issued a statement indicating she was right for two reasons:[38] 'In the first place I am not a member of the Conservative party and secondly, until the Conservative party has worked its passage a very long way, it will not be rejoining me.'

CONTINUING TO FIGHT THE E.E.C.

Powell's early role in the Ulster Unionist delegation was relatively low key and he did not return to public prominence again until the 1975 E.E.C. referendum. Even then he was initially overshadowed on the anti-Market side by Anthony Wedgwood Benn, the Secretary for Industry. Powell's first major speech at Bournemouth in May got no coverage from the B.B.C., prompting a protest from the Get Britain Out campaign.[39] (The B.B.C. responded that the speech had not been reported because they were trying to balance pro- and anti-Market coverage.)[40] In the speech Powell discussed the issue in terms of its effect on the Conservative party. The referendum controversy, he said, made the Conservatives a class party and thus 'doomed it to extinction'.[41] The fact was that the Tory middle class had lost confidence that they could hold their own against an assertive working class and were now bolting for Europe where they hoped, by joining with countries more dedicated to capitalism, they could find a forum in which they would be safe from their own working class. It was a remarkable speech, not merely because of his implicit spokesmanship for a working-class constituency but because the arguments voiced would hardly have been out of place in the *Morning Star*.

In another major speech in London, he made it clear that he regarded the referendum as binding only as long as the present Parliament was in office. Since Britain joined the Market, it has been Powell's contention that Parliament has the right to withdraw the country from the Community at any time. Since Parliament enacted the legislation bringing the country into the Market it also held the power to take the country out of Europe. This speech too received little attention.

At the close of the campaign Powell in a speech in Birmingham argued that only a 'no' vote could prevent the country from suffering a 'moral breakdown'.[42] Membership spelt 'death, the abandonment of all prospects of national rebirth, the end of any possibility of resurgence'.[43] The only way to solve Britain's economic problem was through self-reliance. Powell also attacked British industrialists for trying to influence their employees' vote in what he called a show of 'naked arrogance'. He also participated in a major television debate with a number of leading pro- and anti-Marketeers on the eve of the poll and got prominent play in the newspapers during the week before the vote. Nonetheless it was for him a strangely quiet campaign. There was virtually no change in the polls throughout the campaign, so it is hard to claim that Powell's speeches had much impact. Somewhat surprisingly M.O.R.I. data suggest that less than half the electorate was aware of Powell's anti-Market stance, as Table 7.3 shows:

TABLE 7.3   Percent of electorate correctly identifying leading politicians' position on E.E.C., May–June 1975

Wilson	Heath	Benn	Thatcher	Powell	Foot	Thorpe	Jenkins	Callaghan	
72%	65%	62%	51%	46%	42%	41%	31%	30%	(1569)

Source: M.O.R.I., May–June 1975.

Moreover less than 10% of the sample indicated that Powell might have any influence over the way they might vote, as Table 7.4 shows:

TABLE 7.4   Per cent of electorate saying leading politicians have influence over their referendum vote, May–June 1975

Wilson	Heath	Thatcher	Powell	Benn	Thorpe	Jenkins	Williams	Callaghan	
15%	14%	10%	9%	6%	6%	5%	4%	3%	(1569)

Source: M.O.R.I., May–June 1975.

On the other hand poll data collected during the campaign indicate that Powell may have regained some part of the support he lost during the October 1974 election campaign, as Fig 7.1 shows. An odd feature is Heath's rising popularity (exactly level with Wilson on all three points). The Tory party now had another great and fallen warrior on the backbenches liable to attract dissenting Tory support.

As for the Powellites, a clear 2:1 majority amongst them were anti-Market while an equal proportion of the whole electorate was pro-Market. Moreover, among Powellites in all social classes, anti-Market sentiment was much more intense than among non-Powellite anti-Marketeers, as can be seen from the comparisons evident in the lower half of Table 7.5.

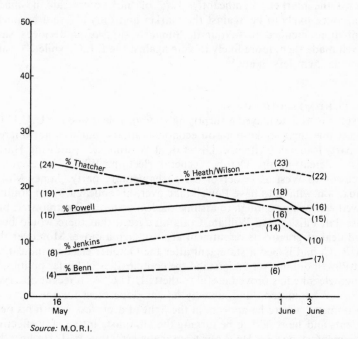

Source: M.O.R.I.

Fig. 7.1   M.P. who best represents electorate's views – referendum campaign, 1975

TABLE 7.5   Powellite attitudes to the Common Market, 1975

	All	Powell-ites	ABC1 all	ABC1 Powell-ites	C2 all	C2 All Powell-ites	DE all	DE Powell-ites
Very strongly in	30	14	40	10	28	17	23	13
Fairly strongly in	21	10	26	20	18	6	17	8
Slightly in	8	5	8	10	7	1	8	6
Total In	59	29	74	40	53	24	48	27
Very strongly out	16	38	8	36	18	37	21	39
Fairly strongly out	7	14	6	10	8	14	8	18
Slightly out	4	6	3	3	6	10	4	4
Total Out	27	58	17	49	32	61	33	61
	(1369)	(261)	(521)	(59)	(517)	(100)	(519)	(97)

Source: M.O.R.I., May–June 1975.

On the other hand, N.O.P. did provide some evidence to indicate that Powell played a role in solidifying the anti-market vote and in winning over undecided voters to this position. A poll they conducted in mid-May showed that 7% of all voters said he made them more likely to vote 'no' with 4% saying he made them less likely to be against the market. Significantly, 12% of 'no' voters said he made them more likely to be against the market and only 2% said he made them more inclined to favour it. Similarly, 9% of undecideds said Powell made them more likely to vote against the E.E.C. while 2% said he made them less likely.[44]

REPRESENTING SOUTH DOWN

Powell has to date played a surprisingly minor role inside the U.U.U.C. He became their spokesman on economic affairs, but was not offered the party leadership either in Ulster or at Westminster following Harry West's defeat in the October general election. While the eventual successor to West as leader of the parliamentary party, James Moly-neaux, was willing to have Powell take over, his colleagues had doubts. Powell was willing enough to assume the leadership at Westminster, but West, Ian Paisley and William Craig all agreed that there would be a good deal of grassroots resentment against such a move. Moreover the U.U.U.C. had issued a statement after the October election indicating that Powell did not yet understand the complexities of Ulster politics.[45] Nonetheless he has proved useful to the U.U.U.C. As a recent observer of Powell has noted, 'undoubtedly he has done most for the party at Westminster, where he appears in the light of a professor with his new students and he is said to be turning the Unionists into a very effective parliamentary party. "He is our team manager", says H. J. Heslip; "he has opened doors we didn't know were there".' [46] Moreover the Ulster

Unionist M.P.s have increasingly turned to him for guidance on critical parliamentary votes.

Because of his anomalous position as the only Englishman among the Unionist parliamentarians, he has been careful not to stray outside his own area of responsibilities, financial affairs. Where his English colleagues all stress his arrogance and aloofness (which they seem to indicate increased after he re-entered the House in October), Unionist M.P.s (with two or three notable exceptions) speak of him in relatively warm terms. Powell has however been dogged by the central question of the future structure of the Northern Ireland Government, where his strong integrationist line continues to sit unhappily with the Unionists' call for devolution.

Early in 1975 he set down what he felt to be the major demands the U.U.U.C. were making on the Constitutional Convention. First, Ulster must remain an integral part of the U.K. and have full parliamentary representation. Second, Ulstermen should have the same right as the rest of the U.K. citizens to democratic local government and thus 'intend to share fully in whatever forms of devolution to regions are consistent with full representation in Parliament'.[47] Finally he also indicated that minorities should enjoy all normal parliamentary and democratic rights. On the other hand in a speech in County Down he tended to see the growth of regional and national separatism in Wales and Scotland as symptoms of the mood of defeat and decline which had swept across Britain. The one place to which defeatism had not spread was Ulster, where the majority remained opposed to any disruption of the U.K.[48]

In a speech at Downpatrick in April Powell again reiterated the U.U.U.C. demand for devolution of power but did express his reservations about it, warning that Unionists had to be wary of a structure that imported a 'top-heavy administration' or made 'unfulfillable demands upon the available manpower and talent'.[49] 'Above all', Powell said, 'we must be on our guard against that parochialism, not of her people, but of some of her politicians, which has from time to time been a curse to Ulster.'[50] Most of all, devolution should not be used as a means of weakening the link between Ulster and the U.K. Powell also expressed reservations about the value of holding a Constitutional Convention in the first place. If Ulster really was an integral part of the U.K. why did it need a special body to plan its local administration? It was a delicate, balanced performance, deliberately leaving his options open.

His delicate balancing act was not successful for long and he found himself in deep trouble with the Unionist leadership following two speeches he delivered in July. Powell made two basic points in the first speech, in County Down, both of which angered the Unionist hierarchy. First, he gave his own definition of Unionism, which to him meant unquestioned obedience to the Crown in Parliament. If Parliament passed a law that Unionists disagreed with, they had no choice but to obey it. This position was clearly unacceptable to most Unionists, who quite correctly realised that if Powell's definition was accepted they would be forced to accept peacefully whatever form of government Westminster imposed on Northern Ireland. Second, Powell also urged the Ulster Unionists to consolidate their leadership under a single person. The Unionist parliamentary party was then led by James Molyneaux and the U.U.U.C. in Northern Ireland was headed by Harry West. Maintaining a balance between the different Unionist factions has always been a difficult enterprise and a consolidation of the leadership along the lines Powell suggested certainly would have provoked controversy at a time when Unionists could ill afford to be divided. Moreover, while Powell made no explicit bid for the leadership himself, the speech could be read as an attempt to assume power.[51] Two weeks later he spoke in County Antrim and said that the Northern Ireland Constitutional Convention was a repudiation of Unionism. His view was that 'the proposition that it is for the people of Northern Ireland to decide the government of Northern Ireland is the most anti-Unionist proposition that could be devised'.[52] The Ulster Unionists naturally wanted to make arrangements for the future government of Ulster in a body where they enjoyed an absolute majority (the Convention at Stormont), rather than at Westminster where they only had 10 of 635 members. So consequently there was outrage at Powell's County Antrim speech.

After the County Down speech, Ian Paisley took issue with Powell's definition of Unionism and dismissed him as a possible Unionist spokesman:[53]

> It is now evident that Ulster will have to look to Ulstermen alone in the coming days for a clear exposition of their principles and an unswerving defence of the same. Any Unionist leadership which imbibed Mr Powell's doctrine of loyalty would be disastrous for Ulster.

Harry West, the leader of the U.U.U.C., issued a slightly less vitriolic statement following the County Antrim speech, suggesting that Powell had not been in Ulster long enough to understand grassroots Unionist opinion. But the Unionists' Chief Whip at the Convention, Captain Austin Ardill, was less kind to Powell. The Antrim speech, Ardill declared, marked a 'betrayal' of his Unionist colleagues.

Perhaps as a result of these criticisms Powell took a stronger pro-devolution line in his next major speech, delivered to the Monday Club of Ulster in September. While warning that devolution was not in itself a panacea, he did set himself unambiguously in support of the U.U.U.C. line exactly as it was set out in the party's manifesto:[54]

I am as deeply and plainly committed as any man to the principle of devolved government for Ulster within the framework of the United Kingdom, exactly as it was set out in the Portrush Declaration and the United Ulster Unionist manifestoes. I do not believe that, if Parliament and Government are to give devolved government to Scotland and Wales, they will find it possible to withhold it from Ulster, and on the same terms and parliamentary principles and with simultaneous full representation at Westminster.

Two weeks later in Banbridge, County Down, Powell returned to these themes. He attacked the press for failing to report that he was a supporter of devolution and indicated he was tired of reading that he favoured the 'direct integration of Ulster', because Northern Ireland was already an integral part of the U.K. Repeating the statement quoted above, he again warned that devolution would not *solve* anything – it would for example provide no assurance that the I.R.A. would finally be defeated.[55]

Powell's attitude towards the press is hard to understand given the different attitudes he has expressed towards devolution in the early 1970s. Had he not once said, 'the mould of Stormont is broken and, like it or not, cannot be put together'? And, two years later, 'I am as deeply and plainly committed as any man to the principle of devolved government for Ulster within the framework of the United Kingdom, exactly as it was set out in the Portrush Declaration and the United Ulster Unionist manifestoes'? By committing himself explicitly to the U.U.U.C. line, he was accepting devolved parliamentary government for Ulster within the context of a federal U.K.

But he has also been outspoken in his opposition to devolved government and to federalism in particular. For example in November 1975 he told the City Conservative forum in London that devolution plans were 'constitutional nonsense'.[56] The creation of local parliaments would necessarily lead to the dissolution of the U.K. or to a federal state. If a federal structure were set up, there would have to be a written constitution and a supreme court to uphold its provisions. Moreover in a federal system each of the parts would have to have identical powers, so a Scottish Assembly could not have more power that a similar body set in Wales. Given the centrality of parliamentary sovereignty to Powell's political ideology, he naturally could not countenance any constitutional alterations which would undermine it. Nor did he believe that the British people would accept the elimination of parliamentary sovereignty and its replacement by an unrepresentative judiciary.

Powell's comments on Ulster in the devolution speech were vague, but he did seem hostile to the idea of resurrecting Stormont. He said it was theoretically indefensible for Ulster to have been governed by a local parliament for fifty years while still enjoying some representation at Westminster. The arrangement was tolerated in practice because the overall effect was minimal. His only reference to the Northern Ireland Convention and its work was to say that the arrangements which were in effect before direct rule need not be recreated. But again he made this point in a rather oblique way:[57] 'This does not mean that Humpty-Dumpty (Stormont) once fallen off the wall – or was he pushed – can be stuck together again.'

The speech put Powell in a particularly difficult position. He now appeared to be an opponent of devolution in Scotland and Wales. Yet only two months earlier he had indicated that he supported devolution to Ulster along the same lines as were being contemplated for other U.K. regions. Synthesis of these two seemingly contradictory positions was difficult, as not a few Unionists have noted. When questioned just after Powell's November speech, Harry West said that Powell continued to say that he supported the U.U.U.C. line. When the obvious divergences were pointed out, West said that as long as Powell did not get too much press attention he would not criticise him publicly.[58]

Powell continued to speak against the U.U.U.C. line in January 1976. Early in the year he told a meeting in Brighton that federalism 'would represent a more radical destruction of the nation than simple amputation of one part'.[59] Two weeks later in Parliament he went even further, stating that he would oppose any constitutional alterations in the structure of the U.K. with the same ardour that he opposed entry into the E.E.C.[60]

> But that this House by its own actions, by its own self-deceptions, should set in frame a course of constitutional action which must lead to the conversion of this country into something totally different and unrecognisable or to the destruction of the unity of whatever this realm is to be, the unity brought to a focus in this House, I say 'No' to that, whether that sovereignty be seen from inside or from outside. That at any rate is the conviction in which I have lived. It is a conviction for which I tore apart the links of my whole political life. It is a conviction from which I will not depart.

All doubts about his position seemingly disappeared early in March when the final report of the Northern Ireland Convention was rejected and an indefinite period of direct rule was introduced. Few Unionist politicians approved of the action (which gave complete authority to Westminster) but Powell seemed almost enthusiastic about the decision. In a Belfast speech he said he approved of the decision because 'for all those who uphold the Union there can be nothing distasteful in being governed as a part of the Union, and sharing the same forms of government, the same rights and duties as the rest of the British people'.[61] So that absolute parity with other regions of the U.K. could be obtained, he said, Northern Ireland should be given full representation at Westminster plus the same form of local government as the rest of the kingdom enjoyed.

The speech was regarded as blasphemous by virtually all shades of Unionist opinion. Since late 1975 he had tried to stick to the Unionist line quite closely, at least while he was in Northern Ireland. But in March Unionists were faced with the spectacle of their only English member coming to Belfast and endorsing direct rule of the province from London. Predictably there were indications from within Powell's own South Down constituency association that some members were eager to find a new parliamentary candidate for the next election. The Unionists have often found Powell personally difficult to work with and the speech in support of direct rule could have been the last straw.

The split between Powell and the Unionists widened in April 1976 when he told his constituency association that the U.U.U.C. no longer existed because of the divisions which had emerged as a result of the dissolution of the Convention. As a supporter of direct integration, he was outspoken in his criticism of men like Ernest Baird, a U.U.U.C. leader who had encouraged direct action and civil disobedience to protest against rule from Westminster. Powell not only said that direct rule should be accepted, but also suggested that the Union was more secure than it had been since 1968.[62] The speech drew an angry response from a number of loyalist leaders, most notably the Rev. William Beattie, second-in-command to Ian Paisley. Beattie said the U.U.U.C. was still alive, and that Powell should be replaced as its member for South Down for intimating that the coalition no longer existed.[63] Two weeks later Powell repeated the controversial argument he developed in the summer of 1975 by telling the Unionists of Banbridge that they were pledged to uphold the sovereign authority of Parliament whether or not they felt it was acting justly. Moreover Powell again warned the supporters of civil disobedience that it was not permissable for them to violate the law to press for their rights. Following the speech, there were published reports that Craig and Paisley were planning to stand a candidate against Powell or, barring that, persuade the official Unionists to replace him.[64]

The split with the loyalists over devolution is not likely to be healed quickly. It is likely that devolution will occupy the British political stage for years to come. Powell does not wish to be left out of such a major debate and his Unionist and nationalist sympathies are strong and shared by many in England. Quite clearly, though, the issue presents a fatal temptation – for he can only speak out on it at the risk of losing his last political redoubt in South Down. Ironically, his very nationalism drove him to seek an extension of his career outside the mainland and the mainstream of British politics. It could just as easily drive him back over the water.

PART II

In Part I we have sought to describe the development of Enoch Powell's career and beliefs during the 1960s and 1970s and to indicate, at least in crude terms, the proportions of the grassroots response to him. No English politician in this period remotely rivalled Powell in the heat, controversy, animosity and loyalty he aroused. The word 'Powellite' quickly entered the language as a truly household word. In Part II we look at the Powellites, focusing on the period of Powell's greatest prominence, 1968–75.

Powellism has never been an organised mass movement – not even within local Conservative constituency associations have organised Powellite factions existed. Nor, often to his followers' frustration, has Powell ever tried to encourage any grassroots organising on his behalf. Rather, the Powellites have existed as a powerful *tendance* within the British body politic, a large and continuing body of opinion which has, perhaps as a form of protest, continued to display admiration and to voice support for Powell quite regardless of – possibly even because of – his isolation at the élite level.

Powellism may be considered as a form of political extremism, not with any implication that either Powell or his supporters have anti-democratic tendencies, but simply in the sense that extremism means 'the tendency to go to the poles of the ideological axis'.[1] Powell has in this sense clearly adopted an extreme position on each of the issues he discussed, moving outside the normal bounds of the British élite consensus. There is no doubt that he has been popularly perceived as an extremist in this sense – when asked which British politician respondents perceived as being most extreme, Powell was the choice of an overwhelming majority.[2] Even among non-Powellites he clearly won high marks for broadening the accepted areas of political discussion and debate. Thus an O.R.C. poll conducted after the 1970 election found that over three-quarters of the electorate praised him for having great courage and sincerity while almost two-thirds disagreed with the contention that he was fanatical and dangerous. On the other hand, while people thought that Powell was by and large performing a useful political function, the fact that he was so far outside the élite consensus did limit the amount of personal support he could win. While 36% of the O.R.C. sample said that Powell was the 'only politician I admire in

Britain' only 19% said the Tory party would be better off with him as leader.[3] Similarly, in 1973, M.O.R.I.'s panel study showed that 25% of the electorate said he was the M.P. who best represented their views while 20% said he would make the best prime minister for the next five years.[4] Thus it seems clear that Powell tapped two separate emotions. On one hand the British were eagerly seeking a politician who could go beyond the confines set by the élite consensus and broaden the realm of political debate. On the other hand they were unwilling to abandon the élite consensus entirely and give Powell unqualified backing. The data would seem to show that even among his most dedicated supporters there were some who doubted whether it would be good for the country as a whole to have him in a position of leadership.

Powellism, then, has been a special sort of extremist protest. Part II will test the utility of the theoretical literature on political extremism in explaining his rise. The approach adopted by most of this literature may be termed 'epiphenomenalist'; that is, an approach which does not treat issues, grievances or the nature of the political system as the first level of analysis, but focuses rather on the social or personal peculiarities of groups or individuals which lead them to espouse extreme positions. We examine in this part of the book the mass society critique developed by William Kornhauser[5]; and the arguments from social mobility, status inconsistency and relative deprivation developed by Lipset, Bell, Lenski, Runciman and Pettigrew.[6] A third epiphenomenal approach – the study of the 'authoritarian personality' – will not be considered owing to a lack of data available for secondary analysis.[7]

Having concluded our examination of Powellism in the light of these theories we turn to a 'phenomenalist' approach which has its roots in economic theories of democracy such as Downs's and in works such as Key's, *The Responsible Electorate*.[8] Rather than take the individual as the level of analysis, such works take the political system as the starting point, and begin by asking how well the system represents the interests of the electorate. Seen from this perspective, 'extremist' and protest movements are liable to arise when the views or interests of significant groups are inadequately represented, causing certain strata to turn to movements or politicians outside the political mainstream. Thus such an approach focuses on the functioning of the political system and the actual issues which protest movements are, at least allegedly, all about.

A classic work of this sort is Michael Rogin's study of Senator Joseph McCarthy's mass base of support. Rogin found, quite simply, that the Wisconsin Senator drew support from Midwestern Republicans upset by their party's failure to take a hard-line anti-communist approach. His supporters were neither more isolated, more authoritarian nor more worried about status than were the rest of the electorate. Nor were his followers part of a vague populist movement willing indiscriminately to support someone on the right or left. Rather, they had a particular interest which had not been taken up forcefully by either of the major parties.[9] Our analysis will ultimately take a line similar to Rogin's and will be complemented by profiles of individual Powellites drawn from interviews. The conclusion will summarise the major arguments and draw some parallels between Powell and Powellism and right wing politics in America during the 1960s and 1970s.

8 A Description of Powell's Social Base of Support in the British Electorate, 1963-75

In this chapter we seek to explore the overall dimensions of Powell's support. First, how many people supported him and over what period? Second, how far was support for him correlated with attachment to (or disaffection from) the major parties and their leaders? Third, what was the social composition of the Powellites and how did this change with time?

A. A COMPOSITE ESTIMATE OF ENOCH POWELL'S OVERALL SUPPORT 1963–75

Drawing a continuous picture of Powell's support over a long period is a difficult task for several reasons. Polling agencies did not ask the same questions about him for more than five years at a time, so comparisons are often hard to draw. The problem is increased by the different types of questions which were asked. Questions measuring levels of agreement or disagreement with his views inevitably produced higher absolute levels of support than did questions asking respondents to choose the best replacement for Mr Heath or the best prime minister for the next five years. Comparisons are difficult even within this latter category. A question asking for a successor to Mr Heath naturally did not include Labour party politicians while a question asking for the best prime minister for the next five years obviously did. Thus in some instances Powell was matched against people like Harold Wilson (who had a natural working-class appeal), while in other cases he was not.

Nevertheless the data available do allow a rough picture to be drawn.[1] Between 1963 and April 1968 the data are fairly clear. All polls measuring Powell's support for the Tory leadership showed that he had well under 10%. Polls conducted during the Tory leadership contests of 1963 and 1965 gave him, respectively, popular rankings between 1% and 3%.[2] An O.R.C. poll in October 1967 showed him to have risen only to 6%, while Gallup's March 1968 survey showed him with only 1%.[3]

Broader questions did show that Powell gained some support between 1964 and 1967. On Gallup's question asking respondents who were the first three people they would put in a Conservative government, Powell's support rose from 0% in December 1964 to 13% in January 1967.[4] Thus a graph of Powell's support between 1963 and 1967 would probably show low levels of support with some slight increase occurring.

It would show a very substantial increase after April 1968. The polls revealed near-unanimous agreement with his immigration views and almost equally firm condemnation of Mr Heath for sacking him from the Shadow Cabinet. He immediately became the leading candidate to succeed Heath in both the Gallup and N.O.P. surveys. A poll in September 1968 showed him running neck and neck with Heath both for the Tory leadership and for prime minister.[5] But after that point Powell's levels of support began to fall off slightly. His position in 'straight fights' against Heath slipped substantially by early 1969 and remained unchanged through the year. A Gallup question measuring agreement or disagreement with his immigration views between April 1968 and June 1970 showed a 26% decline in the percentage agreeing with him.[6] So enormous however had been the impact he made in April 1968, that even this post-1968 decline left him with far more support than in the pre-1968 period. Thus the Gallup question on the first three men to be placed in a Conservative government showed that Powell's support increased from 13% in January 1967 to 36% in October 1969.[7]

However great Powell's contribution to the Tories' 1970 victory, the result served to bolster Heath's support at Powell's expense – an effect deepened by the latter's post-election silence. It was only with Powell's resumption of an active role over the 1971 Immigration Act that his support began to recover. The N.O.P. respondents asked to name their choice for prime minister for the next five years gave Powell 11% support after the election, 9% in October 1970 and 14% in March 1971.[8] He hit his second peak of personal popularity during late 1972 and early 1973 when the Ugandan Asian controversy emerged and disillusionment with the Heath Government's handling of the economy was at a peak. By February 1973 a quarter of M.O.R.I. respondents said that Powell was the M.P. who best represented their views while another 20% said he would make the best prime minister for the next five years. Judging by these extraordinary figures he had surpassed even his April 1968 figures. A later N.O.P. poll in June 1973 showed that his support for the premiership had dropped only slightly to 18%.[9]

In October 1972 Gallup began a series of questions asking their sample which politicians were assets to their parties. Their trend data showed that Powell reached his highest level of support during late 1972 and early 1973. Thus in October 1972 41% rated Powell an asset to his party while a year later only 36% gave a similar response.[10] Thereafter his

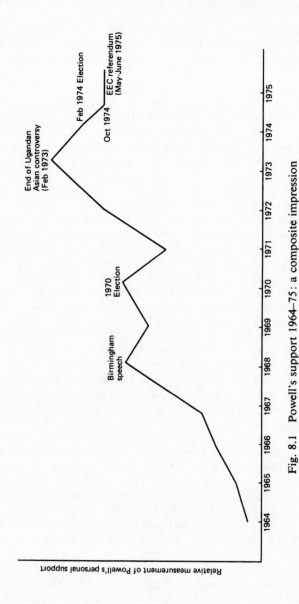

Fig. 8.1 Powell's support 1964–75: a composite impression

support on this question dropped precipitously. But in some ways this question is not particularly useful in measuring his support in the mass electorate. After June 1973 it was hard for anyone (Powell supporter or not) to say that he was an asset to the Conservative party. By threatening to endorse Labour, bitterly attacking the Conservative leadership and then carrying out his threat, he was helping Labour and not the Conservatives. Thus many Powell supporters might have said he was not a Conservative asset, this response being based not on their attitudes towards him but on their perception of his political stance. The second wave of the M.O.R.I. panel study provides evidence that Powell's impact had slipped but not as sharply as the Gallup data may have indicated. While 25% of respondents in February 1973 said that he best represented their views, only 16% gave a similar answer in February 1974. After the ballot, O.R.C. and Gallup both showed that he still had between 10% and 25% of the electorate wanting him to succeed Heath should the Tory leader resign,[11] a level similar to that he enjoyed immediately after his 1968 Birmingham speech. By 1974 he was receiving both much less and more hostile media attention than in 1968. Possibly his support would have been higher in 1974 with greater media attention or, very probably, his following had achieved a certain independence of mere media coverage. Moreover the M.O.R.I. study showed that his support actually increased slightly by July 1974, with 17% of their panel saying he best represented their views compared to 16% in February. So while Powell had slipped from his position of February 1973 he still, remarkably, remained at least as well supported for the Tory leadership in mid-1974 as in April and July 1968, when he had made his first explosive public impact.

Judging by the Gallup and O.R.C. polls (both measuring support for him as a successor to Heath) Powell's move to Northern Ireland did cost him a good measure of support in Britain. After the October 1974 election Gallup showed him falling from 14% to 4% while O.R.C. showed a drop from 21% to 17%.[12] But N.O.P. found that 13% of their sample favoured him to lead a coalition government, placing him in fourth place, 2% ahead of Heath.[13] Moreover data collected during the 1975 referendum campaign showed that he had managed to hold on to his hard-core support, with three M.O.R.I. polls showing 15%, 18% and 15% of their samples saying Powell best represented their views. The impression is strong that roughly one-sixth of the electorate – the same level of support he had achieved in April–July 1968 – was still steadily supporting him seven years later.

The preceding poll results can be used as the basis of a synthetic impression of Powell's levels of support between 1963 and 1975. Because of the different types of questions used, no absolute percentage figures are attached to Fig. 8.1 – which must be regarded as a realistic sketch rather than a statistically accurate picture.

A cursory examination of the data reveals no relationship between support for Powell and the fortunes of the two parties. When Powell first came into public prominence in April 1968 the Tories held a lead of over 20%.[14] In late 1972 and early 1973, when he reached his peak in popularity, the situation was reversed. Between September 1972 and May 1973 Labour held between a 5% and 10% lead over the Tories.[15]

If changing levels of party support do not appear to be related to growth in Powell's support, there does appear to be some correlation between sinking ratings of the party leaders and his emergence. Two weeks before Powell's April 1968 speech Richard Rose wrote in *The Times*, 'Public confidence in the ability of the leaders of the two parties to deal with the nation's problems has reached a post-war low'.[16] With the exception of Sir Anthony Eden after Suez, Wilson's popularity had reached an all-time low for a prime minister in early 1968. When the prime minister's popularity falls, the leader of the opposition party usually profits. But on this occasion, despite the Tory party's massive lead, Heath's rating actually dipped below Wilson's. Indeed Rose's data show a remarkable – and perhaps unprecedented – phenomenon: between 1965 and 1968 there was a steady decline in both leaders' ratings.[17] For example, Heath's average rating between August 1965 and March 1966 was 47%; between January and March 1968 it fell to 31%. The figures during these two periods for Wilson were 60% and 35%.

While satisfaction with the performance of the party leaders was not particularly high, the Government received even lower marks. Wilson's personal ratings may have sagged badly, but they still ran 15% higher than his Government's with even these extraordinarily low levels of popular satisfaction dropping steadily between November 1967 and May 1968. Thus when Powell burst on to the scene in April 1968, he did not so much steal an audience from his rivals as attract one which had already become disillusioned with them.

On the other hand, as Fig. 8.2 shows, there was in the months that followed no simple relationship between Powell's standing relative to Heath's and either Heath's own rating or the Government's. Heath's 'recovery' *vis-à-vis* Powell by January 1969 coincided with slight further drops in both his and the Government's ratings, while a large improvement in both their satisfaction ratings in the course of that year did not see Heath improve his lead over Powell.

In the post-1970 period there was a positive relationship between support for Powell and low satisfaction ratings for the Government and Mr Heath. Nonetheless the correlation remained weak. It is only when we compare support for Powell and Heath as choices for prime

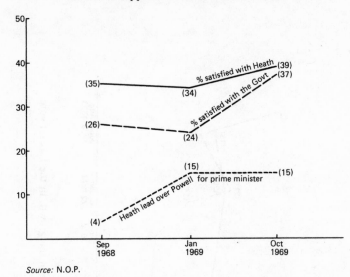

Source: N.O.P.

Fig. 8.2 The relationship between satisfaction with the government and the Conservative leader and support for Heath or Powell for prime minister, 1968–69

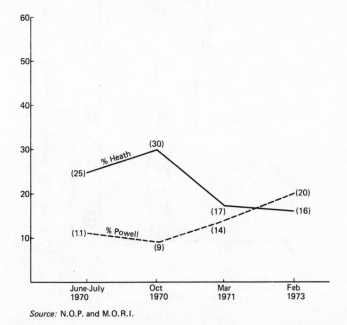

Source: N.O.P. and M.O.R.I.

Fig. 8.3 Support for Heath and Powell for prime minister 1970–73

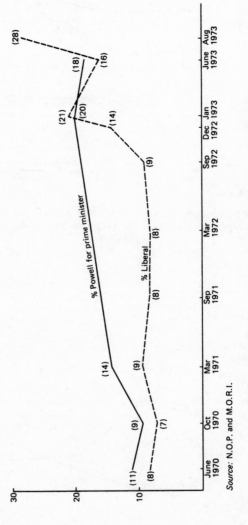

Source: N.O.P. and M.O.R.I.

Fig. 8.4   The relationship between support for Powell and the growth in the Liberal vote

minister (Fig. 8.3) that we find a really clear inverse relationship in movements of opinion.

A number of commentators suggested that both Powell and the Liberals were, in this period, drawing on the same reservoirs of popular dissatisfaction.[18] Figure 8.4 suggests that this was indeed the case, though it is worth noting that the electorate apparently did not see support for Powell or the Liberals as alternatives (which an inverse graphical picture would indicate), but rather as compatible postures, for their support rose together. In part, no doubt, this is a reflection of the fact that Liberals were gaining disproportionately from disaffected Conservatives at this point; but it is also a key indication of how diffuse and generalised was the mood of disillusion on which Powell drew.

A SOCIOLOGICAL ANALYSIS OF POWELL'S SUPPORT, 1962–75: CLASS, PARTY, SEX, REGION AND AGE

1. *Social class*

Before 1968 Powell's base support was heavily weighted towards the upper middle class – not, it would appear (see chapter 1), because of any socially differentiated endorsement of his free-market economic policies, but simply because this was the stratum of the population most likely to be aware of a front-bench Tory M.P.[19] The more obscure a Tory politician, one may hypothesise, the more likely it was that his support should be concentrated within this well-informed and heavily Conservative stratum. This hypothesis is largely borne out by the 1965 N.O.P. poll concerning the 'most outstanding figures' in the Tory party (Table 8.1) and also by a Gallup poll a year later (on the top three figures respondents would place in a Tory government) and by a yet further Gallup poll in January 1967.[20]

TABLE 8.1 Distribution of social class support of leading Tory politicians, Nov 1965

	Per cent of support coming from middle class %	Absolute level of support %
Powell	49	7
Macleod	48	14
Heath	40	50
Maudling	39	36
Hogg	35	7
Douglas-Home	35	16
All respondents	33	(2103)

Source: N.O.P. Poll 65020 supplied by the S.S.R.C. Survey Archive, University of Essex.

TABLE 8.2   Distribution of social class support of leading Tory politicians, Aug 1966

	Per cent of support coming from middle class %	Absolute level of support %
Powell	42	8
Macleod	41	18
Douglas-Home	39	15
Maudling	36	32
Heath	35	52
Hogg	32	15
All respondents	34	(2132)

Source: Roper Center, Williams College.

TABLE 8.3   Distribution of social class support of leading Tory politicians, Jan 1967

	Per cent of support coming from middle class %	Absolute level of support %
Powell	43	13
Maudling	42	45
Macleod	41	19
Hogg	36	19
Douglas-Home	36	21
Heath	33	45
All respondents	34	(2347)

Source: Roper Center, Williams College.

Some of those mentioning Powell were of course Labour identifiers. If however we re-analyse the January 1967 figures, holding party identification constant, the middle-class nature of Powell's support becomes even more apparent (Table 8.4).

Our pre-1968 findings are, then, heavily consistent. Even though Powell significantly increased his overall level of support in this period, he had failed to achieve the proportionate levels of working-class support normal even for other leading Conservative politicians. Had he – like Heath – been able to count two working-class supporters for every middle-class supporter garnered, his overall level of support would have been nearly 17%, instead of 13%, in January 1967.

Powell's Birmingham speech in April 1968 for the first time gave him working-class recognition. Overall, 97% of middle-class and 95% of

TABLE 8.4 Social class distribution of Conservatives and Labour
supporters of Powell, Heath and Maudling, Jan 1967

	All %	Powell %	Heath %	Maudling %
Per cent of Labour support from middle class	13 (851)	20 (46)	11 (164)	18 (129)
Per cent of Conservative support from middle class	44 (907)	55 (62)	42 (216)	47 (203)

Source: Roper Center, Williams College.

working-class respondents told Gallup they had heard or read about the
speech,[21] and the latter were slightly more likely than the former to
agree with the views he expressed. But as Table 8.5 shows, all segments
of the electorate gave him high levels of support. The only question
showing a clearly socially differentiated response came when respondents
were asked whether Heath was right to dismiss Powell.

TABLE 8.5 Per cent of each class agreeing with Powell's views and
disagreeing with Heath's decision to sack Powell Apr 1968

	All %	ABC1 %	C2 %	DE %
Per cent agreeing with Powell's views (Gallup)	75 (928)	70 (296)	75 (340)	78 (292)
Per cent agreeing with Powell's views (N.O.P.)	67	66	71	63
Per cent disagreeing with Heath's decision to sack Powell (Gallup)	69 (928)	59 (296)	70 (340)	76 (292)
Per cent disagreeing with Heath's decision to sack Powell (N.O.P.)	61	56	66	63

Source: *N.O.P. Political Bulletin* (May 1968) 9 and Gallup Poll CQ576 supplied
by Gallup Polls Ltd.

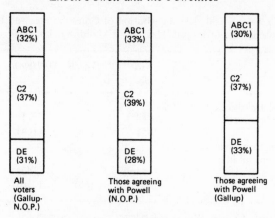

Source: NOP Political Bulletin (May 1968) 9 and Gallup Poll
CQ576 supplied by Gallup Polls Ltd.

Fig. 8.5   Social class distribution of electorate and those in agreement
with Powell's immigration views, Apr 1968

While over two-thirds of those polled expressed agreement with
Powell's immigration views, less than a quarter were willing to make the
stronger commitment of supporting him for the Tory leadership should
Heath resign. Even at this more intense level of support Powellites were,
according to both N.O.P. and Gallup, a fair cross-section of the
electorate – 30% middle and 70% working class.[22]

A month after the Birmingham speech Gallup found that, while 24%
had favoured Powell in this 'strong' sense in April, only 13% did so
now.[23] As Table 8.6 makes clear, those defecting were disproportionately working class. Powell's following was indeed now slightly
weighted towards the middle class again.

TABLE 8.6   Per cent of each social class supporting Powell for the
Conservative leadership, Apr–July 1968

	All %	ABC1 %	C2 %	DE %
April	24 (928)	23 (296)	27 (340)	22 (292)
July	13 (917)	17 (287)	13 (339)	11 (291)
Per cent change	−11	−6	−14	−11

Source: Gallup Polls CQ576 and 585 supplied by Gallup Polls Ltd.

If we now compare the Powellites with the electorate of the three parties (Fig. 8.6) we find that his July 1968 following was more working class than either the Liberals' or the Conservatives', but more middle class than Labour's.

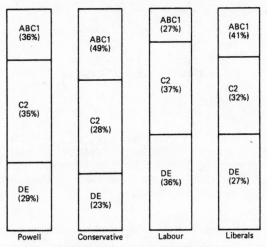

Source: Gallup Poll CQ585 supplied by Gallup Polls Ltd.

Fig. 8.6   Social class distribution of those supporting the Conservatives, Liberals and Labour, July 1968

Powell did suffer a drop in support towards the end of 1968. By late November the percentage agreeing with his immigration views had slipped 16% while the percentage disagreeing had risen 11%. Yet there was almost no change in the distribution of agreement with his views across social classes. In absolute terms he suffered his greatest losses in the working class. The social class profile of those in agreement with Powell's views mirrored the electorate very closely.

During 1968 Powell ran a steady second in a 'straight fight' poll against Heath as a Tory prime ministerial candidate. But, as a comparison of their followings (Table 8.7) shows, Heath was strongest with middle-class respondents while Powell's support was firmest with the skilled working class (C2).

Indeed there appears to have been a transfer effect between the followings of the two men. Prior to 1967 Heath had been best regarded among the working class and Powell among the middle class; after 1968 the position was reversed (Table 8.8).

Gradually the greater staying power of the C2 group in its support for Powell and his views – more pronounced still in the longer time-span

TABLE 8.7   Per cent of each social class supporting Heath or Powell for
prime minister, Jan–Oct 1969

	All %	AB %	C1 %	C2 %	DE %
January					
Heath	49	61	54	43	47
Powell	34	26	29	41	35
Difference	(+15)	(+25)	(+25)	(+2)	(+12)
	(1870)	(265)	(426)	(648)	(531)
October					
Heath	50	64	51	44	48
Powell	35	28	35	41	32
Difference	(+15)	(+26)	(+16)	(+3)	(+16)
	(1835)	(290)	(419)	(648)	(478)

Source: N.O.P. Polls 69021 and 69033 provided by the S.S.R.C. Survey
Archive, University of Essex.

TABLE 8.8   Evaluation of Heath as leader of Conservative party, 1967–70

	All %	AB %	C1 %	C2 %	DE %
Heath as best leader of Tory party (1967)	38	26	32	33	40
Satisfaction with Heath as Tory leader (1970)	45	57	51	39	44

Source: Sunday Times, 14 Oct 1967; and *N.O.P. Political Bulletin* (Feb 1970).

of Fig. 8.7 – altered the composition of his support. While both the
middle class (ABC1) and unskilled workers (DE) fell away from him in
tandem, skilled manual workers (C2), though not his strongest supporters originally, defected from him least and thus bulked increasingly
large in his overall following.

It must of course be remembered that Powell's followers – even
among the C2s – were not an entirely stable group. Like partisans of a
party they suffered a continual process of change, at least on the margin,
through defection and replacement. There is evidence however that
Powell's views continued to gain a more sympathetic hearing within the
C2 milieu. In January 1970 Gallup reported that 33 % of its respondents
claimed to have become more favourable over time to Powell's views and

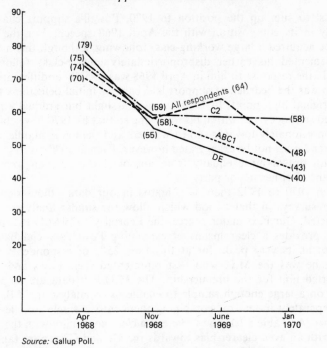

Source: Gallup Poll.

Fig. 8.7 Per cent of each social class agreeing with Powell's immigration views, 1968–70

22% had become less sympathetic. But while among the ABC1 and DE groups 'the favourable margins were narrow, 30–24% and 28–23% respectively, among the C2 group the figure was 40–19%.

These findings are confirmed by the Butler-Stokes panel studies of 1969–70, where respondents were asked to rate politicians on a 0–100 scale. If for our purposes we consider as Powellites only those who gave him ratings of 78–100 a clear bias towards the C1 and C2 groups among his supporters is also visible (Table 8.9).

TABLE 8.9   Support for Powell by class, 1969–70

	All %	*AB* %	*C1* %	*C2* %	*DE* %
1969	23 (1114)	18 (170)	26 (232)	25 (388)	24 (301)
1970	26 (1267)	22 (219)	28 (256)	29 (456)	33 (306)

Source: Butler-Stokes Panel Study, 1969–70.

Thus, to sum up the position to 1970, Powell's support changed sharply in its composition with the April 1968 speech. For the first time he acquired a large working-class following, although this merely complemented his earlier disproportionately middle-class following. Overall, the response to him in April 1968 was socially undifferentiated and so was the bedrock of support laid bare by initial defections from this original high point. In 1969 however a slight but gradually more marked shift occurred within his following so that by 1970 it was biased disproportionately towards skilled workers and the lower middle class. This trend must not be exaggerated however. Even in 1970 his following was still drawn more equally from all social classes than were the partisans of either major party.

From 1970 to 1972 there is a hiatus in our data – there were no further surveys in that period which allow for similar analyses to be conducted. Our next major source, the February 1973 M.O.R.I. panel study, provides a clear means of examining Powell's social base of support at its very peak, for at this time 25% of respondents were saying he was the M.P. who best represented their views and 20% supported him for the premiership. The M.O.R.I. data are, happily, based on a large enough sample to enable us to analyse the ABs and C1s separately instead of combining them into a single middle-class category. As Table 8.10 shows, there is a clear continuity with the 1970 data with an even clearer bias towards the C1 and C2 groups (and an ironing out of the differences between them).

TABLE 8.10   Support for Powell for prime minister and leader of the opposition, Feb 1973

	All %	*AB* %	*C1* %	*C2* %	*DE* %
Choice for prime minister					
Powell	20	16	22	22	17
	(2073)	(280)	(440)	(794)	(559)
M.P. who best represented electorate views					
Powell	25	18	28	28	23
	(2073)	(280)	(440)	(794)	(559)

Source: M.O.R.I. Panel Study, 1973.

Figures 8.8 and 8.9 allow us to compare Powell's constituency at its high point with profiles of the Heath supporters, as well as the whole electorate and the supporters of the three major parties. While Powell's disproportionate C2 support is clear enough, what is really striking still is how much truer a cross-section of the electorate Powellites were than any of the other groups examined. Only the Liberals came close to such mirror-representation of the whole.

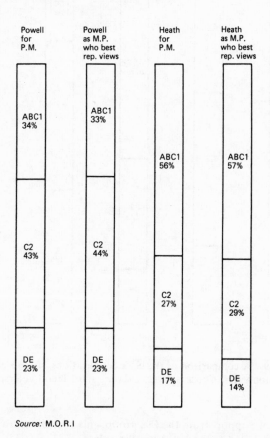

Source: M.O.R.I

Fig. 8.8   Powell and Heath supporters, Feb 1973

In June 1973 came Powell's first sensational hint that he might support Labour in the next election. Not surprisingly, polls taken in June 1973 show a marked and differential fall-off in his middle-class following. As his alignment with the Labour party strengthened into outright support in February 1974 and continued thereafter at least in his harmony with the Labour left over the E.E.C. referendum, so his middle-class support fell away. As a result of this movement – and some compensating

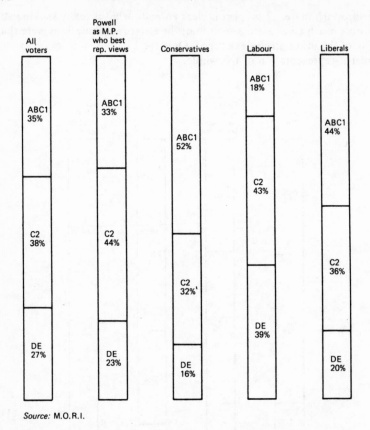

Source: M.O.R.I.

Fig. 8.9 A comparison of the class compositions of the electorate, Powell supporters, Conservatives, Labour, and Liberal voters, Feb 1973

accession of support from the DE group – his overall following became increasingly tilted towards the working class.

The shift within Powell's base – with even some slight attrition in his hitherto solid C2 support – is clearly visible in Figs. 8.11 and 8.12. While only one Powellite in two was a worker in 1965, and only two out of three in 1973, by 1975 better than three out of every four were workers, with unskilled manual workers alone accounting for almost two-fifths of his total support.

Perhaps a clearer picture still of the changing social response to him is achieved by Fig. 8.13 which examines questions which were asked about him over a period of time. This approach allows us to take within our compass the whole range of questions asked in surveys about Powell.

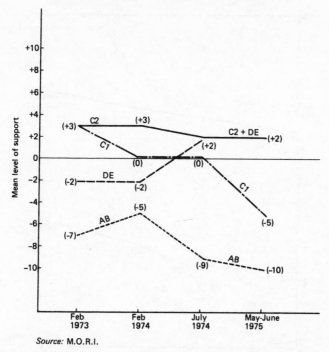

Fig. 8.10 Deviation of each social class from mean level of support given to Powell as M.P. who best represents electorate's views, 1973–75

It is noticeable that his two popularity peaks – in 1968 and in 1972–73 – saw clear convergence in working- and middle-class evaluations of him.

2. *Party*

When Powell's support is analysed by party one finds (Table 8.11) that before 1968 there were no very substantial differences between the supporters of the major parties in their evaluation of him.

While much of the attention he got after the Birmingham speech centred on the working-class (and presumably Labour) dockers and meat-cutters who marched on his behalf, Conservatives generally gave him more support than anyone else, as Table 8.12 shows. Partisans of the different parties were in fairly uniform agreement only in their disapproval of his ejection from the Shadow Cabinet – which may have been viewed as an apolitical question of fair play.

Similarly, questions on Powell as a possible Tory leader (Table 8.13) also showed an initial fairly uniform response across party with a slight Conservative bias – which however became more pronounced a few months after the Birmingham speech as Labour voters, probably affected

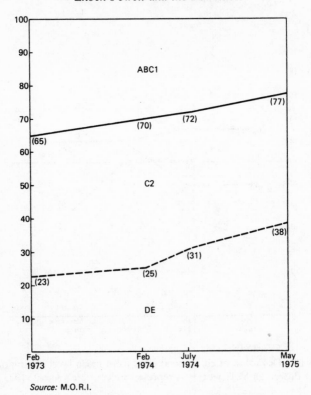

Source: M.O.R.I.

Fig. 8.11   Social class distribution of those saying Powell
best represents their views, 1973–75*

* In each of these surveys between 33% and 35% of the samples were middle
class.

by their own party leader's response to Powell, withdrew some of their
support. The less disciplined partisans – Liberals and 'others' – remained
fairly steady in their support however.

On the other hand Powell *had* had a major impact beyond Tory ranks.
While non-Tory voters pulled away from him when faced with questions
attempting to elicit their support for him nationally against their own
partisan preference, a clearer pattern of favourable response to him is
evident if we select questions which get round that difficulty. If respondents were given only the choice between Heath and Powell (Fig. 8.14) –
i.e. within a Conservative framework only – then Labour and 'other'
respondents frequently felt that Powell was their preferred choice.

Figure 8.14 suggests that large numbers of Labour and Liberal voters
had conceived at least a sneaking regard for Powell after his Birmingham

TABLE 8.11   The evaluation of Powell by party, 1965–67

	All %	*Conservative* %	*Labour* %	*Liberal* %
Nov 1965 – Powell as outstanding figure in Conservative party	7 (2108)	11 (730)	6 (946)	5 (149)
Aug 1966 – Powell as one of first three men for Tory government	4 (2132)	4 (898)	4 (774)	4 (200)
Feb 1967 – Powell as one of the first three men for Tory government	6 (2346)	6 (730)	5 (851)	8 (231)

Source: N.O.P. Poll 65020 supplied by the S.S.R.C. Survey Archive, University of Essex; Gallup data supplied by the Roper Center, Williams College.

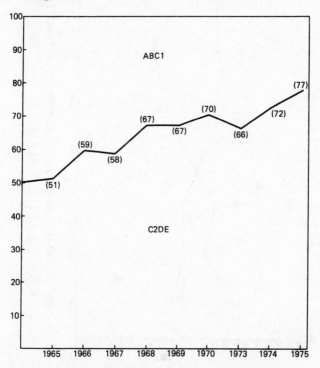

Fig. 8.12   Social class distribution of Powell support, 1965–75*

* In years where there was more than one measure of Powell's class support, an average figure was computed.

Source: N.O.P., Gallup, O.R.C., M.O.R.I.

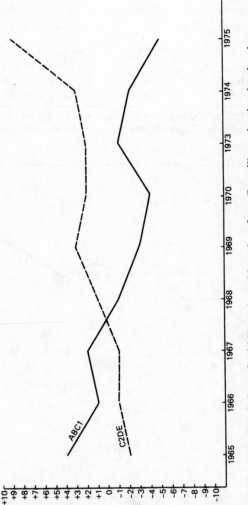

Fig. 8.13   Deviation of middle and working class from Powell's evaluation by the electorate

Source: N.O.P., Gallup, O.R.C., M.O.R.I.

TABLE 8.12   Attitudes to Powell's immigration speech and sacking, by party 1968

	All %	Conservative %	Labour %	Liberal %	Other %
Agree with Powell's immigration views (N.O.P.)	67	75	58	58	—
Agree with Powell's immigration views (Gallup)	74 (928)	80 (443)	70 (218)	59 (99)	74 (168)
Heath's sacking of Powell wrong (N.O.P.)	61	62	60	—	—
Heath's sacking of Powell wrong (Gallup)	69 (928)	68 (443)	68 (218)	64 (99)	72 (168)

Source: *N.O.P. Political Bulletin* (May 1968) 9, and Gallup Poll CQ576 supplied by Gallup Polls Ltd.

TABLE 8.13   Support for Powell as leader of the Conservative party by party, Apr–July 1968

	All %	Conservative %	Labour %	Liberal %	Other %
April 1968 Gallup	24 (928)	25 (442)	25 (218)	15 (99)	25 (169)
N.O.P.	13	13	10	14	—
July 1968 Gallup	13 (917)	16 (402)	9 (264)	14 (98)	11 (153)

Source: *N.O.P Political Bulletin* (May 1968) 9, and Gallup Polls CQ56 and CQ585 supplied by Gallup Polls Ltd.

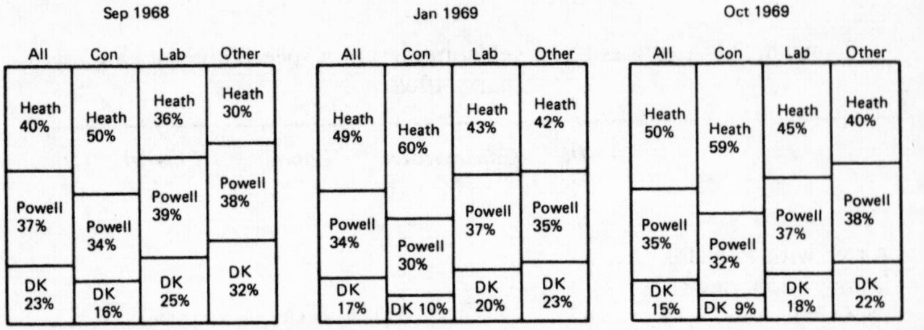

Source: NOP Political Bulletin (Sep 1968) 5; (Jan 1969) 6-7; (Oct 1969) 10; and NOP Polls 69021 and 69033 supplied by SSRC Survey Archive, University of Essex.

Fig. 8.14   Powell or Heath for prime minister 1968–69

speech. They were certainly willing to give him more generous support against Heath than were Tory respondents. For the latter, however, the question was hardly free of partisan considerations, posing as it did questions of loyalty to their official party leadership. When they were simply asked about their agreement with Powell's immigration views – a question on which they faced only the same partisan constraints as other respondents (for *all* party leaders had condemned Powell) – Tory respondents were, as Fig. 8.15 shows, clearly more favourable to Powell than others. Moreover, while Gallup found that a 33–22% plurality of all respondents said they had (by January 1970) grown more favourable to Powell's views, the Conservative and Liberal pluralities were considerably larger (36–22% and 36–21% respectively) than was the Labour margin of 36–26%.

Probably the clearest demonstrations of the Conservative bias in Powell's social base comes from an examination of the Butler-Stokes data from 1969 and 1970 (Table 8.14). In both years he won about twice as much support from Tories as from Labour voters. And in both cases

TABLE 8.14   Support for Powell by party, 1969–70

	All %	Conservative %	Labour %	Liberal %	Non-voter %
1969	23	33	16	19	13
	(1114)	(538)	(298)	(101)	(53)
1970	26	37	19	20	12
	(1267)	(512)	(519)	(103)	(93)

Source: Butler-Stokes Panel Study, 1969–70.

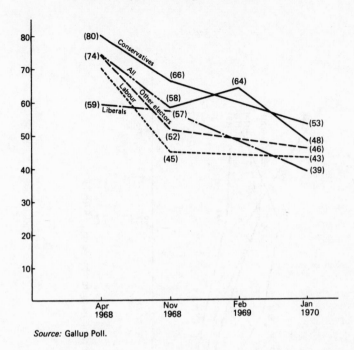

Source: Gallup Poll.

Fig. 8.15   Agreement with Powell's immigration views by party 1968–70

TABLE 8.15   Percent of Conservative, Labour and Liberal voters saying
Powell best represents their views, 1973–75

	All %	Conservative %	Labour %	Liberal %	Other %
Feb 1973	25 (2073)	30 (663)	20 (866)	21 (250)	27 (294)
Feb 1974	16 (1290)	15 (472)	12 (469)	16 (172)	25 (177)
July 1974	17 (827)	15 (266)	17 (346)	15 (115)	20 (100)
June 1975	16 (1569)	14 (621)	17 (572)	14 (154)	25 (222)

Source: M.O.R.I.

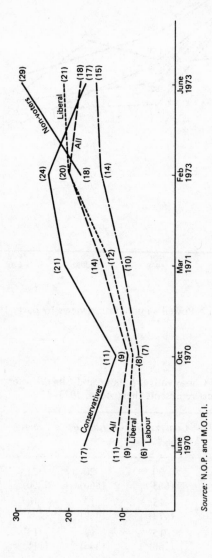

Source: N.O.P. and M.O.R.I.

Fig. 8.16   Powell support for prime minister by party, 1970–73

TABLE 8.16   Powell's support by class and party, 1968–74

	All %	*ABC1*		*C2DE*	
		Con. %	*Lab.* %	*Con.* %	*Lab.* %
May 1968 – successor to Heath (N.O.P.)	11 (1929)	11 (405)	10 (83)	15 (433)	9 (435)
Summer 1970 – Powell 78–100 rating (Butler-Stokes)	32 (988)	33 (260)	13 (98)	39 (198)	19 (329)
Feb 1973 – M.P. who best represents views (M.O.R.I.)	25 (2073)	30 (469)	18 (142)	33 (562)	21 (655)
Feb 1974 – M.P. who best represents views (M.O.R.I.)	16 (1290)	14 (242)	10 (92)	16 (224)	12 (396)

Source: N.O.P. Poll 68016 supplied by the S.S.R.C. Survey Archive, University of Essex; M.O.R.I.; and Butler-Stokes Panel Study, 1970.

he won below average support from non-voters and Liberals – constituencies he should have fared well with if he was directly profiting from a general mood of disenchantment with the two-party system.

If however we run on our data through the 1970 election to June 1973 (when Powell first hinted he might support Labour), we find that the easy advantage he continued to enjoy among Tory voters right through to February 1973 suddenly (and not surprisingly) disappears. On the other hand his support among Labour voters, though still lagging, more than held steady. His really major breakthrough at this point came with Liberal supporters and above all, with non-voters (Fig. 8.16). Perhaps because Powell for the first time gave an indication that he was willing to cast aside his traditional party loyalties, he now could at last emerge as a champion of those least enthused with two-party consensus politics.

Not surprisingly, Conservative support fell away from Powell after his Stockport speech. But his decision to go beyond the limitations placed on him by his membership in the Conservative party was of most benefit to him with voters who had rejected the two-party system (Table 8.15). While he showed a significant fall-off in support among the supporters of all the major parties, between February 1973 and February 1974 'other' respondents were practically unchanged in their evaluation of

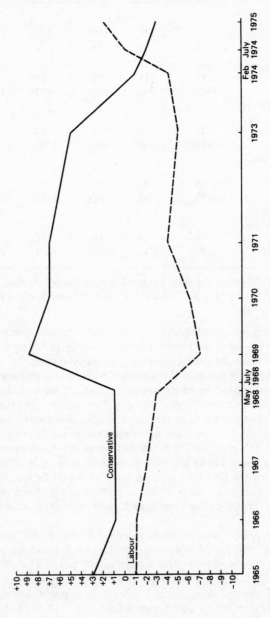

Fig. 8.17   The deviation of Powell's Labour and Conservative support from his rating in the electorate 1965–75

Source: N.O.P., Gallup, O.R.C., M.O.R.I.

him. After February 1974 he maintained his high level of support with 'other' respondents and won an increasing amount of support from Labour voters.

Probably the best way to see how the party structuring of Powell's support changed over time is gained from Fig. 8.17 which seeks to measure deviations by Labour and Tory supporters from the average mean level of support given Powell by all respondents over time. As the figure shows, despite the large accession of working-class support after 1968, Powell fared best among working-class Tories – and possibly of course among working-class Labour voters he brought across to the Tory side. After 1970 there was a gradual fall-off in Tory support, accentuated after 1973. At the same time he picked up Labour support – thus adding more working-class support to his following, so that by 1975 it was largely made up of working-class Tory *and* Labour voters.

Analysing Powell's support by both party and class shows that up to February 1973 he was strongest with working-class Conservatives. Thereafter it is most likely that his base tilted towards working-class Labour voters, though there are no data available for secondary analysis to test this hypothesis.

3. *Region*

While Enoch Powell drew the inspiration for his immigration speeches from conditions in the Black Country, his base of support has been decisively weighted towards the West Midlands only in the period just after his Birmingham speech. Before 1968, as Table 8.17 shows, his

TABLE 8.17   Geographical distribution of Powell supporters, 1965

	All %	London %	East Anglia %	Northern %	S. Wales & West %	Midlands %	North East %	South %	South West %	Scotland %
Those saying Powell one of the outstanding figures in Tory party	7 (2314)	7 (423)	5 (130)	6 (620)	9 (259)	8 (236)	9 (149)	13 (186)	7 (43)	7 (268)

Source: N.O.P. Poll 65020; data supplied by S.S.R.C. Survey Archive, University of Essex.

TABLE 8.18   Geographical distribution of those choosing Powell as a replacement for Heath, May 1968

	All %	London %	East Anglia %	Northern %	Wales & West %	Midlands %	North East %	South %	South West %	Scotland %
Those choosing Powell as successor to Heath	13 (2011)	5 (461)	5 (83)	9 (489)	15 (123)	19 (302)	12 (147)	11 (159)	6 (65)	6 (182)

Source: N.O.P. Poll 68016; data supplied by S.S.R.C. Survey Archive, University of Essex.

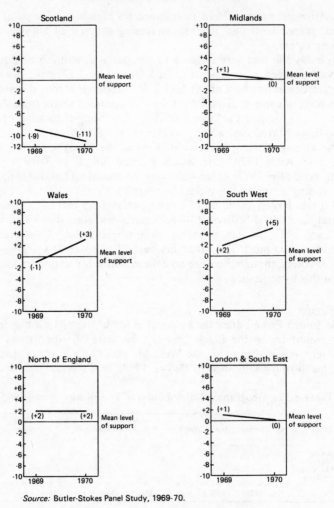

Source: Butler-Stokes Panel Study, 1969-70.

Fig. 8.18 Deviation of each region from Powell's mean level of support 1969-70

support was almost perfectly distributed across the country. But immediately after the 'rivers of blood' speech his base took on a distinctive Midlands bias (Table 8.18).

While immediately after his 1968 address his support did become skewed towards the West Midlands, these differences had largely disappeared by 1969-70, as Fig. 8.18 shows. He was weaker in Scotland than elsewhere but there was no sign of a strong bias towards any

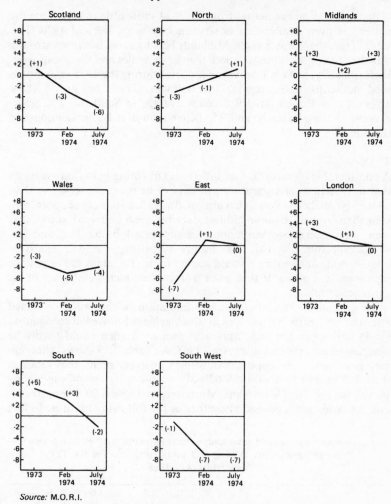

Source: M.O.R.I.

Fig. 8.19 Deviation of each region from powell's mean level of support
as the M.P. who best represents the electorate's views, 1973–74

particular region, certainly not the West Midlands. The same is true
if we explore Powellite strength in 'straight fight' polls for the premiership against Heath in 1968–69. Indeed, not only was he not appreciably
stronger in the Midlands than elsewhere, but January 1969 N.O.P. data
show that while the country as a whole preferred Heath over Powell for
prime minister by a 49–34% margin, Midlands residents backed the
Tory leader by a 54–35% margin.

Similar data on the period from 1973–74 show little change from the pattern of even distribution observable between 1969 and 1970 (Fig. 8.19). True, there was a slight Midlands bias by now, but more striking was the drop in his hitherto 'good' regions of Wales and the South-west. Unfortunately, M.O.R.I. surveys conducted during the 1975 referendum used non-comparable regional breakdowns. These results do show however that Powell fared 9% below average in Scotland, 1% below average in the Midlands, and 2% better than average in London and the South.

4. Sex

A considerable literature on sex differences in voting behaviour suggests that in Britain as elsewhere women tend to be more conservative than men.[24] Nevertheless Powell has almost always drawn more support from men than women. Examination of data for 1966 and 1967 shows that men outnumbered women among his supporters by 62–38% and 60–40% respectively.[25] This was hardly surprising – he was relatively obscure and, since women would appear to be less interested in politics than men, it is probable that fewer women than men were aware of his existence at all.

This argument receives some substantiation in the polls conducted after the 1968 Birmingham speech which achieved universal recognition for Powell. Even the most apolitical men or women could hardly be ignorant of his existence after April 1968. As Table 8.19 shows, although men gave him more support than women on every point, they retained their 3:2 proportions of 1966–67 only on the question of supporting Powell for the Tory leadership. Moreover, as Table 8.20 demonstrates, this sex difference vanished altogether in the following months. In fact

TABLE 8.19   Per cent of men and women agreeing with Powell's views disagreeing with his sacking and supporting him for the Tory leadership, Apr 1968

	All %	Men %	Women %
Agree with views (Gallup)	74	79	70
	(928)	(461)	(467)
Disagree with sacking (Gallup)	69	70	67
	(928)	(461)	(467)
Support for leadership (N.O.P.)	13	14	11
	(1930)	(900)	(1030)

Source: N.O.P. Poll 68016 supplied by the S.S.R.C. Survey Archive, University of Essex and Gallup Poll CQ576 supplied by Gallup Polls Ltd.

it becomes clear that the early defections from this early peak of Powell support was very heavily a male phenomenon. However, a reverse phenomenon appears in Table 8.21 suggesting that women defectors were simply moving away from Powell later than their male counterparts.

TABLE 8.20   Support for Powell for leadership of the opposition, by sex, Apr–July 1968

	All %	Men %	Women %
April 1968	24 (928)	29 (461)	19 (467)
July 1968	13 (917)	13 (436)	13 (480)
Change	(−11)	(−16)	(−6)

Source: Gallup Polls CQ576 and CQ585 supplied by Gallup Polls Ltd.

TABLE 8.21   Agreement with Powell's immigration views, by sex, Apr–Dec 1968

	All %	Men %	Women %
April 1968	74 (928)	79 (461)	70 (467)
December 1968	58 (924)	58 (457)	57 (467)
January 1970	48 (976)	55 (476)	41 (500)
Difference	(−26)	(−24)	(−29)

Source: Gallup Polls CQ576 and CQ607 supplied by Gallup Polls Ltd.

It was only when he was matched against Heath that he appeared to do better among women than among men. In both January and October 1969, Heath led Powell by 15% in polls on support for prime minister. Among men his lead over Powell was 17% while among women it was 13% and 14% respectively.

In the next period where data are available (1973–75) a clear male bias among Powellites is again evident (Table 8.22). By mid-1975 indeed the 3:2 masculine disproportion of the pre-1968 period had been re-established.

TABLE 8.22   Per cent of electorate saying Powell best represents their
views by sex, 1973–75

	All %	Men %	Women %
February 1973	25	27	23
	(2073)	(989)	(1084)
February 1974	16	18	14
	(1290)	(615)	(675)
July 1974	17	19	15
	(827)	(405)	(422)
June–July 1975	17	21	12
	(1596)	(774)	(777)

Source: M.O.R.I.

Therefore Powell never received the predominantly female support
typical of a 'normal' conservative following. Women did rally to him
for a time in numbers not far short of his male followers, and defected
from him more slowly, but ultimately moved away in larger numbers
than men. If feminine conservatism played any role in structuring his
support it seems to have been mainly in constraining women from the
support of a so clearly 'anti-Establishment' figure.

5. *Age*

Partisan attachments tend to harden and become firmer with age,
making older people generally less 'available' to third-party and extremist movements.[26] Younger voters on the other hand, with their partisan
attachments less clearly formed or confirmed, have frequently provided
disproportionate support for such movements.[27] It is for example very
clear that the S.N.P. in the 1970s has received much greater support
from younger Scots than it has from their elders.

Alternatively one might hypothesise that Powell was likely to be
strongest among the most elderly who, for all their firmer partisan
attachments, might have been expected to be more responsive than
others to a politician of his style and views. It is surely the elderly who
have the best-rooted connections with the age of British nationalism and
patriotism which he sought to re-kindle; who were liable to stronger
parochialist and 'Little Englander' responses; whose all-white England
had been most rudely changed by coloured immigration, and who were
often most vulnerably exposed in their social situations to bear the brunt
of such changes. Powell himself, after all, in almost his only appeal to a
specific social group, conjured up the image of the old lady harassed by
immigrant attentions.

Our data disappoint both these expectations. Powell, it seems clear, fared worst among both the youngest and most elderly electors, and has always been strongest among the middle-aged. A slight bias in this direction was clear even before 1968 (Table 8.23) but, as in the case of women, the figures are vulnerable to the argument that Powell was, among the young, suffering mainly from the ignorance of the pre-political.

TABLE 8.23   Support for Powell by age, 1965–67

	All %	16–24 %	25–34 %	35–44 %	45–64 %	65+ %
Those saying Powell one of the outstanding figures in Tory party (N.O.P. 1965)	7 (2108)	4 (91)	8 (360)	7 (445)	8 (839)	6 (373)

	All %	16–34 %	34–44 %	45–64 %	65+ %	
Those saying Powell one of first 3 men for Tory government (Gallup 1966)	4 (2131)	3 (671)	3 (423)	3 (725)	5 (308)	
Those saying Powell one of first 3 men for Tory government (Gallup 1967)	6 (2344)	6 (794)	6 (456)	7 (766)	5 (317)	

Source: N.O.P. Poll 65020 supplied by S.S.R.C. Survey Archive and the Roper Center, Williams College.

After the 1968 speech (Table 8.24) Powell was still clearly stronger with the middle-aged although, initially at least, the speech had the effect of evening out his support in the age groups (in much the same way that it had with the sexes). Even at his peak however he was a great deal less popular among the over-65s than among any other age group. And, as was the case with his women supporters, the initial fall-off in support was less pronounced in these marginal groups than amongst his strongest supporters.

But the pattern was also the same here as we found between the sexes, with a later wave of movement by 1970 producing the greatest defections in the 45–64 and post-65 groups. The result by 1970, as Fig. 8.20 shows,

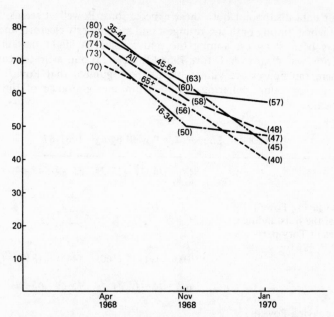

Note: Because of the way in which Gallup reports its figures it was impossible to separate the 16-24s from the 25-34s.

Source: Gallup Poll.

Fig. 8.20 Agreement with Powell's immigration views by age, 1968–70

TABLE 8.24 Support for Powell for leader of the opposition should Heath resign, by age, Apr–July 1968

	All %	*16–24* %	*25–34* %	*35–44* %	*45–64* %	*65+* %
Per cent Powell (N.O.P., April)	13 (1930)	10 (121)	12 (374)	13 (376)	14 (704)	11 (355)

	All %	*21–34* %	*35–44* %	*45–64* %	*65+* %
Per cent Powell (Gallup, April)	24 (928)	24 (292)	27 (171)	26 (317)	17 (148)
Per cent Powell (Gallup, July)	13 (917)	12 (281)	15 (171)	14 (317)	11 (148)

Source: N.O.P. Poll 68016 supplied by the S.S.R.C. Survey Archive, and Gallup Polls CQ576 and 585 supplied by Gallup Polls Ltd.

TABLE 8.25 Support for Powell by age, 1969–70

	All %	*16–24* %	*25–34* %	*35–44* %	*45–64* %	*65+* %
1969	23	16	22	30	24	27
	(1114)	(220)	(163)	(184)	(376)	(167)
1970	26	16	22	31	29	28
	(1267)	(192)	(204)	(204)	(446)	(220)

Source: Butler-Stokes Panel Study, 1969–70.

was to leave Powell weakest of all amongst the elderly and strikingly stronger among the 35–44 age group. Somewhat surprisingly, in view of our earlier data, the figure shows the steepest fall of all among the 45–64 age group. The Butler-Stokes data (Table 8.25) show in the same period a rather dissimilar pattern, with Powell actually gaining significantly *only* among the 45–64 age group. The over-65s in these surveys were also somewhat more favourable to him than our earlier data had suggested. Nonetheless the surveys agree in the general finding that he was strongest among the middle-aged and weakest among the young – by a factor of almost two in this latter survey.

The M.O.R.I. data for 1973–74 (Fig. 8.21) show the same 'ironing out' effect for age as they had on other variables. Nonetheless the relatively greater support among the middle-aged and weakest support among the elderly are still apparent.

We are now in a position to attempt to answer the question with which this chapter started, namely, who were, or are, the Powellites? If we amalgamate our findings we could say they were likely to be male, middle-aged, working-class Conservatives living in the Midlands or the South of England. Such a picture is misleading, however – our chief conclusion must be that the Powellites are distinctive for their lack of distinctiveness. We have noted disproportions in his support where they existed, but they are mainly very small. There is emphatically not a tightly self-contained, socially distinct or regionally concentrated constituency of Powellites. Inasmuch as Powell has been a national politician, addressing himself beyond class or regional issues and often going beyond party itself, he did indeed succeed to an astonishing extent in building a cross-party, inter-regional, cross-class following, a more truly national constituency than that possessed by any of the parties, the Liberals not excepted.

The major factors structuring Powell's support were class and party. Before 1968 his following was disproportionately middle- and even upper- middle class, cutting across party lines. After 1968 his base became more biased towards the working class and had a fairly heavy Conservative cast. His support largely mirrored the social profile of the electorate

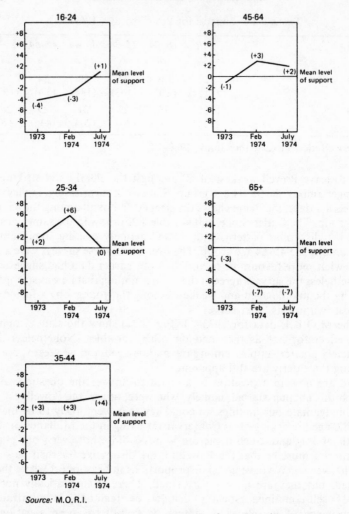

Fig. 8.21 Deviation of each age category from Powell's mean level of support 1973–74

as a whole, a finding notable on two counts. Conservative electoral support does not normally mirror the social profile of the electorate as Powell's following did. While the electorate as a whole is roughly two-thirds working and one-third middle class, the Conservative electorate is made up in roughly equal proportions of these two classes. Also it was not true that his racial appeals, implicit or explicit, raised the greatest echoes of support among the working class (as both popular mythology and a good deal of comparative sociological literature had led us to expect). He *did* receive a great deal of working-class support but no more proportionately than from other classes. On the other hand this finding contrasts sharply with the normal profile of social support for a British Conservative politician. The fact that he had picked up so much extra working-class support after 1968 and yet retained a strongly Conservative following suggests that he must have drawn a very large proportion of working-class Tories. In February 1973 (Table 8.10) no less than 28 % of both the C1 and C2 groups and 23 % of the DE groups said that Powell was the M.P. who best represented their views. Rough estimates suggest that no more than one-third of these groups normally vote Tory; even when we allow for the fact that some of these lower-strata supporters were Labour voters, his hold on working-class Conservatives was considerable. Indeed in the M.O.R.I. February 1973 survey a quarter of the electorate named him as the M.P. who best represented their views while a third of the working-class Tories selected him. But after June 1973 (and Powell's first hint of support for Labour) his following gradually took on a more heavily working-class and Labour complexion.

It is not surprising that Powell's constituency was not more distinct – it was simply too large for that to be probable after 1968. At his peak three-quarters of the electorate professed agreement with his views and a majority continued to do so for long periods. Five years after his 1968 bombshell no less than a fifth of the electorate wanted him to be prime minister. Moreover, his supporters were often enthusiasts – willing to write more than 200,000 letters of support after his sacking from the Shadow Cabinet in 1968, willing to demonstrate on his behalf and willing to write in sufficient numbers to swamp all other candidates in the B.B.C.'s 'Man of the Year' poll in 1972.

The question we must now address ourselves to is how and why did such people respond as they did: what *made* them Powellites?

9 Powellism as Mass Politics

At first blush the theory of mass politics would seem to provide a useful framework for explaining the growth of support for Enoch Powell. Although Hannah Arendt, Erich Fromm, Karl Mannheim and Robert Nisbet have used the mass society critique in their work, the classic account of the rise of extremist movements in terms of mass society theory is found in William Kornhauser's *The Politics of Mass Society*.[1] Kornhauser argues that the electorate becomes susceptible to extremist appeals as a result of a number of fundamental social changes. In particular, the development of mass society is identified with the weakening of voluntary associations and of primary group ties in the lives of the populace. Thus these groups and associations cease to fulfil either of their major functions – the provision of a crucial layer of insulation between the élite and the mass electorate, and the gratification of the populace's psychological needs.

When local associations and primary ties break down, mass theory holds that the political system is necessarily affected. The highly stratified authority system of liberal pluralist democracy, conceived of in the manner of Lipset and Schumpeter,[2] breaks down and a more egalitarian populist system develops. In such a society, 'élites are readily accessible to influence by non-élite and non-élites are readily available for mobilisation by élites'.[3] Thus in mass society one finds individual anxiety, the breakdown of primary social institutions, and a populist system. Kornhauser argues that mass theory leads to the expectation that 'the unattached and alienated of all classes are more attracted to extremist symbols and leaders than all their class-rooted counterparts'.[4] One can thus assume that the strongest response to extremist politics will come from those with the weakest attachments to class organisations or social groupings.

Mass theory has proved helpful in explaining why an earlier movement of the British radical right, Mosleyism, failed to gain a significant base of support during the 1930s. To be sure, mass theory is not the only approach that has been used to explain why fascism did not develop a large base in Britain.[5] But the argument was accorded a prominent role by one of the foremost students of British fascism, Robert Benewick.[6] He has argued that the strong class ties of the electorate to the political parties – particularly of working people to the Labour party and the trade unions – made the development of fascism very difficult. Pluralist institutions were well developed and acted as a buffer between the state and the individual. It is worthwhile to quote from him at some length because his argument is almost a textbook application of mass theory:[7]

> It emerged that there was not a large reservoir of socially isolated, economically depressed and politically frustrated people from whom the fascists could recruit. The established political parties were able to organise and hold the discontented, for the accepted channels for economic and political action were still open and accessible. The state was neither omnipotent nor remote, for the institutional pluralism of British society provided a buffer as well as a link between the state and the individual.
>
> There was also a pluralism of loyalties which meant that interests were represented and loyalties engaged elsewhere. A worker who was a member of a trade union might not have been an active member but he was loyal in that he looked to the trade union to protect his interests. It is also possible that the British class structure militated against the fascist movement. It provided a focal point for loyalty and identification and had thrown up it own organisations to protect its interests. Fascism's ultimate dilemma was the presence of a sense of community which at one and the same time contained and was nurtured by competing interests and loyalties.

Work on post-war British politics has emphasised three aspects of the system which mass theories would argue tend to dampen extremist tendencies. First, many commentators, especially those contrasting America and Britain, have emphasised the hierarchical Burkean nature of the Parliamentary system, serving to insulate the élite from mass influence. Second, many commentators have argued that the British are a deferential people willing to accept the dictates of their leadership. Finally, the strong class basis of the British system has been cited as a possible reason why the mass public has not been available for mobilisation by alternative 'extreme' political élites.

The combination of these habits of deference with the strong integration of the population into class-based politics and organisations thus produces an electorate tied by strong loyalties to their established political élites whom they allow (as McKenzie's analysis of British political parties shows) a considerable freedom of manoeuvre in decision-making.[8]

The point has been very fully and bluntly made by Daniel Bell in his attempt to explain why the McCarthy phenomenon in the U.S.A. had no real British analogue:[9]

> In the élite structure of British politics, control is not in the constituences (or as here among the hundreds of local political bosses who have to be dealt into the game) but in the small parliamentary

caucuses, which have a legal as well as historical independence from mass party control. The British political élite, wedded to a politics of civility, tend to dampen any extremism within the top political structure, while the control system keeps the masses outside and makes it difficult for them to be mobilised for direct pressure on the government.

Other American commentators have tended to concur, suggesting that the climate of public tolerance which has distinguished the British political scene perhaps owes less to any intrinsic traits of national character than to the combination of the Labour party's strong social control over working-class voters and a traditional accordance of privacy and deference to established élites. Latent public intolerance is thereby simply muted and muffled.[10]

Accounting in terms for this comparatively strong tradition of privacy and secrecy in Britain, Edward Shils concludes that the 'magic of secrecy in Britain rests on hierarchy, deference and self-content'.[11] Almond and Verba came to similar conclusions in their monumental *Civic Culture*, finding in their British-American comparisons a predominance of passive over active roles in the former case. They conclude that, 'In Britain the persistently deferential and subject orientation fosters the development of strong and effective government and the maintenance of an efficient and independent state.'[12]

Against this background the widespread support gained by Enoch Powell, popularly, at least, acknowledged as an 'extremist', poses a major set of problems which seem susceptible to explanation within the 'mass society' framework. It is not difficult to piece together the main lines of such an argument: class-based organisations – parties and trade unions alike – have lost to a considerable degree the hold over the electorate they enjoyed during the 1930s; party organisations themselves have declined drastically at the local level. There has been a parallel decline in deference towards established political leaders and institutions, and with this decline has come a new populist orientation in the electorate. The path has thus been cleared for the rise of figures such as Powell.

Whatever the relevance of mass society theory to the explanation of Powellism, it is worth laying out the evidence which can be marshalled behind these points, for it collectively provides a valuable contextual framework within which to view the rise of Powellism. Evidence of the decline of the class alignment in British electoral politics has been provided mainly in the work of Richard Rose.[13] Rose's A.I.D. analyses of Gallup polls indicate a continuing decline in the ability of social characteristics and particularly occupational class to structure partisanship.[14]

Butler and Stokes in their second edition of *Political Change in*

TABLE 9.1 Amount of variance explained by social structural variables, class and trade union membership, 1959–70

	Social structural variables %	*Class* %	*Trade union membership* %
1959	21·8	12·5	3·8
1964	20·6	11·5	3·2
1966	18·1	1·7	3·4
1970	12·0	—	3·3

Source: Richard Rose, *The Problem of Party Government*, p. 48.

Britain concur with the finding that there is a declining relationship between class and party.[15] They suggest a variety of possible reasons for this development: the less intense class content of politics in the 1960s; the increasing youth of the electorate; and Labour's efforts to move away from its close ties with the unions and the increasing social convergence in patterns of élite recruitment by the parties. At the very least these factors have produced less stable (and less intense) relations between class and party and have ushered in an era of greater volatility in public opinion, not only in the polls but in a whole series of election results, particularly at the local level and in by-elections. By 1973 these prognostications had been largely confirmed in the huge electoral surge towards the Liberals and Nationalist third parties, a movement not susceptible to explanation in terms of the class alignment.

The decline of local party constituency associations is also clear – they have suffered large losses in membership and a continuing fall in the number of party agents. Enoch Powell's comment after the 1964 election that the Conservative party 'in many constituencies is represented by a couple of dowdy rooms and an ill-paid agent' probably applies equally well to the Labour party.[16] Rose's data show that only about 5% of the electorate belong to a political party. In terms of individual rather than trade union membership, the Labour party – which makes the most explicit class appeals – has only one-fifth the Tory membership.[17]

There is also a considerable recent literature suggesting that deference is a waning aspect of British political culture. Bob Jessop, after a careful examination of categorisation of deferential attitudes in Britain, found that deference in any tightly defined sense (regarding the 'socially ascribed élite' as being uniquely qualified for political office, or the holding of exaggerated respect for the high-born and wealthy) was both extremely limited in its incidence and in its power to explain voting behaviour. Only a third very general type of deference – involving acceptance of the traditional 'social and moral order' – appeared to have any clear relationship with Tory voting and even this form of tradition-alism fell far short of explaining all the variance in partisan choice.[18] Not surprisingly, Butler and Stokes among others have argued that this concept of deference is too all-embracing to be useful in the analysis of political behaviour.

Another recent critique of the concept of deference by Dennis Kavanagh has gone further, questioning its continuing utility as a term of analysis.[19] Moreover there is evidence that the number of working-class people who vote for the Conservatives for deferential reasons are declining relative to secular or pragmatic Tory voters.[20] Rose has speculated indeed whether it is still useful to speak about the deferential working-class Tory. His analysis of the 1970 Gallup data shows that working-class Conservatives are more accurately regarded as a cross-section of Tory supporters rather than as an isolated social group. They are no more or less deferential than other voters. Rose found a plurality of British voters in 1970 believing that the best leaders were found in the Labour and not the Conservative party. The upper middle class showed the highest regard for the Conservative leadership, while manual voters favoured Labour's leaders. Rose suggested that the pattern here reveals not deference but the simple fact that voters pre-ferred political leaders who were similar to them. Only an insignificant proportion of Labour voters preferred Tory leaders.[21]

Kavanagh in his critique also questioned how far the strong govern-ment/apathetic population analysis goes in explaining recent British political history, citing the strength of pressure groups, trade unions and public opinion in the post-war period as phenomena hardly conson-ant with such a picture. The British public, and particularly the working class, he argues, places a high regard on its ability to influence Govern-ment policy and has higher rates of political participation than the populations of most other countries. Kavanagh suggests that Almond and Verba's Anglo-American comparisons of political culture are in this sense misleading. The British may be passive in comparison to the Americans, but in contrast with the Mexicans, the Italians and the Germans they are activist.

Both academic and non-academic commentators, sensing a waning in deferential attitudes, spoke of a new wave of populism in the British body politic.[22] Voters were increasingly demanding more control over party and Government policy: there was a heightened awareness of the gap between mass and élite attitudes, the feeling that 'no one in Government represents my views' had become both widespread and very strong. These factors, themselves perhaps partly born of the failure of either party to solve the country's major problems, created a climate of scepti-cism, even disillusion, about political leaders and parties in general.

One study of the influence of public opinion on politicians has noted that 'the deferential politician seems to be well on the way to replacing the deferential voter'.[23] In the view of the author, Rudolf Klein, government is increasingly becoming a job of trying to respond to public opinion, rather than winning consent from the public. Klein notes that Government reports and Royal Commissions have begun recommending that attempts should be made to measure public opinion before decisions are taken. The decision to hold a referendum on Common Market membership was, in this view, merely an extension of such trends.

Within both major political parties have come calls for more influence over party policy. The assertiveness of the left wing of the Labour party has been well documented and needs no further discussion here. There have also been quieter rumblings within the Conservative party. After complaints that the selection of prospective M.P.s was carried out too secretly, two constituency associations in 1969 opened the selection process to a democratic vote of all dues-paying members of the association.[24] Even the Tory party conference – hitherto the scene of sedate and stage-managed demonstrations of support for the leadership – began to know stormier days in the 1960s.

A mass society theorist would also doubtless make much of the famous studies of the affluent workers of Luton to suggest that large segments of the new working class and white-collar workers are susceptible to extremist political behaviour. A brief review of accounts by Goldthorpe, Lockwood and others of the new life-styles reveals a close convergence with the ideal type of the people Kornhauser believed were most likely to respond to extreme appeals.[25] The workers had a strong and uncomplicated economic pragmatism; many had been willing to incur grave dislocation of their kinship networks in order to come to Luton at all; their life-style was privatised, with social life centred on the home and immediate family; there was little workplace fraternisation and little activity in social organisations. Union membership remained high because it provided specific benefits, not because the union was perceived as a social or political institution. White-collar workers in Luton had also developed privatised life-styles to the point where they and manual workers lived in 'near isolation' with their families.[26] Little class or status consciousness was manifested. Whatever sort of hierarchy that was perceived was based on monetary criteria.

The authors of the Luton study offer two hypotheses as to the implications of these new life-styles for political attitudes. Workers might develop conservative and individualistic tendencies or they would become alienated and dissatisfied and be susceptible to some mass political activity.[27] The first alternative is dismissed on the grounds that the workers had not broken away from the Labour party or their trade unions. While those ties may now be more instrumental than they once were, no swing to the right was perceptible. Their discussion of alienation theories is limited to those of the Left – Marx, Gorz and

Mallet – whose arguments all derive from a consideration of the worker's reaction to his job and the workplace atmosphere. To rebut them, Goldthorpe, Lockwood and others suggest that the affluent worker is willing to accept dull, boring jobs as a necessary evil to the primary end of making money. Thus, because of economic instrumentalism – plus sheer inertia – they retain their loose but overwhelming support for the Labour party. A possibility not voiced – though one clearly compatible with their findings – is that Conservative attitudes on non-economic issues could easily co-exist with vaguely Labour attitudes on economic questions.[28] Workers could, in short, support Powell over immigration and still maintain their links to the Labour party and trade unions. Partisan choice is not unidimensional and in certain circumstances non-economic issues can clearly influence political behaviour. It is strange that the only theories of radicalism which Goldthorpe and his co-authors take into account are those associated with the left, although the mass society critique, centring not on workplace frustrations but on mass life-styles, meshes very closely with their picture of the affluent workers of Luton.

Thus, the critique of Britain as a mass society is complete: People are more isolated, belong to fewer organisations, are less deferential and more distrustful of Government. How far, though, does Kornhauser's analysis of the roots of extremist movements find substantiation in an examination of the Powellites? Are Powell's supporters concentrated disproportionately in any isolated area, such as the countryside? Second, are they weaker class-identifiers than the rest of the population? Third, do they show any less tendency to join voluntary associations, participate in politics or join trade unions? Finally, do they have any tendency to be weaker identifiers with the major parties than the rest of the electorate?

In fact our data show that on every index of isolation, participation and class identification the Powellites are either very similar to the whole electorate or, apparently, better integrated. They have maintained a strong interest in politics – indeed it was precisely for this reason that Powell's early supporters were particularly disturbed by the direction British politics took during the 1960s and 1970s. As will be shown in the next chapter, concern over immigration was essential in forging Powell's initial constituency. However, the reaction was probably as intense as it was precisely because his supporters were not isolated, detached and aimless individuals. Rather they were intensely interested and involved participants.

A review of the data on the geographical distribution of Powellites has already shown (chapter 8) that they have never been concentrated disproportionately in one part of the country. If anything, there was a slight tendency for Powell's support to be slightly weaker in rural and outlying areas than in urban areas.

On two other indices of isolation, the Powellites are very similar to the whole electorate. An N.O.P. survey in October 1969 showed that car ownership (a key index of mobility and ability to sustain widespread social networks) was slightly higher (at 56%) among Powellite house-holds than among the population at large (53%). On another potential index of social integration, telephone ownership, the 1969 wave of the Butler-Stokes survey showed that 36% of Powellites owned a telephone, as against 34% of the electorate as a whole. Since the Powellites in the 1969 wave of the Butler-Stokes data were strong Tory supporters, controls were employed to determine whether Powellites were less likely to own phones when class and party were held constant. When the controls were applied, no significant difference emerged.

When we turn to voluntary association membership – viewed by mass theorists as a key index of both participation and integration – we again find Powellites undistinctive. Questions about voluntary association membership, using three sets of criteria to define 'activism', were posed to respondents in the three waves of the M.O.R.I. panel study. The results are summarised in Table 9.2.

TABLE 9.2   Activism in politics and voluntary associations, 1973–74

	All %	*Feb 1973* *Powell-ites* %	*Non-Powell-ites* %	*All* %	*Feb 1974* *Powell-ites* %	*Non-Powell-ites* %	*All* %	*July 1974* *Powell-ites* %	*Non-Powell-ites* %
% activist	7 (2073)	6 (521)	7 (1552)	22 (1290)	22 (285)	22 (1085)	26 (827)	30 (140)	25 (687)

Source: M.O.R.I.

If we break down the M.O.R.I. data (Table 9.3) to examine the separate indices of group activity, we not only find that Powellites were generally as active as the rest of the electorate, but they were significantly more so in the field of trade union affairs. Not only were Powellites more likely than others to belong to a trade union but Powellite trade unionists were more active in their unions than were trade unionists as a whole. This finding is confirmed by the 1970 wave of the Butler-Stokes data, with Powellites more likely than the rest of the electorate to belong to unions, even though they gave a disproportionate amount of support to the Conservatives. This relationship remained unchanged when party and class were held constant. Particularly noteworthy was the high level of trade union membership of Labour and DE Powellites.

Calculating backwards from these figures we find that 28% of all trade unionists in the 1970 Butler-Stokes sample who rated Powell supported him (as against 26% of all respondents) while in 1973, 28% of all trade unionists were Powellites (as against 25% of all M.O.R.I. respondents).

TABLE 9.3   Political activity and voluntary association membership
of Powell's supporters, 1973

	All electors %	Powell's supporters %	Non-Powellites %
Presented views to local councillor	11	9	12
Written letter to an editor	5	6	5
Urged someone else to vote	17	16	17
Urged someone to get in touch with M.P.	16	17	16
Made speech before organised group	7	8	7
Elected officer of organisation	13	12	13
Stood for public office	0	1	0
Took active part in political campaign	4	2	5
Helped in any fund-raising activity	74	72	75
Voted in last council election	58	59	58
Been to local political party meeting	7	7	7
Member of trade union	26	29	25
Been to trade union meeting	16	20	16
Been to interest group meeting	17	16	17
Taken part in demonstration/ sit-in	5	6	5
None of these	12	12	12
	(2073)	(521)	(1552)

Source: M.O.R.I Panel Study, 1973.

Nor do Powellites appear to be weaker class identifiers than the rest of the electorate. In 1969 41% of the Powellites in the Butler-Stokes panel said they thought of themselves in class terms while the figure for all respondents was only 36%. By 1970 this gap had vanished, with 42% of the Powellites and 43% of the sample saying they thought of themselves in class terms, but again the data hardly support the hypothesis that Powellites were more detached than others from their social classes.

On the other hand Powellite consciousness of class did not imply a class conflict model. Fifty-three per cent of the Powellites in the 1970 Butler-Stokes sample said that class differences were not wide while only 43% of all respondents thought similarly. By a 63%–55% margin Powellites were also more convinced than others that social class differences

TABLE 9.4 Trade union membership of Powell supporters, 1970

	All %	*AB* %	*C1* %	*C2* %	*DE* %	*Con.* %	*Lab.* %	*Liberal/ other* %
Per cent of all voters in trade unions	41 (762)	26 (124)	24 (152)	49 (288)	52 (188)	26 (266)	56 (269)	32 (55)
Per cent of Powellites in trade unions	43 (207)	26 (27)	20 (45)	49 (85)	61 (46)	28 (101)	62 (52)	20 (10)
Per cent of non-Powellites in trade unions	40 (555)	26 (97)	25 (107)	28 (203)	49 (142)	26 (165)	55 (217)	35 (45)

Source: Butler-Stokes Panel Study, 1970.

were narrowing. Equal percentages of Powellites and non-Powellites (63%) said that the classes in Britain could get along.

It is more difficult to test hypotheses that Powellites were more or less deferential than others. As Kavanagh has shown, there are many different ways to define the concept and many different empirical tests may be used to measure it. Moreover the statistical tests are subject to differing interpretations. For example, support for high-status leaders may simply reflect the electorate's trust in people with good education rather than any degree of deference to an élite. Thus one must proceed cautiously in trying to evaluate this hypothesis. On one measure of deference – attitudes to the Royal family – the Powellites in all groups appeared to be more deferential than the electorate. As Table 9.5 shows, the difference was most particularly striking in the DE social group and among those not supporting any of the three major parties (groups with a considerable overlap).

On the other hand Powellites were less likely than others to accept the dictates of their political leaders passively. Market & Opinion Research International found that in 1973 78% of all respondents, 76% of non-Powellites but 83% of Powellites agreed that they did not have enough to say in Government decisions. The February 1974 wave of the M.O.R.I. panel study found that 71% of the electorate, 70% of non-Powellites but 74% of Powellites felt they were capable of exercising more responsibility than they were allowed. During the E.E.C. referendum M.O.R.I. found Powellites less likely than others to accept the judgement of their political leaders on most questions. For example,

TABLE 9.5 Attitudes towards Royal family by class and party, 1969

	All %	*AB* %	*C1* %	*C2* %	*DE* %	*Con.* %	*Lab.* %	*Lib.* %	*Other* %
Per cent of sample saying Royal family very important	54 (1094)	59 (168)	58 (230)	50 (381)	54 (245)	67 (459)	48 (346)	52 (97)	34 (184)
Per cent of Powellites saying Royal family very important	62 (258)	67 (30)	65 (60)	55 (93)	68 (71)	69 (151)	53 (58)	53 (17)	45 (31)
Per cent of non-Powellites saying Royal family very important	52 (832)	57 (138)	55 (170)	48 (288)	50 (224)	66 (308)	47 (288)	51 (80)	32 (153)

Source: Butler-Stokes Panel Study, 1969.

71% of the electorate, 68% of non-Powellites but 83% of Powellites agreed that there should have been a referendum before Britain entered the Common Market in the first place.

The data therefore are somewhat contradictory on deference. In a sense the section above raises questions about the utility of the standard twofold scheme of classification developed by McKenzie and Silver,[29] of traditionalists and secular pragmatists. Powellites, to the extent that they differed from others, might be typified as assertive traditionalists.

Probably the most serious deficiencies in the mass society critique with regard to Powellism lie in its assumptions about their political activity and interest. According to mass theory, one would expect that Powellites would be the least informed, least interested members of the electorate. In fact the opposite appears to be the case, as Tables 9.6 and 9.7 show very clearly.[30]

Moreover the Powellites were stronger identifiers with the major parties than the whole electorate. Forty-nine per cent of 1970 Powellites identified very strongly with one of the major parties while only 42% of the whole sample had similarly strong party ties. The 1974 data show that identical proportions of Powellites, non-Powellites and all respondents (30%) identified very strongly with one of the political parties. It is still possible of course that the theory is of some value but that our

TABLE 9.6   Political interest of Powellites, 1969–74

	1969			1970			1974		
	All	Powell-ites	Non-Powell-ites	All	Powell-ites	Non-Powell-ites	All	Powell-ites	Non-Powell-ites
Per cent which follow politics in press	43 (779)	49 (194)	41 (585	71* (1266)	73* (331)	70 (935)	50 (1094)	52 (269)	49 (825)
Per cent which follow politics on television	49 (1091)	57 (260)	47 (831)	65 (1266)	73 (331)	65 (935)	58 (1096)	65 (270)	48 (826)
Per cent which follow politics on radio	17 (1092)	17 (259)	16 (833)	25 (1264)	28 (330)	23 (934)		(not asked)	
Per cent with good deal of interest in politics	17 (1095)	22 (260)	15 (835)	38 (1265)	47 (331)	34 (934)	53 (1096)	53 (270)	53 (826)
Per cent which care a good deal who wins	66 (1099)	80 (260)	62 (839)	68 (1265)	76 (331)	69 (934)	75 (1095)	77 (270)	74 (825)

Source: Butler-Stokes Panel Study, 1969–74.
* The question in 1970 was changed to "Do you read a morning paper?"

empirical tests are inadequate. As Wolfinger has asked in a study of the radical right in California, can group memberships be used as an index of class attachment? That is, can one really say that people without formal group memberships are less class-rooted than people who belong to six or seven organisations?[31] Is membership in a local association evidence that an individual is well integrated? These are questions that our relatively straightforward empirical tests cannot hope to answer.

It may be indeed that group membership is not, or is no longer, an indicator of social integration. Perhaps compulsive 'joiners' of civic associations and clubs do so because of unsatisfying home and family lives. People with high levels of group memberships might actually be the least well integrated members of society. Also, more fundamental arguments could be made about the changing nature of voluntary association membership. In terms of aggregate figures, membership in virtually all intermediate associations has increased since 1945. These increases may have nothing to do with social integration. People may have joined trade unions and pressure groups for purely instrumental reasons (i.e. achieving a specific goal such as winning higher wages) which have little to do with their personal lives. Nor do high levels of group membership and activity necessarily imply that people feel strong commitments to the institutions and associations they belong to. The Butler-Stokes data provide some evidence for the last point. Despite the Powellites' higher levels of trade union membership and activity, they were more likely than non-Powellites to say that unions had too much

TABLE 9.7 Political interest of Powellites and non-Powellites by party and class, 1970

	AB %	C1 %	C2 %	DE %	Con. %	Lab. %	Lib./ other %
Follow election on T.V.							
Per cent of all respondents	71 (219)	70 (255)	66 (455)	64 (306)	74 (471)	70 (437)	63 (104)
Per cent of Powellites	83 (48)	67 (72)	71 (132)	75 (69)	79 (168)	75 (77)	71 (21)
Per cent of non-Powellites	68 (171)	72 (183)	74 (323)	60 (237)	72 (303)	68 (360)	71 (83)
Read morning paper							
Per cent of all respondents	79 (219)	71 (255)	72 (455)	66 (306)	74 (471)	72 (438)	70 (104)
Per cent of Powellites	79 (48)	68 (72)	74 (132)	75 (69)	71 (168)	81 (71)	62 (21)
Per cent of non-Powellites	79 (171)	73 (183)	71 (323)	63 (237)	76 (303)	70 (361)	72 (83)
Follow campaign on radio							
Per cent of all respondents	34 (218)	32 (255)	19 (454)	21 (306)	29 (469)	24 (437)	21 (104)
Per cent of Powellites	38 (47)	42 (72)	21 (132)	19 (69)	35 (167)	20 (77)	19 (21)
Per cent of non-Powellites	32 (171)	28 (183)	18 (322)	22 (237)	26 (302)	24 (360)	22 (83)
Talk to others about election							
Per cent of all respondents	79 (219)	69 (255)	71 (453)	66 (306)	75 (470)	73 (436)	67 (104)
Per cent of Powellites	71 (48)	75 (72)	76 (132)	78 (69)	79 (168)	74 (77)	67 (21)
Per cent of non-Powellites	81 (171)	66 (183)	70 (321)	62 (237)	73 (302)	73 (359)	67 (83)
Good deal of interest in campaign							
Per cent of all respondents	59 (219)	43 (254)	31 (455)	32 (306)	50 (470)	39 (437)	27 (104)
Per cent of Powellites	69 (48)	49 (72)	38 (132)	42 (69)	57 (168)	44 (77)	29 (21)
Per cent of non-Powellites	57 (171)	41 (182)	28 (321)	29 (237)	46 (302)	38 (360)	26 (83)

Source: Butler-Stokes Panel Study, 1970.

power in society. Among trade unionists the differences between Powellites and non-Powellites were particularly striking (Table 9.8). Powellites, then were seemingly both more active in and more alienated from trade unions than non-Powellites. Clearly membership and activity in unions do not necessarily imply a positive commitment to the role they play in society. This evidence would seem to suggest that a model of group memberships and activity necessarily demonstrating social integration is probably too simple.

It is also possible that mass conditions do not in and of themselves lead to extremist political behaviour. David Riesman and C. Wright

TABLE 9.8   Attitudes to trade union power of Powellites and non-Powellites by trade union membership, 1969–70

	1969					
	All %	Powellites %	Non-Powellites %	All TUs %	Powellite TUs %	Non-Powellite TUs %
Trade unions Have too much power	62	70	59	47	56	44
Don't have too much power	28	21	30	47	39	50
Don't know	10	9	11	6	5	6
	100	100	100	100	100	100
	(688)	(160)	(528)	(249)	(57)	(192)
	1970					
	All %	Powellites %	Non-Powellites %	TUs %	Powellite TUs %	Non-Powellite TUs %
Trade unions Have too much power	65	76	61	49	64	43
Don't have too much power	28	19	31	44	31	50
Don't know	7	5	8	7	5	7
	100	100	100	100	100	100
	(758)	(206)	(552)	(310)	(87)	(223)

Source: Butler-Stokes Panel Study, 1969–70.

Mills have both suggested that mass conditions may lead to conformity and passivity rather than political extremism.[32] Edward Shils has also denied that mass culture leads to militancy and has stressed the positive qualities of mass society.[33] Joseph Gusfield has gone further still, indicating that mass society may help prevent extreme movements from developing.[34] In this view mass society provides sources of 'supra local' institutional links. People may thus become attached to a national culture and not be isolated from major social and political changes. Mass culture therefore can enhance the possiblity of consensus because the issues open for political conflict are limited to intensity and scope since people have similar interests, outlooks and backgrounds. Groups are not isolated in mass society in the way that small-town racists in the American South were during the 1960s or rural Nazis during the 1920s and 1930s.[35] Mass society actually may increase the links between groups, maximising the possibility that individuals will be cross-pressured, and thus leading them to be less inclined to pursue single ends to extreme conclusions.

Such points suggest very major revisions – indeed almost total inversions – of the original mass society theory of Kornhauser, and need not detain us here. What does seem clear is that the theory in its present form can hardly explain or even accommodate the phenomenon of Powellism.

10 Powellism as Status Politics

The critique of 'extremist' movements offered by Kornhauser and other 'mass society' theorists has, as we have suggested, important differences from other epiphenomenal approaches to the study of political movements: it offers a sweeping contextual theory of social development and is more ambivalent in its epiphenomenalism. More thorough-going in their epiphenomenalism but less ambitious in their theoretical 'reach' are the various theories attributing political extremism to a variety of possible changes in class position and social status. While the Kornhauserian view seeks to explain extremism by reference to a theory which posits a global change in the whole nature of a society, these latter theories seek more medium-range explanations by reference to intrasociety changes. Four particular hypotheses are apparent, relating political extremism respectively to social mobility (up or down); status inconsistency; economic insecurity; and relative deprivation. In this chapter we shall examine the applicability of each of these approaches to the phenomenon of Powellism.

1. SOCIAL MOBILITY

Students of social mobility have argued that rising or falling in the social hierarchy leads to alterations in an individual's entire political outlook and social life. For example social mobility has been related to increases in rates of mental illness and suicide.[1] It has also been related to the growth of extremist political tendencies – be they of the left or the right.

Probably the most inclusive theory of the effect of social mobility on political attitudes comes from Seymour Martin Lipset and Hans L. Zetterberg.[2] With regard to upward mobility they argue that in countries where shifts from one class to another entail major alterations in lifestyles, people are likely to retain links to their class of origin. However, in countries with a relatively fluid social structure, like America, people will tend to identify with the class they move into. Because the upwardly mobile often suffer status rejection and discrimination, skilled workers in highly stratified countries like Germany and Sweden were found to identify intensely with the working class. Hence they actually developed more radical ideologies than those who remained in the manual stratum.

However, Lipset and Zetterberg found that in countries where class divisions were not so intense, skilled workers experienced less resentment when they advanced to the middle class. Hence they become more conservative than those below them.[3] Unfortunately Lipset and Zetterberg present no data on Britain except to point out that skilled workers there were more conservative than unskilled workers. The presumable inference that the class system in Britain is more open than that of Germany and Sweden is not argued by Lipset, who gives prominence instead to the notion of continuing deference to an élite in explaining the relative conservatism of the British working-class.[4] While Britain emphasises achievement and egalitarianism in its economic and political life, the class system is characterised by ascription, élitism and particularism. According to the basic Lipset-Zetterberg thesis, these elements of the British class system should encourage leftism in the upwardly mobile. However, because of the lingering power of deference, Lipset suggested that the British working-class has been willing to accept an ascriptive class system. Working-class people have no strong desire to attain élite status and are relatively content with the system. Thus they are willing to give support to the Conservative party.

As we have seen, the more recent literature on deference and the British social structure raises doubt about the continued validity of this approach. A perhaps more plausible theme in much recent British social comment and analysis has been one of increasing social fluidity with the shrinkage of income, status and life-style differences between the manual and non-manual workers.[5] One recent investigator has suggested that it is useful now to concieve of British society in terms of three strata – an upper class, a working class and a broad middle, encompassing clerical non-manuals and skilled members of the working-class.[6] We may certainly accept that something of the sort has been happening without necessarily having to embrace the (largely discredited) theories of the *embourgeoisement* of the working-class. This process has probably gone less far and less fast in Britain than in America. The very gradualness of the process is such that one would expect upwardly mobiles to become extreme conservatives unless altogether new frustrations arose out of their changed life-styles and expectations or unless they were led to experience strong resentment in their actual pursuit of middle-class life-styles. There is strong American evidence of such groups – the 'new rich' of Texas oilmen, for example – reacting to such resentment by turning sharply rightward.[7]

The available literature does not seem to indicate that upward mobility in Britain has made people more prone to extremist activity, though it does indicate that they have become more conservative in their partisan choice.[8] There is no suggestion in the literature that the British middle-class has strongly resisted the upwardly mobile. In fact the relative openness of the British élite has been offered as one of the possible reasons why facism did not gain a foothold in Britain.[9] On the other hand the idea that the upwardly mobile working class had an intense desire to 'become middle class' has been largely discredited. There has been no suggestion that the upwardly mobile from the British working class possessed attributes similar to these possessed by the people who, as Bell and his associates suggested, offered support to Joseph McCarthy in America.[10] Status anxiety of the dimensions found by some political sociologists in America does not seem to have an important force in the British social structure, or at least British political sociologists have not found it to be so.

The other direction of social mobility – downwards – has generally been assumed to be a source of political conservatism, in Britain and elsewhere.[11] The simplest explanation for the pronounced conservatism of the downwardly mobile is that they continue to identify with the party dominant within their former class. They are thus more conservative than most members of the class they formerly belonged to. Downward mobility often entails a loss of status and people undergoing such changes often turn to the radical right as a means of seeking to preserve their position in society. As Lipset and Raab note:[12] 'If there has been one constant, it has been the perception of extreme rightist movements as those which have risen primarily in reaction against the displacement of power accompanying change.'

The view that extremist movements rise primarily in reaction to the displacement of power and status has been used to explain the emergence of the radical right in America as well as the Nazis in Germany.[13] Runciman also speculated that the upward mobility of British manual workers might cause similar frustrations to develop amongst British clerical workers who felt that their position in the social hierarchy was thereby threatened.[14]

Mobility can be measured in a number of different ways. One can examine the respondents' class position at two different points using standard market research class divisions based on occupation. Or one can use the evaluations of class position that the respondent himself offers. Or one may compare the respondents' class position to that of their parents. The Butler-Stokes data provide a means of relating a number of these tests of mobility to support for Powell (defined here as giving him a 78–100 rating on a 100-point scale).

Tables 10.1 and 10.2 below show that there was in fact no consistent relationship between mobility and support for Powell in either 1969 or 1970. True, 1969 respondents who showed the greatest degree of downward mobility gave Powell his highest level of support, but this finding is reversed in the 1970 wave, where downwardly mobiles gave Powell as much support as the non-mobiles. Also those who dropped from the middle class to the skilled working class in 1969 gave Powell less support than those who remained working class. The slightly upwardly mobile from the working class to the lower middle class in both years gave Powell higher levels of support than those who had remained in the working class since their childhood. But 1969 respondents who showed the greatest degree of upward mobility (moving from the working class to the upper middle class) were less likely to support Powell than people who were born in the working class and subsequently became skilled members of the manual stratum (C2s). Also 1970 respondents who moved from the working class to the upper middle class offered Powell less support than those who were consistently middle class. The 1974 data (Table 10.3) show a very powerful relationship between upward mobility and support for Powell. But there were virtually no differences between mobile and non-mobile working-class respondents.

TABLE 10.1   The effect of social mobility on support for Powell: present class position by recollection of class when young, 1969

	Present class position†			
	AB	C1	C2	DE
	Per cent for	Per cent for	Per cent for	Per cent for
Class when young*	Powell	Powell	Powell	Powell
Middle	15 (75)	20 (74)	18 (60)	47 (30)
			downwardly mobile	
	upwardly mobile			
Working	23 (84)	29 (141)	26 (318)	22 (261)

* Based on respondent's subjective categorisation.
† Based on respondent's occupation.

Source: Butler-Stokes Panel Study, 1969.

The Butler-Stokes data also allow us to push the analysis of mobility back a generation, comparing respondents' social positions with those of their fathers' when *they* were young. In 1969 (Table 10.4) those showing the most extreme degrees of downward mobility were once again the most prone to give support to Powell. However, the downwardly mobile were not uniformly higher in their levels of support for him than the non-mobiles. For example, those with fathers originally (at least) from the middle class, who themselves had gone into the lower middle class, were more likely to back him than those children of middle-class fathers who themselves dropped into the skilled manual stratum. Among those respondents with working-class fathers, people who

TABLE 10.2   The effect of social mobility on support for Powell:
present class position by recollection of class
when young, 1970

	Present class position†			
	AB	C1	C2	DE
	Per cent	Per cent	Per cent	Per cent
	for	for	for	for
Class when young*	Powell	Powell	Powell	Powell
Middle	22	27	27	20
	(50)	(37)	(30)	(15)
			downwardly mobile	
Working	upwardly mobile		26	21
	17	29	(156)	(102)
	(47)	(75)		

* Based on respondent's subjective categorisation.
† Based on respondent's occupation.

Source: Butler-Stokes Panel Study, 1970.

TABLE 10.3   The effect of social mobility on support for Powell:
present class position by recollection of class
when young, 1974

| | Present class position† | | | |
Class when young*	AB	C1	C2	DE
Middle	13	12	27	29
	(60)	(89)	(34)	(38)
Working	22	24	27	30
	(87)	(190)	(373)	(198)

* Based on respondent's subjective categorisation.
† Based on respondent's occupation.

Source: Butler-Stokes Panel Study, 1974.

remained in the skilled working class actually gave Powell more support
than those who were upwardly mobile.

Analysis of the 1970 data (Table 10.5) again leads one to question how
important downward mobility was in structuring attitudes to Powell.
Again we find the odd pattern of the less steeply upwardly mobile giving
him greater support than those experiencing more dramatic movement.

The only time we found an unambiguous relationship between social
mobility and support for Powell was in 1969 when subjective measures
of present class position were combined with subjective measures of past

class position. In these instances those who experienced upward and downward mobility were more likely than the non-mobiles to support Powell. But the 1974 data were not consistent with these findings, there was only a weak relationship between upward mobility and support for Powell while the downwardly mobile gave Powell almost half as much support as those who remained in the working class.

TABLE 10.4   The effect of social mobility on support for Powell: present class position by recollection of father's class when he was young, 1969

| | Present class position† | | | |
| | AB | C1 | C2 | DE |
Father's class when* he was young	Per cent for Powell	Per cent for Powell	Per cent for Powell	Per cent for Powell
Middle	15 (61)	20 (64)	25 (56)	45 (38)
			downwardly mobile	
	upwardly mobile			
Working	21 (91)	23 (147)	26 (292)	20 (228)

* Based on respondent's subjective categorisation.
† Based on respondent's occupation.

Source: Butler-Stokes Panel Study, 1969 wave.

TABLE 10.5   The effect of social mobility on support for Powell: present class position by recollection of father's class when he was young, 1970

| | Present class position† | | | |
| | AB | C1 | C2 | DE |
Father's class when* he was young	Per cent for Powell	Per cent for Powell	Per cent for Powell	Per cent for Powell
Middle	13 (38)	30 (30)	23 (31)	24 (17)
			downwardly mobile	
	upwardly mobile			
Working	23 (52)	30 (74)	26 (144)	18 (98)

* Based on respondent's subjective categorisation.
† Based on respondent's occupation.

Source: Butler-Stokes Panel Study, 1970 wave.

TABLE 10.6   The effect of social mobility on support for Powell:
present class position by recollection of class
when young, 1969

	Present class position†	
	Middle	*Working*
Class of family when young*	*Per cent for Powell*	*Per cent for Powell*
Middle	18 (174)	35 (57) downwardly mobile
Working	upwardly mobile 27 (150)	25 (632)

* Based on respondent's subjective categorisation.
† Based on respondent's subjective categorisation.

Source: Butler-Stokes Panel Study, 1969.

TABLE 10.7   The effect of social mobility on support for Powell:
present class position by recollection of class when young, 1974

	Present class position†	
	Middle	*Working*
Class of family when young*	*Per cent for Powell*	*Per cent for Powell*
Middle	16 (166)	16 (45) downwardly mobile
Working	upwardly mobile 19 (126)	29 (699)

* Based on respondent's subjective categorisation.
† Based on respondent's subjective categorisation.

Source: British Election Study at Essex University, 1974.

Thus the data on social mobility do not show a consistent relationship with support levels for Powell. The only time when the hypothesis was clearly confirmed was in (1969) when two subjective measures of class position at different points in time were combined. But this clear relationship disappeared by 1974. In all other instances when a subjective measure of past class position was combined with an objective measure of present position, the results were less clear. In some cases (1969) the downwardly mobile seemed more prone to be favourable to Powell, but

TABLE 10.8   The effect of social mobility on support for Powell:
present class position by recollection of father's
class when he was young, 1969

| | *Present class position†* | |
Class of family when young*	*Middle* *Per cent for Powell*	*Working* *Per cent for Powell*
Middle	21 (119)	36 (87) downwardly mobile
Working	upwardly mobile 24 (177)	24 (558)

* Based on respondent's subjective categorisation.
† Based on respondent's subjective categorisation.

Source: Butler-Stokes Panel Study, 1969.

this did not hold true in 1970. Moreover there was no clear relationship
between upward mobility and support for Powell. In none of the tests
used above did respondents showing the greatest amount of upward
mobility offer him a disproportionate amount of backing. If anything
data suggest (tentatively) that those who had made the small move across
the manual/non-manual line (from skilled working to lower middle
class) were the most likely to rally to his support. This finding is
complicated of course by the fact that this is precisely the area of the
social structure where, it is claimed, social convergence has been most
striking. Nonetheless the consistency of the disproportionately high
support given to Powell by this moderately upwardly mobile group is
impressive.

2.   STATUS INCONSISTENCY

Status inconsistency is analytically distinct from social mobility for, as
Hope notes, mobility implies comparisons between one's status at
different moments in time while inconsistency means 'concurrent
measurement of different aspects of status'.[15] Inconsistency becomes
a source of stress for individuals when they think of themselves in
terms of one aspect of their social position which entitles them to high
status and the rest of the population sees them in the light of another
element of their social position entitling them to a lower status. For
example a West Indian doctor might think of himself in terms of his
status as a physician while the rest of the population might tend to view
him as an immigrant and ascribe to him a lower status.

The leading student of status inconsistency, Gerhard Lenski, has argued that a common response to inconsistency is antagonism against the social order, often expressed through support for political parties advocating radical social change.[16] Lenski and others provide evidence that, particularly when the inconsistency is between an ascribed status (e.g. ethnicity) and an achieved status (e.g. education), the tendency for the inconsistents to support the left wing is particularly intense. In America status inconsistencies of this sort appear to have been productive of support for the Democratic party.[17]

While much of Lenski's work has been concerned with showing that status inconsistency leads to left-wing political attitudes, he holds out the possibility in footnotes that it might also lead to rightist behaviour.[18] Other studies appear to confirm this hunch – one analyst of the Wallace vote in America for example has found that tension between ascribed and achieved statuses led to high levels of support for the Alabama Governor.[19]

Very little work has been done on the effect of status inconsistency on British society and politics. The fact would seem to be that class has been such a powerful force in British society that all other distinctions have been relegated to secondary importance. In part, of course, the force of class has been so great precisely because, by the 1960s at least, it existed in such a straightforward, thorough-going form, uncomplicated to any important extent by 'second-order' factors such as religion and ethnicity. The possibility of status inconsistency affecting political choice must have existed to a greater extent in the later 19th century when the religious cleavage was more intense, but in contemporary Britain few people have been placed in the situation of the West Indian doctor discussed above. Indeed in the four-nation study of status inconsistency Lenski found that his argument that incongruity predisposed people to support parties advocating social change did not work for Britain. He hypothesised that the homogeneity of Britain was such that ethnic and religious differences were not particularly salient.[20] Given the persistence of the class alignment (even though it too has been weakening), it is likely that the most fruitful way to examine status inconsistency in Britain is to look for incongruent class evaluations. That is, are people whose self-evaluation does not match their objective classification more prone than the rest of the population to support extremists?

The empirical studies on class inconsistency show that manual workers who place themselves in the middle class are more likely to be Conservative supporters than those whose self-evaluation matches their objective working-class categorisation. Identification with a higher stratum does, it seems clear, predispose people to greater political conservatism, but there has been no discussion of its effect on extremist attitudes.

Our data allow us to test both the 'pure' Lenski thesis relating social position to inconsistencies of religious status, education and income, and also the suggested modification of incongruent class self-evaluations.

Religion

Lenski suggests that in societies where Protestants hold the dominant positions and Catholics are secondary, people whose class position did not match their religion's in the social hierarchy would be more prone to support social change. Confirmation of this hypothesis was certainly found in some societies, but the British evidence was not particularly strong. If we attempt to operationalise the theory in regard to Powellism we might hope to find greater Powellite support among middle-class Catholics (compared to middle-class Anglicans) or among working-class Anglicans (compared to working-class Catholics). The data from 1969 and 1970 do not completely confirm the hypothesis, as Table 10.9 shows. Middle-class Anglicans were more likely in both years to rate Powell favourably than middle-class Catholics. But in both years working-class Anglicans more likely to support him than working-class Catholics. The major finding is simply that Catholic support for him (across both classes) fell in dramatic fashion between 1969–70. While he lost little Anglican support in this period, he lost half his working-class Catholic support and two out of every three middle-class Catholic supporters. The data should be treated with some caution because of the small number of respondents involved. Still, this phenomenon is probably largely attributable to the strong fall-off in Powellite support among Labour voters in this period – Catholics being quite disproportionately Labour in sympathy.

TABLE 10.9   The effect of status inconsistency on support for Powell: class by religion, 1969 and 1970

| | Present class position | |
| | ABC1 | C2DE |
	Per cent supporting Powell	Per cent supporting Powell
1969		
Church of England	28	29
	(231)	(372)
Catholics	21	22
	(28)	(55)
1970		
Church of England	26	28
	(115)	(210)
Catholics	6	11
	(42)	(38)

Source: Butler-Stokes Panel Study, 1969 and 1970.

Another way to test the effect of status inconsistency on support for Powell is to examine inverse relationships between educational attainment and class position (Table 10.10). Again the picture is mixed. Among middle-class respondents, the status inconsistency hypothesis holds strikingly well. Those who left school before the age of 15 were almost twice as likely to support him as those who were educated to or beyond the age of 18. However, in the working class the anticipated relationship was not found. What is much more striking is the clear and strong inverse relationship between educational attainment and Powellite support, even when class is held constant. Table 10.10 furnishes no evidence to support the status inconsistency hypothesis but it does point up the strength of the educational factor in structuring attitudes to Powell.

TABLE 10.10   The effect of status inconsistency on support for Powell: class by educational attainment, 1969

| | Present class position | |
| | ABC1 | C2DE |
Age leaving school	Per cent supporting Powell	Per cent supporting Powell
15 or less	33	26
	(36)	(27)
16–17	24	21
	(101)	(61)
18 or greater	17	11
	(41)	(14)

Source: Butler-Stokes Panel Study, 1969 wave.

A further test of the status inconsistency hypothesis, furnished by our data on income and social class (Table 10.11), again provides only partial confirmation of the argument. Middle-class respondents with low incomes were most likely to offer support to Powell, but the relationship was not clear in the working class. The most affluent working-class respondents did give him the most favourable response but the difference between them and the least affluent was only 1 %. Moreover the range of differences between both classes and income levels was simply too narrow to support strong conclusions of any kind.

The final measure of status inconsistency, matching the respondents' social self-evaluations with their objective (occupational) status, provided some support for the hypothesis (Table 10.12). In both 1969 and 1970 those with non-congruent self-ratings tended to give Powell more support than those with congruent self-ratings, with only one out of eight inconsistent groups (the 1969 C2s) a clear exception to this

TABLE 10.11   The effect of status inconsistency on support for Powell: class by income, 1969

| | Present class position | |
| | ABC1 | C2DE |
Present income	Per cent supporting Powell	Per cent supporting Powell
£750 or less	29 (58)	26 (207)
£750–£1200	28 (90)	23 (234)
£1200 or more	22 (148)	27 (128)

Source: Butler-Stokes Panel Study, 1969 wave.

TABLE 10.12   The effect of inconsistent class evaluation on support for Powell, 1969, 1970 and 1974

	AB Per cent for Powell	C1 Per cent for Powell	C2 Per cent for Powell	DE Per cent for Powell
Self-evaluation (1969)				
Middle class	16 (104)	26 (191)	19 (68)	28 (54) *Inconsistents*
Working class	25 (48) *Inconsistents*	29 (119)	26 (291)	23 (231)
Self-evaluation (1970)				
Middle class	19 (137)	27 (113)	31 (103)	29 (65) *Inconsistents*
Working class	29 (59) *Inconsistents*	29 (121)	30 (321)	21 (224)
Self-evaluation (1974)				
Middle class	12 (92)	15 (110)	24 (50)	26 (47) *Inconsistents*
Working class	26 (54) *Inconsistents*	25 (161)	28 (353)	30 (186)

Source: Butler-Stokes Panel Study, 1969–74.

general rule. But in 1974 the relationship, if anything, grew stronger in the middle class, but among working-class respondents the anticipated pattern did not appear.

3. ECONOMIC INSECURITY AND RELATIVE DEPRIVATION

While we may discuss these last two epiphenomenenal approaches together, they are of course analytically distinct from one another and from the phenomenon of downward social mobility, even though the same person may well experience all three. While feelings of relative deprivation depend upon the choice of reference groups (independent of change in one's own status), feelings of frustration arising from downward mobility entail a comparison of one's changing status at two different points in time. Economic insecurity on the other hand implies concern over one's financial position at a single point in time, without reference necessarily either to one's own social status or that of others.

The argument relating economic insecurity to political extremism is simply that concern over economic well-being may lead people to turn to extreme alternatives to alter society to their benefit. Again, little attention has been given to this approach in the study of British politics. One *Economist* article did hypothesise that much of Powell's support among dockers was due to concern over their economic position:[22]

> The most vociferous support for Powell has come from industries whose workers are reactionary and restrictive about a great many matters quite distinct from racial prejudice. Like all right-wing demogogues, he finds support among men who feel insecure because their positions are industrially indefensible. The London St Catherine docks and the Smithfield meat plants are due for destruction and with them go the workers' highly paid, protected jobs.

The best study of relative deprivation in Britain is Runciman's and his approach can be applied to the study of political extremism. Runciman argues that while inequalities of class and status have steadily narrowed in Britain, relative deprivation of status has grown more powerful in the working class. Having achieved similar living standards to non-manuals, working-class people want the same opportunities that middle-class people have, and experience feelings of relative deprivation when they are denied them. Such feelings, he believes, 'have not led to political militancy, because they relate to experiences without necessary implications for class-consciousness.' Relative deprivation was 'egotistic' rather than 'fraternal' largely because the Labour movement was well integrated into the social structure. It was hard for working-class people to develop strong feelings of resentment when their representatives were well established (and accepted) at Westminster. As Runciman noted:[23]

But the seeming achievement of a greater equality of power was itself one of the influences which made working-class aspirations in general less a common resentment of the subordinate position of manual work as such and more an individual pursuit of middle-class perogatives. This pursuit did not have to be motivated by a deliberate imitation of non-manual workers; but it was accompanied by an increasing detachment from the lateral loyalties of a proleteriat still resentful of its powerlessness as well as its poverty or lack of social esteem.

Runciman's approach does not seem to leave much place for radical politics in Britain. In fact he suggested that only manual workers who were working-class fraternalists would be likely to support extreme policies. That is, only the people who feel a sense of deprivation on behalf of their membership reference group rather than within that group would be likely to support radical activity. Runciman cites data collected by Thomas Pettigrew showing that the key dependent variable in support for Wallace was fraternalistic deprivation rather than simple relative deprivation.[24] Pettigrew's test of this theory stands virtually alone and it is impossible to replicate his test using the available data. Still it will be interesting if there is any relationship between simple relative deprivation and support for Powell.

The available data do not permit us to carry out relative deprivation tests similar to Runciman's. The M.O.R.I. data enable us to test the theory on its most simple level. One might hypothesise that those who felt their standard of living had deteriorated while that of other people had improved would be most likely to support Powell. In fact the data (Table 10.13) more or less reverse the relative deprivation hypothesis. Those most clearly feeling relatively deprived were the *least* likely to support him. The only group giving him disproportionate support was that which felt its own and others' economic positions both to be deteriorating. The Butler-Stokes data from February 1974 also showed that those who were most clearly relatively deprived offered Powell a very low level of support while the most economically insecure offered him the highest levels of support.

Simple poll data do suggest a slight relationship between support for Powell and respondents' feelings of economic insecurity. In a May 1968 N.O.P. survey, 53% of those who favoured him for the Tory leadership said they expected their incomes to be lower next year while only 44% of the whole sample gave this answer. An exactly similar proportion of Powell supporters in December 1969 (in an N.O.P. 'straight fight' against Heath) said that they were dissatisfied with their standard of living, as against 50% of the whole sample.

To test the hypothesis further an index of economic insecurity was constructed from the Butler-Stokes data. Respondents were asked a series of four questions about their economic position: whether they felt

TABLE 10.13   The effect of relative deprivation on support for Powell,
Feb 1974

	All %	*Self worse,* *others better* %	*Self worse,* *others same* %	*Self worse,* *others worse* %
Powell as M.P. who best represents views (M.O.R.I.)	16 (1284)	8 (38)	15 (83)	19 (420)
	All %	*Self worse,* *nation's* *economy* *better* %	*Self worse,* *nation's* *economy* *same* %	*Self worse,* *nation's* *economy* *worse* %
Powell 8–10 rating on 0–10 scale (British Election Study)	25 (1070)	13 (39)	8 (60)	23 (100)

Source: M.O.R.I. and British Election Study at Essex University, 1974.

better off financially than in the past; whether they felt they would be
better off in the future; whether unemployment was a problem in their
family and whether unemployment was a problem in their community.
The economically insecure were defined as those giving two or more
'insecure' answers out of four. On comparing Powellites with non-
Powellites on this basis (Table 10.14) we find a positive relationship in
1969, which weakened in 1970 and reasserted itself in 1974.

TABLE 10.14   The relationship between economic insecurity and support
for Powell, 1969, 1970 and 1974

	1969			1970			1974		
	All	*Powell-* *ites*	*Non-* *Powell-* *ites*	*All*	*Powell-* *ites*	*Non-* *Powell-* *ites*	*All*	*Powell-* *ites*	*Non-* *Powell-* *ites*
Per cent giving 2 or more answers indicating economic insecurity	20 (1076)	25 (256)	18 (820)	18 (1013)	21 (266)	17 (747)	38 (1096)	44 (270)	36 (826)

Source: Butler-Stokes Panel Study, 1969–74.

The relationship was unchanged when class was controlled, with
no group of Powellites consistently showing high levels of economic
insecurity.

TABLE 10.15 Difference between the percent of Powellites and all respondents giving two or more answers indicating economic insecurity, controlling social class, 1969, 1970 and 1974

	1969 %	1970 %	1974 %
AB (Powellites – all respondents)	23	10	−2
C1 (Powellites – all respondents)	6	6	10
C2 (Powellites – all respondents)	5	5	7
DE (Powellites – all respondents)	4	−1	5

Source: Butler-Stokes Panel Study, 1969 and 1970 waves.

The M.O.R.I. study provides another means of relating economic insecurity to support for Powell at a later stage. In each of their three surveys they asked respondents whether they were better off or worse off than a year ago and whether they expected to be better off in three or four years' time. As Table 10.16 shows, Powellites (here defined as those who said Powell best represents their views) seemed to be much more pessimistic about the future than the whole sample, and indeed to become disproportionately more concerned as time went on.

TABLE 10.16 The relationship between economic insecurity and support for Powell, 1973–74

	All respondents %	Powellites %	Non-Powellites %
Change in income from a year ago			
Feb 1973 – worse	33 (2073)	32 (521)	33 (1552)
Feb 1974 – worse	42 (1290)	46 (205)	41 (1085)
July 1974 – worse	37 (827)	36 (140)	37 (687)
Expected change in income 3–4 years from now			
Feb 1973 – worse	30 (2073)	35 (521)	28 (1552)
Feb 1974 – worse	28 (1290)	36 (205)	26 (1085)
July 1974 – worse	32 (827)	44 (140)	28 (687)

Source: M.O.R.I. Panel Study, 1973–74.

Because both the Butler-Stokes and M.O.R.I. panels asked similar questions about concern over economic position, one can examine the effect of these questions on support for Powell over time. Multiple regression analysis provides a means of analysing the effect of economic insecurity on support for Powell, holding racial attitudes and party affiliation constant. The coefficients in Table 10.17 thus measure the effect of each variable on support levels for Powell with the other two held constant. In each of the equations three separate contrasts were used. In each case the effect of Conservative versus Labour partisanship was tested. Also those who felt strongly about the number of immigrants in the country were contrasted with those who did not feel strongly about the issue. Finally, on the two questions dealing with economic insecurity, those saying they were better off in the past were contrasted with those who said they were worse off in the past and those who said they would be better off in the future were contrasted with those who said they would be worse off. Table 10.17 makes clear how minor was the role of feelings of economic insecurity compared to either race or party in structuring attitudes to Powell. Concern over future economic position was always a better indicator than concern over the past, but it never overtook race and only became more important than party affiliation in February 1974. This last result of course coincided with a large shift in Powell's support towards Labour-voting workers and is probably more a reflection of that shift than of any secular change of mood among Powellites.

TABLE 10.17   Multiple regression analysis of the effect of race, party and economic insecurity on support for Powell, 1969–74

	Con.	Racialist	Past economic insecurity	Con.	Racialist	Future economic insecurity
1969 (B & S) Things worse economically	·76	1·41	·14	·70	1·30	·22
Feb 1973 (M.O.R.I.) Things worse economically	·44	1·04	·12	·39	·95	·27
Feb 1974 (M.O.R.I.) Things worse economically	·31	·92	·25	·24	·85	·47

(All coefficients significant at 0·1 level).

Source: Butler-Stokes Panel Study, 1969 and M.O.R.I.

We may summarise our findings as follows:

Social mobility
This factor did have some marginal explanatory power in that the upwardly or downwardly mobile were on the whole more likely to support Powell (especially when subjective indices of class position were used exclusively). But this was clearest in cases of limited upward mobility, of working-class respondents climbing to C1. There was also some evidence that extreme downward mobility (in 1969) produced an outpouring of support for him. It is worth remembering that our data are drawn from 1969–70 when his support was based largely on anti-immigrant feelings; it is likely that the disproportionate support given by the downwardly mobile and more particularly the upwardly mobile stemmed from their heightened consciousness of and response to this issue. Those who had risen from the bottom of the heap to the lower middle class were perhaps particularly affronted at finding their new status threatened by the arrival of coloured immigrants, 'bringing down' the social standing of the entire neighbourhoods in which they found homes, reducing their hard-won gains. Similarly the smaller number of DEs claiming a sad descent from middle-class parentage – distressed gentlefolk in their own eyes if not perhaps in statistical fact when their parents' occupations were examined – might also have been particularly susceptible to anxieties over race and immigration, the new arrivals confirming their worst fears about how far they had fallen.

The picture is of course conjecture, but it *would* explain the odd pattern of limited mobility having the larger effect – workers who had fully risen into the top of the middle class may well have removed themselves entirely from the social stress-points where the impact of the new arrivals was felt most keenly. This would for example tend to be the case for those who had moved from council to private housing estates.

The argument must not be pressed too far. We have no direct evidence for this hypothesis, likely though it seems. Moreover the difference between the mobile and non-mobile in support for Powell was not so pronounced as to allow arguments about mobility to carry too much weight. And above all, only a fifth of the 1969 panel and a third of the 1970 panel were mobiles. The overwhelming bulk of Powell's support at both points came, naturally, from the non-mobile majority and no hypotheses from social mobility can begin to explain *their* support.

Status inconsistency
The same overall consideration must be borne in mind when we examine our status inconsistency data. The strength of the British stratification system is such that the consistents preponderated heavily over the non-consistents in all cases. On the most revealing inconsistency

for our purposes (self-rated class compared to occupation-based class) only 28% were inconsistents. While those with inconsistent self-rated status were more likely to support Powell, the bulk of his followers came from the consistent 72%. The differences we found were in any case seldom very striking, but the main point is that arguments from status inconsistency are useless for an explanation of the major section of Powell's support.

Two other unrelated points did emerge from this exercise, however – Powell's substantial decline in Catholic support between 1969 and 1970 and the across-the-board explanatory power of educational attainment in differentiating Powellites from non-Powellites.

Relative deprivation and economic insecurity
Our single and rough test of the relative deprivation hypothesis actually produced an inverse result. Those most likely to compare themselves with other reference groups were the least likely to support Powell. What emerged instead was a rather better correlation between Powellite support and generalised economic insecurity, particularly middle-class insecurity (at least until 1974). But this factor too paled against the variables of party and race.

Thus the various 'epiphenomenal' hypotheses tested in this chapter have failed to emerge as powerful explanatory tools for our under-standing of Powellism. In our next chapter we attempt to confront the Powellite phenomenon more directly.

11 Towards an Explanation of Powellism

The relative sophistication of the mass society and status based theories we have thus far examined has not been matched by a corresponding success in explaining satisfactorily the phenomenon of Powellism. In this chapter we have found it useful to consider the phenomenon as having two separate phases.

The first phase (1968–70), we suggest, occurred during a period of growing general political disillusionment. In this period, very simply, Powell drew the support he did because of his stand on immigration and as a Tory. He benefited perhaps from the climate of disillusion, but only in the most general sense, for his supporters were no more disillusioned than those who failed to support him.

In the second phase – after 1970 – Powell's support changed. While his following was never wholly independent of public feeling on specific issues, it became more diffuse and evolved into a general coalition of those dissatisfied with the political system – of which Powell himself was the staunchest defender and advocate. In this period political disillusion grew to be almost as important as racial attitudes in structuring opinions toward Powell. Conservative party identification became of almost negligible importance after his turn away from the Tory party in June 1973.

A. 1968–70
1. The role of disillusionment
The disillusionment which developed in Britain in the 1960s was not divisive. That is, it did not set one part of the electorate against another in the way that debates over religion or capitalism do. Indeed this was almost its problem – alienation was a general cross-class phenomenon; it weakened existing partisan attachments but did not create clear new lines of cleavage. Thus the Lipset-Rokkan model is not really of use in analysing the breakdown of consensus during the 1960s.[1] The dissatisfaction people felt resulted simply from the failure of Government to perform – that is, to solve the problems facing the country.[2] Disillusionment arose not out of partisan considerations but rather because of a general breakdown in the political system.

A simple but useful way to think about recent British political history is to consider the functions a democratic system must perform and then evaluate its success.[3] At the most simple level a democratic system must both represent interests and be responsive to the people's wishes. All major segments of the electorate must feel that their interests are being adequately represented. Voters must also feel that the choices presented by the political parties are meaningful. If neither of these functions is performed, the result is likely to be protest, apathy or support for third parties and extreme movements. But finally voters must also feel that there is some point in the whole game – that their exercise of the franchise is capable of producing a government with a real executive efficacy in tackling the problems of the polity.

This latter issue of managerial performance is not divisive and for this very reason can have the effect of making party competition appear irrelevant. It matters little after all if the Conservatives or Labour are offering different solutions to current economic problems if both are equally incapable of delivering the goods. Most voters are no doubt aware that at different points during the 1960s and 1970s both parties adopted similar approaches to inflation and neither achieved much success. Both parties have, quite simply, been unable to escape from stop-go economics, to defend the currency or to construct a 'modernised' Britain capable of holding its own with all-comers.

On top of this, politicians appeared insensitive to issues such as immigration, despite their very real impact on the voters' lives. Moreover the rise of organised interests and pressure groups in British politics has increasingly given the average elector the sense that he counts for little in the system.[4]

A useful 'snapshot' way to chart the growth of this mood of political dissatisfaction is provided by the descriptive analyses of the Nuffield election studies.[5] The tone of the 1964 study was very different from that of the 1959 work. The authors of the 1964 work, David Butler and Anthony King, noted that 'the mood of buoyant self-satisfaction which characterised Britain during the 1950s suddenly seemed to give way to a mood of self-doubt and angry introspection'.[6] Neither the Tories nor Labour seemed able to restore confidence in the system:[7]

> The political parties seemed like helpless spectators at a game they insisted in putting on but which they could no longer control. All three parties reacted to events far more than they determined them. Labour's share of the vote actually fell for the third election running; Labour's authority to govern was further weakened by having the lowest share of any majority government since 1922.

The 1966 election brought no wave of enthusiasm for the Labour Government despite their increased majority. Butler and King noted that 'Enthusiasm for the Government with Labour was only a little higher than the proportion satisfied with the Conservatives before the 1964 election.[8] The Labour victory should probably be attributed more to dissatisfaction with the Tories than to any measure of confidence in Labour's ability to govern'. Butler and King concluded by noting that 'By 1966 Labour had indisputably asserted its will to govern, but the eagerness of the first few weeks had largely vanished, and so had much of the confidence'.[9]

In the 1970 study Butler and Michael Pinto-Duschinsky emphasised the continuation of these earlier trends. The Conservatives might not have had an enviable record on performance issues during the early 1960s but, as the Nuffield study flatly puts it, 'Mr Wilson had an unenviable record of disaster'.[10] The Government had been forced to withdraw two major Bills in one parliamentary session; had been compelled to devalue the pound; had had finally to withdraw from East of Suez; and had amassed a record balance of payments deficit.

The 1964–70 period was a particularly important one. During the thirteen years of Tory rule one might at least have hoped that Labour could succeed where the Conservatives failed. By the middle of Labour's second government this hope too had been thoroughly extinguished, with no corresponding revival of confidence in the Conservatives. Butler and Pinto-Duschinsky note that the evidence they collected showed that Labour's deficit in the polls was due almost entirely to dissatisfaction with the Government; there were few conversions to the Conservative party.

Butler and Pinto-Duschinsky also pointed to the lack of disagreement along the traditional basis of cleavage (class) and the apparent convergence of party policies as leading to a weakening of voting loyalties and support for party leaders.[11] The effects may even have been more important than they suggest. The policy convergence of the parties and the increased social homogeneity of the two party élites noted by Johnson and Rose gave many the feeling that the political élite was a remote and closed circle of like and limited ideas.[12]

There is almost no end to the impressionistic evidence of disillusion which one could produce, but the evidence is more than impressionistic. Perhaps the most basic measure of apathy is electoral participation. Turnout dropped steadily in Britain from 79 % in 1959 to 72 % in 1970, with predictably steep falls in traditional Labour strongholds such as mining seats and urban working-class districts.[13] In such areas abstention is probably the only way voters can express discontent, Tory or third-party voting being virtually pointless as well as (historically) unthinkable.

The weakening hold of the major parties over the electorate was also evidenced in increased electoral volatility. General election swings were twice as high in the 1960s as they were in the 1950s. Moreover, the highest swing was recorded between 1966 and 1970 – the period when Powell first reached public prominence. Confirming this, Butler and Stokes showed that there was a steady decline in the percentage of people voting for the same party between 1964 and 1970. While 26% of the electorate changed their voting behaviour between 1964 and 1966, 35% altered their choice between 1966 and 1969. Between 1969 and 1970 no less than 45% of the electorate changed parties in the space of a year.[14]

Another sign of dissatisfaction with the major parties has been the shrinking two-party share of the total vote in general elections. Since 1969 there has been a reasonably steady decline in the major parties share of the two-party vote, though the real Liberal revival did not come until after the 1970 election. The decline in this period was particularly noticeable in Scotland and to a lesser extent Wales where the Nationalists made inroads. Plaid Cymru won a by-election in 1966 and achieved an average vote of 40% in three by-elections between 1966 and 1968. In Scotland the S.N.P. won the 1967 Hamilton by-election and averaged 30% in by-elections of the 1967–70 period.[15]

English by-election voters deserted the Government too. Between 1966 and 1970, the Government lost 20% or more of the votes they had received in the 1966 election in 34% of all by-elections, while swings of this magnitude against the Macmillan Government (1959–64) had occurred in only 18% of all by-elections.

Popular discontent and disillusionment with politicians and (major) parties had risen particularly high in the period of Powell's emergence in April 1968. An N.O.P. survey in February 1968 showed that M.P.s were considered the most useful members of the community by only 4% of the respondents – 3% more approbation than dustmen received.[16] A majority of respondents thought that there were no great men in any of the parties and that politicians were in government only to get out of it what they could. A Gallup poll taken just after Powell's speech confirmed the impression given by these results.[17] On the three questions relating to Government performance about two-thirds of respondents said they did not have enough say in government, making it the institution thought by far the least responsive to the public. Only 7% of respondents thought M.P.s had much influence over the country's future, and nearly 70% said certain issues should be decided by popular vote (presumably by referenda).

Politics abhors a vacuum as much as any other part of nature and, as we have already suggested, there was in April 1968 a clear political vacuum into which Powell could step. Just two weeks before Powell's speech, Richard Rose wrote in his previously cited *Times* article that 'Public confidence in the ability of the leaders of the two major parties to deal with the nation's problems has reached a post-war low'.[18]

Rose's data (Table 11.1) showed that the averages of the leaders' rating had declined steadily.

Journalistic commentary of the time (including an article on Powell by Ronald Butt,[19] before the Birmingham speech) held that Powell

TABLE 11.1   Average combined ratings of the major party leaders
1965–68

Aug 1965/Mar 1966 %	Apr/Dec 1966 %	1967 %	Jan/Mar 1968 %
53·5	46	39·5	33

Source: Richard Rose 'Voters Show their Scepticism of Politicians' *The
Times*, 9 Apr 1968.

attracted the support he did in this climate of disillusion largely because
he had broken a stale consensus, and 'sounded different'.

The gap between mass and élite opinion had grown so wide, the argument ran, that the electorate responded to Powell simply because he was
echoing commonly held views which no other leader had yet expressed,
and because he was not afraid to do so. Others suggested that the
reaction to him was attributable to structural aspects of the British
parliamentary system. Perhaps too much, not too little, had been 'taken
out of politics' with M.P.s playing administrative rather than political
roles. The system insulated M.P.s from an electorate they could afford to
ignore. It was important only that they should not offend their party
leaders.

The *Financial Times* political correspondent, David Watt, took up this
line of argument but suggested that while these features of the British
system served in good part to stifle the development of any extremist
or populist movements, they also made the system more vulnerable:[20]

> But in another sense the ponderous effectiveness of the whole arrange-
> ment is profoundly disturbing. For it is one of the main ingredients in
> the present troubles. The isolation of politicians, the ingroupness of
> Westminster, the blandness of the establishment, the tendency to keep
> unpleasant facts under the carpet for the best of motives (as well as
> the worst), the irrelevance of many of the old party divisions to
> modern problems – these are the main characteristics of the conven-
> tional system as the man in the street sees it. The balance and stability
> of constitutional machinery – which are protections against revolution
> and tyranny – often seem less important than its increasing remote-
> ness, irrelevance or incompetence.

More conservative analysts (notably Peregrine Worsthorne and
Angus Maude) came close to echoing Powell's own views about the
demoralising effects of the end of Empire: there was, particularly among
the working class, a sense of lost nationalism as well as a lost sense of
nationalism. Changes in moral values propounded by the élite were met
with hostility by a public fearful of the erosion of traditional standards of

discipline and authority. Powell's appeal, in this argument, rested on a public sense of his shared concern with them about the need to maintain traditional British values.[21]

Interestingly, Powell himself subscribed to a variant of the general disillusionment thesis as a means of explaining why he received such a tremendous outpouring of support. In a September 1968 *Sunday Times* interview, Powell said he viewed his role as being a representative in the Burkean sense, rather than just a delegate whose job is merely to voice the people's sentiments.[22] Nevertheless he said he felt he must voice the people's feelings, especially if they ran counter to fashionable opinion or the élite consensus. He explained that he too saw a gap between the people's and politicians' views and said that the reaction to his Birmingham speech revealed evidence of deep frustration about a number of issues including immigration, overseas aid, trade and taxation policy. People did not feel that their views were getting through to the élite; his purpose was to ensure that they did.

There was another aspect to Powell's impact which he could hardly comment upon; the quite evident hero-worship of some, going far beyond mere support. Many not merely applauded what he said but his bravery in saying it; in risking his career, in affronting the Establishment; for standing alone. A *Spectator* editorial said: 'Mr Powell is the only consistent and powerful voice of dissent . . . [He] is the only politician from either major party who stands apart; therein lies his strength.'[23]

As we have already suggested, Powell was rewarded for 'standing up for the man in the street', for being unafraid of voicing the real fears affecting the lives of 'little people'. It says much for the electorate's view of its own Establishment that there should be this slightly self-righteous, slightly fearful attitude to the forthright expression of grass-roots feelings. To many his message appeared as a legitimation of their sentiments, an appeal to feel no guilt or embarrassment about their expression, a summons to stand up and be counted. The title of Powell's books, *A Nation Not Afraid* and *Freedom and Reality*, are deliberately and powerfully suggestive of this mood.

A number of empirical tests can be employed to measure the degree to which political disillusionment actually affected support for Powell in the period from 1968 to 1970. First, one can measure the extent to which Powellites were more or less disillusioned than the rest of the electorate by examining the percentage believing that the Government, party leaders and M.P.s were out of touch with the people, or that they failed to present the electorate with distinct policy alternatives. We are also able to test the hypothesis that Powellites were particularly sensitive and hostile to the liberalisation of the country's social and cultural values.

As Table 11.2 shows, the Powellites were more likely to say the Government and M.P.s paid little attention to the people, a finding which

TABLE 11.2   Attention government and M.P.s pay to the people, 1969

	All			Conservative			Labour			Liberal			Other		
	All %	Pow. %	Non-Pow. %	All %	Pow. %	Non-Pow. %	All %	Pow. %	Non-Pow. %	All %	Pow. %	Non-Pow. %	All %	Pow. %	Non-Pow. %
Government does not pay much attention to the people	62 (1092)	69 (258)	59 (834)	68 (458)	72 (151)	65 (307)	55 (345)	62 (58)	53 (287)	66 (97)	65 (17)	66 (80)	56 (184)	68 (31)	54 (153)
M.P.s do not pay much attention to the people	36 (1077)	47 (245)	33 (822)	38 (453)	45 (148)	34 (305)	35 (348)	48 (63)	33 (285)	32 (92)	50 (16)	28 (76)	37 (183)	52 (31)	34 (152)

	All			AB			C1			C2			DE		
	All %	Pow. %	Non-Pow. %	All %	Pow. %	Non-Pow. %	All %	Pow. %	Non-Pow. %	All %	Pow. %	Non-Pow. %	All %	Pow. %	Non-Pow. %
Government does not pay much attention to the people	62 (1092)	69 (258)	59 (834)	63 (166)	73 (30)	60 (136)	63 (230)	63 (60)	63 (170)	62 (382)	73 (94)	59 (288)	60 (294)	66 (70)	58 (224)
M.P.s do not pay much attention to the people	36 (1077)	47 (254)	22 (823)	35 (164)	43 (28)	34 (136)	40 (226)	49 (59)	37 (167)	34 (375)	42 (93)	31 (282)	37 (292)	53 (70)	32 (222)

Source: Butler-Stokes Panel Study, 1969.

remains true when party and class are controlled. But the margins were relatively slight on both questions used: 69%–62% and 47%–36%. The differences widen somewhat if we compare only Powellites and non-Powellites (69%–59% and 47%–33%). These margins are certainly not insignificant but they do not properly allow one to talk of the Powellites having a systematic alienation from the whole political system. On the question where the margin was greatest between Powellites and others (M.P.s' attention to the people) still less than half of all Powellites gave the 'alienated' answer.

Moreover Powellites were more likely than the whole sample by a 50%–47% margin to say that parties made the Government pay at least some attention to what the people think, and by a 71%–70% margin to say that elections made the Government pay at least some attention to the people.

Similarly one might have supposed the more disillusioned would be the most likely to see little or no difference between the parties, but Powellites were actually more likely than the whole sample (by a 40–32% margin) to have said there was a good deal of difference between the parties and were also more likely (by 24%–19%) to believe that the differences had become wider in recent years. These differences were undisturbed when party and class were controlled.[24]

One of the postulated measures of disillusionment that the Powellites *did* appear to score highly on was dissatisfaction with the leaders of the major parties. In 1969 45% of the Powellites wanted Wilson replaced as Leader of the Labour party against only 35% of all respondents. Also 52% of the Powellites supported Heath's removal while only 41% of all respondents took this position. These differences were virtually unaffected·when party was controlled: 32% of Labour Powellites and 23% of all Labour respondents wanted Wilson removed, while 57% of Tory Powellites and 47% of all Conservatives wanted Heath replaced.

2. The 'social issue'

The Worsthorne/Maude argument that Powellites were reacting against the liberalisation of social and moral values is very similar to the approach Scammon and Wattenberg and Phillips took in analysing American politics during the late 1960s and early 1970s.[25]

The argument in essence is that a whole complex of social and cultural changes had opened the way to a new sort of political alignment, based not on the old economic issues but on the 'social issue' – conceived of as an amalgam of 'silent majority' resentments, against students, radical chic of all kinds, permissiveness and the general 'over-liberalisation' of public *mores*. (Typically the race issue was in practice a powerful though half-submerged component of social issue politics but it was always quite clearly an independent and separable element.)

There does seem to be some evidence that Powellites reacted more intensely than others to such social changes. One of the major components of the backlash reaction in America was a reaction against student campus demonstrations. In Britain one might expect the reaction to have been even more intense because such a small percentage of the population experienced higher education. Anti-student feeling did indeed run strong – and was marginally stronger among the Powellites than among all respondents. By a 79–71 % margin Powellites were more prone to say students were not justified in participating in demonstrations on political subjects. Powellites were also more willing to take harsh measures if students participated in demonstrations. By a 49–43% margin all respondents felt that students who engage in political demonstrations should lose their grants. Among Powellites the more severe view was favoured by a much larger margin (65–32%). These differences were unaffected when party and class were controlled.[26]

In America one of the major components of Scammon and Wattenberg's 'social issue' politics has been a strong 'law and order' position. Supporters of strong measures to curb crime invariably supported longer gaol sentences, tougher judges and often the death penalty. The Powellites in Britain were also stronger supporters of the retention of the death penalty (by 84%–9 %) than the whole sample, among whom 73 % were for retention and 18 % were for abolition. Powell's own abolitionist stand throughout his career seems to have weighed little with his supporters – indeed, interviews with Powellites in the London area even in 1975 showed that none were aware that Powell opposed the death penalty. Powellites were also more concerned about trade union power – 77 % of them in 1970 (as against 65 % of all respondents) thought the power of unions too great. This remained true when party was controlled. – 87 % of Tory Powellites (against 81 % of all Conservatives) and 57 % of Labour Powellites (against 52 % of all Labour supporters) held this view. These anxieties were focused on trade unions in particular – not on the power of organised groups in general, for Powellites were no more likely than others to say that the power of big business was too great.

It seems clear that general disillusionment was important to the Powellite phenomenon, playing a preparatory role in making the electorate more receptive to those who took up positions outside the mainstream of British politics. Thereafter the 'social issue' probably played a secondary role in helping Powell solidify his constituency during the 1970 campaign. (The data cited were collected before 1971.) But its role was slight. It was only at the close of the 1970 campaign that Powell first stressed the social issues during his 'enemy within' speech.[27] Given the strength of Powellite concern about the 'social issue', it seems likely that Powell reinforced his base by stressing these concerns. But his own use of the issue was relatively slight. He did explicitly channel popular resentments against immigrants, student demonstrators, Whitehall bureaucrats, Irish terrorists, over-mighty trade unionists and liberal do-gooders. But he could have stressed these themes far more than he did; he remained a strong opponent of the death penalty (even against terrorists); he consistently defended industrial wage bargaining even during the miners' strike. And of course he of all people was unlikely to inveigh against 'pointy-headed professors' in the style of George Wallace. In fact Powell's relative lack of stress on these issues may paradoxically have made the 'social issue' more important than it might otherwise have been, for his supporters were thereby left free to assume that their hero shared their prejudices across the board. Even so it is difficult to assign 'social issue' politics much prominence in the forging of Powellite support. It was a thin overlay, not a basic element.

3. *Immigration*

Quite indisputably however Powellism between 1968 and 1970 was an immigration-related phenomenon. No amount of oblique analysis from mass society, status, relative deprivation, the 'social issue' or disillusionment can hide this very direct and simple fact. The huge leap in Powell's support directly after the April 1968 speech needs little elaboration. Moreover, in the years that followed, the evidence confirmed that this continued to be true. Powellites in 1969 and 1970 were more sharply distinctive in their views on immigration (Table 11.3) than on any other issue for which we have data.

One can indeed emphasise the point by reading Table 11.3 the other

TABLE 11.3   Attitudes toward immigration of the electorate and Powellites

	1969			1970		
	All %	*Powellites* %	*Non-Powellites* %	*All* %	*Powellites* %	*Non-Powellites* %
Too many immigrants let in	85 (1092)	99 (260)	81 (832)	84 (737)	97 (203)	80 (534)
Feel very strongly about the number of immigrants	54 (1071)	78 (258)	47 (813)	49 (1206)	74 (325)	40 (881)
Immigration a neighbourhood problem	13 (1073)	28 (258)	9 (815)	11 (1204)	16 (323)	9 (881)
Against anti-discrimination legislation	30 (1065)	38 (257)	27 (808)	(not asked in 1970)		

Source: Butler-Stokes Panel Study 1969–70.

way round. Of those presumably most affected by immigration (those who felt it posed a neighbourhood problem) no less than 45% were Powellites in 1969. (At this point the proportion of Powellites in the whole electorate was 23%.) Of those who felt very strongly about the number of immigrants in 1969 (an overall majority did) again 45% were Powellites. The 1970 figures are not very different. The almost total unanimity of Powellites on the first question, producing figures (99% and 97%) seldom seen in any poll on *any* questions, tell their own story: for many, answering this way and supporting Powell were simply synonymous.

We extended our analysis by constructing an index of racial conservatism (based on the 1969 data) to measure the intensity and strength of racial attitudes. Respondents were given one point for every affirmative answer they gave to the four questions in Table 11.3 and their scores were then cross-tabulated by the respondents' rating of Powell on the 0–100 scale (Table 11.4). The clear correlation between Powellite sympathies and racial conservatism was not affected when class and party were held constant. Race was particularly important in separating Powellites from the rest of the electorate among ABs, and supporters of the Liberals and minor parties.

TABLE 11.4   Powell rating by score on racial conservatism scale, 1969

	0–34 %	35–54 %	55–77 %	78–100 %
Scores on racial conservatism				
scale				
0	22	15	4	1
1	37	41	26	17
2	34	36	53	50
3	7	9	17	32
	(196)	(323)	(317)	(260)

Source: Butler-Stokes Panel Study, 1969.

In the 1970 survey Butler and Stokes asked respondents for their own views and their perceptions of Powell's views on what should be done about immigration. They gave their respondents five possible choices and asked them to state which came closest to their position and to Powell's position. As Table 11.6 makes clear there was a general convergence as well as some specific divergences between people's own views on immigration and their perception of Powell's. Working from Table 11.6 makes it easy to understand why the Birmingham speech was so well received, but provides only a partial clue as to how the electorate made their assessment of Powell personally.

TABLE 11.5 Powell rating by score on racial conservatism scale, controlling class and party, 1969

	All			AB			C1			C2			DE		
	All %	*Pow.* %	*Non-* *Pow.* %	*All* %	*Pow.* %	*Non-* *Pow.* %	*All* %	*Pow.* %	*Non-* *Pow.* %	*All* %	*Pow.* %	*Non-* *Pow.* %	*All* %	*Pow.* %	*Non-* *Pow.* %
Per cent of each group scoring 3 on racial conservatism scale	17 (1096)	33 (260)	12 (836)	16 (168)	37 (30)	10 (138)	14 (230)	27 (60)	10 (170)	17 (383)	33 (95)	12 (288)	19 (295)	35 (71)	14 (224)

	All			Conservative			Labour			Liberal			Other		
	All %	*Pow.* %	*Non-* *Pow.* %	*All* %	*Pow.* %	*Non-* *Pow.* %	*All* %	*Pow.* %	*Non-* *Pow.* %	*All* %	*Pow.* %	*Non-* *Pow.* %	*All* %	*Pow.* %	*Non-* *Pow.* %
Per cent of each group scoring 3 on racial conservatism scale	17 (1096)	33 (260)	12 (836)	20 (460)	33 (152)	13 (308)	15 (347)	27 (59)	13 (288)	8 (97)	36 (17)	13 (80)	14 (184)	42 (31)	8 (153)

Source: Butler-Stokes Panel Study, 1969.

While a clear 70% of respondents (irrespective of attitude towards Powell) supported the more drastic solutions (1 and 2), no less than 93% believed Powell favoured such solutions. While he was most particularly identified with the first solution, the oddity is that those most likely to make that identification were the least likely to support him. Moreover even his strongest supporters divided clearly against repatriation, though they too identified him with it.

Nonetheless Powellites clearly showed the highest level of preference for repatriation, and those who were most antagonistic towards him were least favourable to assisting in sending immigrants home. But the similarities between the different categories were perhaps more striking than the differences. Over 50% in the last three categories supported solution 2 and so did a plurality in the first category. Powellites were

TABLE 11.6   Electorate views towards immigrants and their perception of Powell's position, by rating of Powell, 1970

Solutions	Respondent's own view Powell rating				Respondent's perception of Powell's position on immigration Powell rating			
	0–34 %	35–54 %	55–77 %	78–100 %	0–34 %	35–54 %	55–77 %	78–100 %
1. Favours repatriation	7	14	22	34	77	71	71	71
2. Stop immigration but allow those here to stay	32	50	53	51	9	20	24	24
3. Allow dependents to enter and skilled workers	30	24	22	13	2	2	3	2
4. New workers allowed to enter	13	4	2	1	0	0	0	0
5. Free entry	6	2	1	0	0	0	0	0
	(225)	(302)	(488)	(331)	(225)	(302)	(488)	(331)

Source: Butler-Stokes Panel Study, 1970.

clearly the most racially conservative. But the uniformly high awareness of Powell's views and the very considerable consensus in attitudes towards immigration leaves problematic the very question why one group came to give him high levels of support and the others did not.

4. *Party identification*

While race clearly played a decisive role in structuring attitudes towards Powell during this period, party identification was also important. Despite the publicity focused on Powell's working-class support his following initially was heavily Conservative.

The Tory bias in Powell's base can be seen from N.O.P.'s survey of preferences for the Tory leadership conducted immediately after the Birmingham speech. Respondents who preferred Powell favoured the Tories by a 46–20% margin, while the entire sample gave the Tories only a 43–27% lead. This Tory bias of Powellites was evident within every social class but was most pronounced in the working class (Table 11.7).

TABLE 11.7 Support for Powell by party, controlling class, 1968

	Con.	Lab.	Tory lead over Lab.	Lib.	Other
AB					
Powellites	76%	14%	(+62)	5%	5% = 100% (21)
All	68%	9%	(+59)	10%	13% = 100% (242)
C1					
Powellites	58%	10%	(+48%)	14%	18% = 100% (52)
All	57%	14%	(+43%)	10%	19% = 100% (432)
C2					
Powellites	39%	23%	(+16%)	11%	27% = 100% (102)
All	36%	32%	(+4)	12%	20% = 100% (735)
DE					
Powellites	39%	26%	(+13)	5%	30% = 100% (85)
All	32%	37%	(−5)	6%	25% = 100% (528)

Source: N.O.P., May 1968 survey; table computed by S.S.R.C. Data Archive, Essex University.

When party instead of class was controlled, the working-class bias of the Powellites appeared, with 59% of Conservative Powellites coming from the working class against 52% of all Conservatives in the poll; 64% of Liberal Powellites and 62% of all Liberals were from the manual stratum, while 84% of Labour Powellites and all Labour voters were working class.

The Butler-Stokes data from 1969–70 also showed a strong Tory bias among Powellites. In 1969 68% and in 1970 63% of the people who gave Powell a 78–100 rating were Tories. By contrast, only 28% in 1969 and 16% in 1970 of those who gave Powell a 0–34 rating in these two years were Conservatives. Table 11.8 shows the relationship between party and the evaluation of Powell as well as the Powellites' working-class bias when party was held constant.

TABLE 11.8 The evaluation of Powell by party, 1970

	0–34 %	35–54 %	55–77 %	78–100 %
Conservative	16	35	57	63
Labour	70	52	35	29
Liberal	12	10	5	6
Other	2	3	3	2
	100	100	100	100
	(225)	(302)	(488)	(331)

	Conservative		Labour		Liberal		Other	
	Pow. %	All %	Pow. %	All %	Pow. %	All %	Pow. %	All %
Per cent of support from ABC1 (middle class)	47	54	16	20	52	54	41	38
Per cent of support from C2DE (working class)	53	46	84	80	48	46	59	62
	100	100	100	100	100	100	100	100
	(168)	(663)	(77)	(665)	(17)	(106)	(69)	(377)

Source: Butler-Stokes Panel Study, 1970.

Partisan loyalties and attitudes to race and immigration thus clearly emerge as the major explanatory variables of Powellite support in this period, with a certain working-class bias also apparent. A multiple regression analysis was conducted to measure the effect of a number of different variables on the support level for Powell. The coefficients in Table 11.9 measure the relative effect of each variable on support for Powell with the others held constant. The number of respondents in the survey allowed only three variables to be tested together.

In all three equations party and race were independently important in explaining support for Powell. In equations 1 and 2, which used two different measures of alienation as the third independent variable, racial attitudes appeared to be twice as important as party. When social class was used as the third variable (equation 3) racial attitudes were still one and a half times more important than party. As equations 1 and 2 show, there was only a statistically insignificant relationship between support for Powell and general alienation (with race and party controlled).

There was also a weak but statistically significant relationship between working-class status and support for Powell. The evidence suggests quite clearly that attitudes to race and immigration were overwhelmingly the most important factors in structuring support for Powell in this period. This support was then passed (as it were) through a second major filter – that of party, with social class playing a much more final role as well. Disillusionment with the system does little to explain Powellite support in this period.

TABLE 11.9   Multiple regression on support for Powell, 1969

Equation	Explanation of third independent variable	Conservative	Racist	Disillusionment	Social class
1.	Government pays no attention to people when taking decisions	·77*	1·37*	0·05†	
2.	No difference between parties	·74*	1·36*	0·08†	
3.	Manual	·92*	1·41*		·29*

* Significant at ·01 level.
† Insignificant.

Source: Butler-Stokes Panel Study, 1969.

B.   1970–75
The character of Powellism from 1968 to 1970 thus seems clear enough. There are however grounds for believing that after 1970 the Powellite phenomenon underwent a gradual change, with attitudes to immigrants and party playing a diminishing role in structuring Powell's following.

1.   *Party identification*
Conservative party identification certainly remained important in structuring attitudes toward Powell up to June 1973 – when Powell gave the first indication that he might support the Labour party in the next election. Until this point Powell had received far better ratings from Conservatives than from Labour voters. In March 1971 he received more than twice as much support for prime minister from Conservatives as he did from Labour voters. His relentless criticism of the Heath Government led to only minor attrition of this support and in February 1973 he was still winning a quite disproportionate amount of his support from Conservative voters. There was a clear change after June 1973. An N.O.P. poll after the Stockport speech showed that Conservative and

Labour voters gave Powell practically the same amount of support for prime minister.[28] Gallup also found a sharp decline in the number of Tories saying he was a party asset, from 44% in April 1973 to 35% after Stockport, and to 32% by October, while among non-Conservatives he lost practically no ground.

Conservative support continued to ebb away from Powell thereafter – not just in 1974 when he backed Labour but into the 1975 referendum campaign as well. Although by July 1975 he was better supported by Labour than Tory voters, the former by no means made up for the Conservatives who had defected since February 1973, meaning that he had suffered a significant overall drop in support. (See Table 8.15, p. 183.)

2. *Disillusionment*

The election of a Tory Government in 1970 did not bring an upswing in popular confidence in the political leadership. Mr Heath lacked popular appeal, many of his Ministers were less well known than their Labour 'shadows', inflation mounted, house prices raced away from home buyers, the Government was publicly and visibly vanquished by the trade unions on more than one occasion and, by 1972, the Government's U-turn on economic policy served to confuse and disquiet the party faithful. The stock of Mr Wilson and the Labour party obstinately refused to rise. After a very brief honeymoon the mood of disillusion was again widespread. Even in 1970 Heath had had an average satisfaction rating of only 51% (according to N.O.P.) while the Government's average rating was 39%. By 1973 Heath's average rating had dropped to 38% while the Government was down to 34%. For the first time since the early 1960s the Liberal party began to make headway in the polls, reaching 10% by mid-1972. By August 1973 they exceeded 25%,[29] a phenomenon clearly reflected in a series of by-elections in February 1973. There seems little doubt that Powell too was a beneficiary of this mood.

As the *Spectator* editorial said just after the 1973 by-elections:[30]

> The discussion of the recent by-election results is conducted with hardly any reference to Mr Powell, and Mr Thorpe and Mr Wilson are discussed as the alternative to Mr Heath, when the probability is that the alternative the public yearns for is Mr Powell. Those who seek an alternative to the policies of these men (Heath and Wilson) may express their resentment at the present set-up by voting for Mr Thorpe and his merry men, but how many would remain loyal to the Liberal party were a new standard to be raised (by Powell)?

In contrast to the pre-1970 period, Powellites after 1972 began to demonstrate higher levels of political disillusionment than the whole electorate. In February 1973 40% of those whom M.O.R.I. considered 'alienated' said Powell best represented their views.[31] No other group supported him so heavily – only 30% of Tories, 20% of Labour voters and 25% of all respondents gave the similar response. The February 1974 data showed a similar position, with 31% of the alienated saying Powell best represented their views against 15% of all respondents, 16% of Conservatives and 12% of Labour voters. By July 1974 the differences had grown further still, with 36% of the alienated now feeling best represented by Powell against 17% of all respondents, 15% of Conservatives and 17% of Labour supporters.

Examination of the responses to separate questions reveals the extent of the difference between Powellites and the electorate. By February 1973 Powellites were more likely than others to say that it was difficult to see any difference between the Conservative and Labour parties (Table 11.10), a clear reversal from 1969–70 when the Butler-Stokes surveys had shown Powellites as *more* likely than others to say there were differences between the major parties. Moreover the differences between Powellites and others had widened by 1974, as Table 11.10 also shows. The industrial and political confrontation of early 1974 produced a considerable and predictable hardening of the party blocs and of the feeling that they represented different things – but the Powellites were affected hardly at all by this change.

TABLE 11.10   Political disillusionment and support for Powell, 1973–74

	Feb 1973			Feb 1974		
	All %	*Pow.* %	*Non-Pow.* %	*All* %	*Pow.* %	*Non-Pow.* %
It is difficult to see any difference between the Conservative and Labour parties						
Agree	35	42	33	30	42	28
Neither the Conservative or Labour party represent the views of people like me						
Agree	39	52	35	31	49	28
Both the Conservative and Labour governments have failed to solve the most important problems facing Britain						
Agree	49	56	47	52	61	50
	(2073)	(521)	(1552)	(1290)	(205)	(1085)

Source: M.O.R.I. Panel Study, 1973–74.

While Powell may not have drawn a disproportionate amount of support from Liberals, he was generally very well received by other voters who were not satisfied with the two major parties. In the February 1973 wave of the M.O.R.I. panel he did extremely well with floating voters (people who had supported at least two different parties in the last three general elections). While only 25% of the whole sample said he best represented their views, a third of the floating voters gave this response.

3. Immigration and the E.E.C.

Immigration and the E.E.C. were both independently important in structuring attitudes to Powell in the period after 1970. A Gallup poll in June 1973 showed that 48% of those who said Britain made the wrong decision in entering the E.E.C. said Powell was an asset to the Tory party while only 29% of those who said the country made the right decision gave him a similar rating. Similarly the poll showed that 44% of those believing immigration to be a serious problem rated him a Conservative asset while only 28% of those who said it was not serious considered him an asset.[32]

More persuasive evidence of the importance of both issues come from the 1974 wave of the Butler-Stokes panel study. Their data show a clear relationship between taking an anti-E.E.C. posture (advocating a pull-out if fundamental re-negotiations are not conducted or a withdrawal regardless of the negotiated terms) and awarding Powell a high rating on a 0–10 scale (Table 11.11). The anti-Market position of the Powellites was not merely a function of their working-class or Labour party bias. Even with class and party controlled, the Powellites were more prone to be against the E.E.C. than other respondents (especially among middle-class and non-Labour voters). Powellites were once again more likely

TABLE 11.11   The relationship between anti-Market beliefs and support for Powell, 1974

	Powell rating			
	0–2 %	3–5 %	6–7 %	8–10 %
Sorry Britain entered the E.E.C.	37	50	63	75
Believe Britain should withdraw unless fundamental re-negotiations take place or withdraw regardless of the terms negotiated	28 (303)	41 (287)	54 (211)	64 (270)

Source: British Election Study at Essex University, 1974.

TABLE 11.12 The relationship between anti-Market beliefs and support for Powell, controlling class and party, 1974

	All %	*AB* All %	*AB* Pow. %	*AB* Non-Pow. %	*C1* All %	*C1* Pow. %	*C1* Non-Pow. %	*C2* All %	*C2* Pow. %	*C2* Non-Pow. %	*DE* All %	*DE* Pow. %	*DE* Non-Pow. %
Believe Britain should withdraw unless fundamental re-negotiations take place or withdraw regardless of the terms negotiated	46 (1096)	31 (152)	59 (27)	26 (125)	39 (288)	68 (60)	31 (228)	54 (415)	68 (113)	49 (302)	50 (241)	57 (70)	47 (171)

	All %	*Labour* All %	*Labour* Pow. %	*Labour* Non-Pow. %	*Conservative* All %	*Conservative* Pow. %	*Conservative* Non-Pow. %	*Liberal/other* All %	*Liberal/other* Pow. %	*Liberal/other* Non-Pow. %
Believe Britain should withdraw unless fundamental re-negotiations take place or withdraw regardless of the terms negotiated	46 (1096)	62 (436)	71 (128)	59 (308)	25 (371)	44 (61)	22 (310)	43 (194)	68 (57)	33 (137)

Source: British Election Study at Essex University, 1974.

Table 11.13   The relationship between racial conservatism and support
for Powell, 1974

	Powell rating			
	0–2	*3–5*	*6–7*	*8–10*
	%	%	%	%
Per cent scoring two or more on racial conservatism scale	61	68	75	87
	(303)	(287)	(211)	(270)

Source: British Election Study at Essex University, 1974.

than other respondents to advocate conservative positions on immigration. A racialism scale was once again constructed with respondents
given one point for each affirmative answer they gave to the following
questions: Are there too many immigrants in Britain? Do you feel very
strongly about the problem? Is immigration a neighbourhood problem?
Do you favour repatriation of coloured immigrants? The data in Table
11.13 show that the higher the rating Powell was accorded the more
likely it was for the respondent to give two or more affirmative answers
to the questions listed above.

It is of course impossible to measure the relative importance of both
issues without holding the effect of each one constant when examining
the effect of the other on support for Powell. Still, the strength of the
E.E.C. issue in explaining Powell's support is evident from the greater
differences between Powellites and non-Powellites on that question than
on immigration and race relations.

4. *Summary*

Multiple regression analysis again provides a convenient way of measuring the effect of a number of different independent variables on attitudes
toward Powell. By replicating a number of the tests performed on the
1969 Butler-Stokes data, a comparative assessment of the effect of
different variables can be conducted. The beta coefficients in the table
measure the relative effect of each variable on support for Powell with
the others held constant. As with the Butler-Stokes data, only three
variables were tested together. Because party and racial attitudes were
the most important variables in 1969, they were kept in each of the
regression equations which were computed for 1973 and 1974. An
examination of Table 11.15 shows that in virtually every test the importance of party identification and racial attitudes declined in importance
over time, so that by February 1974 Conservative party identification
was of only minimal importance in structuring attitudes to Powell. Only
when attitudes to the Common Market were controlled did Conservative identification play anywhere near the role it had previously.
Similarly all the equations for 1973 and 1974 show a significant decline

TABLE 11.14 The relationship between racial conservatism and support for Powell, controlling class and party, 1974

				AB			C1			C2			DE		
	All %	Pow. %	Non-Pow. %	All %	Pow. %	Non-Pow. %	All %	Pow. %	Non-Pow. %	All %	Pow. %	Non-Pow. %	All %	Pow. %	Non-Pow. %
Per cent scoring 2 or more on racial conservatism scale	72 (1096)	87 (270)	68 (826)	56 (152)	82 (27)	50 (125)	68 (288)	88 (60)	63 (228)	76 (415)	86 (113)	72 (302)	81 (241)	90 (70)	78 (171)

				Labour			Conservative			Liberal/other		
	All %	Pow. %	Non-Pow. %	All %	Pow. %	Non-Pow. %	All %	Pow. %	Non-Pow. %	All %	Pow. %	Non-Pow. %
Per cent scoring 2 or more on racial conservatism scale	72 (1096)	87 (270)	68 (826)	76 (436)	89 (128)	7 (308)	72 (371)	87 (61)	69 (310)	65 (194)	81 (57)	59 (137)

Source: British Election Study at Essex University, 1974.

TABLE 11.15 Multiple regressions on support for Powell, 1969–74

Equation	Explanation of third independent variable in equation 1969	Con-servative	Racialist	Dis-illusion-ment	Social class	Common Market
1.	Government pays no attention to the people when taking decisions	·77*	1·37*	(0·05)		
2.	No difference between the parties	·74*	1·36*	(0·08)		
3.	Manual	·92*	1·41*		·29*	
4.	Anti-Market	·86	1·50*			0·00‡
	1973					
1.	Neither party represents the views of people like me	·47*	1·12*	·64*		
2.	Little difference between the parties	·49*	1·12*	·33*		
3.	Average person has no say in government decisions	·57*	1·12*	·53*		
4.	Manual	·54*	1·13*		·14*	
5.	Anti-Market	·86*	1·50*			0·00‡
	1974					
1.	Neither party represents the views of people like me	·27*	1·02*	1·21*		
2.	Little difference between the parties	·27*	1·01*	·71*		
3.	Manual	·26*	·93*		·13†	
4.	Anti-Market	·63*	·97*			·59*

* Significant at ·01 level.
† Significant at ·05 level.
‡ Insignificant.

Source: Butler-Stokes Panel Study, 1969 and M.O.R.I. Panel Study, 1973–74.

in immigration's importance. It was still the most important variable in all but one equation, but it too showed a steady decline in importance from 1969. With the decline of party identification and to a lesser extent racial attitudes, general political disillusionment came to play an increasingly substantial role in structuring attitudes toward Powell. By 1974, indeed, the 'disillusionment' test (equation 1) was actually the most powerful independent variable in structuring attitudes to him. Other equations testing the effect of general political disillusionment showed its increase in importance after 1973. For example in 1969 there was no statistically significant relationship between having the sense that Government paid no attention to the people (equation 1) and support for Powell. By February 1973 there was a clear relationship between believing the average person had no say in Government decisions (equation 3) and support for Powell. By February 1974 it is probably fair to say that general disillusionment had replaced Conservative party identification as the second most important variable in structuring attitudes to Powell. Also for the first time the data show a strong relationship between anti-Market sentiments and support for Powell.

Summary and Grass Roots View of the Powellites

Thus to sum up: from 1968 to 1970 Powellism was a phenomenon most heavily based on attitudes to race and immigration, with Conservative party identification also a major determinant and social class a weaker third. The phenomenon of Powell burst to life in this period of general disillusionment but Powellites were not notably more alienated or disillusioned than others.

After 1970 – and particularly by 1973–74 – the most powerful single determinant of Powell's support was still racial attitudes, with disillusionment now a close second. Party identification had ceased to play an important role and class continued to be a weaker predictor. This very diffusion of Powellite support away from a party and single-issue based phenomenon should not be considered surprising. By 1973–74 the Powellites had become increasingly alienated from the political system. Given that their hero had achieved such scant success and given their probable feelings of frustration over the two issues which mattered most to them – the E.E.C. and immigration – their disillusionment is understandable enough.

To gain some insight into how Powellites *did* feel by the mid-1970s we include below material drawn from a number of interviews carried out in the London area during March 1975. All names are fictitious but all were real enough people who told interviewers at an earlier stage that Powell was the M.P. who best represented their views. Throughout the preceding chapters the Powellites appear as rows of statistics or lines on a graph. It is perhaps only fair to let the Powellites speak for themselves. As even this brief interview material shows, human reality can be more striking than the most clear-cut correlation.

George and Joan Jefferson

George and Joan Jefferson live in a three-room flat in Southfields (London S.W. 18). Their flat does not have a toilet – they share a public W.C. in their hallway. But the flat itself is very clean and bright; they've clearly done a lot of work to make it that way. They are a good-looking, cheerful couple in their late 20s, with a three-month-old son. They would like – but can't afford – to own their own house. While the Jeffersons have been on the waiting list for four years for a council house, they don't think they have any chance of getting one.

George works for the Electricity Board as a cable-joiner's mate and is reasonably happy with the pay. He has never voted in his life, saying when interviewed that he was neither favourable nor unfavourable to any of the three major parties. He was strongly anti-Communist and had some regard for the National Front – though he did say he knew little about these two parties. His wife is a regular Conservative voter but she did not cast a ballot in the February 1974 election – 'out of disgust' she says.

When interviewed George said that he felt the major problem facing Britain was inflation. 'People should realise that they can only make so much money; everybody must take a drop, but nobody is willing to.' Asked if there was another problem which concerned him, he replied quickly: 'immigration and population. It won't affect us in my time, but maybe in my baby's time. It's all due to unwanted babies. Not that you can force people to have only two, but it's a question of not being educated. At the rate they're going, the world will be over-populated.'

When George was asked who among Britain's leading politicians best represented his views, he wife, who was busy feeding the baby, chimed in 'Enoch Powell!' George smiled and said his wife was given to enthusiasm. As for himself, 'I don't vote for any of them, but right now Willie Whitelaw impresses me the most.' On a previous interview he had said Enoch Powell, but when asked now, 'I agree with most of his views, but if he had his way there would be blood in the streets.'

Without any prompting, George turned to his views on immigration: 'You should look after your own people first. When immigrants come into a country, they should expect you to look after your own kind first. For example, I wanted to go to New Zealand to move there. But if I went there, I'd expect to be treated less well than the people who were already there.'

When asked about what could be done about immigration, he said: 'Obviously you can't stop it right away. Those who want to go back, and there are a lot of them, ought to be given assistance. If we threw them out, and all the English people living in other countries all over the world came back, they say there would be more people here. I don't know. They don't live our way of life. Sure they have eyes, a nose and a mouth. I know the argument. But it's a different culture.'

Why didn't he vote in the last election? 'I was puzzled by the bickering. I agree with some of the things Labour says, and some of the things the Conservatives say. I don't believe in the Labour party. They always want to help people who don't help themselves.' Would he have voted in the last two elections if Powell had been the Tory leader? No, not really. Some of the things he stands for I agree with, and some I don't. He lost his argument, he went about it the wrong way. He was slanging people. "Vote Labour", he said. This was childish. He made some good statements in his day, but I'm going away from him. He's gone off crying. He's hurt inside, and won't let anybody forget it.'

What would he think of Powell for prime minister? 'I wouldn't say Enoch Powell. He's so strong. With that type of man as prime minister in the situation of the miners, he would stand firm. That's right. I was for the miners from the word go. I think they're pushing their luck, though.' But George did have great respect for what Powell has said about immigration. 'I think he brought that issue to the fore. The majority of the people are for it, for what he said. I admire him. He had everything going for him. He's lost a lot. If he had foreseen what would happen, he would have done the same thing.'

Throughout the discussion with George, his wife had only occasionally interjected a comment while she served coffee and biscuits and tended to the baby. But after George was finished with his comments, Joan took her turn to answer our questions. She was far more concerned with immigration and over-population than her husband. She felt that the politicians really did not understand the problem in the way that she and her husband did.

'Immigration is the main problem. M.P.s don't have to live with them. They live in their £30,000 houses out in Surrey. Their kids don't go to comprehensive schools. Their kids go to public schools. I don't want council houses and comprehensive schools. That's why I'm not Labour. We want to live our life like they do.' Pointing to her son, she said, 'I want him to go to a private school. I want him to be a lawyer or something. Not a labourer. That's why I vote Tory. But the politicians, they don't represent the view of the ordinary person.'

When asked what politician best represented her views, she replied firmly, 'Enoch Powell. The fact is that if he promises to do something, he stands by it. He's the only man who really stands by it. He's forceful.' Was there anything she disliked about Powell? 'He's a bit extreme, though I don't really know. He's a bit frightening. Public opinion would have nothing to do with him. He's fortunate. He talks the one issue that people agree with him on, immigration.' She expressed support for some type of repatriation plan. 'I'd support repatriation of those that didn't want to work. We've had to work hard for what we've got. Life's too short to worry about anything else.'

Why didn't she vote in February or October 1974? 'I was disgusted with the lot of them. I tried to get help to get a new house and got nowhere. We've been on the housing list for four years. Four years! To get help you have to be poor. It's things like that which make you go to the extreme, to Enoch. The underdog always gets on.' Had Powell been the Conservative leader, she might have acted differently. She might have voted Conservative then, but she was careful to say that at that time she was thoroughly disgusted with all politicians. Nor was Joan particularly enthusiastic about the prospect of Powell becoming prime minister. 'No, he doesn't have the sort of attitude we need. But he should have a big voice in government. He should definitely be brought into

Mrs Thatcher's inner circle. Mrs Thatcher is for people who want to help themselves, we ought to give her a try.' She also disapproved of Powell's statement in support of Labour in February and October. 'If he really is a Conservative, he should be loyal. Voice your views to change the party.'

Did either George or Joan feel that some groups in society were rising at their expense? George did not think so. 'No. No, people are not rising at my expense. I work for a nationalised industry. If it were private, it would be broke, so much money's being wasted.' Still, he thought it was necessary to have public utilities nationalised.

To Joan talk of 'groups in society' had a more restricted meaning. 'We should help the people who've lived here, not people who've just come in. They get national health, council houses. People know all anyone has to do to get help is to be poor and have kids. We were sensible, planning our child, got ourselves a house while we were waiting, and what have we got? We're paying because we were sensible.'

'Look', her husband broke in, 'my brother had two kids by a woman he wasn't married to. They moved into a half-way house and they got a council flat in six months. They're O.K., but it's the system that's wrong. I like my brother, we get on well with him', his wife nods, and they both smile. 'Maybe he's cleverer than we were,' he says, 'they had the kids and got their house.'

Winifred Winston

Winifred Winston has lived for the last thirty years as a widow in Ealing (London W. 13). She keeps her small two-room flat immaculately clean, as if she were expecting guests. She's an open and friendly person with very clear opinions about what has been happening to her neighbourhood over the past few years.

'I've lived in this neighbourhood over the past thirty years; and the neighbourhood has been getting steadily worse. The foreigners have interfered with our lives. . . . These people claim they have passports. So what, anyone can get a British passport. We wouldn't be treated as well as they are if we went to a foreign country.'

Mrs Winston is also disgusted with the way the major political parties have handled immigration. Despite the immigration control legislation of the 1960s and 1970s, she contends, 'The problem is that all the parties want the immigrants in. There's no real difference between them. For the present, we should cut immigration completely.'

But despite her concern over the deterioration of Ealing and the coloured children who she claims are always playing on her small front lawn, Mrs Winston does not believe that immigration is the most important problem facing Great Britain. 'The main problem in Britain today is money. I've never known anything as terrible as it is now. Neither the Liberals, the Conservatives nor Labour have any answers. I don't agree with the people who say our problems have nothing to do with politics; I'll support someone who will do something for the entire country.'

Mrs Winston voted Labour in February but did not seem to have voted in October. She was dissatisfied with all the parties and took little interest in the campaign. 'I really can't remember if I voted in October. I really don't think I did, I was so disgusted. It's all such a waste of time now.'

But when Mrs Winston was asked if anyone in Britain understood the problems facing the country, her eyes lit up. 'Enoch Powell is the man', she said. 'He's seen it all. He's got it at his finger tips. But I really don't understand what he did last year. I really don't understand too much about these political things. Maybe he did it because everyone in the Conservative party turned against him. He just wanted to get at the Conservatives.'

She is also confused about why Powell now represents South Down in Parliament. She wishes he was still the member for Wolverhampton South West. 'I really don't understand why Enoch left England. It's certainly a loss to us. As I've said, I really don't know much about politics. I felt Enoch spoke his mind on immigration over the years. I really don't like them (the immigrants); they want their own way. The West Indians keep a neat house, but the Pakistanis are dirty, you ought to go up to Southall. It's like being in Asia.'

Britain would 'be at the top of the tree' with Powell as prime minister, according to Mrs Winston. But she did not believe that he should join Mrs Thatcher's Shadow Cabinet. 'Those two could never get on, there would be such clashes. Anyway, I don't believe in a woman being the supreme being.'

Mrs Winston has little recollection of what Powell has said over the years about Britain's economic problems, but she did know he was anti-Common Market. 'I don't remember anything Enoch has said about our economic crisis. He doesn't want to take orders from Brussels, does he? I'm definitely against the Market, and plan to vote 'out' in the referendum. That's one thing Enoch is definitely right about.'

Mary Wills

Mary Wills also lives in Ealing, sharing a flat with her sister Eleanor. Miss Wills has never been married and consequently has had a lot of time free for social and fraternal activities. She qualifies as a political activist, having voted in all general and council elections as well as making speeches to organised groups and attending numerous local civic association meetings.

Like the other people that were spoken to, Miss Wills also agreed that the economic crisis and inflation were the main problems facing the country. But she seemed to place greatest emphasis on immigration.

'The most important issues are inflation and immigration. Immigration has to be controlled, especially with 50,000 people coming in every year. We also have to do something about inflation. Eleanor and I can hardly afford to eat even though both of us bring home a decent salary each week.'

Like Mrs Winston, Miss Wills is particularly concerned about the situation in Ealing. 'I've lived here 35 years and life in this neighbourhood has got much worse. There's too much noise with the foreigners. Mind you, I haven't got anything against them, there's bad and good in every race. When I first came here there was quiet, and no children in the streets. Now its cosmopolitan, there are late parties until 6 a.m., its so bad that the walls and my bed vibrate. We just can't go where we want any more. Why should they get National Health Service benefits? I couldn't just pick up and go to their countries and expect to be treated like a first-class citizen. There is no real difference between the political parties on the issues, they've simply done nothing to keep the immigrants out.'

Miss Wills is an admirer of Enoch Powell, but with some reservations. She likes what he has been saying about keeping Northern Ireland in the U.K., but is afraid of what would happen if he ever got into power. She shared the Jeffersons' sense that Powell was a bit too extreme.

'It would be a good thing for Britain if Enoch were prime minister provided he didn't get too mad. In some of these things he's like an upcoming Hitler, a dictator. He's sometimes too extreme, you can see his eyes rolling. I also don't think he'd fit into Mrs Thatcher's Shadow Cabinet. He's just too powerful for the poor lady.'

In November 1975 Enoch Powell had said on television that he felt his Birmingham speech had made little impact in the effort to control coloured immigration. Miss Wills agrees with this view. 'Enoch had the right idea on immigration, but I can't honestly say he's helped the situation because there has been no improvement. They are still pouring in.'

Miss Wills respects Powell because he has been one of the few people willing to discuss the problem directly. 'Enoch understands the problem like few politicians do. I think he sees things the way I do. The problem with this country is that if you have a row with coloured people you're always in the wrong. With race relations legislation, you're more inclined to let things slide. Immigrants have to realise they must abide by a country's rules too.'

She voted Liberal in February and October out of dissatisfaction with Labour and the Conservatives. The problem with the major parties according to her was that the Tories were only out for their own interests while Labour was too left-wing and trade-union minded. To her mind, none of the parties really had a dynamic leader. The only person who could conceivably have persuaded her to vote Conservative was Powell, though she did develop second thoughts about him after he endorsed Labour. 'That's just something I couldn't figure out. How can a Conservative tell people to vote for the Socialists?'

'They've got to try to get prices stable. Something in the shop went up 8½p. this week. There's nobody in the Government worth voting for. The only man who talks sense is Enoch Powell.'

But her support for Powell did not imply agreement with his position on economic issues – she said that she did not know much about such things. 'My support for Enoch is just general approval. Mostly I agree with what he said about coloured people. There's a crowd of them over the way. These people came over and got all they could out of national assistance. And they get so much money from the Government that they can go out and buy cars. The daughter of the Pakistani over there is learning to drive. I've worked all these years and I can't afford a car.'

Mary Whyle

Mrs Whyle did not vote in either the October or February elections. She too was disgusted with the major parties. She also was one of Enoch Powell's strongest supporters during 1974 though she did not understand quite what he was trying to do. 'I would have voted if Enoch Powell had been head of the Tories. Because Powell's not afraid of what he thinks, and doesn't give a damn about the other people. I was canvassed by this lady from the Tories here in Ealing and I told her I wasn't voting, but that I would if Powell were the Tory leader. She said, "but he's much too controversial". I replied: "You silly thing, that's just what we need! He's an honest man." And the last time (February 1974), why did Heath want to go out and have an election?'

Immigration was clearly her central concern and she responded directly when asked if any groups were advancing at her expense. 'It's the immigrants. I'm helping them see their bloody kids through. Two or three or more. I never agreed with the children's allowance. I saw a woman collect the allowance, and give it to her kid as pocket money. It's all wrong.'

Without pausing, Mrs Whyle related what had happened to her when she went to get her pension. 'I wanted to find out how to get on pension so I went into the office and got the coloured bloke who couldn't even speak English! A young coloured bloke. I told him to get someone who could speak English to talk to me. He knew nothing whatsoever, but he spoke to me like he was the King of England. I know they are people the same as we are, but we're getting the rough kind around here.'

What should be done about immigration? 'Enoch was right when he said that a whole lot of them should be sent back. As it stands now, they're sending money back to their own countries! Money they're earning here, they're sending back!'

While she shared Powell's views on immigration, she was less sure of his actions during 1974. Mrs Whyle was unsure why Powell stood as a United Ulster Unionist in South Down and she did not understand why he endorsed Labour. 'I don't quite understand the whole Northern Ireland business. It's the only time I wondered what the hell he was up to. I don't quite agree with that. I also don't quite understand him with Labour.' With a laugh in her voice she said, 'I guess I don't understand much about his policies.'

She was not too optimistic about his prospects of joining Mrs Thatcher's Shadow Cabinet. 'I'd like to see him do it, but I don't think he'd get along. They'd strike him down. The Conservatives are out to get him.'

Conclusion

Many views are possible of Enoch Powell's career. He has been variously regarded as a rigid unbending ideologue, a rank opportunist, a shrewd and calculating tactician, a mere political maverick using any means possible to attack his party's leadership, an ivory tower academic and a 'people's tribune'. How can these varying impressions be reconciled?

A. PRINCIPLES AND OUTCOMES

Our contention here will be that throughout most of his career Powell certainly has been ideologically consistent, particularly in regard to his central belief in *laissez-faire*, free-market capitalism.[1] His beliefs and arguments on this point have emerged sufficiently clearly in the preceding chapters not to warrant extensive re-summary here. He believes quite simply that the public interest has been best served by market forces working themselves out. The economic system can be analogised to a continuous general election with consumers constantly registering their votes by only buying goods they want or need. Hence, business is forced to tailor its offerings to what consumers want. If businesses or industries are uprofitable, it is in the public interest for them to be allowed to go out of business. Powell has accepted a degree of Government regulation of the economy – the state maintains the right to lay down universal health and safety regulations, for example. But he is positively opposed to any state efforts either to plan or influence economic choice, not merely because a purely capitalist system would produce the most efficient division of labour, but because there is maximum individual freedom when consumers and producers are free from Government control.

On matters not involving economic decisions (defined here as choices between alternatives which can be compared on a monetary scale), Powell accepts the need for a limited amount of state intervention. Thus he acknowledges the need for state involvement with the military, the educational system and health care planning. Even here he is far from accepting a 'universal state' – favouring private education, selective-on-need social services, and, most recently, advocating the creation of a 'people's army' of citizen volunteers. But it should be noted that by accepting state intervention in non-economic areas he gives himself wide latitude in defining what particular issues entail non-economic choice.

His belief that inflation can only be controlled through Government

264

regulation of the money supply stems directly from these arguments. Prices and incomes policies are always ineffective when applied selectively; they can only work when *every* price and income is controlled. Accepting the full implications of what an incomes policy entails accordingly requires an excessive surrender of individual liberty. Blame for inflation lies not with consumers or producers in any case. Wage and price rises are an effect, not a cause, of inflation. The solution was to cut expenditure and/or raise taxes, and establish a floating rate for sterling. By doing this a sound monetary system would be created and the free society maintained.

It is from these relatively simple arguments that Powell has undeviatingly generated his entire economic critique and analysis over two decades. The ideas are neither new nor unusual, but he has expounded them with a rigour, logic and passion quite untypical of most Conservative economic thought. His ideas have enjoyed notable success. He has seen the Conservative party turn first to Selsdon-man and, later, repudiate the heritage of Heath and opt for the Joseph-Thatcher brand of monetarist, free-enterprise Conservatism. He has seen the Tory party twice and the Labour party once turn against the idea of a statutory prices and incomes policy. He has seen both parties accept the floating of sterling. Both parties have accepted the necessity of increased taxes, public expenditure cuts and control of the money supply in the fight against inflation. It is doubtful whether Powell can be said to have directly caused these shifts but he certainly deserves credit for his advocacy and prophecy of them.

On immigration Powell has, since 1967 at least, been equally consistent. Despite the great and continuous hail of abuse to which he was subjected on this question he has stuck unwaveringly to his guns and not sought to trim before the wind. To be sure, he has in recent years been more preoccupied with other issues, but when he returned to the subject in February 1975, after a period of 18 months silence on the issue, his position had changed not at all. He again spoke strongly in favour of the repatriation of immigrants as the only way to avert future racial conflict in English cities. Britain would provide economic incentives to immigrants and their mother countries to make it profitable for a large-scale movement of the population to begin. His vehemence has hardly cooled in seven years. Indeed, after the speech there was some talk of prosecuting him for violation of the Race Relations Act but the Attorney General announced that no action would be taken.[2]

Again, Powell had achieved some success on this issue, not only in the form of the increasingly restrictive immigration laws enacted by both Labour and Tory Governments but by the virtual collapse of liberal opposition to such restrictions.

Moreover, Powell's statistical prophecies have been at least partially vindicated. Official estimates of the number of coloured immigrants in the country *have* had to be continually upwardly revised and the growth of inner-city black ghettoes, with all their attendant problems, is indeed visible. Even Powell's apparently wilder allegations have received some substantiation. When in 1970 and 1971 Powell alleged that Home Office civil servants had deliberately underestimated the number of coloured immigrants coming into Britain, he was accused of making McCarthyite allegations. Yet in early 1976 Mr Jenkins, the Home Secretary, was forced to concede in answer to a parliamentary question that the correct inflow of immigrants for 1973 was not 17,000 as originally reported, but 86,000. Powell wondered aloud whether this 'clerical error' had been made with other years' figures. He reported that immigration was running at 90,000 a year with more than 250,000 people having been added in the last three years alone. The position is not yet entirely clear (an official inquiry is currently being held) but it *does* seem that Powell's figures are probably roughly correct. Referring to his 1968 Birmingham speech when he said watching the flow of immigrants into Britain 'was like watching a nation busily engaged in heaping up its own funeral pyre', Powell said in January 1976:[3] 'What never occurred to me, even in my gloomiest forebodings, was that eight years later we should still be heaping the funeral pyre not just at the same rate but twice as fast.'

Powell again accused 'a considerable ring' of Home Office civil servants of 'cooking' the immigration figures. Specifically absolving Jenkins of any blame, Powell alleged that Home Office civil servants had adjusted the 1974 figures to compensate for the error on the 1973 figures. A 'cover-up' was operating in the Home Office to deny the Home Secretary, the Permanent Under-Secretary and his deputies access to the corrected figures 'until the last possible moment sixteen months later'.[4]

Nonetheless, Powell got little credit. The *Economist*, *The Times* and the *New Statesman* gave Powell passing credit for pointing out the error but concentrated on criticising him for his use of statistics in making projections about the current and future size of the immigrant population.[5] Powell's own major journalistic supporter was the *Spectator* columnist Patrick Cosgrave (political adviser to Mrs Thatcher), who wrote a column explaining in detail why Powell was right and admitting that he, Cosgrave, must now withdraw the criticisms he had earlier made of Powell.[6]

Powell's other central concern has been to forge a new national identity for Britain. His views were set out most completely, as we have seen, in 1964 in his St George's Day and Trinity College, Dublin, speeches. We have seen too how this conception has underlain Powell's attitude to defence policy, immigration, Northern Ireland and the E.E.C. It is difficult to evaluate his relative success on this front. Writing in 1976 it is hard to assert that the mood and the reality of British national decline have not merely continued but deepened. On defence, Powell's ideas have been followed by policy-makers, but not as a matter of conviction, merely as a *faute de mieux* in the face of the shrinkage of British world power. The Northern Ireland situation is still confused but, as Powell predicted, power-sharing has collapsed and the I.R.A.'s strength has been enormously reduced. It is unclear what form of government Ulster will ultimately be given, but it is not likely that her parliamentary representation will be made proportionate with its population, as Powell has repeatedly urged. Britain entered the E.E.C. and Powell's defeat there at least seems quite straightforward. But the battle may well not be over, even there. The world recession of the 1970s has brought strains on the unity of the E.E.C. The virtual collapse of the Community's monetary policy by early 1976 has made the prospect of financial and monetary union by 1980 seem increasingly remote. The issue of direct elections to a European parliament in 1978 promises to be contentious in a number of countries. Moreover the E.E.C.'s weaker members, Italy and Britain, are under even greater internal pressure to bolt for protectionism as the recession cruelly exposes their weak competitive position *vis-à-vis* their partners. Such a move would of course entail a complete abrogation of the Treaty of Rome and might amount to their virtual exit from the E.E.C. altogether. It is still too soon, in other words, to say that hostility to the E.E.C. is a horse which Powell may not ride again.

Where Powell has most singularly failed however is in his over-riding hope of rekindling a regenerated sense of British nationalism. By 1976 the very opposite – a fragmentation into regional nationalisms and particularisms – seemed more likely. Even here the game is not lost. It seems by no means impossible that these tendencies will produce a strong 'Unionist' reaction, particularly in England (which Powell could champion). One casualty of such a clash of tendencies might well be Powell's hold on a Unionist seat in Northern Ireland (lost either through rejection by the South Down Unionist association or through rejection by the voters of the constituency at the next general election should he be renominated). Ironically, a rejection by the South Down Unionist association could force him to reconcile himself with the Tory leadership. Since returning to Parliament he has done everything he can to block an alliance between the Tories and the Ulster Unionists and was instrumental in getting the Unionists to abstain in the no confidence vote against the Government following its defeat over public expenditure cuts in March 1976. It is hard to imagine Powell begging anyone, much less the Tory leadership, for forgiveness, but it is not outside the realm of possibility for a reconciliation to be effected. Deep-seated resentments aside, the prospect of seeing his political career end unceremoniously in Ulster could drive Powell to reach out for the Tories again. Regardless of his disloyalty in 1974, the Tories are no doubt aware of Powell's still strong electoral appeal and might consider taking him back should he be willing to make concessions himself. If Powell's antagonism toward the Conservatives does not moderate, he might stand in England as an independent supporting Labour nationally.

B. *Pragmatism and opportunity*

While Powell has undoubtedly been a man of principle, it should not be inferred that he ignored practical considerations. In fact Powell has on a number of occasions argued explicitly against any party or government adopting an unbending adherence to principle and eschewing compromise. Ideological consistency is clearly not the only (or highest) political virtue:[7]

> Whatever the principles that a party enshrines, its actions in office are circumscribed by practicality . . . and principle must be diluted and compromised both by the situation inherited from the past and by the limits of time, space and opinion.

Powell's personal goal has been to become leader of the Conservative party and he has employed a number of different strategies to achieve this ambition. Initially he sought to play the role of the party maverick, and to advance within the parliamentary party by developing alternatives to party policy which other M.P.s might find attractive. In varying forms Powell employed this strategy throughout the period from his entry into Parliament in the 1950s until his 1968 Birmingham speech. This strategy involved maintaining a delicate balance between adherence to the party line and personal independence. He did not seek confrontation with the leadership, but inevitably fell into disfavour whenever the hierarchy felt he had stepped too far out of line. Between 1962 and 1968 he clashed with Reginald Maudling, Edward Heath and Sir Alec Douglas-Home over different aspects of party economic and defence policy. At least over economic policy Powell was of some influence in moving the party away from an interventionist policy. However on the personal level, he won little if any support from M.P.s, as was made clear in the 1965 Tory leadership contest. Part of his problem was that he simply refused to try to organise his own faction of back-bench Tory M.P.s committed to his policies. During the 1965 Tory leadership contest the *Economist* wrote about him:[8]

> Some would call Mr Powell a leader of a possible lurch to the right, but he is the antithesis of the sort of political boss for whose favours other contenders might manoeuvre in the hope he will throw blocks of support their way. Mr Powell hugs principles, not supporters, to himself.

Similarly, Richard Rose has pointed out that:[9]

> Powell is not a factional leader in the way that Aneurin Bevan was within the Labour party. Powell does not associate himself with

colleagues in the House of Commons. Most of his major statements are made away from the House and his friends and followers there are few.

Nor were there factions inside the Tory party which could naturally coalesce behind Powell.[10] The New Right in the party was always more of a political tendency than a stable faction.[11] Moreover Powell himself did not make an attempt to carve out a limited set of policies which members could rally to. He moved back and forth between different tendencies within the party, supporting right-wing economic policies, but endorsing homosexual law reform and supporting the abolition of capital punishment. Thus people likely to support him on one issue were more than likely to oppose him on others. For example, by joining the anti-Market cause Powell did not automatically win personal support from others taking this position. As one Tory M.P. put it:[12]

> Take Enoch Powell. I suppose I am slightly on the left wing, if you can call it a wing of the Tory party, on social matters, and I certainly am on immigration. Now, having done this anti-Common Market thing for years and years, I made it quite clear to Enoch, when he came into the group that, super, he's on the side of the anti-Marketeers and we're glad to have him, but so far as I was concerned that didn't imply that I sympathised with him over all his other things. Just because we were working together on this one thing, he mustn't expect me to be one of his cohorts.

Further, the very nature of Powell's political style alienated his colleagues in the House. Rose has noted that:[13]

> By his readiness to speak to rank and file constituency association meetings almost everywhere, by his journalistic sense of newsworthiness and by his statements, Powell has succeeded in making himself a major political figure. Yet he has never succeeded in establishing himself as a leader of the Conservative party, for the very actions that make him a political celebrity also make him distrusted among his parliamentary colleagues as a man of unsound judgement.

Powell's refusal to organise a faction of back-bench M.P.s sheds some light on his own brand of political pragmatism. While he always believed that he should try to maximise his own influence, it has also always been his contention that events and accidents of history thrust men into positions of leadership. The right sort of political calculations can put a person in the right position to take power, but political calculation and manoeuvring are not enough. Hence he believed that between 1962 and 1968 his speeches on economics plus the inevitable fiscal crisis would lead M.P.s to turn to him. However by early 1968 he realised that the party was accepting a number of his basic principles about incomes policy and economic planning without turning to him for leadership.

Powell's belief that it would be a crisis which would ultimately lead the Tory party to turn to him did not change in 1968. But his approach and choice of issues did. By April 1968 his emphasis turned away from attempting to win élite support through the careful development of policy alternatives. Rather he chose to go outside the parliamentary framework to win enough mass support on immigration to force other M.P.s to turn to him if the problem reached crisis proportions. To be sure, while he was developing his own critique of economic policy he did travel across Britain spreading his message. True, he often drew large crowds. While on economics he was preaching largely to Tory activists and the upper middle class, on immigration he found – as he must have anticipated – a sympathetic response from well over a majority of the electorate. The immigration speeches certainly increased Powell's personal stature, but the problem itself was never serious enough to unseat Edward Heath. Moreover Heath moved the Tory party closer to Powellite positions on immigration to undercut his potential impact.

Because immigration has always been such an emotional issue, its impact on the mass electorate has always been uneven. During some periods passions have been excited while at other times there has apparently been little popular concern. Consequently it was not surprising that, when the turmoil over the Race Relations Bill and the Kenyan Asians died down, Powell began to see his support eroding. He then turned to the anti-E.E.C. cause. But the E.E.C. never really helped him expand his mass base. The issue was much more remote than immigration and it was actually taken out of the political arena for a time in 1970 and 1971 when Mr Heath conducted the Brussels negotiations as if there was no question that Britain would join.

Immigration also became less salient politically after the passage of the 1971 Commonwealth Immigrants Act. Despite the fact that the Act eventually proved largely unworkable and needed substantial revision, it did incorporate two of Powell's major policy positions, voluntary repatriation and control over the right of dependents to enter. Once again he needed another issue. He chose Northern Ireland, with the hope of forging a broad constituency to pressure the Tory Government not to shirk from its responsibility to keep Ulster in the U.K. However, people in England were always more concerned with ridding themselves of the problem rather than adopting a specific policy position. Thus Powell's speeches on the question won him no new mass support in Britain.

The 1970–74 period of the Heath Government must have been a time of terrrible personal frustrations for Powell. Both the approaches he had adopted to win power in the Tory party had failed. He saw the Government abandon a *laissez-faire* approach, implement a statutory incomes policy and take Britain into the E.E.C. Despite the fact that he still had massive popular support and some continuing influence over immigration policy, on other fundamental questions he seemingly had no influence. Moreover, he was totally isolated from the Government on the back-benches. It is difficult to avoid the conclusion that he reacted to his increasing isolation on the élite level as well as to Heath's success in implementing policies he disagreed with by trying to bring down the Leader and the Government. When the Government introduced statutory wage and price controls, Powell asked publicly if Mr Heath had taken leave of his senses. A year later (November 1973) he defended that statement and said he feared for his Leader's emotional and mental stability. By June 1973 he was threatening publicly to desert the Tories in the next general election over the E.E.C., a warning he continually reiterated until February 1974, when he carried it out. Not surprisingly, M.P.s close to Mr Heath were convinced that Powell would do anything to embarrass the Prime Minister:[14]

> After 1971 Enoch sought any issue he could find to build his popularity. When we wanted to reform local government, he opposed the plan hoping to win support. When he got no response Powell supported our position in divisions. He did the same thing on the Housing Finance Bill. His hatred of Ted Heath was extraordinary.

The February 1974 election presented him with a grave crisis. His principles clearly made it impossible for him to support the Tories nationally. Heath had committed the party to staying in Europe and called the election to test his will against the miners. Powell was afraid that if Britain stayed in the E.E.C. much longer, European institutions would be created which would irrevocably destroy the sovereignty of the British Parliament. He also felt it was absurd to call an election to win support for a policy which, he believed, had no effect in curbing inflation, had no legal standing and was likely to be scrapped immediately after the poll. Purely practical considerations might have led him to stand as an independent or an independent Conservative in Wolverhampton South West, running on his own election manifesto. There is even some indication Central Office would not have opposed him had he taken this course of action.[15] Alternatively Powell could have simply stood down and not taken an active role in the campaign. Either way he would have been a potential leadership candidate after the Tories' national defeat. But despite pleadings from his few back-bench supporters, he refused to take this course of action. As a believer in party government he felt it would be inconsistent for him to stand as an independent. Since Labour was committed to fundamental re-negotiation of the terms of E.E.C. entry and a subsequent consultative referendum, he felt compelled to support them despite his disagreement with them over economics. Socialist policies could always be reversed, but once parliamentary sovereignty was surrendered it could never be regained. He had, moreover, a considerable amount of 'face' at stake.

Thus when principle collided with pragmatism in February 1974, Powell stuck to his convictions. But after February 1974 for the first time ideological principle had to give way to pragmatism. The only way he could regain a seat in Parliament was to stand in Northern Ireland as a U.U.U.C. candidate. But the U.U.U.C. was committed by its election manifesto and Portrush Declaration to significant devolution to Stormont within the context of a federal United Kingdom, to be carried out within the context of devolution to the other regions of the U.K. By his often repeated acceptance of the manifesto and the Portrush Declaration, Powell appeared to be accepting these positions as his own. Yet he has also set himself unambiguously against federalism for the same reason that he opposed E.E.C. membership: the sovereignty of Parliament would be undermined. Despite the fact that he stood on a manifesto committed to federalism, he set himself firmly against any constitutional alterations of that sort in a speech early in 1976. That he could have defended a manifesto which explicitly called for a federal structure and also speak against federalism so forthrightly seems to be the most fundamental contradiction of his career.

Also, if the British Government had accepted the Northern Ireland Convention's report and devolved power back to Stormont, he would have been forced to accept devolved government for Scotland and Wales, were he to remain consistent with the Unionist manifesto. Yet since 1968 he has continuously set himself against limited devolution of legislative power to Wales and Scotland, arguing that those regions must either be part of the U.K. in the same way that Cornwall and Devon are or that they must be totally independent.

For the first time in his career, Powell has been on both sides of an issue at the same time. Since his re-entry into Parliament in October 1974 he has taken a reasonably firm Unionist line (though his few deviations have brought him sharp criticism from the leadership and the grassroots). In England he has maintained a firmer anti-devolution position and pushed for increasing Northern Ireland's representation at Westminster to demonstrate that the province is an integral part of the U.K. In the past, when he has changed his position – for example on the E.E.C. – the reversal has been unambiguous. In this instance it has been very difficult to determine what his personal position is on devolved government in Ulster.

Powell seemingly answered the question in March 1976 when, in a Belfast speech, he defended the British Government's plan to govern Northern Ireland directly from Westminster after the dissolution of the Convention. Direct rule was perfectly acceptable because it brought Northern Ireland's government closer to that which other U.K. regions enjoyed and thus strengthened the Union. Powell cannot hope to maintain his position in Northern Ireland politics on this basis, and his reassertion of fundamental principles yet again suggests that his pragmatism has definite limits.

C. POPULISM

Powell's use of the immigration issue after 1968 raises the question of how he viewed his own role. In a limited sense, he saw himself as a populist politician, not in the sense that he accepted the doctrine that what the majority of people believed was the only basis for the formation of policy,[16] but that politicians had to voice the people's feelings *especially* if they ran counter to fashionable opinion or the élite consensus. Part of the politician's job was to 'provide people with words and ideas which will fit their predicament better than the words and ideas they are using at the present'.[17] At another point he stated that 'the politician in the end is a voice and the political parties a chorus of voices. We hope that what we speak may be what others have been thinking and are ready to hear so we may be a chord which will reverberate.'[18] But if the politicians and the parties did not happen to be saying exactly what the people are thinking, it was not their task to abandon their positions to suit the popular will. Thus he has never been willing to support the death penalty, despite its massive popular appeal, though he has said that if public support for it ever became overwhelming he might change his position.

Powell ultimately viewed his role as being a representative in the Burkean sense, rather than just a delegate whose job was merely to voice the people's sentiments.[19] Nevertheless he felt a special responsibility to voice popular fears and concerns and eagerly sought issues on which he could bridge the gap between the people's and politicians' views.

Immigration was thus an ideal issue for him. It was highly emotional and no British politician of his Shadow Cabinet rank and obvious intellectual stature had ever given respectability to what most élites considered to be nothing more than popular prejudices. By speaking out as he did, he commanded national media attention and demonstrated to his many sympathisers that there was at least one person in a position of some authority who understood the problem as they experienced it. Because so few British politicians have ever done what Powell did, he won significant mass support with his anti-immigration activities. His support in public opinion polls reached its peak when he was speaking on racial questions during controversies over immigration in 1968 and then again in late 1972 and in early 1973.

Powell also tried to cast himself in a populist role on other major issues, but had little success in winning new popular support. A large part of his justification for a free-market economy was that it gave ordinary people, and not just politicians, the ultimate voice in making economic decisions. For Powell, the difference between Conservative and Labour principles lay in the fact that the Tories 'trust the people' while Labour believed that virtually all economic decisions had to be taken in Whitehall and Westminster. (Interestingly, Powell's 1963 slogan for the Tories – 'Trust the People' – was adopted by the Governor of Alabama, George Wallace, for the 1976 American Presidential election.) Sometimes, despite his academic background and élite status, his deep distrust of state mandarins and his confidence in the people could produce even a hint of anti-intellectualism:[20]

> The collective wisdom and the collective will of the nation reside not in any little Whitehall clique but in the whole mass of the people. In the producers, listening to the voice of the customers at home and abroad; in the savers and investors, using their eyes and their brains to lay out their resources to best advantage; in the consumers themselves, expressing through the complex central nervous system of the market their wishes, their needs, their expectations. In short, the true national economic plan is being made all the time by the very people and institutions which intellectually arrogant Socialists affect to despise. What a world of contempt for the ordinary man and woman one finds in Labour [party propaganda].

Superficially at least the E.E.C. provided the same sort of conditions as immigration. Through much of the first three years that Powell opposed entry (1969–72) a majority of the public shared his negative views of the E.E.C. while the élite consensus by and large supported E.E.C. entry. But Powell did not win on the E.E.C. issue popular support comparable to that he had gained on immigration. People were simply far more willing to take their cues from established political leaders on the E.E.C. than they were on immigration. Thus, when the negotiations were concluded favourably in July 1971, support for entry jumped significantly. Also when the leaders of the three major parties combined to support the 'yes' position in the 1975 referendum, the public accepted their judgement. Moreover the aspect of E.E.C. membership Powell was most concerned with aroused little concern in the mass electorate. On immigration, he had discussed the question in the same fashion that ordinary people did, infusing it with the same strong emotions they felt. When people heard Powell describe what immigrant settlement could do to a neighbourhood, many were able to feel that he understood the problem as they experienced it. But, though Powell came to share popular opposition to the E.E.C., he was mainly concerned with the effect membership had on parliamentary sovereignty, while the electorate was concerned primarily with its effect on prices and the cost of living. Moreover, polls found the least interest in the sovereignty question among the working-class electors that Powell simply *had* to reach if the issue was to 'take off'. Instead, the lower down the social scale one went the more disproportionately was concern focused on bread-and-butter issues like prices. It was only among the (few) upper middle class anti-Marketeers that one found any evidence of concern about relatively abstract concerns like loss of parliamentary sovereignty. The British people, as Richard Rose has noted, have never been particularly insecure about their Englishness:[21]

> So secure are Englishmen in their personal and national identity that ineptitude does not stimulate a fear of national disintegration, a fear facing many newly formed nation-states. The outlook is summed up in the motto 'There will always be an England'. Confidence in national identity is as impressive when it is an obstacle to adaptation as it is when easing the assimilation of change.

Powell also tried to create a broad nationalistic constituency dedicated to keeping Northern Ireland in the U.K. Here again he received a weak response; by and large people seemed unconcerned about the fate of Ireland. Never more than a quarter of British public opinion poll respondents supported Powell's own integrationist solution to the problem. Popular feeling against terrorism and violence was at least sporadically intense, but it was not translated into similar levels of concern on constitutional questions. It is important therefore to distinguish the impact immigration and the E.E.C. had on British politics from the effect Northern Ireland had. Immigration and the Common Market were both 'position issues' which pitted vast segments of the electorate against the political élite.[22] But feelings only ran deep on the immigration issue – on the E.E.C. popular feelings were never really very intense, so the issue was difficult to exploit for political gain.

Whereas immigration and the E.E.C. were position issues, Northern Ireland was a 'valence issue'. Voters were not deeply divided about what policy the Government should adopt and were willing to endorse any plan which would produce tranquility. The Northern Ireland problem of the late 1960s and early 1970s was very different from the Irish question at the turn of the twentieth century when its divisive force was sufficiently strong for Joseph Chamberlain to be able to reshape the party system in his opposition to Gladstone's Home Rule policy. Powell may perhaps have been over-impressed by his own strong consciousness of history and the possible parallels between Chamberlain's career and his own. But it is impossible to argue that he took up the issue only through a mis-calculation as to its popular appeal. In a number of his early speeches on the issue, he acknowledged that the British did not really care much about the problem, paraphrasing the predominant British emotion as being:[23] 'The same old trouble with Ireland and the Irish, Protestants and Catholics, the former centuries over again – we thought we had got rid of all that at last, but apparently not.'

Powell was to great a realist not to see the issue's limitations; it seems clear he took it up despite those known problems. It was a matter of conviction and principle, straightforwardly enough – though it is also true that by 1971 he needed a new issue. The Heath Government had co-opted his views on immigration and economics and the E.E.C. was not yet a domestic political issue. Given his principles he was always likely to take up the issue, but his timing, at least, was probably influenced by more tactical considerations.

*   *   *

It may be stated fairly bluntly that politicians outside the leadership strata of the major parties have rarely won much lasting popular support in British politics.[24] The most singular exception to that generalisation has been Enoch Powell. The 1968 Birmingham speech was delivered at a time when Powell was a relatively obscure member of the Heath Shadow Cabinet; from May 1968 to February 1974 he was merely a back-bench M.P.; after that he was either not in the House of Commons or he was representing a minor party on the back-benches. He has nonetheless retained enormous popular support.

He has clearly been one of the three leading politicians in the eyes of the British electorate since 1968, regardless of his position *vis-à-vis* the political Establishment. This is still the situation at present, despite the departure into Irish politics. He was very close to Willie Whitelaw as the electorate's choice to succeed Heath as Conservative Leader and in 1974 has apparently held on to the support of some 15% of the electorate in polls conducted up to the summer of 1975.

Moreover Powell's impact has not just been limited to public opinion polls. The Butler-Stokes data from 1970 and 1974 clearly demonstrated that Powell played a decisive role in winning the 1970 election for the Tories and came back to make an important contribution to the Labour victory in February 1974. He has been able to mobilise his supporters in opposite directions at two different elections four years apart without the benefit of a political organisation or a strong base in the leadership of either political party; influence of this sort is probably unprecedented in British political history.

His electoral impact only hints at the commitment of large numbers of his followers in the mass electorate. In the early 1960s he became something of a hero to Tory activists because of his unrestrained advocacy of the free-market system. Friends of Powell, as well as Powell himself, recall the large number of people that used to turn out at his meetings, well before the Birmingham speech (during a time when most politicians had trouble getting people away from their television sets and out to political gatherings). After Birmingham, Powell's supporters proved the tenacity of their commitment to him by staging demonstrations and marches to protest against his dismissal from the Shadow Cabinet, and by writing hundreds of thousands of letters in his support to newspapers, to Mr Heath, to local M.P.s and to Powell himself. His ability to fill a hall was unrivalled in British politics between 1968 and 1974.

What is especially interesting about his support is that it was derived from all segments of the electorate, in all parts of the country. Unlike Mosley's fascist movement of the early and mid-1930s Powell's support has never been concentrated in one stratum of society or in one geographical area.[25] Through most of the late 1960s and early 1970s his support mirrored the electorate. It was only after June 1973 that his base began shifting toward the working class.

Powell's mass constituency is also distinctive because of the broad range of issues he drew support on. Up to 1970 he won backing largely because he was a Conservative and because of his position on immigration. After that people turned to him because of his stance on the E.E.C. and because he was the one man outside the élite consensus whom the disillusioned could show any confidence in. He was thus able to cut across the traditional divisions of party identification in forging his mass constituency.

So we have seen that he was clearly a man of rigid principle. His tactical abilities were second to none. He was one of the leading parliamentarians in the House and was able to build a very broad and lasting mass following. Yet while he was able to influence the outcome of two elections, contribute significantly to the development of Conservative party policy and play a major role in bringing down the Government and leadership of Edward Heath, Powell is now (and is likely to remain) a political outcast. For all its brilliance his career has, in this sense, been a failure. Given his enormous and obvious strengths we must ask why that should be so.

The simplest answer is that Powell himself never was willing to do any of the necessary grassroots organisational work to organise his supporters in the electorate. In 1969 he did nothing to encourage the consortium of Midland businessmen who were trying to persuade him to stand against Heath for the Tory leadership. In 1973 he was also cool to an attempt by the leader of the Brent Conservative constituency association to build support for him in the country by circulating copies of his speeches to the leaders of other associations. There has never been any Powellite organisation either inside Tory constituency associations or in the population at large.

Another more significant reason why Powell has not been more of a force in British politics is that the population by and large has not shared his concern over parliamentary sovereignty and the more general issue of U.K. nationalism. Except when they have been directly threatened (as in war), the English public has never been susceptible to mobilisation over questions of sovereignty and nationhood in the way that the Americans have. There was no English variant of Mc-Carthyism in the 1950s. Nor can the political parties win sizeable numbers of votes by playing on themes like 'England's declining position in the world'. By contrast American politicians such as Ronald Reagan and Henry Jackson have based their Presidential campaigns in 1976 largely on the debateable assertion that America's position in the world has been severely eroded, hoping to emulate John Kennedy's success with his stress on the (fictitious) 'missile gap'. If the sovereignty of the American Congress were threatened in the same way that the sovereignty of the U.K. Parliament has been by the E.E.C., there would have been a far fiercer reaction than the one which was found in Britain. None of the issues Powell has stressed over the late 1960s and 1970s was critical enough to the British people for him to be catapulted into a position of leadership through mass agitation.

But while there has been no fundamental crisis in British government over the past eight or so years, disillusionment has surely grown. One of Powell's tactical failings has been his unwillingness to play on the disillusionment theme. In America the Governor of Alabama, George Wallace, has successfully played on middle-class dissatisfaction with the functioning of the political system to broaden his base beyond hard-core Southern segregationists. Powell has used this approach only sparingly, but at the mass level his constituency did change in the same way that Wallace consciously sought to mould his following. The evidence seems to suggest that had Powell tried to build an anti-system movement using racial antagonism and general disillusionment as the central elements, he might have had more success. But his commitment to the parliamentary system has been so strong that he has been unable to bring himself to emphasise the weaknesses in something he is resolutely committed to.

Beyond Powell himself, there are aspects of the British political system which have retarded his development. First, there are the purely structural elements. In the end it is the parliamentary party, and not the mass electorate, which determines the leadership of the political parties, and hence the government. Only in times of dire crisis can public opinion 'make' a party leader or prime minister. Also, unlike American presidential nominations, elections for leadership of the parliamentary parties are often the result of chance and historical accidents. A British politician cannot do what Barry Goldwater did in 1964 or George McGovern did in 1972: spend two years cultivating support in anticipation of a nominating convention to be held at some fixed date in the future. Margaret Thatcher was able to win the Tory leadership largely because Edward Heath failed to resign immediately after the October 1974 election. Had Heath resigned before the first ballot it is very likely that Whitelaw would have won the contest. Mrs Thatcher emerged not so much because of her stature in the party or with the public but because she positioned herself properly within the élite context in the short period of time between the October defeat and her ultimate election in February 1975. A defeat in 1970 very possibly could have made Powell the leading contender for the Tory leadership. As it was, the Tory victory probably ended his chances of ever leading his party.

Another factor weakening Powell's claims on national leadership has been that the growth of general disillusionment has not been accompanied by a basic questioning of British political institutions. People apparently feel that their institutions have not been working properly, but they are not willing to abandon them. Powell has been seen as someone who can make these institutions work more effectively because of his outspoken posture and willingness to go beyond the confines of the élite consensus. Yet his very willingness to be different and challenge the Establishment has undoubtedly cost him support. The growth of disillusionment has not completely eroded the conventional English belief in the virtues of moderation and compromise. Many people have welcomed his efforts to make the Establishment more responsive, but even among those admiring him there have been loudly voiced questions about his ability to unify the country and prevent divisions.

Powell's successes over the 1960s and 1970s are in large part a tribute to his own very substantial abilities and the frustrations of many British people with the performance of their political system and leaders. His failure to head either a government or a political party is evidence of the underlying strength and stability of the system, popular discontent with it notwithstanding.

Bibliography

1 *Periodicals and Newspapers Consulted*
The Times, 1962–76
Guardian, 1968–76
Financial Times, 1965–76
Daily Telegraph, 1963–76
Daily Mail, 1968–75
Daily Sketch, 1968
Daily Mirror, 1968–70
Sun, 1968–70
Daily Express, 1962–76
Economist, 1962–76
Spectator, 1962–76

2 *Television and Radio Transcripts*
All available B.B.C. radio and television interviews with Enoch Powell
between 1962 and 1975 were consulted.

3 *Interviews*
Dr Rhodes Boyson, M.P., 28 October 1975, Westminster
Richard Body, M.P., 30 October 1975, Westminster
Reginald Maudling, M.P., 4 November 1975, Westminster
Nicholas Ridley, M.P., 4 November 1975, Westminster
William Ross, M.P., 4 November 1975, Westminster
Douglas Hurd, M.P., 11 November 1975, Westminster
James Molyneaux, M.P., 11 November 1975, Westminster
Peter Walker, M.P., 17 November 1975, Westminster
John Laird, Treasurer, Official Unionist Party, 25 November 1975, Belfast
Norman Hutton, Secretary, Official Unionist Party, 25 November 1975, Belfast
Harry West, Chairman, United Ulster Unionist Coalition, 25 November 1975, Belfast
William Craig, M.P., 25 November 1975, Belfast
Airey Neave, M.P., 1 December 1975, Westminster
John Biffen, M.P., 1 December 1975, Westminster
William Whitelaw, M.P., 1 December 1975, Westminster

James Douglas, former Director of Conservative Research Department, 11 January 1976, Princeton, New Jersey, U.S.A.

Sarah McCallum, long-time Chairwoman of Wolverhampton South West Conservative women, 2 February 1976, Wolverhampton

William Clark, Chairman of Wolverhampton South West Conservative Association, 2 February 1976, Wolverhampton

Robin Pollard, Agent for Wolverhampton South West Conservative Association, 2 February 1976, Wolverhampton

Peter Wesson, former Vice-Chairman of Wolverhampton South West Conservative Association, 3 February 1976, Wolverhampton

Peter Farmer, President of Wolverhampton South West Conservative Association, 3 February 1976, Wolverhampton

Allen Garner, Chairman of Wolverhampton South West Labour Party, 3 February 1976, Wolverhampton

George Wilkes, former Chairman of Wolverhampton South West Conservative Association, 3 February 1976, Wolverhampton

W. G. Morrison, Chairman of Conservative Group on Wolverhampton Borough Council, 3 February 1976, Wolverhampton

David Howell, M.P., 12 February 1976, Westminster

Barney Hayhoe, M.P., 12 February 1976, Westminster

Nicholas Budgen, M.P., 12 February 1976, Westminster

David Watt, political columnist of the *Financial Times*, 20 February 1976, London

John Wood, Deputy Director, Institute for Economic Affairs, 20 February 1976, London

Diana Spearman, author of articles on Powell's election and immigration letters, 24 February 1976, London

Sir Geoffrey Howe, M.P., 24 February 1976, Westminster

Colonel E. H. Brush, Chairman, South Down Unionist Association, 18 April 1976 (telephone)

4 *Books and Articles Consulted*

Adorno, T. W., Frenkel-Brunswik, Else, Levinson, Daniel and Sandford, R. Nevitt, *The Authoritarian Personality* (New York, Harper & Row, 1950)

Alexander, Andrew and Watkins, Alan, *The Making of the Prime Minister 1970* (London, Macdonald, 1970)

Alford, Robert, *Party and Society* (Chicago, Rand McNally, 1963)

Almond, G. A. and Powell, G. Bingham, *Comparative Politics: A Developmental Approach* (Boston, Little, Brown, 1966)

Almond, Gabriel and Verba, Sidney, *The Civic Culture* (Princeton, N.J., Princeton University Press, 1963)

Arendt, Hannah, *The Origins of Totalitarianism* (London, Allen & Unwin, 1960)

Banks, Arthur (ed.), *The Political Handbook of the World: 1975* (New York, McGraw Hill, 1975)

Beer, Samuel, *Modern British Politics* (London, Faber, 1969)

Bell, Daniel (ed.), *The Radical Right* (New York, Doubleday, 1963)

Benewick, Robert, *Political Violence & Public Order* (London, Allen Lane, 1969)

Benham, John, *The Middle Class Vote* (London, Faber, 1954)

Boyd, Andrew, *Brian Faulkner and the Crisis of Ulster Unionism* (Tralee, County Kerry, Anvil Books, 1972)

Butler, David and Stokes, Donald, *Political Change in Britain* (2nd ed.) (London, Macmillan, 1975)

—— and Rose, Richard, *The British General Election of 1959* (London, Macmillan, 1960)

—— and King, Anthony, *The British General Election of 1964* (London, Macmillan, 1966)

—— and King, Anthony, *The British General Election of 1966* (London, Macmillan, 1966)

—— and Pinto-Duschinsky, Michael, *The British General Election of 1970* (London, Macmillan, 1970)

—— and Kavanagh, Dennis, *The British General Election of February 1974* (London, Macmillan, 1974)

—— and Kavanagh, Dennis, *The British General Election of October 1974* (London, Macmillan, 1975)

Butt, Donald, 'The Importance of Being Enoch', *Crossbow*, 9 (Apr–June 1966) 9–11

Christie, R. and Jahoda, M. (eds.), *Studies in the Scope and Method of the Authoritarian Personality* (New York, The Free Press, 1954)

Churchill, Randolph, *The Fight for the Tory Leadership* (London, Heinemann, 1963)

Converse, Philip, 'The Nature of Belief Systems in Mass Publics', in David E. Apter (ed.), *Ideology and its Discontents* (New York, Macmilllan, 1964) pp. 206–61

Deakin, Nicholas, *Colour and The British Electorate 1964* (London, Pall Mall Press, 1965)

Deakin, Nicholas and Bourne, Jenny, 'The Minorities and the General Election, 1970', *Race Today*, 2 (July 1970) 205–6

—— 'Powell, the Minorities and the 1970 Election', *Political Quarterly*, 40 (Oct–Dec 1970) 399–415

Deutsch, Richard and Magowan, Vivien, *Northern Ireland 1968–1973: A Chronology of Events (Vols. I and II)* (Belfast, Blackstaff Press, 1974)

Downs, Anthony, *An Economic Theory of Democracy* (New York, Harper & Row, 1957)

Durkheim, Emile, *Suicide* (New York, The Free Press, 1966)

Eitzen, Stanley, 'Status Inconsistency and Wallace Supporters in a Mid-Western Town', *Social Forces*, 49 (1970) 493–8

Finer, S. E., Berrington, Hugh and Bartholomew, D. J., *Backbench Opinion in the House of Commons, 1955–1959* (Oxford, Pergamon Press, 1961)

Foot, Paul, *The Rise of Enoch Powell* (Harmondsworth, Middlesex, Penguin, 1969)

Fraser, Peter, *Joseph Chamberlain: Radicalism and Empire 1868–1914* (London, Cassell, 1966)

Frasure, Robert C., 'Backbench Opinion Revisited', *Political Studies*, 20 (1972) 375–8

Fromm, Erich, *Escape from Freedom* (London, Routledge & Kegan, 1942)

Gamble, Andrew, *The Conservative Nation* (London, Routledge & Kegan, Paul 1974)

Goffman, Irving, 'Status Inconsistency and Symptoms of Stress', *American Sociological Review*, 27 (1962) 275–81

Goldthorpe, John, *et al.*, *The Affluent Worker in the Class Structure* (vol. 3) (Cambridge University Press, 1969)

Goot, Murray and Reid, Elizabeth, *Women and Voting Studies: Mindless Matrons or Sexist Scientism* (London, Sage, 1974)

Gusfield, Joseph, 'Mass Society and Extremist Politics', *American Sociological Review*, 27 (Feb 1962) 19–30

Guttsman, W. L. *The British Political Elite* (London, MacGibbon and Kee, 1968)

Harbinson, J. F., *The Ulster Unionist Party 1882–1973* (Belfast, Blackstaff Press, 1973)

Herberle, Rudolf, *From Democracy to Nazism* (New York, Grosset & Dunlop, 1970)

Hindess, Barry, *The Decline of Working Class Politics* (London, MacGibbon & Kee, 1971)

Hollingshedd, A. B., Ellis, R. and Kirby, E., 'Social Mobility and Mental Illness', *American Sociological Review*, 19 (1954) 577–84

Hoogvelt, Ankie M., 'Ethnocentrism, Authoritarianism and Powellism', *Race*, 11 (July 1969) 1–12

Hope, Keith (ed.), *The Analysis of Social Mobility* (Oxford University Press, 1972)

Humphry, Derek and Ward, Michael, *Passports and Politics* (Harmondsworth, Penguin, 1974)

Ionescu, Ghita and Gellner, Ernest (eds.), *Populism: its meaning and national characteristics* (London, Weidenfeld and Nicolson, 1967)

Jessop, Bob, *Traditionalism, Conservatism and British Political Culture* (London, Allan & Unwin, 1974)

Johnson, R. W. 'The British Political Elite 1955–1972', *European Journal of Sociology*, 14 (1973) 35–77

Kavanagh, Dennis, 'The Deferential English: A Comparative Critique', *Government and Opposition*, (Summer 1971) 333–60

Kenny, Paul J., 'The Affluent Worker Project: Criticism and a Deprivation Study', *The Sociological Review*, 20 (Aug 1972) 373–89

Key, V. O., *The Responsible Electorate* (New York, Vintage Books, 1966)

King, Anthony, 'Overload: Problems of Governing in the 1970s', *Political Studies*, 23 (1975) 162–74

—— *British Members of Parliament* (London, Macmillan, 1974 ed.)

—— *The British Prime Minister* (London, Macmillan, 1969)

Kitzinger, Uwe, *Diplomacy and Persuasion* (London, Thames and Hudson, 1973)

Klein, Rudolf, 'The Case for Elitism: Public Opinion and Public Policy', *Political Quarterly*, 45 (Oct–Dec 1974)

Kohn, Hans, *Nationalism: Meaning and History* (Princeton, N.J., Van Nostrand, 1966)

Kornhauser, William, *The Politics of Mass Society* (Glencoe, The Free Press, 1959)

Lenski, Gerhard, 'Status Inconsistency and the Vote: A Four Nation Test', *American Sociological Review*, 32 (1967) 941–54

—— 'Social Participation and Status Crystallisation', *American Sociological Review*, 21 (1956) 458–64

—— 'Status Inconsistency: A Non-Vertical Dimension of Social Status', *American Sociological Review*, 19 (1954) 405–13.

Lindsay, T. F. and Harrington, Michael, *The Conservative Party, 1918–1970* (New York, St. Martin's Press, 1974)

Lipset, Seymour Martin and Raab, Earl, *The Politics of Unreason: Right Wing Extremism in America 1790–1970* (New York, Harper Torchbooks, 1973)

—— and Rokkan, Stein, *Party Systems and Voter Alignments* (New York, The Free Press, 1967)

—— *The First New Nation* (New York, Basic Books, 1963)

—— *Political Man* (London, Mercury Books, 1960)

—— and Bendix, Reinhard, *Social Mobility in Industrial Society* (Berkeley, University of California Press, 1959)

Mac Eoin Gary, *Northern Ireland: Captive of History* (New York, Holt Rinehart and Winston, 1974)

McKenzie, R. T. and Silver, Allan, 'Conservatism, Industralism and the Working Class Tories in England' in Richard Rose (ed.), *Studies in British Politics* (London, Macmillan, 1969)

Mackintosh, John P., *The British Cabinet* (London, Stevens, 1968)

—— *The Government and Politics of Great Britain* (London, Hutchinson, 1974)

Mansback, Richard W. (ed.), *Northern Ireland: Half a Century of Partition* (New York, Facts on File Inc., 1973)

Marrinon, Patrick, *Paisley: Man of Wrath* (Tralee, Co. Kerry, Anvil Books, 1973)

Mills C. Wright, *The Power Elite* (New York, Oxford University Press, 1956)

Moore, Barrington, *The Social Origins of Dictatorship and Democracy*, (London, Penguin University Books, 1974)

Mosley, Oswald, *The Greater Britain* (Bungay, Suffolk, Richard Clay, 1932)

Nairn, Tom, 'Enoch Powell: The New Right', *New Left Review*, 61 (May–June 1970) 3–27

Newton, Kenneth, *The Sociology of British Communism* (London, Allen Lane, 1969)

Noble, Trevor, 'Social Mobility and Class Relations in Britain', *British Journal of Sociology*, 23 (Dec 1972) 403–36

Nordlinger, Eric A., *The Working Class Tories* (London, MacGibbon & Kee, 1967)

Penniman, Howard R. (ed.), *Britain at the Polls: The Parliamentary Elections of 1974* (Washington, American Enterprise Institute for Public Policy Research, 1974)

Philips, Kevin J., *The Emerging Republican Majority* (New Rochelle, N.Y. Arlington House, 1969)

Powell, Enoch, *The Common Market: Renegotiate or Come Out* (Kingswood, Surrey, Elliot Right Way Books, 1973)

—— *Still to Decide* (Kingswood, Surrey, Elliot Right Way Books, 1972)

—— *The Common Market: The Case Against* (Kingswood, Surrey, Elliot Right Way Books, 1971)

—— *Freedom and Reality* (Kingswood, Surrey, Elliot Right Way Books, 1969)

—— *Medicine and Politics* (London, Pitman, 1966)

—— 'Conservatives and the Social Services', *Political Quarterly*, 24 (Apr–June 1953) 156–66

Pulzer, Peter, *Political Representation and Elections in Britain* (London, Allen & Unwin, 1967)

Riesman, David, *The Lonely Crowd* (New Haven, Yale University Press, 1964)

Rogin, Michael Paul, *The Intellectuals and McCarthy* (Cambridge, Mass., MIT Press, 1967)

Rose, Hannan, 'The Immigration Act 1971: A Case Study', *Parliamentary Affairs*, 26 (Winter 1972–73) 69–91

—— 'The Politics of Immigration After the 1971 Act', *Political Quarterly*, 44 (1973) 183–96

Rose, Richard, *Politics in England Today* (London, Faber, 1974)

—— *The Problem of Party Government* (London, Macmillan, 1974)

—— (ed.), *Electoral Behaviour* (New York, The Free Press, 1974)

—— *Governing Without Consensus* (Boston, Beacon Press, 1971)

—— 'Class and Party Divisions: Britain as a Test Case', *Sociology*, 2 (1968) 129–62

—— 'Parties, Factions and Tendencies in Britain', *Political Studies*, 12 (1964) 33–46

Roth, Andrew, *Enoch Powell: Tory Tribune* (London, Macdonald, 1970)

—— *Heath and the Heathmen*, (London, Routledge & Kegan Paul, 1972)

Runciman, W. G., *Relative Deprivation and Social Justice* (Harmondsworth, Penguin, 1972)

Rush, Gary, 'Status Consistency and Right Wing Extremism', *American Sociological Review*, 32 (1967) 86–92

Scammon, Richard and Wattenberg, Ben J., *The Real Majority* (New York, Coward, McCann and Geoghegan, 1970)

Schneider, William, 'Issues, Voting, and Cleavages: A Methodology and Some Tests', *The American Behavioural Scientist*, 18 (Sep 1974) 112–17

Schoenberger, Robert (ed.), *The American Right Wing* (New York, Holt, Rinehart and Winston, 1969)

Schumpeter, Joseph, *Capitalism, Socialism, and Democracy* (New York, Harper & Row, 1947)

Segal, David and Knoke, David, 'Class Inconsistency, Status Inconsistency and Political Parties in America', *Journal of Politics*, 133 (1971) 941–54

—— 'Social Mobility, Status Inconsistency and Partisan Realignment', *Social Forces*, 47 (1968) 154–7

Seyd, Patrick, 'Factionalism within the Conservative Party: The Monday Club', *Government and Opposition*, 7 (1972) 464–87

Seymour-Ure, Colin, *The Political Impact of Mass Media* (London, Constable, 1974)

Shils, Edward, *The Torment of Secrecy* (New York, The Free Press, 1956)

Stokes, Donald, 'Spatial Models of Party Competition', in Angus Campbell *et al.*, *Elections and the Political Order* (New York, John Wiley, 1966) pp. 161–79

Studlar, Donley T., 'British Public Opinion, Colour Issues, and Enoch Powell: A Longitudinal Analysis', *The British Journal of Political Science*, 4 (1974) 371–81

Sunday Times Insight Team, *Ulster* (Harmondsworth, Penguin, 1972)

Teer, Frank and Spence, James, *Political Opinion Polls* (London, Hutchinson, 1973)

Utley, T. E., *The Lessons of Ulster* (London, Dent, 1975)

—— *Enoch Powell: the man and his thinking* (London, Kimber, 1968)

Wallace, Martin, *Northern Ireland: Fifty Years of Self-Government* (Devon, David & Charles, 1971)

Weber, Eugen, *The Varieties of Fascism* (Princeton, N.J., Van Nostrand, 1964)

Weiss, John, *The Fascist Tradition* (New York, Harper & Row, 1967)

Winchester, Simon, *In Holy Terror* (London, Faber, 1974)

Wood, John (ed.), *Powell and the 1970 Election* (Kingswood, Surrey, Elliot Right Way Books, 1970)

—— (ed.), *A Nation Not Afraid: The Thinking of Enoch Powell* (London, Batsford, 1965)

Wright, Frank, 'Protestant Ideology and Politics in Ulster', *European Journal of Sociology*, 14 (1973) 213–80

Young, Kenneth, *Sir Alec Douglas-Home* (Teaneck, N.J., Farleigh Dickinson Press, 1971)

Notes

Introduction
1   Arthur Wise, *Who Killed Enoch Powell?* (New York: Harper & Row, 1971).

Chapter 1
1   For accounts of Powell's career see Roth, *Enoch Powell: Tory Tribune*, and Utley, *Enoch Powell: the man and his thinking*. The material on Powell's early life is drawn from Roth, pp. 9–61.
2   Roth, *Enoch Powell*, p. 116.
3   *Ibid.*, p. 215.
4   The promotion got only a scant mention in *The Times*. See 14 July 1962. For an account of the events of July 1962 see Mackintosh, *The British Cabinet*, pp. 439–40.
5   After finishing his term as Minister of Health, Powell wrote a book on the relationship between medicine and politics. See Powell, *Medicine and Politics*.
6   See, for example, *Spectator*, 209 (20 July 1962) 71–2.
7   Cited by Roth, *Enoch Powell*, p. 278.
8   *Ibid.*, pp. 278–88 for an account of Powell's role in the Profumo affair. Also *The Times*, 17 and 19 June 1963.
9   Roth, *Enoch Powell*, p. 294.
10 See *Daily Express*, 20 June 1963. For the Gallup and *Daily Express* data on Powell's support among M.P.s see Roth, *Heath and the Heathmen*, p. 178.
11 This account of Powell's role in the October leadership struggle draws heavily on Roth, *Enoch Powell*, pp. 279–304, and Utley, *Enoch Powell*, pp. 90–4.
12 *The Times*, 21 Oct 1963.
13 *Ibid.*
14 For the N.O.P. data see *NOP Political Index* (July and Oct 1963). See *Daily Telegraph*, 1 Nov 1963 for the data on the electorate's attitudes towards Powell's refusal to serve in Sir Alec's Cabinet.
15 *The Times*, 21 Oct 1963.
16 Utley, *Enoch Powell*, p. 94.
17 *The Times*, 19 Nov 1963.
18 *Ibid.*, 29 Jan 1964.
19 *Ibid.*, 30 Jan 1964.
20 *Ibid.*, 13 Apr 1964.
21 *Ibid.*, 6 Apr 1964.

22 See Ian Gilmour, 'Enoch Powell's Pipe Dream', in *Spectator*, 212 (10 Apr 1964) 477–9.

23 For the texts of those speeches see Wood, *A Nation Not Afraid*, pp. 20–3, 26–8, 89–91, 91–3, 143–6; and Powell, *Freedom and Reality*, pp. 18–21.

24 Wood, *A Nation Not Afraid*, pp. 86–91.

25 See *The Times*, 17 June and 30 July 1964; for the text of those speeches see Wood, *A Nation Not Afraid*, 119–22 and Powell, *Freedom and Reality*, pp. 200–3.

26 On this point see also Gamble, *The Conservative Nation*, p. 117.

27 *The Times*, 29 Oct 1964.

28 *Ibid.*, 28 Nov 1964.

29 *Ibid.*, 30 Nov 1964.

30 Roth, *Enoch Powell*, p. 319.

31 For his Royal Society of St George speech see Wood, *A Nation Not Afraid*, pp. 143–6; for his Trinity College, Dublin, speech, see pp. 136–43.

32 *Ibid.*, p. 143.

33 *Ibid.*, p. 144.

34 This quote comes from an anti-Market speech made in 1972. See Powell, *The Common Market: Renegotiate or Come Out*, p. 56.

35 Wood, *A Nation Not Afraid*, p. 145.

36 *Ibid.*

37 See *The New Anatomy of Britain* (London, Hodder & Stoughton, 1971) p. 673.

38 Wood, *A Nation Not Afraid*, p. 145.

39 *Ibid.*

40 *NOP Political Bulletin* (June 1964).

41 In December 1964 Gallup asked the electorate: 'If you were making up a Conservative Government, who are the first three men you would put in for Prime Minister and the other jobs?' Home (41%) got the most support followed by Maudling (36%), Butler (33%), Heath (14%), Hogg (10%) and Macleod (7%). Gallup fortunately repeated the question a number of times over a five-year period making comparisons possible. See the *Gallup Political Index* (Dec 1965) 177.

42 *Financial Times*, 1 Mar 1965, cited by Roth, *Enoch Powell*, p. 320.

43 *The Times*, 8 Mar 1965.

44 See Roth, *Enoch Powell*, pp. 321–2.

45 *The Times*, 22 May 1965.

46 Cited by Roth, *Enoch Powell*, p. 327.

47 Data supplied by the Social Science Research Council (S.S.R.C.) Survey Archive, University of Essex and the *NOP Political Bulletin* (Nov 1965).

48 Roth, *Enoch Powell*, p. 331.

49 *The Times*, 26 July 1965.

50 *Ibid.*

51 See the special supplement to the *NOP Political Bulletin*, (Nov 1965) 7–9.

52 Iain Macleod, 'Enoch Powell', *Spectator*, 215 (16 July 1965) 76.

53 *Sunday Times*, 20 June 1965, cited by Roth, *Enoch Powell*, p. 324.

54 *The Times*, 31 May 1965 cited by Roth, *ibid.*, p. 325.

55 *The Times*, 26 July 1965.

56 Alan Watkins, 'How Heath Pulled it Off', *Spectator*, 215 (30 July 1965) 142; and 'The Tasks Before Mr Heath,' *Spectator*, 215 (22 Sep 1965) 503.

57 Much of this argument is drawn from Anthony King, 'New Stirrings on the Right', *New Society*, 6 (14 Oct 1965) 7–11. David Butler has suggested this article overestimates Powell's influence. See Butler and King, *The British General Election of 1966*, p. 64.

58 On the appointment see *The Times*, 5 Aug 1965; for the *Telegraph* quote see Roth, *Enoch Powell*, p. 332.

59 Roth, *Enoch Powell*, p. 334.

60 *The Times*, 11 Nov 1965.

61 *Ibid.*, 5 Nov 1965.

62 See the special supplement to the *NOP Political Bulletin* (Nov 1965).

63 *Gallup Political Index*, 68 (Dec 1965) 177.

64 Alan Watkins, 'The Tasks before Mr Heath', for a discussion of the response Powell got at the conference.

65 See *The Times*, 13 Jan 1966.

66 *The Times*, 19 Jan 1966.

67 *Swinton Journal*, 12 (1966) 3–4.

68 See *The Times*, 19 Jan 1966.

69 *Ibid.*, and *Economist*, 218 (22 Jan 1966) 291.

70 See *The Times*, 15 Jan 1966.

71 *Ibid.*, 5 Mar 1966.

72 See Roth, *Enoch Powell*, pp. 336–7.

73 *The Times*, 11 Mar 1966.

74 Roth, *Enoch Powell*, pp. 337–8.

75 *The Times*, 16 Mar 1966.

76 Alan Watkins, 'The Future of Heath', *Spectator*, 216 (1 Apr 1966), 393.

77 See Paul Foot, *The Rise of Enoch Powell*, pp. 67–97.

78 *Ibid.*, and *The Times*, 18 Apr 1966.

79 For a text of the speech see Powell, *Freedom and Reality*, pp. 115–17.

80 Foot, *The Rise of Enoch Powell*, p. 98.

81 See for example Powell, *Freedom and Reality*, pp. 29–30, 56–9, 127–33, 136–9, 159–61, 206–9.

82 *The Times*, 8 Sep 1966.

83 *Ibid.*, 20 July and 15 Oct 1966.

84 *Ibid.*, 13 Dec 1966.

85 *Spectator*, 216 (4 Feb 1966) 127.

86 *NOP Political Bulletin* (July 1966).

87 The data used for further analysis of the August 1966 Gallup Survey come from the Roper Center, Williams College, Williamstown, Mass. There are discrepancies between the figures in the Gallup Opinion Index and those in the data made available by Roper. The Gallup report showed that 8% of the electorate named Powell as one of the first three men it would place in a Conservative government while the Roper data place the figure down at 3%. Attempts to clarify this problem through Gallup Poll Ltd proved unfruitful because Gallup does not maintain data on this question in their files.

88 Foot, *The Rise of Enoch Powell*, p. 99, and *The Times*, 17 Jan 1967.

89 Foot, *The Rise of Enoch Powell*, p. 98.

90   *The Times*, 13 Feb 1967.
91   See *The Times*, 2 and 7 Mar 1967, as well as his 'Nuclear Weapons and World Power', *Listener*, 75 (1966) 227–8.
92   Alan Watkins 'How Safe is Ted?', *Spectator*, (27 Jan 1967) 92.
93   *The Times*, 20 Mar 1967.
94   Auberon Waugh, 'Stumbling into Powellism', *Spectator*, 220 (8 Mar 1968) 228.
95   Alexander and Watkins, *The Making of the Prime Minister 1970*, pp. 87–8; see also *The Times*, 14 and 19 July 1967.
96   Alexander and Watkins, *The Making of the Prime Minister 1970*.
97   *Sunday Times*, 15 Oct 1967.

Chapter 2

1   On this point see Roth, *Enoch Powell*, pp. 206, 209–10.
2   See Michael Hartley-Brewer, 'Smethwick', in Deakin (ed.), *Colour and the British Electorate 1964*, pp. 77–105 for a discussion of the Gordon Walker-Griffiths campaign.
3   Cited by Foot, *The Rise of Enoch Powell*, p. 67.
4   A. W. Singham in 'Immigration and the Election' in Butler and King, *The British General Election of 1964*, p. 365, reported that Powell cancelled the engagement.
5   Foot, *The Rise of Enoch Powell*, p. 69.
6   *Sunday Times*, 14 July 1964; also cited by Foot, *The Rise of Enoch Powell*, p. 67.
7   On Powell's concept of nationalism see Foot, *The Rise of Enoch Powell*, pp. 1–42; Tom Nairn, 'Enoch Powell: The New Right' in *New Left Review* 61 (May–June 1970) 3–27; and Gamble, *The Conservative Nation*, pp. 119–22.
8   *The Times*, 6 Oct 1964.
9   *Wolverhampton Express and Star*, 10 Oct 1964, cited by Foot, *The Rise of Enoch Powell*, p. 69.
10   Foot, *The Rise of Enoch Powell*, p. 71.
11   Butler and King, *The British General Election of 1964*; p. 299.
12   See Roth, *Enoch Powell*, pp. 321–2.
13   Foot, *The Rise of Enoch Powell*, p. 78.
14   *Ibid.*, p. 79.
15   *The Times*, 22 May 1965.
16   The *Sun* cited by Foot, *The Rise of Enoch Powell*, p. 89.
17   *Ibid.*, p. 90; see also *The Times*, 22 Nov 1965.
18   *The Times, ibid.*
19   Foot, *The Rise of Enoch Powell*, p. 96.
20   See *Wolverhampton Express and Star*, 26 Mar 1966, cited *ibid.*, p. 94.
21   Foot, *The Rise of Enoch Powell*.
22   Cited by Foot, *ibid.*, p. 102.
23   *Spectator*, 220 (23 Feb 1968) 225–6.
24   See *The Times*, 9 and 19 Oct 1967.
25   For a text of the speech see Powell, *Freedom and Reality*, pp. 290–2.
26   Foot, *The Rise of Enoch Powell*, p. 110, and Roth, *Enoch Powell*, p. 347.

27 Roth, *Enoch Powell*, p. 347.
28 *The Times*, 16 Feb 1968.
29 *Ibid.*, 17 Feb 1968.
30 Foot, *The Rise of Enoch Powell*, p. 111.
31 Butler and Pinto-Duschinsky, *The British General Election of 1970*, p. 76.
32 Interview with Tory M.P.
33 Interview with Tory M.P.
34 See Utley, *Enoch Powell*, p. 11–44 for a discussion of the background behind the speech. For a text of the speech see pp. 180–90.
35 *Sunday Telegraph*, 21 Apr 1968.
36 See *Sunday Mirror*, and *Sun*, 21 Apr 1968.
37 *Evening Standard*, 20 Apr 1968.
38 See *The Times*, 22 Apr 1968, and *Listener*, 7 (25 Apr 1968) 536 for Heath's public remarks when he dismissed Powell. In the Cabinet reshuffle which followed, Maudling replaced Powell as Defence spokesman and Douglas-Home assumed responsibility for Commonwealth and Foreign Affairs.
39 *The Times*, 23 Apr 1968.
40 See Utley, *Enoch Powell*, p. 190.
41 See for example David Wood's article in *The Times*, 22 Apr 1968.
42 *Daily Express*, 23 Apr 1968.
43 *Economist*, 227 (27 Apr 1968) 14.
44 *Daily Mail*, 23 Apr 1968.
45 See *The Times*, 15 July 1968 for a discussion of the vote on the third reading on the Race Relations Bill. See *Daily Mirror*, 23 Apr 1968 and *Evening News*, 21 Apr 1968 for discussions of the split inside the Conservative party on race relations.
46 *The Times*, 26 Apr 1968.
47 *Guardian*, 26 Apr 1968.
48 *Sunday Times*, 28 Apr 1968.
49 *The Times*, 23 Apr 1968.
50 *The Times*, 27 Apr 1968. See *Wolverhampton Express and Star*, 1 May 1968, for a report that the Bristol Conservative association passed a resolution in support of Powell. See also *Guardian*, 6 May 1968, for a report of Powell's support in Bradford, Brixton and Deptford, and Greenock.
51 Bulter and Pinto-Duschinsky, *The British General Election of 1970*, p. 78.
52 *The Times*, 25 Apr 1968.
53 See Alexander and Watkins, *The Making of the Prime Minister 1970*, pp. 101–2.
54 *Evening Standard*, 6 May 1968 and *Daily Express*, 6 May 1968.
55 *Guardian*, 6 May 1968.
56 The mixed editorials generally praised Powell for speaking out but suggested he had acted at the wrong time and/or used the wrong sort of language. The 45 editorials were read at the Institute of Race Relations, Pentonville Road, London.
57 For accounts of the dockers' march on Westminster see *The Times*, 25 and 26 Apr 1968.
58 Chapter 8 provides a detailed analysis of the reaction to Powell's speech by party, class, region, sex and age.

59   See Gallup Poll CQ585 – data supplied by the Roper Center, Williams College.

60   Studlar, 'British Public Opinion, Colour Issues, and Enoch Powell', *The British Journal of Political Science*, 4 (1974) 371–81.

61   See *The Times*, 11 July 1968 for an account of the debate on the third reading of the Race Relations Bill.

62   *The Times*, 13 and 19 Sep 1968.

63   *Ibid.*, 16 Sep 1968.

64   *Ibid.*, 28 Sep 1968.

65   *Ibid.*, 20 Oct 1968.

66   *Ibid.*, 4 Oct 1968.

67   *Ibid.*, 4 Oct 1968.

68   See *The Times*, 11 Oct 1968, and Alexander and Watkins, *The Making of the Prime Minister*, pp. 101–2.

69   See *Sunday Times*, 17 Nov 1968 for a report of the data.

70   See *NOP Political Bulletin* (Sep 1968) 7–11.

71   Powell, *Freedom and Reality*, pp. 298–314 for a text of the speech; see also *The Times*, 18 Nov 1968, pp. 1, 3.

72   Powell, *Freedom and Reality*, p. 300.

73   Angus Maude, 'Enoch Declares War', *Spectator*, 221 (22 Nov 1968), 726–7; and *The Times*, 18 Nov 1968.

74   See *The Times*, 18 Nov 1968.

75   *Ibid.*, 22 and 23 Nov 1968.

76   The editorials were read at the Institute of Race Relations, Pentonville Road, London.

77   See *Birmingham Post*, 3 Dec 1968 and *Cardiff Western Mail*, 3 Dec 1968.

78   Since O.R.C. did not have data on the precise age, sex and class background of the immigrant population, they had no way of knowing whether their sample of immigrants was truly representative.

79   See for example *The Times*, 16, 17 and 18 Jan 1969.

80   *Ibid.*, 4 Jan 1969.

81   *Ibid.*, 22 Jan 1969.

82   *Ibid.*, 23 Jan 1969.

83   *Ibid.*, 27 Jan 1969 for a text of Heath's Walsall remarks.

84   *Gallup Political Index* (Feb 1969) 28.

Chapter 3

1   Roth, *Enoch Powell*, p. 374.

2   *Ibid.*, p. 377.

3   See Powell, *The Common Market: The Case Against*, pp. 9–16.

4   See Roth, *Enoch Powell*, pp. 362–71 for a discussion of Powell's role in the fight against reform of the House of Lords.

5   *The Times*, 10 June 1969.

6   See p. 42 above.

7   *The Times*, 10 June 1969.

8   *Ibid.*, 14 June 1969.

9   *Ibid.*, 19 July 1969.

10   *Ibid.*

11   *Gallup Political Index* (Feb 1970) 37.

12 See *The Times*, 30 Sep, 3 and 4 Oct 1969.

13 *Ibid.*, 9 and 10 Oct 1969.

14 Quoted by Alexander and Watkins, *The Making of the Prime Minister, 1970*, p. 112.

15 See *The Times*, 19 Jan 1970.

16 *Ibid.*, 24 Jan 1970; and Alexander and Watkins, *The Making of the Prime Minister, 1970*, pp. 113–14.

17 *Gallup Political Index* (Feb 1970) 37.

18 *The Times*, 2 Feb 1970.

19 Powell made his remarks 2 Feb 1970 on the B.B.C.'s *Money Programme*.

20 *The Times*, 10 Mar 1970.

21 *Ibid.*, 9 Mar 1970.

22 See Butler and Pinto-Duschinsky, *The British General Election of 1970*, p. 232, Table 1 for data from 1970 public opinion polls on the *Sun*'s readership broken down by social class.

23 *Sun*, 7 Mar 1970.

24 See *NOP Political Bulletin* (May 1968) 1.

25 *Sunday Times*, 24 May 1970.

26 *The Times*, 27 May 1970.

27 See Powell's 1966 and 1970 election addresses published by R. N. Pollard, 38 Tettenhall Road, Wolverhampton.

28 *The Times*, 1 June 1970.

29 *Ibid.*, 4 June 1970; Alexander and Watkins, *The Making of the Prime Minister 1970*, p. 178; and Butler and Pinto-Duschinsky, *The British General Election 1970*, p. 160.

30 Much of this argument is drawn from Alexander and Watkins, *The Making of the Prime Minister 1970*, pp. 179–95.

31 John Wood (ed.), *Powell and the 1970 Election*, pp. 97–104.

32 *Ibid.*, p. 98.

33 Alexander and Watkins, *The Making of the Prime Minister 1970*, pp. 188–9.

34 Wood, *Powell and the 1970 Election*, pp. 104–12. See also *The Times*, 15 June 1970.

35 See *The Times*, 15 June 1970.

36 See Butler and Pinto-Duschinsky, *The British General Election of 1970*, p. 239, Table 2.

37 Powell, *The Common Market: Renegotiate or Come Out*, pp. 20–1.

38 See *The Times*, 17 June 1970; see also Wood, *Powell and the 1970 Election*, pp. 119–24.

39 See Deakin and Bourne, 'The Minorities and the General Election, 1970', and their 'Powell, the Minorities and the 1970 Election' (see Bibliography). See also Michael Steed, 'The Results Analysed', in Butler and Pinto-Duschinsky, *The British General Election of 1970*, pp. 406–8.

40 Steed, 'The Results Analysed', and Deakin and Bourne, 'The Minorities and the General Election, 1970', p. 205.

41 *Observer*, 21 June 1970.

42 Steed, 'The Results Analysed', p. 408.

43 Louis Harris Research Ltd, *The 1970 General Election: What Happened?* (London, mimeographed, 1970) pp. 9–10.

44 *Gallup Political Index* (June/July 1970) 98.
45 Butler and Stokes, *Political Change in Britain*, pp. 290–2.
46 *Ibid.*, p. 306, Table 14.9.
47 Donley T. Studlar, 'The Impact of the Coloured Immigration Issue on British Electoral Politics 1964–1970' (Indiana University, Ph.D. thesis, 1975) p. 261.
48 *Ibid.*, p. 265.
49 *Ibid.*, p. 260.
50 Butler and Stokes, *Political Change in Britain*, p. 308.
51 *Ibid.*, p. 307.
52 Studlar, 'The Impact of the Coloured Immigration Issue on British Electoral Politics, 1964–1970', p. 349.
53 *Ibid.*
54 This involves amendment of the term 'Powellite' that we have used elsewhere in this book. When basing our calculations on the 0–100 scale elsewhere we have termed 'Powellites' only those who gave him scores of 78–100.
55 A perfectly possible supposition given Powell's relative weakness among the young (Chapter 8) but, even if so, of relatively little significance. Turnout in 1970 among 18–21-year-olds was well below the overall average and they constituted only about 10% to 15% of the electorate.
56 The precise construction of this racial conservatism index is explained in greater detail in Chapter 11.
57 *The Times*, 20 June 1970.
58 See *Sunday Times*, 21 June 1970.
59 *The Times*, 1 Oct 1970.
60 *Ibid.*, 8 July 1970, p. 8.
61 *Ibid.*, 6 Oct 1970, pp. 2, 12.

Chapter 4
1 *Ibid.*, 13 Nov 1970.
2 *Ibid.*, 23 Nov 1970.
3 He only adopted this approach in April 1976 in a speech to the national police conference.
4 *Ibid.*, 26 Sep 1970. For discussions of the 1971 Commonwealth Immigrants Act see Hannan Rose, 'The Immigration Act 1971' and 'The Politics of Immigration After the 1971 Act', (see Bibliography).
5 *The Times*, 16 Feb 1971.
6 *Ibid.*
7 *Ibid.*, 17 Feb 1971.
8 *Sun, Sketch, Daily Mail*, and *Mirror*, all 16 Feb 1971.
9 *Sun*, 17 Feb 1971, p. 1.
10 *Ibid.*, 21 Feb 1971.
11 *The Times*, 8 and 9 Mar 1971.
12 *Ibid.*, 2 and 3 Apr 1971.
13 *Ibid.*, 26 May 1971.
14 *Ibid.*, 28 May 1971.
15 *Ibid.*, 3 May 1971.

16 *Ibid.*, 17 June 1971.
17 *Ibid.*, 9 Sep 1971.
18 Powell, *Still to Decide*, p. 209; and *The Times*, 5 Nov 1971.
19 *The Times*, 18 Nov 1971.
20 *Sunday Express*, 12 Dec 1971.
21 Quoted by Roth, *Enoch Powell*, p. 148.
22 See Powell, *The Common Market: The Case Against*, p. 9.
23 See Powell, *The Common Market: The Case Against;* see also Roth, *Enoch Powell*, pp. 375–6.
24 Powell, *The Common Market: The Case Against*, p. 11.
25 *Ibid.*, p. 16.
26 *Ibid.*, pp. 25–8.
27 *Ibid.*, p. 28.
28 Quoted by Roth, *Enoch Powell*, p. 377.
29 Powell, *The Common Market: The Case Against*, pp. 17–25.
30 *Ibid.*, p. 18.
31 *Ibid.*, p. 17.
32 Quoted by Roth, *Enoch Powell*, p. 11.
33 On Powell's role at the 1969 conference (where he only spoke on economic questions) see *The Times*, 6 and 9 Oct 1969.
34 Powell, *The Common Market: The Case Against*, pp. 28–34.
35 *Ibid.*, p. 33.
36 *Ibid.*, p. 34.
37 *Ibid.*, pp. 35–41.
38 Kitzinger, *Diplomacy and Persuasion*, pp. 354–8 for trend data on this point.
39 Cited by Kitzinger, *Diplomacy and Persuasion*, p. 357.
40 In June 1971, before the negotiations were concluded, 26% of N.O.P.'s sample approved of membership. After the agreement was reached, approval rose to 34%, while those opposing dropped from 58% to 44%. See Teer and Spence, *Political Opinion Polls*, p. 116 for a report of these data.
41 See Powell, *The Common Market: The Case Against* and *The Times*, 16 Jan 1971.
42 Powell, *ibid.*, p. 48.
43 *Ibid.*, pp. 48–53.
44 *Ibid.*, p. 49–50.
45 *Ibid.*, p. 50.
46 *Ibid.*, p. 50–1.
47 *Ibid.*, p. 52–3.
48 *The Times*, 21 Apr 1971.
49 Powell, *The Common Market: The Case Against*, pp. 54–70; for this quote see p. 55.
50 *Ibid.*, p. 56.
51 *Ibid.*, pp. 71–8.
52 *Ibid.*, pp. 97–110; and *Daily Telegraph*, 18 May 1971.
53 *Ibid.*, pp. 111–18.
54 *Ibid.*, pp. 112–13.
55 Teer and Spence, *Political Opinion Polls*, pp. 116–20.

56 See Kitzinger, *Diplomacy and Persuasion*, pp. 165–6.
57 See Powell, *The Common Market: Renegotiate or Come Out*, pp. 26–9.
58 Kitzinger, *Diplomacy and Persuasion*, p. 168.
59 *Ibid.*, p. 185.
60 *The Times*, 23 Oct 1971.
61 Kitzinger, *Diplomacy and Persuasion*, p. 168.
62 *Ibid.*, pp. 187–8, 371–3.
63 *The Times*, 29 Nov 1971.
64 *Ibid.*
65 *Ibid.*, 22 Nov 1971.
66 Kitzinger, *Diplomacy and Persuasion*, p. 371.
67 *Ibid.*, p. 373.
68 See Teer and Spence, *Political Opinion Polls*, p. 114.
69 See Powell, *The Common Market: Renegotiate or Come Out*, pp. 29–31.
70 *Ibid.*, p. 30.
71 *Ibid.*, pp. 44–53.
72 *Ibid.*, p. 45.
73 On the Government's E.E.C. legislation, see Kitzinger, *Diplomacy and Persuasion*, pp. 374–82.
74 *The Times*, 18 Jan 1972.
75 *Ibid.*, 21 Jan 1972.
76 *Ibid.*, 18 Feb 1972.
77 *Ibid.*, 14 Feb 1972.
78 *Ibid.*, 4 Mar 1972.
79 *Ibid.*, 15 Mar 1972.
80 Powell, *The Common Market: Renegotiate or Come Out*, pp. 60–8, 117–18.
81 *Ibid.*, p. 117.
82 *Ibid.*, p. 118.
83 *Ibid.*, p. 32.
84 *Ibid.*, p. 33.
85 *Ibid.*
86 *The Times*, 28 Feb 1972.
87 *Ibid.*, 11 Mar 1972.
88 See *ibid.*, 19 Apr 1972.
89 *Ibid.*
90 Kitzinger, *Diplomacy and Persuasion*, pp. 387–96.
91 Powell, *The Common Market: Renegotiate or Come Out*, pp. 101–6.
92 *Ibid.*, p. 105.
93 *Ibid.*, p. 34.
94 *The Times*, 24 June 1972.
95 See *Economist*, 234 (17 June 1972) 24.
96 *The Times*, 17 Aug 1972.
97 See Humphry and Ward, *Passports and Politics*, for a discussion of the Ugandan Asian controversy. On this point see pp. 28–38, esp. p. 35. See also *The Times*, 11 Oct 1972.
98 Humphry and Ward, *Passports and Politics*, p. 37.
99 *The Times*, 15 Sep 1972.
100 Humphry and Ward, pp. 79–80.
101 *The Times*, 11 Oct 1972.

102 See Humphry and Ward, *Passports and Politics*, pp. 73–85.

103 See *The Times*, 12 Oct 1972.

104 Patrick Cosgrave, 'Love and the Tory Party', *Spectator*, 229 (14 Oct 1972) 574 and his 'The Rediscovery of Tory Liberalism', *Spectator*, 229 (21 Oct 1972) 619. See also *The Times*, 13 Oct 1972.

105 Cosgrave, 'Love and the Tory Party', 575.

106 Cosgrave, 'The Rediscovery of Tory Liberalism', 618.

107 *Spectator*, 229 (21 Oct 1972) 620.

108 *The Times*, 23 Nov 1972.

109 *Ibid.*, 9 Dec 1972.

110 *Ibid.*, 19 Dec 1972.

111 See *Economist*, 246 (27 Jan 1973) 19.

112 *The Times*, 28 Sep 1972.

113 *Ibid.*, 9 Oct 1972.

114 *Ibid.*, 9 Nov 1972.

115 *Ibid.*, 20 Dec 1972.

116 *Ibid.*, 4 Dec 1972.

117 *Ibid.*, 28 Dec 1972.

Chapter 5

1 See *ibid.*, 28 Sep 1968.

2 For a text of the speech see Powell, *Still to Decide*, pp. 170–5.

3 *Ibid.*, p. 170.

4 *Ibid.*, p. 172.

5 *Ibid.*, p. 175.

6 One of the most valuable works on contemporary Ulster politics is Deutsch and Magowan's *Northern Ireland 1968–1973; A Chronology of Events*. Their two volumes profile a chronological account of Ulster politics on a day-to-day basis. On the U.D.I., see pp. 52, 98, 163, 177.

7 Cited by Tom Nairn, 'Enoch Powell: The New Right', *New Left Review*, 61 (1970) 19.

8 *Ibid.*

9 For a text of the speech see Wood, *Powell and the 1970 Election*, pp. 104–111.

10 *The Times*, 16 and 18 Jan 1971.

11 See Deutsch and Magowan, *Northern Ireland*, p. 89 and the *Sunday Times* Insight Team, *Ulster*, pp. 239–42.

12 Powell, *Still to Decide*, p. 179.

13 *Ibid.*

14 *Ibid.*, p. 180.

15 For a text of that speech, see *ibid.*, pp. 181–3.

16 *Ibid.*, p. 181.

17 On the setting up of 'Free Derry' see the *Sunday Times* Insight Team, *Ulster*, pp. 115–20.

18 As late as 11 Feb 1971 Ian Gilmour, Under Secretary of State for Defence, told the Commons that there were no areas of Northern Ireland which the security forces would not enter. The existence of areas like 'Free

Derry' made statements like Gilmour's highly questionable. See Deutsch and Magowan, *Northern Ireland*, p. 93.

19 Powell, *Still to Decide*, p. 182.
20 Deutsch and Magowan, *Northern Ireland*, p. 98.
21 For the text of that speech see Powell, *Still to Decide*, pp. 183–8.
22 *Ibid.*, p. 186.
23 *Ibid.*, p. 188.
24 See *NOP Political Bulletin* (Apr 1972) 9.
25 On the imposition of direct rule and the events immediately thereafter see Harbinson, *The Ulster Unionist Party 1882–1973*, pp. 174–7.
26 *The Times*, 25 Mar. 1972.
27 *Ibid.*, 29 Mar 1972.
28 See Deutsch and Magowan, *Northern Ireland*, p. 166.
29 *The Times*, 24 Apr 1972.
30 *Ibid.*, 12 June 1972.
31 See *NOP Political Bulletin* (Apr 1973) 9.
32 In early May 1972 Powell spoke to a Unionist rally in Newtownards and in June he spoke to the East Belfast Unionist association. See Deutsch and Magowan, *Northern Ireland*, pp. 175, 182, for brief accounts of these addresses.
33 *Ibid.*, p. 184.
34 *Ibid.*, p. 195.
35 *Ibid.*, p. 198.
36 *Ibid.*, p. 205.
37 *Ibid.*, pp. 202–4 for an account of the entry into the 'no go' areas. See also *The Times*, 1 Aug 1972.
38 See *NOP Political Bulletin* (Aug 1972) 16.
39 Hugh Macpherson, 'A Particularly Awkward Customer', *Spectator*, 229 (29 July 1972).
40 Deutsch and Magowan, *Northern Ireland*, p. 242.
41 Wallace, *Northern Ireland: Fifty Years of Self-Government* pp. 27–43.
42 *Ibid.*, p. 39.
43 See Deutsch and Magowan, *Northern Ireland*, p. 222.
44 *Ibid.*, pp. 163, 183.
45 *Ibid.*, p. 223.
46 *Ibid.*, p. 226.
47 For a summary of the White Paper see *ibid.*, p. 282.
48 See *The Times*, 30 Mar 1973.
49 *Ibid.*, 25 May 1973.
50 *Ibid.* On the Northern Ireland Constitution Bill, see Deutsch and Magowan, *Northern Ireland*, p. 300.
51 See *The Times*, 15 June 1973.
52 See Deutsch and Magowan, *Northern Ireland*, p. 319.
53 *Ibid.*, p. 303.
54 Speech to the Londonderry Imperial Unionist Association, 18 Sep 1973 (italics added).
55 For a report of the data see *The Times*, 5 Oct 1973.
56 Deutsch and Magowan, *Northern Ireland*, pp. 345, 362.
57 *Ibid.*, p. 360.

58   *Ibid.*, p. 230.
59   *The Times*, 15 Oct 1973.

Chapter 6
 1   *The Times*, 13 Jan 1973.
 2   *Ibid.*, 19 Jan 1973.
 3   *Ibid.*, 24 Jan 1973.
 4   *Ibid.*, 30 Jan 1973.
 5   *Ibid.*, 24 Feb 1973.
 6   *Ibid.*
 7   *Ibid.*
 8   *Ibid.*, 1 Mar 1973.
 9   *Ibid.*, 14 June 1973.
10   *Ibid.*, 26 Mar 1973.
11   *Ibid.*, 8 Apr 1973.
12   Powell, *The Common Market: Renegotiate or Come Out*, pp. 110–11.
13   See *The Times*, 11 June 1973.
14   *Ibid.*
15   See *ibid.*, 9 June 1973 for Wilson's response and 19 June 1973 for Heath's.
16   *Economist*, 247 (16 June 1973) 11–12.
17   *Spectator*, 231 (25 Aug 1973) 239. '
18   *The Times*, 16 July 1973.
19   *Ibid.*, 25 Sep 1973.
20   *Ibid.*, 12 Oct 1973.
21   *Ibid.*, 18 Dec 1973, and *Guardian*, 24 Jan 1974.
22   *Guardian, ibid.*
23   *Economist*, 248 (2 Sep 1973).
24   See *NOP Political Bulletin* (Oct 1973) 18.
25   See *Gallup Political Bulletin* (Feb 1974) 242.
26   *The Times*, 3 Nov 1973.
27   *Ibid.*
28   *Ibid.*, 8–9 Nov 1973.
29   *Ibid.*, 30 Nov 1973.
30   *Ibid.*
31   *Ibid.*, 1 Dec 1973.
32   *Ibid.*, 2 Jan 1974.
33   *Ibid.*, 16 Jan 1974.
34   *Ibid.*, 9 Jan 1974.
35   *Ibid.*, 24 Jan 1974.
36   *Ibid.*, 2 Feb 1974.
37   *Ibid.*, 8 Feb 1974.
38   *Ibid.*
39   *Ibid.*
40   *Ibid.*, 9 Feb 1974.
41   The material in this section is based on interviews with Wolverhampton
     political activists. The interviewing was done in February 1976.
42   *Guardian*, 14 Feb 1974.
43   *Ibid.*, 25 Feb 1974.
44   *Ibid.*

45 See *Financial Times*, 26 Feb 1974.
46 *Ibid.*
47 *Ibid.*
48 Michael Steed, 'The Results Analysed', in Butler and Kavanagh, *The British General Election February 1974*, p. 331.
49 *Ibid.*, pp. 331–2.
50 See Steed, 'The Results Analysed', in Butler and Pinto-Duschinsky, *The British General Election of 1970*, pp. 406–8.
51 *Daily Telegraph*, 28 Feb 1974.
52 *NOP Political Bulletin* (Feb 1974) 37–8.

Chapter 7
1   *The Times*, 8 Apr 1974.
2   See the United Ulster Unionist Council, 'Policy Document' (Belfast, Puritan Printing Co., 1974) which was published after the Portrush conference.
3   *The Times*, 18 May 1974.
4   *Ibid.*, 20 May 1974.
5   *Ibid.*, 26 June 1974.
6   Harbinson, *The Ulster Unionist Party, 1882–1973*, pp. 97–105.
7   *Economist*, 251 (27 Apr 1974) 15.
8   *Spectator*, 232 (4 May 1974) 537.
9   Utley, *Lessons of Ulster*, pp. 118–22.
10 *The Times*, 14 June 1974.
11 Speech at a Unionist rally at Enniskillen, 3 June 1974.
12 *The Times*, 31 Aug 1974.
13 *Ibid.*, 31 Aug 1974.
14 *Ibid.*, 2 Sep 1974.
15 *Ibid.*, 21 Sep 1974.
16 A recent profiler of Powell has written that 'the machine-like precision of his campaigns clashed with the rather more happy-go-lucky approach of his followers'. See Caroline Moorehead, 'A Would-Be Leader Deserted by Destiny', *The Times*, 12 May 1975.
17 Speeches at Banbridge, Co. Down, 25 Sep 1974; at Newcastle, Co. Down, 7 Oct 1974; and at Ballynahinch, Co. Down, 8 Oct 1974.
18 See also *The Times*, 27 Sep 1974.
19 *Ibid.*, 30 Sep 1974.
20 *Ibid.*, 4 Oct 1974.
21 *Ibid.*
22 *Ibid.*
23 Speech at Newcastle, Co. Down, 7 Oct 1974.
24 See *The Times Guide to the House of Commons, October 1974* (London, Timesbook, 1974) p. 109.
25 *Daily Mail*, 5 Sep 1974.
26 *NOP Political Bulletin* (Oct 1974) 34.
27 *The Times*, 12 Nov 1974.
28 *Gallup Political Index* (Nov 1974) 5.
29 *The Times*, 4 Oct 1974.

30 *Ibid.*, 14 Oct 1974.
31 *Ibid.*, 23 Nov 1974.
32 See for example *Economist*, 254 (15 Feb 1975) 13; *The Times*, 6 and 13 Feb 1975; and *Financial Times*, 14 Feb 1975.
33 Martin Walker, 'Nation's Shepherd Calls his Errant Flock', *Guardian*, 31 May 1975, p. 6.
34 *Daily Telegraph*, 30 Jan 1975.
35 *Ibid.*
36 *The Times*, 8 Feb 1974.
37 *Ibid.*, 28 Feb 1975.
38 *Ibid.*, 15 Feb 1975.
39 *Guardian*, 12 May 1975.
40 *Ibid.*
41 *Ibid.*
42 *Financial Times*, 3 June 1975.
43 *Ibid.*
44 David Butler and Uwe Kitzinger, *The 1975 Referendum* (London, Macmillan, 1976), p. 257.
45 *The Times*, 14 Oct 1974.
46 *Ibid.*, 12 May 1975.
47 Speech to a United Ulster Unionist Rally at the Queen's Hall, Holywood, Co. Down, 9 Jan 1975.
48 Speech to the Iveagh Unionist association, Dromore, Co. Down, 25 Jan 1975.
49 Speech in Killyleagh, Downpatrick, 19 Apr 1975.
50 *Ibid.*, pp. 4, 5.
51 Speech to Unionist rally at Kilkeel, Co. Down, 5 July 1975.
52 Speech to a Unionist rally at Ballyhill, Co. Antrim, 26 July 1975.
53 *Economist*, 256 (12 July 1975) 26.
54 Speech to the Monday Club of Ulster at Unionist headquarters, Belfast, 11 Sep 1975.
55 Speech at Banbridge, Co. Down, 30 Sep 1975.
56 See *The Times*, 13 Nov 1975.
57 Speech to the Conservative City Forum, Houndsditch, London, 12 Nov 1975.
58 Interview, 25 Nov. 1975.
59 *The Times*, 7 Jan 1976.
60 *Hansard*, 903 (19 Jan 1976) cols 998–1006.
61 *Sunday Telegraph*, 7 Mar 1976.
62 *Financial Times*, 23 Apr 1976.
63 *Guardian*, 24 Apr 1976.
64 *Ibid.*, 10 May 1976.

Part II
Introduction

1 This definition of extremism is taken from Lipset and Raab, *The Politics of Unreason*, pp. 4–7.
2 In a June 1973 Gallup Poll 45% of the electorate said Powell took extreme positions while Michael Foot (12%) and Anthony Wedgwood

Benn (11 %) were far behind. See Gallup Poll CQ822, provided by Gallup Polls Ltd.

3 For a report of these data see *Sunday Times*, 21 June 1970.

4 Data supplied by Robert M. Worcester, Managing Director of Market & Opinion Research International.

5 See *The Politics of Mass Society*.

6 For these arguments see Lipset and Bendix, *Social Mobility in Industrial Society*, pp. 64–75; Lenski, 'Status Inconsistency: A non-Vertical Dimension of Social Status'; Runciman, *Relative Deprivation and Social Justice*; Robert T. Riley and Thomas F. Pettigrew, 'Relative Deprivation and Wallace's Northern Support', (San Francisco, paper presented at the American Sociological Association meeting, 1969) and Bell (ed.), *The Radical Right*.

7 On the authoritarian personality see Adorno, Frenkel-Brunswik, Levinson and Sandford, *The Authoritarian Personality*; Christie & Jahoda (eds.), *Studies in the Scope and Method of the Authoritarian Personality*; Seymour Martin Lipset, 'Working Class Authoritarianism', in *Political Man* (New York, Doubleday, 1960) pp. 97–103; and Hoogvelt, 'Ethnocentrism, Authoritarianism and Powellism', for an application of this approach to the study of Powellism.

8 See Downs, *An Economic Theory of Democracy* and V. O. Key, *The Responsible Electorate*.

9 Michael Paul Rogin, *The Intellectuals and McCarthy* (Cambridge, Mass., The MIT Press, 1967), pp. 219–51.

Chapter 8

1 Figure 8.1 (p. 162) is an attempt to synthesise a wide variety of different types of data on Powell's support. It should not be considered to be anything more than an impressionistic sketch of how his support changed with time.

2 See *Daily Express*, 20 June 1963; N.O.P. Poll 65010, data supplied by the S.S.R.C. Survey Archive, University of Essex; and the special supplement to the *NOP Political Bulletin* (Nov 1965).

3 For the O.R.C. data see *Sunday Times*, 14 Oct 1967 and for the Gallup data see *Gallup Political Index* (May 1968) 47.

4 See *Gallup Political Index* (Dec 1965) 177; (Sep 1966) 117; and (Feb 1967) 30 for a report of these data.

5 See *NOP Political Bulletin* (Sep 1968) 5.

6 See Gallup Polls CQ576, 607 and 670 for a report of these data.

7 For a discussion of Powell's impact which makes use of these data see Studlar, 'British Public Opinion, Colour Issues, and Enoch Powell', 371–81.

8 See *NOP Political Bulletin* (June/July 1970); (Sep/Oct 1970) 5; and (Mar 1971) 5, for a report of these data.

9 See *NOP Political Bulletin* (June 1973) 8.

10 See Gallup poll CQ720 and the *Gallup Political Index*, (Oct 1973) for a report of these data.

11 See *The Times*, 14 June 1974 for the O.R.C. data and *Gallup Political Index* (Nov 1974) 5.

12   See *The Times*, 12 Nov 1974 for the O.R.C. data and *Gallup Political Index* (Nov 1974) 5, for a report of these data.

13   *NOP Political Bulletin* (Oct 1974) 11.

14   According to *NOP Political Bulletin*, the Tories held a 24% lead in April and a 23% lead in May.

15   See *NOP Political Bulletin*, between September 1972 and May 1973 for a report of the exact figures.

16   Richard Rose, 'Voters show their scepticism of politicians', *The Times*, 9 Apr 1968.

17   *Ibid.*

18   See for example *Spectator*, 231 (25 Aug 1973) 239.

19   For a comparison of the Gallup and N.O.P. class divisions see Peter Pulzer, *Political Representation and Elections in Britain*, p. 100. In the Gallup scheme, 6% of the sample was 'average +' or well-to-do. Another 22% were rated 'average', representing the middle and upper middle class. Sixty-one per cent were considered 'average −', representing a small share of the lower middle class and the bulk of the working class. Another 11% was called 'Group D', representing unskilled workers and pensioners. In the standard market research categorisations used by N.O.P. 12% were rated AB (upper middle class). Another 22% were placed in the C1 category (lower middle class). Thirty-seven per cent were skilled manual workers (C2) and 29% were DEs (semi- and unskilled workers as well as pensioners).

20   The data in Tables 8.2 and 8.3 are presented with the Gallup percentages transformed on to the standard market research categories. This was done by use of the following ratios. It was assumed that the 'average +' and 'average' categories represented the middle class. Thus the per cent of a politician's support coming from the middle class was taken to be the sum of the contribution of these two categories. Because the 'average −' category includes some lower middle-class respondents, the sum of the average + and average categories actually understates the politician's middle-class support. To partially compensate, a politician's middle-class support on the Gallup scale was divided by the per cent middle class in their whole sample (28%). That figure was taken to be the amount by which his base was biased towards the middle class. That figure was then multiplied by the per cent of the N.O.P. sample which was middle class (34%). That product yielded an estimate of the per cent of the politician's support which would come from the middle class using the N.O.P. categories.

     For example, in the August 1966 Gallup Poll 35% of Powell's support came from average + and average respondents. Dividing 35% by 28% yields 1.25. Multiplying 1.25 by 34% yields 42%, which is the figure one finds on the first line of Table 8.2.

21   See *Gallup Political Index* (May 1968) 52.

22   See Gallup Poll CQ576 supplied by the Gallup Polls Ltd, and N.O.P. Poll 68016 supplied by the S.S.R.C. Survey Archive, University of Essex.

23   See Gallup Polls CQ576 and 585 supplied by the Gallup Polls Ltd, for a report of these data.

24   As Lipset has noted, 'In practically every country for which we have data

(except perhaps the U.S.), women tended to support the Conservative parties more than men do'. See Lipset, *Political Man*, p. 221. For a comprehensive, if tendentious, discussion of the political behaviour of women see Goot and Reid, *Women and Voting Studies: Mindless Matrons or Sexist Scientism*. On the greater conservatism of women than men in Britain, see the Nuffield election studies from 1959 to October 1974.

25 See Gallup Polls CQ489 and 512 supplied by the Roper Center, Williams College.

26 See Butler and Stokes, *Political Change in Britain*, pp. 48–66.

27 For evidence on this point with regard to the Nazis, see Reinhard Bendix, 'Social Stratification and Political Power', in Reinhard Bendix and Seymour Martin Lipset (eds.), *Class, Status and Power* (Glencoe, The Free Press, 1956), p. 605. On Italian Fascism, see Lipset, *Political Man*, p. 165.

Chapter 9

1 See Erich Fromm, *Escape From Freedom*; Karl Manheim, *Man and Society in an Age of Destruction* (New York, Harcourt & Brace, 1944); and Arendt, *The Origins of Totalitarianism*.

2 See S. M. Lipset, *Political Man*, p. 45. See also Joseph Schumpeter, *Capitalism, Socialism and Democracy* (New York, Harper & Row, 1947) pp. 232–302.

3 Kornhauser, *The Politics of Mass Society*, p. 39.

4 *Ibid.*, p. 180.

5 For other arguments on why fascism did not flourish in Britain, see Weiss, *The Fascist Tradition*, p. 76; Arendt, *The Origins of Totalitarianism*, pp. 250–5; Barrington Moore, *The Social Origins of Dictatorship and Democracy*, pp. 422–44; and Weber, *The Varieties of Fascism*, p. 112.

6 Benewick, *Political Violence and Public Order*.

7 *Ibid.*, pp. 304–5.

8 Robert T. McKenzie, *British Political Parties* (London, Mercury Books, 1963) pp. 510–15.

9 Daniel Bell, 'The Dispossessed 1962', in Bell (ed.), *The Radical Right*, p. 38 n. 23.

10 Herbert Hyman, 'England & America: Climates of Tolerance and Intolerance' in Bell, *The Radical Right*, pp. 227–50.

11 Shils, *The Torment of Secrecy*, p. 53.

12 Almond and Verba, *The Civic Culture*, p. 493.

13 Rose has written widely on the decline of the class alignment since 1968. The most recent statement of this theme will be found in his 'Britain: Simple Abstractions and Complex Realities' in Rose (ed.), *Electoral Behaviour*, pp. 481–541.

14 Richard Rose, *The Problem of Party Government*, Appendix A.

15 *Political Change in Britain*, pp. 197–208.

16 Butler and King, *The British General Election of 1964*, p. 299.

17 Richard Rose, *The Problem of Party Government*, pp. 157–69.

18 See Jessop, *Traditionalism, Conservatism and British Political Culture*, pp. 34–5, 124–63.

19 Dennis Kavanagh, 'The Deferential English: A Comparative Critique', *Government and Opposition*, 6 (Summer 1971) pp. 333–60.
20 See McKenzie and Silver, 'Conservatism, Industrialism and the Working Class Tories in England', pp. 32–5.
21 Richard Rose, 'Britain: Simple Abstractions and Complex Realities', p. 530.
22 See an article by the influential maverick Tory M.P., Dr Rhodes Boyson, lamenting the weakening of deferential working-class Tory voting, in *The Times*, 31 Dec 1974.
23 Klein, 'The Case for Elitism: Public Opinion and Public Policy'.
24 *The Times*, 14 July 1969.
25 John Goldthorpe *et al.*, *The Affluent Worker in the Class Structure* (Vol. 3).
26 *Ibid.*, p. 107.
27 *Ibid.*, p. 165.
28 See Lipset and Raab, *The Politics of Unreason*, pp. 456–82, for a documentation of this point in the American case.
29 McKenzie and Silver, 'Conservatism, Industrialism and Working Class Tories in England', pp. 33–5.
30 Powellites in 1974 were defined as respondents who gave Powell an 8–10 score on a 0–10 scale.
31 Raymond Wolfinger *et al.*, 'America's Radical Right: Politics and Ideology', in Schoenberger, *The American Right Wing*, p. 29.
32 See Riesman, *The Lonely Crowd* and Mills, *The Power Elite*.
33 Edward Shils, 'Mass Society and its Culture', *Daedalus*, 89 (Spring 1960) 288–344.
34 Joseph Gusfield, 'Mass Society and Extremist Politics'.
35 See Philip Converse, 'The Nature of Belief Systems in Mass Publics', pp. 206–61 and Gusfield, 'Mass Society and Extremist Politics', p. 27.

Chapter 10
1 On suicide rates see Durkheim, *Suicide*, pp. 246–54, and on mental health see Hollingsheed, Ellis and Kirby, 'Social Mobility and Mental Illness'.
2 S. M. Lipset and Hans L. Zetterberg, 'A Theory of Social Mobility' in L. A. Coser and Bernard Rosenberg, *Sociological Theory* (New York, Macmillan, 1964). See also their revision of this essay in Lipset and Bendix, *Social Mobility in Industrial Society*, pp. 64–75.
3 Lipset and Bendix, *Social Mobility in Industrial Society*, pp. 66–7.
4 Lipset, *The First New Nation*, p. 217.
5 W. G. Runciman, *Relative Deprivation and Social Justice*, pp. 65–142.
6 Kenny, 'The Affluent Worker Project'.
7 See Lipset and Raab, *The Politics of Unreason*.
8 See Butler and Stokes, *Political Change in Britain*, pp. 95–102.
9 See Barrington Moore, *The Social Origins of Dictatorship and Democracy*, pp. 442–4.
10 See the essays in Bell (ed.), *The Radical Right*, for the argument that status anxiety led people to support Senator Joseph McCarthy.
11 See Lipset and Bendix, *Social Mobility in Industrial Society*, p. 69; and Butler and Stokes, *Political Change in Britain*, pp. 95–102.

12 Lipset and Raab, *The Politics of Unreason*, p. 3.
13 Herberle, *From Democracy to Nazism*.
14 See Runciman, *Relative Deprivation and Social Justice*, p. 138.
15 See the introduction to Hope (ed.), *The Analysis of Social Mobility*, p. 9.
16 The basic statement of this thesis can be found in Lenski, 'Status Crystal-lisation: A Non-Vertical Dimension of Social Status'.
17 Segal and Knoke, 'Social Mobility, Status Inconsistency, and Partisan Realignment' and Segal and Knoke, 'Class Inconsistency, Status Inconsistency and Political Parties in America'.
18 See Lenski, 'Social Participation and Status Crystallisation', p. 459, n. 3 and his 'Status Inconsistency and the Vote: A Four Nation Test', p. 299, n. 4.
19 Eitzen, 'Status Inconsistency and Wallace Supporters in A Midwestern Town'. Rush, 'Status Consistency and Right Wing Extremism'.
20 See Lenski's 'Status Inconsistency and the Vote: A Four Nation Test', p. 300.
21 Runciman, *Relative Deprivation and Social Justice*, pp. 201–21; and Bonham, *The Middle Class Vote*, p. 180.
22 See *Economist*, 227 (27 Apr 1968) 49.
23 Runciman, *Relative Deprivation and Social Justice*, p. 161; Lipset also makes this point in his *First New Nation*, pp. 213–49.
24 Runciman, *Relative Deprivation and Social Justice*, p. 390.

Chapter 11
1 See Lipset and Rokkan's introduction to *Party Systems and Voter Alignments* for their approach to understanding the political cleavages in Western democracies.
2 See Schneider, 'Issues, Voting and Cleavages: A Methodology and Some Tests'.
3 The use of this approach is one that Schneider is employing in his *The Meaning of Elections* (forthcoming).
4 Beer, *Modern British Politics*, pp. 318–51 and Mackintosh, *The Government and Politics of Great Britain*, pp. 87–9.
5 The studies drawn on here are Butler and Rose, *The British General Election of 1959*; Butler and King, *The British General Election of 1964*; Butler and King, *The British General Election of 1966*; and Butler and Pinto-Duschinsky, *The British General Election of 1970*.
6 *The British General Election of 1964*, p. 30.
7 *Ibid.*, p. 270.
8 *The British General Election of 1966*, p. 265.
9 *Ibid.*, p. 270.
10 *The British General Election of 1970*, p. 45.
11 *Ibid.*, p. 349.
12 R. W. Johnson, 'The British Political Elite, 1955–1972', and Richard Rose, 'Class and Party Divisions: Britain as a Test Case' provide documentation of the decline in working-class representation in Labour's parliamentary membership.
13 Butler and Stokes, *Political Change in Britain*, p. 206.
14 *Ibid.*, p. 269.

15 *Ibid.*, p. 112.
16 See *Daily Mail*, 9 Feb 1968.
17 See *Daily Telegraph*, 13 July 1968.
18 Richard Rose 'Voters Show their Scepticism of Politicians', *The Times*, 9 Apr 1968.
19 Ronald Butt, 'The Importance of Being Enoch'.
20 *Financial Times*, 26 Apr 1968.
21 See *Sunday Telegraph*, 28 Apr and 5 May 1968 and *Spectator*, 220 (3 May 1968) 627.
22 *Sunday Times*, 3 Sep 1968.
23 *Spectator*, 220 (21 June 1968) 842.
24 All data used in this section are from the 1969–70 Butler-Stokes panel study, unless otherwise specified.
25 See Scammon and Wattenberg, *The Real Majority* and Phillips, *The Emerging Republican Majority*.
26 Table computed from May 1968 N.O.P. Omnibus Survey by S.S.R.C. Survey Archives, University of Essex.
27 See Wood (ed.), *Powell and the 1970 Election*, pp. 104–11.
28 See *NOP Political Bulletin* (June 1973) 8.
29 These data are taken from *NOP Political Bulletin* (1970–73).
30 See *Spectator*, 231 (11 Aug 1973) p. 171.
31 The alienated were defined as those who agreed with the statement that 'neither party represents the views of people like me'.
32 Gallup Poll CQ855 (June 1973); supplied by Gallup Polls Ltd.

Conclusion

1 For discussion of Powell's economic philosophy see Utley, *Enoch Powell: the man and his thinking*, pp. 114–67 and Gamble, *The Conservative Nation*, pp. 116–19.
2 *The Times*, 28 Feb 1975.
3 *Ibid.*, 6 Jan 1976.
4 *Ibid.*
5 *Economist*, 258 (10 Jan 1976) 22–3; *New Statesman*, 91 (9 Jan 1976) 29–30; *The Times*, 6 Jan 1976.
6 *Spectator*, 236 (10 Jan 1976) 5.
7 *The Times*, 3 Dec 1973.
8 *Economist*, 215 (19 June 1965) 1368.
9 *The Problem of Party Government*, p. 326.
10 For discussion of the absence of stable factions within the Conservative party see Finer, Berrington and Bartholomew, *Backbench Opinion in the House of Commons 1966–1959*, pp. 76–131 and Richard Rose 'Parties, Factions and Tendencies in Britain'. For a view that Conservative backbench opinion might be coalescing towards more stable factions see Frasure, 'Backbench Opinion Philip Revisited' and C. Norton, 'Test your own Powellism' *Crossbow*, 17 (Feb 1976) 10–11.
11 Gamble, *The Conservative Nation*, pp. 87–123.
12 Quoted by King, *British Members of Parliament*, p. 44.
13 Rose, *The Problem of Party Government*, p. 349.
14 Interview with Conservative M.P.

15   Interview with Conservative M.P.

16   To Edward Shils there were two basic principles which were fundamental to populism. The first was the supremacy of the people's will 'over every other standard, over the standards of traditional institutions and other the will of other strata. Populism identifies the will of the people with justice and morality.' He also said populism necessitated direct links between the people and the leadership strata without intermediate institutions. See his *Torment of Secrecy*, pp. 98–104.

17   See *Crossbow* (Apr–June 1968) 26, quoted by Colin Seymour-Ure, *The Political Impact of Mass Media*, p. 114.

18   See *Illustrated London News*, 252 (1968) 13.

19   See report of interview with Powell in *Sunday Times*, 3 Sep 1968.

20   Wood (ed.), *A Nation Not Afraid: The Thinking of Enoch Powell*, p. 3.

21   Richard Rose, *Politics in England Today*, p. 123.

22   For the initial statement of the difference between position and valence issues see Angus Campbell *et al.*, *Elections and the Political Order* (New York, John Wiley, 1966) pp. 161–79.

23   Powell, *Still to Decide*, p. 176.

24   Butler and Stokes, *Political Change in Britain*, pp. 353–5.

25   Robert Skidelsky, *Oswald Mosley* (London, Macmillan, 1975) pp. 317–337.

Index